DISAFFILIATED MAN

DISAFFILIATED MAN

Essays and bibliography on
skid row, vagrancy, and outsiders

edited by

HOWARD M. BAHR

University of Toronto Press

CONTENTS

CONTRIBUTORS

Theodore Caplow is Professor of Sociology, Graduate Faculties, Columbia University. His books include The Sociology of Work, Principles of Organization, and Two Against One. He has been interested in the problems of disaffiliation since publication of a paper on transiency in 1940. He has conducted numerous studies of transient and homeless populations including a large-scale study in New York City which is now in its 7th year.

James F. Rooney has crossed the United States by freight train three times and has lived in many skid rows in the course of field work on homeless men. He co-authored The Men on Skid Row, a research report about Philadelphia's skid-row population, and has written numerous reports and articles on problems of poverty and homelessness. Currently research director of the OEO (Poverty) program in Camden, New Jersey, Mr. Rooney is completing work on his doctorate in sociology at the University of Pennsylvania

Howard M. Bahr is Associate Professor of Sociology and Associate Rural Sociologist at Washington State University. Since 1965 he has worked with Theodore Caplow as project director of the studies of homeless men and women conducted at Columbia University's Bureau of Applied Social Research. His articles on disaffiliation and skid-row problems have appeared in several sociological journals.

Felix M. Berardo is Associate Professor of Sociology at the University of Florida. He is co-author of Emerging Conceptual Frameworks in Family Analysis .

His research on widowhood includes the technical report Social Adaptation to Widowhood Among a Rural-Urban Aged Population and a number of articles in professional journals. He has also conducted research on the influence of migration on kinship interaction.

Armand L. Mauss is Assistant Professor of Sociology at Washington State University. His published work includes articles on drug abuse, political sociology, intergroup relations, and the sociology of religion. He is the editor of a special issue of the Journal of Social Issues on "New Left Versus Old Left."

INTRODUCTION

This book has two main objectives: to facilitate access to an extensive literature on homelessness, chronic inebriety, and related forms of disaffiliation, and to increase the utility of this literature by highlighting its relevance to more general social problems and processes. The annotated bibliography is directed primarily to the first objective; the introductory essays are more pertinent to the second.

Some of the essays deal with skid row and its men. Others treat more common forms of disaffiliation such as widowhood or defection from membership in voluntary associations. The discussion of topics beyond the traditional boundaries of the "homelessness" literature is an attempt to encourage the explicit generalization of findings from research on transiency and skid-row life to other areas of inquiry. The massive disaffiliation of the skid-row man represents the final stages of the focalization in a single life history of the same processes that accompany unemployment, widowhood, or less dramatic changes in patterns of social activity and affiliation.

Everett Hughes once remarked that the study of the lowest statuses was profitable because it revealed social relationships stripped of much of the complexity that attends higher positions. At the lower levels the bones of the social system are barer, and layers of social veneer are fewer in number and perhaps thinner. If this is so, the skid-row man is an extremely profitable object of study, for by almost any criterion of social class he represents the extreme lower end of scale; he lacks political power, social esteem, economic power, and self-respect.

Consideration of the antecedents and concomitants of skid-row life may illuminate the personal and social consequences of powerlessness or provide insight into what is specifically human and social in our activities regardless of the status level at which they occur. But if the lowest statuses have been studied because of their simplicity or accessibility, the findings must be interpreted with reference to the more numerous population of higher status, less accessibility and greater complexity of social organization.

Unfortunately this kind of interpretation of findings rarely is found in the research literature on transiency, skid row, and excessive alsohol use. The study of disaffiliation has not been distinguished by theoretical sophistication. Most researchers have been oriented to social "problems," intent on describing the disaffiliate and discovering what was "wrong" with him, and have not concerned themselves with generalizing to the wider perspective of human society in general. In part, the theoretical sterility of much of the skid-row research has been due to the lack of a theoretical unifying principle; in part, it has stemmed from the ad hoc nature of the research, related to the need to "do something" about a highly visible social problem. Also, many of the skid-row surveys have been designed to provide data for social planners and urban developers, and concern for extending scientific knowledge has been secondary.

The essays in the present volume have several functions. They introduce the bibliography, summarize certain aspects of the literature, and point to research opportunities. Perhaps their most important function is that, taken together, they underscore the relevance of the extensive research on homelessness and its synonyms to the understanding of social order.

In the first essay Caplow notes the important part skid-row research has played in the historical development of sociology as a discipline, and enumerates some of the ambiguities attending the condition of homelessness. Despite almost a century of research, the critical problems of etiology and successful rehabilitation continue to puzzle the experts.

Rooney reviews the factors affecting the growth and decline of skid rows in the United States, and points to historical changes in the character and behavior of skid-row men. He contrasts the present skid row with that at the turn of the century, and makes some predictions about the future of skid row in American society.

Bahr discusses the various definitions of homelessness used by researchers and identifies disaffiliation as a common element in them. The concept of disaffiliation is linked to retreatism and anomie theory. It is proposed that retreatism be operationalized so that retreatists may be identified independently of their place of residence.

Berardo states that researchers have paid little attention to the study of widowhood status and the problems that accompany it. He outlines the social consequences of widowhood, including mortality, mental illness, social isolation, and suicide. His discussion of the problems of the widower demonstrates that the widower is very much like the skid-row man, who also is isolated from kin and other social ties and bears the negative personal consequences of that isolation.

In the final article, Mauss asserts that the study of religious defection has been neglected by sociologists of religion. His discussion illustrates the application of the study of disaffiliation to a specific voluntary association, the church. The principles he discusses are generalizable to other voluntary associations, but the church is particularly relevant to the study of homeless man. A tie to organized religion frequently is the only social affiliation maintained by the skid-row resident.

The published work about social disaffiliation cuts across many disciplines, including sociology, psychology, law, medicine, gerontology, social work, police science, and urban planning. In practice this means that it is easy for important works to be "lost" because they are published in journals outside the purview of most students or researchers. The task of mastering the literature is complicated further by the fact that much skid row research is disseminated only in the form of unpublished agency reports that receive, at best, limited distribution. Thus there is a "hidden literature," often unknown to the student lacking long-term familiarity with the field, and frequently inaccessible even when one knows that the specific documents exist.

The annotated bibliography is an attempt to make both the published literature and the unpublished "other works" more accessible to the interested reader. The intention has been to provide, within the limitations of a brief annotation, information about the author's general thesis and conclusions, and for works reporting empirical research, to identify the problem studied, the research site, sample size, methods applied, and major findings. As a general rule unpublished studies and materials not available in English translation were annotated in greater detail than other works. Most of the studies cited were conducted in the United States, but there is a substantial representation of Canadian and British studies, and a conscious effort was made to include material from as many national settings as possible.

In areas where the study of disaffiliation intersects other major substantive fields the present bibliography is quite incomplete. For example, much of the literature on aging is relevant to the study of disaffiliation; only a fraction of that extensive literature is included in the present work. Similarly, works most relevant to disaffiliation have been selected from the fields of social psychology, the sociology of work, the sociology of the family, and many other specialties within disciplines. The aim has been to provide enough links between the study of disaffiliated man and the literature central to these professional specialties that the interested reader will have several starting points available to him.

Early versions of the bibliography were compiled between 1965 and 1967, as part of the Homelessness Project, a program of research sponsored by the National Institute of Mental Health (MH-10861) and conducted at the Bureau of Applied Social Research, Columbia University. I am indebted to Theodore Caplow, principal investigator of that project, for encouragement and invaluable advice, both during the course of the Homelessness Project and since that time. His insistence that the annotations receive a high priority has been a major factor in bringing this work to completion. In addition, Professor Caplow read an earlier draft of the manuscript and made many helpful suggestions.

Annotations were contributed by several staff members of the Homelessness Project. The work of Nan Markel Sigal, Stanley K. Henshaw, Stephen J. Langfur, B. Luise Margolies, Michael A. Baker, J. Edward Hawco, Harry E. Conklin, N. Jefferson Garrett, Martha Gershun, Rita Aronow and Marcia J. Cebulski is acknowledged. Miss Aronow and Miss Cebulski deserve special mention, Miss Aronow for her painstaking typing of earlier drafts of the bibliography and Miss Cebulski for supervising research assistants and editing their annotations during the final months of the project.

Sources of items include several mimeographed bibliographies by Earl Rubington, an annotated bibliography by Samuel E. Wallace, a listing of relevant doctoral dissertations from a "Datrix" search conducted by University Microfilms, listings, reprints, and bibliographies kindly mailed to me by the Addiction Research Foundation of Ontario, a bibliography of studies on aging and mental health supplied by Marjorie Fiske Lowenthal, and the Classified Abstracts of the National Council on Alcoholism. Special thanks are owed to Mrs. Aline Young of the National Council on Alcoholism Library. Other libraries used extensively include the New York Public Library and the university libraries at Columbia, the University of Washington, and Washington State University.

Substantial revision and extension of the bibliography was supported in part by funds provided for biological and medical research by the State of Washington Initiative Measure No. 171. The research assistance of James Wood, Nancy Camp, Karen Brady, and Eugenie Hoggard is acknowledged with thanks. The typing of the final manuscript was supported by Project 1960, Department of Rural Sociology, College of Agriculture, Washington State University. F. Ivan Nye provided solid administrative support and intellectual encouragement. I wish to express appreciation to Julie Fisher, Rosemary Guse, and Janee Roche, who patiently and competently typed and retyped the manu - script. Finally, the efforts of those who contributed essays are acknowledged with gratitude. Permission to reprint the Mauss and Berardo articles was obtained from the authors and publishers.

H. M. B.

DISAFFILIATED MAN

THE SOCIOLOGIST AND
THE HOMELESS MAN

Theodore Caplow

Every field of scientific or scholarly investigation has certain topics that fascinate the professional investigator and that are studied more often and more closely than their importance may warrant. Hamlet is such a topic for literary scholars; the fruitfly has occupied such a place in genetics. The study of homeless men, as Professor Bahr's bibliography shows, has attracted sociologists since the earliest days of social research for reasons that have nothing to do with the relative urgency of homelessness as a social problem.

 The oldest statistical study of homelessness in the United States reported in these pages is John McCook's "Tramp Census" (1893). The oldest work cited which may be said to contain empirical data is the Liber Vagatorum, edited in 1528 by Martin Luther, of all people (Hotten, 1860).

 Although the rise of sociological research in the United States is generally dated from the publication of The Polish Peasant (Thomas and Znaniecki, 1918-1920) at least half a dozen serious, sociological studies of homeless men were published earlier, including Solenberger's One Thousand Homeless Men (1911), a landmark work referring to the period 1901-1903, and Stuart Rice's Bowery study (1918) based on participant observation in 1916 and 1917. Rice, a future president of the American Statistical Association, was one of a long line of sociologists--Anderson (1923), Minehan (1934), Locke (1935), Wallace (1965), and Lovald (1960) were some of the others--to roam skid row disguised as hoboes and derelicts. Nor was he alone in eminence among skid-row scholars. The reader will encounter Park (1925), Sutherland (Sutherland and Locke, 1936), Riis (1904), and many of their peers in the bibliography that follows.

The geographical scope has been equally wide. Besides Chicago's West Madison Street and New York's Bowery, both classic observation sites, empirical studies of similar districts have been carried out in Philadelphia, Detroit, Boston, Los Angeles, St. Louis, San Francisco, Baltimore, Minneapolis, Cincinnati, Pittsburgh, Rochester, Sacramento, Montreal, and a number of European cities.

The decrease of the skid-row population observed nearly everywhere during the past decade has not brought about any perceptible diminution of interest; quite the contrary. Although homeless men on the Bowery now constitute only about six one-hundredths of one percent of New York City's population and their number is declining from year to year, at least four major studies of Bowery men have recently been published. The Bowery has lost many of the basic institutions of skid row—it no longer contains a barber college, a pawnshop, or an all-night theatre—but it does not seem to have lost any of its magnetism for sociologists.

Even the most casual review of this vast sociological literature suggests two related questions. What is there about the homeless man that fascinates the sociologist? How has the sociologist's work affected the homeless man?

Historically, American skid-row districts have sheltered a predominantly male, predominantly adult population made up of several distinct elements: 1) vagrants, wanderers and seasonal laborers--hoboes, in the now-obsolete term; 2) chronic inebriates, some partly employed and others unemployable; 3) old men retired from manual employment and living on meagre pensions or savings; 4) steadily employed men without family or community affiliations. These four types--the hobo, the drunk, the old-timer, and the loner--made up the primary population of skid row, supplemented at various times by cripples, fugitives, temporarily unemployed workers, soldiers, petty criminals, and even a few women. The proportions of each type present vary from time to time and from place to place. Today, the hoboes have nearly disappeared and there are relatively more old-timers

than ever before. Recent studies show a very low proportion of young men, a sizeable Negro minority, a high
proportion of the whites native-born, median education
at about the eighth-grade level, a minority of total abstainers, and very few family affiliations. About half of
the homeless men interviewed in recent studies describe
themselves as never married. The majority have no contact with relatives. Those who have been married report
a great deal of marital discord. Their job histories are
characterized by low status, low pay, and brief tenure.

Skid row traditionally provided an oasis within the
larger community where the subsistence cost of living
was lower than anywhere else and the ordinary norms
of urban behavior were suspended. These protective
features of the environment are not very well maintained
under current conditions. The cost of a bed in a lodging
house is often more than the rental of a furnished room
elsewhere in the city. The prices in skid-row restaurants
are sometimes higher than in the cheap restaurants of
other districts. A drunken man on a skid-row street is
much more likely to be arrested than if he makes a similar appearance in a residential district. The risk of
being robbed or assaulted when drunk is very much greater in skid row than out of it. The environment does not
offer the homeless man comfort or safety or even freedom from interference, but it does permit him to live in
a certain style, whose major components are isolation
from women, wine-drinking, the free disposition of one's
time, and the absence of compulsory obligations toward
others.

Whether skid row is a specialized community or
subculture, as some investigators believe, or an organizational vacuum, as others maintain, is a semantic
question. Almost all observers agree that there are
characteristic, acquired patterns of behavior in such
districts, that considerable social interaction occurs
among the homeless men on skid row, and that the system
is sufficiently cohesive that it may be difficult to leave,
and once left, may be difficult to stay away from. On
the other hand, there is no reliable report of a skid-row
population engaging in collective action or even in mutual

self-defense.   Although some observers claim to see a
status hierarchy, there is no corresponding structure of
rights, duties and relationships.   Above all, there are
no common goals.

Can refusal to act be considered a form of action?
Skid row as a social system adapts to the external environment by not reacting to it, achieves its goals by
having none, maintains its external adaptations by leaving them to chance, and screens its membership by accept-
ing everyone who applies.   It is perhaps unique among
human communities in presenting no problem of entree
for the sociologist.   Like the policeman, the social worker, the evangelist, and the thug, he can enter and leave
skid row as he pleases.

Whatever else he may be, the skid-row man is not
his brother's keeper.   Nor his brother's opinion-leader,
norm-enforcer, or action-initiator.   That is to say, he
is about as different from Homo Sociologus as it is possible to be while still remaining human.   Therein lies
skid row's fascination for the sociologist.   For the price
of a subway ride, he can enter a country where the accepted principles of social interaction do not apply.

The same phenomenon can move the ordinary citizen to fury.   Anyone who has worked on the problem of
redeveloping a skid-row district or relocating a population of homeless men can testify to the extraordinary
hostility aroused by the prospect of a settlement of homeless men in a residential or business district.   This
sentiment is institutionalized in what Pittman and Gordon
(1958) call "The Revolving Door"--the practice or arresting, convicting and quickly releasing homeless men for
intoxication, vagrancy and other nominal offenses, which
continues without apparent purpose in most major cities.
At the time the Columbia Bowery Project began its inquiries, this curious institution accounted for about one-
fourth of all police arrests in New York City.   Homeless
men were arrested according to a quota system, not
necessarily when intoxicated. They were almost invariably released the following morning.   No one connected
with the system, from the presiding judge down to the
driver of the police van, had any clear idea of what it

was intended to accomplish. Its persistence reflects the extent to which the settled community perceives skid row as threatening. Even though the crime rate of homeless men with respect to outsiders is close to zero, the image of the dangerous tramp who sets fire to the barn still lurks somewhere in the collective consciousness.

The sociological literature is not entirely free of punitive attitudes. Some of the early observers wanted to "eliminate the tramp" by incarcerating him in a labor colony, and one fairly recent study, under social-work auspices, advocated permanent confinement for homeless men who refused to cooperate with a rehabilitation program. At the other extreme are those like Colin Wilson (1956) who describe the homeless man as a moral hero defying the snares of organized society.

The majority of sociological observers have perceived the homeless man as victim of circumstances, ripe for social therapy. In other words, they have developed explanations of homelessness and suggested cures accordingly. If we compare the various explanations that have been offered, taking account of divergent terminologies, we discover that there is not really much disagreement nowadays about the etiology of homelessness. Whether the homeless man is described as undersocialized, sociopathic, anomic, nonaffiliated, kin-isolated, attitudinally passive, non-addictively alcoholic, having a negative ego-image, or economically marginal, the diagnosis reflects substantial agreement about his condition and its origins. The typical homeless man has had a long history of social undernourishment which has discouraged him from seeking satisfaction in family relationships, self-improvement, voluntary associations, or work. Alcohol has played a large part in his life, either to dissolve his social relationships or to console him for their absence.

That much of the puzzle is easy. It is much harder to explain why certain individuals select themselves or are selected to follow this developmental route. As in the study of other types of deviance, we face a blank wall here which research has not penetrated very far. Certainly there are factors predisposing to deviant behavior.

Coming from a broken home, having a father who was not regularly employed, dropping out of school, drinking at an early age, being Irish rather than Ukrainian, are all conducive to homelessness, but the rub is that most of the men with these characteristics do not become homeless. Why A spends most of his years on skid row while his brother B, with a similar background and early experience, goes to work, marries, raises a family, buys a house, sends his children to college and runs for office remains, for the moment, an undecipherable mystery. A century of intensive research has hardly advanced us toward a solution. One after another, most of the plausible explanations have been tried and found wanting. Homeless men, on the average, are of average intelligence, and among them are many whose homes were unbroken, whose childhood was easy, who did graduate from school and who never had any dramatic disappointments. Yet there they sit on a curb in an alley, sipping the rotgut wine.

The question of rehabilitation involves similar ambiguities. Rehabilitation is a curious goal for the homeless man who was never "habilitated," and who cannot be restored to normal life and a steady job because he has never had either. Nevertheless, there are many men on skid row who have drunk themselves out of established social roles, and even for the others, it makes sense to ask what treatment or incentive would transform them from homeless men to ordinary men. Hundreds of programs have been launched at one time or another--compulsory labor, compulsory abstinence, salvationism, job-training, psychotherapy, group therapy, halfway houses, guaranteed employment, hospitalization, dispersion, rehousing, communal gardens; even hypnotism and group-singing. Every method shows a few successes (mostly among men who have not been homeless for long or who have experienced unusual downward mobility) and many failures. Since every program provides a living for its practitioners, many programs fit into the pattern of skid-row life and persist indefinitely. An antique institution like a revival mission can often be found next door to something as modern as a group therapy center. Either type of program is effective with a motivated client and a few such clients can almost always be found.

Meanwhile, the mass of homeless men sedulously avoid treatment, even when cajoled by free food, medical care, protection from arrest, or occupational training.

To some sociologists, any attempt to lure the homeless man back into a defective society is the sign of a graver malady than his own. As Mills (1943) wrote in his famous essay on "The Professional Ideology of Social Pathologists," sprinkling the page with quotation marks to show his scorn,

> . . . another conception in terms of which "problems" are typically discussed is that of adaptation or "adjustment" and their opposites. The pathological or disorganized is the maladjusted. This concept, as well as that of the "normal," is usually left empty of concrete, social content; or its content is, in effect, a propaganda for conformity to those norms and traits ideally associated with small town, middle-class milieux.

This opinion probably commands wider agreement now than when it was written. It is currently fashionable to criticize would-be reformers of deviant behavior. They are accused of imposing solutions dictated by the Establishment on subjects whose problems are caused by the existing social structure and whose legitimate needs can only be satisfied in opposition to it. The criticism may fit some of the writers who have discussed the problems of homeless men, but its fit to most of the sociological literature on homelessness is surprisingly poor.

To begin with, no one has ever been able to discover why certain men fall out of the habit of goal-seeking and exclude themselves from the benefits and constraints of organized society. Secondly, as far as the research evidence goes (and there is now considerable evidence on this point) homeless men do not usually express anomic attitudes. They reject neither the accepted cultural goals nor the available means of goal achievement. The general attitudes of homeless men towards the social structure are practically indistinguishable from those of their settled contemporaries. What makes the difference is the lack of intermediaries be - tween them and society; they have no intimates to embody social expectations. Although they interpret their own presence on skid row as symbolizing failure, there are no social agents to whom they must apologize for that failure. If the characterization of homelessness as a pathological condition and skid row as an unfortunate place to be were an expression of middle-class morality , then the values of men on skid row would have to be classified as middle-class.

In fact, they are nothing of the sort. The overwhelming majority of homeless men have had only working class affiliations, and their norms of personal and occupational achievement are those prevalent in the settled working class. With respect to deviance, as scores of studies have shown, working class morality is essentially the same as middle-class morality and places similar emphasis on the fulfillment of interpersonal obligations, self-improvement, staying out of trouble, and a rising standard of living. These goals probably come as close to universal acceptance in our society as did the predominant goals in any large-scale society of the past. The typical deviant shares them to the extent of regarding himself as a deviant for not being moved by them. If future research on deviance produces a therapeutic method, it may turn out to be not a scheme for the repression of deviance, but a formula that enables individuals to reject some of the prevailing social goals without committing themselves to a losing battle against organized society.

REFERENCES

Anderson, Nels.
    1923   The Hobo: The Sociology of the Homeless Man.
           Chicago: University of Chicago Press.

Hotten, John C.
1860   (trans.) The Book of Vagabonds and Beggars:
        With a Vocabulary of Their Language (Liber
        Vagatorum). London: John Camden Hotten.
Locke, Harvey J.
1935   "Unemployed Men in Chicago Shelters." Soci-
        ology and Social Research 19 (May-June):
        420-428.
Lovald, Keith Arthur.
1960   "From Hobohemia to Skid Row: The Changing
        Community of the Homeless Man." University
        of Minnesota, unpublished doctoral dissertation.
McCook, John J.
1893   "A Tramp Census and Its Revelations." Forum
        15 (August): 753-766.
Mills, C. Wright
1943   "The Professional Ideology of Social Patholo -
        gists." American Journal of Sociology
        49 (September): 165-180.
Minehan, Thomas.
1934   Boy and Girl Tramps of America. New York:
        Farrar & Rinehard.
Park, Robert E.
1925   "The Mind of the Hobo: Reflections Upon the
        Relation Between Mentality and Locomotion. "
        Pp. 156-160 in Robert E. Park, Ernest W.
        Burgess and Roderick D. McKenzie, The City.
        Chicago: University of Chicago Press.
Pittman, David J. and Wayne T. Gordon.
1958   Revolving Door: A Study of the Chronic Police
        Case Inebriate. Glencoe: Free Press.
Rice, Stuart A.
1918   "The Homeless." Annals of the American Acad-
        emy of Political Science 77 (May): 140-153.
Riis, Jacob A.
1904   How the Other Half Lives. New York: Scrib -
        ners.
Solenberger, Alice Willard.
1911   One Thousand Homeless Men: A Study   of
        Original Records. New York: Russell Sage
        Foundation.

Sutherland, Edwin H. and Harvey J. Locke.
   1936   Twenty Thousand Homeless Men.   Chicago:
          J. B. Lippincott.
Thomas, William I. and Florian Znaniecki.
   1818-   The Polish Peasant in Europe and America.
   1920   Boston: Gorham Press
Wallace, Samuel E.
   1965   Skid Row as a Way of Life. Totowa, New Jersey:
          Bedminister Press.
Wilson, Colin.
   1956   The Outsider.   Boston: Houghton Mifflin.

SOCIETAL FORCES AND THE UNATTACHED MALE: AN HISTORICAL REVIEW

James F. Rooney

In the historical experience of the United States, a variety of social and economic forces have operated to produce and sustain homelessness among certain segments of the labor force. Structural factors contributing to homelessness have included the transition from an agrarian to an industrial economy, large scale unemployment, and poverty stemming from personal injuries or misfortunes. The first section of this paper considers each of these factors separately. It is followed by a discussion of the changes in skid-row institutions and life styles that seem related to variation in extent of industrialization, unemployment and personal misfortune.

STRUCTURAL FORCES AND DISAFFILIATION

Transition to an Industrial Economy

Rostow (1960) has identified several stages in the process by which a traditional society may become industrialized. Initial stages involving the development of economic and technological institutions necessary for growth are followed by a "take-off" or expansionary phase in which the gross national product increases sharply due to the systematic application of sciences and technology. This "take-off" stage of economic growth is a period of extremely rapid social change, and the accompanying shift from agricultural to industrial employment coupled with industrial relocation may necessitate the uprooting of large portions of the labor force.

The "take-off" stage of the United States economy occurred between 1843 and 1900 (Rostow, 1960). The human dislocation accompanying this stage of economic growth was intensified because it occurred simultaneously with the development of the western frontier.

A critical resource for the initial industrial development of the frontier was the availability of large numbers of unskilled men without families. Logging, mining, and railroad construction industries required a labor force of unskilled males who were willing to take employment on a seasonal or irregular basis in widely separated and often isolated areas, to accept crude living conditions, and to labor long hours for low pay.

The frontier work camps and their satellite institutions altered traditional systems of community relationships and social control through the aggregation and ecological separation of low-status, unattached males. For these men, occasional drinking sprees in nearby towns compensated for the bleak life of the work camps.

The frontier open town provided temporary residence and recreation to loggers, miners, cowboys, farmhands, and railroad construction workers, and at the same time served as a supply center for farms and for logging and mining industries (Asbury, 1933; Morgan, 1951). The recreational interests of the unattached men were not extensive, and consequently the recreational offerings of these towns were generally limited to the concert saloon and dance hall, prostitution, and open gambling. During a brief but rousing period in town, most men spent every penny earned since the last spree. Among loggers it was considered ethically indefensible for a man to return to camp "until he had spent his last dollar, lost his hat, and awakened with his coat pleated from sleeping against a radiator in some river-front hotel" (Holbrook, 1938:7). Similarly, my own experience during the 1950's among "gandy dancers" (railroad seasonal track laborers) upholds the truth in their folklorism, "When a gandy goes to town, you don't expect him back 'til you see him coming."

Unattached men were the dominant majority in frontier towns. San Francisco, the archetypical frontier town of the mid-nineteenth century, served as the recreation center first for miners and later for farm workers, construction laborers, loggers, and visiting sailors from all ports of the world. Its history illustrates the process by which the norms of the unattached wanderers became dominant in a community.

When gold was discovered in California in 1848 San Francisco was a quiet hamlet with a population under 1,000. The gold rush swelled the population tremendously, and the majority of the new arrivals were unattached men. Old residents feared trouble or violence, and the town council reflected those fears in an ordinance which prohibited card playing in public. The casino owners and their customers ignored the ordinance and public gambling was not curtailed. Unable to enforce the ordinance, the town council elected to save face and rescinded the statute at its next meeting (Asbury, 1933: 19). Clearly, power had passed to the new majority group of unattached men.

San Francisco was the crossroads of the western United States and the gateway to the inland gold fields. A perennial shortage of ships' crewmen developed as large numbers of incoming sailors jumped ship to join the search for gold. As a consequence, gangs were active in shanghaiing men to fill crew shortages for visiting ships. During the 1850's there were at least 23 gangs of this kind in the "Barbary Coast," that section of San Francisco where the unattached men were concentrated (Asbury, 1933).

For more than 40 years efforts by the more "responsible" citizens to control activities in the Barbary Coast were unsuccessful. For example, laws prohibiting women in saloons were passed in 1869 and again in 1876, but the people of the Barbary Coast never knew that such regulations existed. In 1890 there was a licensed saloon for every 96 San Franciscans, but there were also at least 2,000 speak-easies operating without licenses, the largest number of these being located in the Barbary Coast (Asbury, 1933: 106, 123).

Most unattached men were subject to seasonal unemployment, and they migrated to cities during periods of idleness. Many of them arrived in autumn and wintered in the city. Prior to 1880 the unattached male population in eastern cities was distributed principally in rooming houses in working class districts. Beginning about 1890 new shelter facilities began to appear. Warehouses were converted into dormitory space and large hotels for unattached men were constructed near city centers (Solenberger, 1911: 9, 314). These facilities served to centralize the low-income, unattached male population, with the result that it became an associational group whose members had the opportunity for daily contact and for the development of a distinctive subculture.

Becoming a conspicuous social entity in a distinctive urban ecological area, the unattached men were labeled members of "hobohemia." Later their neighborhood was dubbed "skid road," the term deriving from the logging camp road down which logs were skidded to a body of water for convenient transportation to a sawmill (Holbrook, 1938: 163; Morgan, 1951: 9). Via simultaneous diffusion over the country and phonetic drift ("road" became "row") the urban areas containing unattached male outcasts acquired the name they now bear: "skid row."

Workers came to the urban skid-row areas to seek on a larger scale the rapid-paced recreation found in the frontier open towns, and skid-row facilities were used for brief recreation sprees as well as for spending the winter. Of those wintering in the area, only the provident paid advance room rent until spring before "blowing it in" at the saloons, whorehouses, and gambling halls. Among the less provident majority, it was not unusual to find a man penniless after spending three months' wages in three days. Most had to skimp along on odd jobs, begging, and eating in rescue missions and soup lines.

Cities which served as central distribution centers for their economic region also played the role of employment centers. Because the skid-row area served as a nucleation of low-skilled migratory workers, employment agencies were established to fill the demand for seasonal labor throughout the hinterland served by the urban center. These agencies were called "slave markets" and the employment clerks were dubbed "man catchers," based upon the occasional practice of signing up and putting drunken men on a train for a distant hard-to-fill job.

As these cities industrialized, another niche developed in the labor market: day labor was needed to fill the fluctuating short-term employment needs of local industry. In terms of occupational skills and psychological orientation, skid-row residents were ideally suited for this economic role. Initially, short-term employment referrals were handled by gospel missions. Later casual labor offices of state employment services and private employment agencies were established in the skid-row area.

Thus seasonal employment needs in rural areas and a continuous need for casual labor in urban industry led to the establishment of skid-row areas in most large cities in the United States. The concentration of large numbers of working men in a central area permitted the development of additional institutions, including outfitting stores selling outdoor clothing and work supplies, checkrooms where baggage could be stored safely during a brief stay in town, pawn shops for obtaining quick cash when necessary, barber colleges where cheap haircuts were available to men willing to serve for student practice, and gospel missions which offered free food and lodging to men who would endure their religious services.

The availability of both food and lodging at minimal or no cost and tolerance of begging contributed to the development of an additional function of skid row, that of refuge for drop-outs from the working class. Men who were either unwilling or unable to maintain positions in the working class due to age, disease, disability, alcoholism, lack of ambition, seasonal unemployment or economic depression could find a niche

somewhere in the skid-row social system because requirements for membership were minimal. The system
was wide-open at the bottom, and nearly everyone could
fit in somewhere.

In summary, skid row came to serve a number of
major functions for single men separated from the
institutions of the stable, family-oriented community;
it was an employment center for migratory workers, a
place of "hibernation" during the winter, a locale for
recreation at any season, a supply and outfitting center,
a year-round residence for casual workers, and a refuge
for drop-outs from the working class.

After the turn of the century this collection of
employment, recreation, service and charitable institutions fused into a distinctive configuration characterized by a distinguishing set of life styles which constituted
a new community form in America (Lovald, 1960: 443).
The dominant life style was that of the hobo or migratory
casual worker, and the flamboyant world of hobohemia
flourished in urban skid-row areas and on the open road
from approximately 1900 until 1930 when great numbers
of disconsolate unemployed men invaded skid row and
changed its character.

The continuous development of a distinctive single
man's culture was associated with increasing differentiation, isolation, and opposition from the stable, family-
oriented community. The unattached men could not be
included in the status groups of the resident community
because of the differences of values stemming from the
former's lack of structured responsibility, particularly
as expressed in the lack of restraint in recreation,
pursuit of immediate pleasure, and lack of concern for
the future. The differentiation of the unattached men
from the more stable community was reinforced by
their ecological concentration. Migratory casual workers formed a separate status group quite distinct from
the settled working class.

Along with the differentiation from the working
class came three interrelated changes which greatly
diminished the size of the unattached group and markedly reduced its power: 1) in many industries mechan-

ization produced a decline in the demand for unskilled employment, particularly on a seasonal basis; 2) certain occupations experienced collective upward mobility; and 3) shifts occurred in the sex and marital composition of the population of frontier areas. Each of these changes will be discussed briefly.

The declining demand for unskilled and seasonally mobile labor is apparent in census figures. The proportion of all employed   workers engaged in unskilled non-farm labor declined from 12.5 percent in 1900 to 9.4 percent in 1940 and to 4.8 percent in 1960 (U. S. Bureau of the Census, 1960: 75-78). Furthermore, the industries employing the greatest number of unattached men were among those suffering the greatest relative decline in number of employees due to increased mechanization. For example, the relative proportion of gainfully employed workers in logging declined more than 50 percent between 1900 to 1960, and the relative proportion in metals, mining, and quarrying declined more than 80 percent (U.S. Bureau of the Census, 1902: Table 91; 1964: Table 202). The proportion of the labor force employed in agriculture decreased from 64 percent in 1850 to 38 percent in 1900. By 1940 the farm labor force included less than 19 percent of the gainfully employed, and by 1960 the figure was 6.6 percent (U. S. Bureau of the Census, 1943a: Table 18; 1964: Table 91).

Not only did many seasonal industries experience a loss in the number of employees due to mechanization, but mechanization itself lengthened the working season, and in turn diminished the demand for seasonal workers.

Collective upward mobility of whole occupational groups occurred among loggers, miners, construction workers and seamen. The critical occupational groups of logging and mining experienced large-scale unionization relatively early. Between 1897 and 1900 the number of unionized miners increased from 21,000 to 131,000. The latter figure represented over half of all metals miners. Similarly, the number of unionized loggers increased; by the turn of the century one of every four loggers was a union member (U.S. Bureau of the Census, 1960: 98; 1902: Table 91).

The combination of increased industrial production and mass unionization raised wage levels and employment stability. A lengthened working season and
higher, more stable income permitted a new style of
life among workers in formerly seasonal occupations.
Two important results were increased residential stability and a higher incidence of marriage among workers. By 1920 the majority of loggers were domesticated
family men, and the remaining single loggers tended
to be somewhat unstable persons with drinking problems
(Hayner, 1945).

Changes in technology and in the labor force were
functionally related to a change in the composition of
the population of the frontier. Although the United States
as a whole maintained a proportion of approximately
51 percent males from 1850 through 1920, corresponding figures for the Western Division (Mountain
and Pacific Regions) indicate a continual decline in
proportion of males from nearly 75 percent in 1850 to
approximately 53 percent in 1920 (U. S. Bureau of the
Census, 1892: Table 9; 1923: Table 37). At the same
time the proportion of married males increased. In
1890 only 41 percent of the males 15 years of age and
over in the western states were married; by 1920 the
figure had increased to 55 percent (U. S. Bureau of the
Census, 1943b: 104).

The change in the sex ratio and marital composition of the population led to a shift in the community
norms. The values of the frontier open town came to
be held by a decreasing minority of citizens. Gradually
the laws and law enforcement came to reflect standards
based upon the norms of the family-oriented, residen-
tially stable, home-owning, steadily employed segment
of the community.

The passing of the frontier norms may be set at
the start of the second decade of the twentieth century .
Although after 1870 the activities flourishing in San
Francisco's famed Barbary Coast were increasingly
opposed by the various church and civic groups, only
sporadically were any of the offending practices curtailed in any way. It was not until 1911 that the election

of a new mayor committed to a strong reform program presaged change. Complete repression of gambling, prostitution and unlicensed liquor sales was not accomplished immediately, but by 1917 offending establishments were completely closed down (Asbury, 1933: 309).

The year 1911 also marked the apparent demise of frontier norms in Seattle. In that year the mayor and city council sponsored construction of a 500-bed brothel designed especially for the attraction and comfort of visiting loggers. Since approval of the building site involved the donation of a 20-foot protrusion along a 100-foot frontage of public street, the city fathers obviously considered the enterprise a form of public utility. Although the building was constructed, opposition on the part of organized women's and church groups was so strong that the brothel never opened for business (Morgan, 1951: 176-180). In other cities the frontier type saloon gradually disappeared. By 1940 Nels Anderson observed that workingmen's saloons "no longer put sawdust on the floor for the comfort of drunks with rebellious stomachs" (1940: 13).

The decline in the economic need for unattached men continued until in the public view they were considered unnecessary for the maintenance of the economy. Steady employment and family group membership had become the hallmarks of the decent citizen. The unattached men of skid row were effectively set apart from the rest of the community, ecologically isolated, and labeled deviant. Defined as inferior, alien, or malicious, the skid-row men were placed outside the network of contractual obligations and emotional controls of the community. Despite the retention of economic roles by many of them, their predominant status changed from worker to outcast.

The label of outcast, however, did not obviate the lingering economic need for a smaller number of unattached workers. Even today, the unattached are needed in vacation resorts and farm work. In 1968 there were 279,000 migratory farm workers (U.S. Dept. of Agriculture, 1969: Table 4). The economic circumstances of these workers are not greatly different from those

of laborers on the frontier. They still confront extreme
seasonality of work (migratory farm workers averaged
a total of 120 days of farm work in 1968 (U. S. Dept .
of Agriculture, 1969: Table 9); are not covered by minimum wage legislation (U.S. Dept. of Labor, 1955: Section 210), and in most states lack coverage by disability
insurance (Myers, 1959: 5). As a consequence, most
migrating workers are extremely poor. In 1968 migratory farm workers received an average of $11.15 for
each of the 120 days they worked, producing a yearly
average total income of $1711 per person (U. S. Dept. of
Agriculture, 1969: Tables 4, 8 and 9). The continuation
of poor working conditions among farm workers, in contrast to lumbermen, miners, and seamen, is due to the
fact that agriculture has not experienced the unionization
which raised the wages and living standards of the other
occupational groups. Furthermore, agricultural workers
have been deliberately excluded from much federal leg -
islation designed to improve the conditions and security
of citizens.

Large Scale Unemployment

One adjustment to the severe poverty resulting from
sustained unemployment has been the dissolution of ties
with family and local community and the adoption of a
different way of life either on skid row or on the open
road where living costs are greatly diminished, soup
lines readily available, and casual employment more
easily found.
        The relationship of employment cycles and depend-
ency may be illustrated in news releases from the
Bowery Mission in New York City. It reported a huge
increase in clients during the high unemployment period
of 1915, when up to 1, 000 men per day were fed. The
following year this number dropped more than 90 percent to 85 men per day (New York Times: 1922),
and in 1917 employment was so readily available that
the breadline was closed entirely (New York Times:
1917). In 1920 over 500 men per day were fed, and
this increased to more than 1, 700 daily in the depres-

sion of 1921 (New York Times: 1921). The size of the unattached worker group diminished greatly during the 1920's, but thousands were impoverished by the large-scale unemployment occurring during the Great Depression. In 1930 the Bowery Mission reported that conditions were worse than they had ever been. Not only were the numbers large, but many men were in rags and weak from hunger (New York Times: 1930).

During the Great Depression the number of men "on the road" increased tremendously. Between 1928 and 1932 the number of men riding freight trains of the Missouri Pacific Railroad increased more than tenfold, rising from 13, 000 to 150, 000 (Lovald, 1960: 177). Comparable increases occurred on almost all railroads in the land. The migrants of the 1930's differed from those of prior decades in that travel was not an essential and continuing part of their way of life. Instead, migrancy was necessary in the search for employment, preferably steady employment.

Until the Great Depression of the 1930's the typical American view of unemployment was that it was due to individual failure. It was held that 1) any able-bodied man who really wanted work could find it, and 2) only those too thriftless to save suffered from the effects of unemployment (Calkins, 1930).

Able-bodied unemployed persons were accorded the status of deviants regardless of their economic condition and without consideration of the degree to which they were responsible for their plight. Upon joining the wandering army of unattached males, the newly unemployed were immediately stereotyped as outcasts and ne'er-do-wells, as the frontier workers had been stigmatized a generation earlier. They were considered to be untrustworthy, shiftless, and unworthy of the basic rights granted to responsible citizens (Kazarian, 1933; Sutherland and Locke, 1936: 170).

Workers in certain age classes, racial groups, and geographic regions may experience particularly high rates of unemployment somewhat independently of nationwide economic conditions. Differentials by race in unemployment have been well documented in recent years. The differential rates of unemployment by age have received somewhat less attention.

The age grouping which experiences the greatest difficulty in finding employment includes workers over 45 years of age. Age per se is a definite handicap; employers tend to prefer younger men regardless of equal or greater skill among older workers.

Age-biased hiring practices are especially detrimental for the unskilled and semi-skilled workers who experience frequent lay-offs and thus must often seek new work. Age discriminatory hiring prevents a relatively high proportion of low-skilled workers from obtaining employment and subjects them to the disaffiliating forces that accompany poverty and unemployment.

A brief review of historical trends in the magnitude of unemployment in the United States and its effects on the population of unattached men is relevant at this point. Estimates of unemployment rates are available for years since 1901. Changes will be noted for the period since that time in terms of the maximum and minimum unemployment rates and the degree of fluctuation in employment cycles. For the period since 1939 changes in the proportion of the labor force covered by unemployment insurance may be cited.

A study of the rates of cyclical unemployment demonstrates that unemployment was much more severe between 1901 and 1944 (hereafter referred to as **Period I**) than in the years following World War II (Period II). Although both periods have similar average minimum unemployment rates (4.0 percent and 3.9 percent, respectively) the average annual maximum rate for Period I was 10.5 percent of the labor force compared with 5.6 percent during Period II. The highest annual maximum unemployment rate during Period I was 24.9 percent (1933), almost four times greater than that for Period II (6.8 percent, 1958). In addition to maximum rates of lesser magnitude, the employment cycles since World War II have involved smaller fluctuations in the unemployment rates. The average percentage of change in the unemployment rate between cyclical minima and maxima declined from 6.5 percent in Period I to 2.0 percent in Period II (U.S. Bureau of the Census, 1960:73 ; 1966:218; 1968:215). With smaller fluctuations in employment rates, fewer individuals find themselves periodically out of work.

Part of the reduction in the annual variation in unemployment is due to the active federal fiscal policy of maintaining high rates of employment. In addition to federal monetary controls, the economic and social stability of unemployed workers was strengthened by the initiation of the national unemployment insurance program in 1939. In recent years this source of economic stability has been extended to cover a greater proportion of the civilian labor force, rising from 41 percent iń 1940 to 60 percent in 1965 (U. S. Dept. of Health, Education and Welfare, 1961: 39, 40; U. S. Dept. of Health, Education and Welfare, 1967: Tables 5-20, 21). Taken together, the fiscal programs for control of cyclical unemployment combined with government aid to the unemployed have greatly reduced the socially disintegrative effects of unemployment on the national scale.

Old Age, Disability, and Sickness

Exclusion from the labor market due to permanent or temporary disability, sickness, or old age may produce severe financial problems, especially for persons who have no kinsmen to whom they may turn for help. The problems of illness are compounded for low-income persons because 1) they experience more days of sickness per year than do persons with higher incomes, and 2) they have fewer dollars to spend for health care.

Data gathered by the National Center for Health Statistics show an inverse relation between income and three measures of illness (restricted activity days, bed disability days, and work-loss days for males). Men having annual incomes under $2,000 experience approximately 70 percent more restricted activity and bed disability days and **over 40 percent** more work-loss days than do men in the $2, 000 to $3, 999 income group. In contrast, the latter group suffers a 30 percent greater occurrence in each of these disability categories than do men in the $4, 000 to $6, 999 income group (U. S. Public Health Service, 1963: Tables 1, 2, 4).

Moreover, families with incomes between $7, 000 and $9, 999 spend $145 per person per year in health expenditures, while those with incomes below $2, 000 spend only $96 per person (U. S. Public Health Service, 1966: Table 3). But in the latter households this smaller expenditure amounts to 5 percent or more of total income per person, in contrast to 1. 7 percent of annual income per person for the more affluent families. Thus, in comparison with those in higher-income categories persons with low incomes face the dilemma of suffering illness more frequently and at the same time have fewer resources to cope with it.

Prior to the passage of the Social Security Act (1935) and the diffusion of health insurance programs after World War II, sickness and long-term disability could leave persons in a most desperate situation. Sometimes sickly, disabled, and aged men had to live in the areas of the city where rents were lowest; frequently that meant skid row. One alternative was going to the municipal poor house, but that was considered a sign of giving up. For many, life on skid row was preferable (Lovald, 1960: 301).

Today almshouses have nearly disappeared in the United States. The availability of the Old Age Assistance program for all low-income persons 65 years of age and over permits large numbers of the aged to maintain themselves in the community, albeit at a low-income level.

Since many aged and disabled men have very low incomes and lack the assistance of family resources, these men are more prone to enter skid row than younger or non-disabled persons. Thus, the proportion of the aged on skid row is much higher than in the national population. In 1960 the proportion of the male population of the United States aged 65 and over was 8.4

percent (U. S. Bureau of the Census, 1964: Table 45). In contrast, surveys of skid rows have found between 17 and 35 percent of the residents to be 65 and over (Caplow et al., 1958: 22; Bogue, 1963: 14; Blumberg et al., 1960: 3; Bahr, 1968: 301).

The widespread prevalence of handicaps is an important factor in the disadvantageous economic position of skid-row men and is partly responsible for their residence in the skid-row area. Survey data from Chicago illustrate the link between physical impairments and social detachment. Eleven percent of Chicago skid-row residents were found to be severely handicapped, and another 27 percent were moderately handicapped. In fact, only 28 percent of the skid-row men of working age were considered to be completely free of any handicaps (Bogue, 1963: 217).

The socially disruptive effects of illness have been diminished during the past generation by the widespread diffusion of various forms of health insurance. The proportion of the population covered by hospitalization insurance increased from 9 percent in 1940 to 83 percent in 1965. At the same time the proportion covered for surgical expenses increased from 4 percent to 77 percent (Health Insurance Institute, 1968: 19; U.S. Bur - eau of the Census, 1968: Table 2). These large-scale changes in health insurance coverage severely reduce the possibility that destitution and impoverishment will result from long-term illnesses. Further increases in health insurance coverage coupled with more comprehensive programs of financial assistance to aged and disabled persons should lessen the influence of these factors in impelling men to live on skid row.

One consequence of the social and economic changes described is a substantial decrease in the number of skid-row residents. Anderson (1923:3) estimated that during the winter months of the 1920's the Chicago homeless man population attained a magnitude of 75, 000. A survey of the same population group during the winter of 1957-58 found approximately 12, 500 persons, an 83 percent decrease (Bogue, 1963: 82). Although data regarding the size of the unattached male

population are not available for other cities prior to
World War II, surveys of skid rows in Minneapolis,
Philadelphia, and New York indicate a decline of about
25 percent between 1950 and 1960 (Caplow et al., 1958: 21-
23; Rubington, 1958; Blumberg et al., 1960: 208; Nash
and Nash, 1964: Table 5; Nash, 1964: C-5). Partly in
response to the declining population, during the early
1960's Minneapolis and Philadelphia launched urban renewal projects designed to eliminate the concentrated
skid-row area.

CHANGES IN SKID-ROW INSTITUTIONS
AND LIFE STYLES

Long-term observers agree that since the 1920's
there have been several substantial changes in the composition of skid row and the activities of its residents.
For one thing, skid row is no longer primarily a haven
for migratory workers. Anderson (1923: 96) estimated
that in 1920 over half of the Chicago skid-row population
took employment out of the city each year. A 1958 survey of the same area found that the skid-row population
consisted largely of permanent residents: only about
16 percent shipped out for seasonal work (Bogue, 1963:
237). Surveys in Minneapolis and Philadelphia also
reveal a low proportion of seasonal workers (Caplow
et al., 1958: 79-82; Blumberg et al., 1960: 32).

Another important change has occurred in the
institutions by which men are recruited into skid row.
Originally persons entered skid row chiefly through
economic institutions, either by being engaged in seasonal or day labor or as casualties of economic depression. Since World War II welfare institutions have
played a relatively greater role in drawing men to skid
row. From its origin the skid-row area has served
several functions, but the relative importance of each
function has changed. Skid row no longer is mainly a
base of operation for seasonal workers; instead, it
serves as a haven for dropouts from the working class.

As a result of these changes the range of personality traits found among the skid-row population has

narrowed. The exodus of most of the actively militant migratory workers has left behind weak, passive men, of whom approximately one-third are alcoholics. In contrast to the past, skid-row men seek only to be left alone at a minimum subsistence level.

Skid row has always contained many men who were not reliable, year-round employees, who were misfits in family-oriented communities, and who acknowledged themselves to be "losers" in the struggle for economic success. But contemporary residents of skid row differ from their predecessors in that they attribute their failure chiefly to shortcomings in themselves, such as little education, a lack of employment skills, or inability to control drinking (Bogue, 1963: 397). This attribution of responsibility to the personal faults of individuals rather than the injustices of the social system is a radical change in perspective from that expressed more than 50 years ago in hobo ballads. An individualistic interpretation of failure has replaced a socioeconomic ideology of oppression.

This change in emphasis on causal factors has contributed to a basic change in the perspective by which members view the group. In the early part of this century skid-row men saw themselves as sharing potentially unifying economic interests which separated them from the resident working class. For many, skid row was a positive reference group. Today's skid-row residents perceive individual failure as the common denominator which separates them from the working class; but the perception of common individual failure, unlike that of common exploitation, has not been the basis for any kind of organization among them. Instead, it has served to increase personal distance. For many residents skid row has become a most negative reference group.

Accompanying the change from a positive to a negative reference group is a change in the definition of the legitimacy of skid-row norms. Formerly the behavior patterns of the unattached men were defined as legitimate and those of the outside society as oppressive and unfair. Furthermore, through radical fraternal and labor organizations, the skid-row men challenged the prevailing social order and offered alternative principles of social organization for the restructuring of society. In Merton's terms, the early skid-row men were rebels in that they publicly dissented, challenged the legitimacy of the norms they rejected, and sought to change these norms by appealing to a transcendent system of justice (Merton, 1957: 360-61).

Today skid-row residents label the behavior of their peers as deviant and accept the ultimate validity of the values of the middle class. In place of attempting to change a normative system they do not follow, they now seek to hide their departure from institutionalized norms and thereby to escape their sanctions. In relation to society's major institutions the behavior of skid-row men has shifted from rebellion to retreatism.

The change from protest to passive acquiescence may be illustrated in a brief historical review of the organized activities of skid-row residents. Early in this century the radical labor and political movements had great appeal among homeless men. The largest and most active labor organization among them was the militant labor union, the International Workers of the World (I. W. W.), more commonly known as the "Wobblies." Founded in Chicago in 1905, this free-swinging radical union organized for the first time occupational groups such as longshoremen in Philadelphia, lumberjacks in remote work camps, and migratory farm workers in the midwest wheat belt (Taft, 1960). Because of the lack of stable leadership the I. W. W.'s operating methods paralleled the behavior of hobo workers. A labor historian reports that the union could not maintain a viable on-the-job organization. "It was much better adapted to engaging in colorful battles with police and local authorities than to recruiting and organizing stable and steady workers" (Taft, 1960: 55). Anderson observes that the great attraction of the I. W. W. and all other radical organizations was principally a psychological appeal to the spirit of unrest which was part of every hobo's make-up. Thus, the antisocial attitudes of rebellious individuals were sublimated into radical idealism (Anderson, 1923: 249).

Based almost entirely on fundamental Marxism, the I. W. W. enjoined its members to organize, agitate, overthrow capitalism, and to carry on production after the revolution. Although never more than mildly successful on a sustained basis, it was a vehicle for uniting unattached men who shared common occupational interests and discontent with the existing social order. Less radical hobo organizations such as the International Brotherhood Welfare Association (sponsor of the Hobo College from approximately 1910 until 1930) and the Migratory Workers' Union also served to define and express the interest of the mobile workers and to develop collective goals for the group(Anderson, 1923: 235-249). However, by 1940 the labor and fraternal organizations in skid row had disappeared. No new groups have arisen around similar or other interests; instead the orientation toward collective goals has been lost.

Similarly, interest in political issues was high in the first decades of this century. Many skid-row men favored the various socialist parties. The loss of political vitality has been gauged by Dunham's historical analysis of the voting patterns in the Detroit skid row. In 1912, 45 percent of the votes cast by skid-row residents were for minor parties such as the Socialist National Progressive (Bull Moose) and the Prohibition parties. In 1952, minor party candidates received only one percent of the votes of skid-row men (Dunham, 1953: 41). However, the most striking change in political interest is revealed, not by the move to the support of dominant parties, but by the current practice of selling votes to competing precinct committeemen. The Philadelphia skid-row area contains two precincts, one dominated by Republicans and the other by Democrats. In recent times votes have been sold at 50 cents each for primary elections and one dollar for general elections. The old-time avid interest in political, social, and economic issues has disappeared completely, and voting has changed from a vehicle for expressing opinion on vital public issues to a means for obtaining the cost of a bottle of wine or a meal in a skid-row restaurant.

The changing orientation of skid-row men also is manifested in their choice of reading material. Radical newspapers such as Industrial Solidarity, Voice of Labor, Weekly People, and the Liberator used to be popular. Although the metropolitan daily papers were also read, the majority of unattached men did not endorse them. During the 1920's the Chicago skid-row population supported book stores which sold pocket-sized editions of works on economics, politics, sociology, and history, as well as novels of adventure and travel (Anderson, 1923: 186). Forty years later the survey of the Minneapolis skid row found that nearly everyone read the metropolitan newspapers and about half of the men read magazines, usually the mass news magazines or detective and sports periodicals. No respondent read anything more radical than Life, Newsweek, and True. Books were read by 42 percent of the population but were limited to popular fiction, especially detective stories and westerns. This change to conservative reading habits may be attributed to the lack of class-based political institutions on skid row (Lovald, 1960: 405).

Early in the century the streets of skid row were alive with an assortment of "soap-box" orators advocating economic change and betterment of conditions for the working class. Although soap-box speakers never started a mass movement and may not have made a permanent impression on listeners, they did succeed in making audiences think and contributed to a sense of community by giving voice to the ill-defined sentiments shared by unattached men (Anderson, 1923: 229).

By the end of World War II the only street speakers were preachers from gospel mission advocating reform of individuals for failure to adjust to society. Nowadays there are few street meetings on skid row, but inside the missions the preachers continue to assail individual sinners with an intensity equaling or surpassing that with which radical orators of the past generation condemned the injustices of the economic system.

Today skid-row residents privately condemn the missions, but publicly no one presents an alternative to the perspective of individual depravity. This disappearance of protest activity can be interpreted as signifying one of the following conditions: 1) Skid-row men implicitly accept the message of the missions, i.e., the culpability of wayward individuals and the validity of middle class morality; or 2) Although they do not accept the message of the missions as valid, the men feel powerless to attempt to control the institutions which govern them. Either of these conditions is evidence for a shift from a rebellious to a passive world-view.

The demise of political movements among unattached working men has been paralleled by the disappearance of hobo songs and poems. Many of the ballads expressed themes of protest and of wanderlust. Anderson (1923: 198-214) cites examples such as "Harvest War Song," The Preacher and the Slave," "Portland County Jail," "The Slave Market," "The Wanderer," and "Nothing To Do But Go." These songs have disappeared from the culture of the homeless, and nothing has taken their place. Contemporary disaffiliated men, when assembled either on skid row or in a work camp, do not join together to sing even popular or traditional American songs. Similarly, the hobo poets and novelists have disappeared.

In summary, there have been marked changes in the attitudes and behavior of skid-row men. They are no longer an aggregate of aggressive working men with a great sense of pride, self-reliance, and independence, but rather a concentration of passive, inept men largely dependent on public institutions and bearing a very diminished sense of self-worth. Formerly, skid-row residents actively confronted and challenged the social order, but now they passively seek to avoid the demands of society and have withdrawn from all major responsibilities.

CONCLUSION

Future changes in the nature of the unattached population can be inferred from a projection of past trends. Whereas formerly one's "selection" to skid row was primarily the result of structural forces, today psychological factors seem most important. The availability of social service and insurance programs has diminished the migration to skid row attributable to exigencies such as unemployment, sickness, disability, and old age. Furthermore, skid row has largely lost the function of an employment center for either migratory or resident casual workers. Its continued existence appears to depend upon one important remaining function: providing a refuge for drop-outs from the working class who have psychic disabilities, a significant proportion of which involve alcoholism. If present trends continue, the population of skid row will continue to decline, and the proportion of psychically disabled skid-row men will increase. Consequently skid row may come to function primarily as an open asylum.

REFERENCES

Anderson, Nels.
    1923   The Hobo: The Sociology of the Homeless Man. Chicago: University of Chicago Press.
    1940   Men on the Move. Chicago: University of Chicago Press.
Asbury, Herbert.
    1933   The Barbary Coast: An Informal History of the San Francisco Underworld. New York: Knopf.
Bahr, Howard M.
    1968   Homelessness and Disaffiliation. New York: Columbia University Bureau of Applied Social Research.
Blumberg, Leonard, et al.
    1960   The Men on Skid Row: A Study of Philadelphia's Homeless Man Population. Philadelphia: Department of Psychiatry, Temple University School of Medicine.
Bogue, Donald J.
    1963   Skid Row in American Cities. Chicago: Community & Family Study Center.

Calkins, Clinch.
 1930   Some Folks Won't Work. New York: Harcourt,
         Brace & Company.
Caplow, Theodore, Keith A. Lovald and Samuel E. Wallace.
 1958   A General Report on the Problem of Relocat-
         ing the Population of the Lower Loop Redevelop-
         ment Area. Minneapolis: Minneapolis Housing
         & Redevelopment Authority.
Dunham, H. Warren.
 1953   Homeless Men and Their Habitats. A Research
         Planning Report. Detroit: Wayne University.
Hayner, Norman S.
 1945   "Taming the Lumberjack," American Socio-
         logical Review 10 (April): 217-225.
Health Insurance Institute.
 1968   Source Book of Health Insurance Data. New
         York: Health Insurance Institute.
Holbrook, Stewart.
 1938   Holy Old Mackinaw: A Natural History of the
         American Lumberjack. New York: Macmillan.
Kazarian, John.
 1933   "Starvation Army," Nation 136 (April): 396-398,
         443-455, 472-473.
Lovald, Keith A.
 1960   "From Hobohemia to Skid Row: The Changing
         Community of the Homeless Man." University
         of Minnesota, unpublished doctoral dissertation.
Merton, Robert K.
 1957   Social Theory and Social Structure. New York:
         Free Press.
Morgan, Murray.
 1951   Skid Row: An Informal Portrait of Seattle.
         New York: Viking Press.
Myers, Robin.
 1959   The Position of Farm Workers in Federal and
         State Legislation. New York: National Advi-
         sory Committee on Farm Labor.
Nash, George.
 1964   A Preliminary Estimate of the Population and
         Housing of the Bowery in New York City. New
         York: Columbia University, Bureau of Applied
         Social Research.

Nash, George and Patricia Nash.
   1964   A Preliminary Estimate of the Population and
           Housing of the Bowery in New York City. New
           York: Columbia University, Bureau of Applied
           Social Research.
New York Times.
   1917   "Bowery Mission Announces Discontinuation
           of Breadline Because of Prosperity Caused by
           Demand for Labor for Government Work,"
           December 26.
   1921   "Bowery Mission Tells of Great Need Among
           Unemployed," September 3.
   1922   "Bowery Mission Young Men's Home," March 29.
   1930   "Bowery Mission Appeals for Aid," August 16.
Rostow, W. W.
   1960   The Stages of Economic Growth. London: Cam-
           bridge University Press.
Rubington, Earl.
   1958   A Research Design for Dealing with the Human
           Side of Philadelphia's Skid Row Problem.
           Philadelphia: A report submitted to the Greater
           Philadelphia Movement.
Solenberger, Alice Willard.
   1911   One Thousand Homeless Men. New York: Rus-
           sell Sage Foundation.
Sutherland, Edwin H. and Harvey J. Locke.
   1936   Twenty Thousand Homeless Men.   Chicago:
           J. B. Lippincott.
Taft, Philip.
   1960   "The I. W. W. in the Grain Belt,"   Labor
           History 1 (Winter): 53-67.
United States Bureau of the Census
   1854   Compendium of the Seventh Census. Washing-
           ton, D. C. : A. O. P. Nicholson, Public Printer.
   1892   Compendium of the Eleventh Census: 1890:
           Part I, Population. Washington, D. C. : U. S.
           Government Printing Office.
   1902   Twelfth Census of the United States, Taken in
           the Year 1900: Population: Part II. Washing-
           ton, D. C. : U. S. Government Printing Office.

1902   Twelfth Census of the United States, Taken in the Year 1900: Population: Part II. Washington, D.C.: U.S. Government Printing Office.

1923   Abstract of the Fourteenth Census of the United States: 1920. Washington, D.C.: U.S. Government Printing Office.

1943a Sixteenth Census of the United States: 1940, Population. Vol. II, Characteristics of the Population, Part 1: United States Summary and Alabama-District of Columbia. Washington D.C.: U.S. Government Printing Office.

1943b Sixteenth Census of the United States: 1940, Population. Vol. IV, Characteristics by Age. Part 1: United States Summary. Washington, D.C.: U.S. Government Printing Office.

1960   Historical Statistics of the United States Colonial Times to 1957. Washington, D.C.: U.S. Government Printing Office.

1964   U.S. Census of Population: 1960. Vol. I. Characteristics of the Population. Part I, United States Summary. Washington, D.C.: U.S. Government Printing Office.

1966   Statistical Abstract of the United States: 1966. Washington, D.C.: U.S. Government Printing Office.

1968   Statistical Abstract of the United States: 1968. Washington, D.C.: U.S. Government Printing Office.

U.S. Department of Agriculture.

1969   The Hired Farm Working Force of 1968. Washington, D.C.: Economic Research Service.

U.S. Department of Health, Education and Welfare.

1961   Health, Education and Welfare Indicators (August).

1967   Health, Education and Welfare Indicators (January).

U.S. Department of Labor.

1955   Fair Labor Standards Act, as Amended. Washington, D.C.: U.S. Government Printing Office.

U. S. Public Health Service.
1963   Family Income in Relation to Selected Health Characteristics: United States. Washington, D. C. : National Center for Health Statistics.
1966   Personal Health Expenses: Per Capita Annual Expenses. Washington, D. C. : National Center for Health Statistics.

HOMELESSNESS, DISAFFILIATION, AND RETREATISM

Howard M. Bahr

Most research about homelessness has focused on residents of skid row. Often investigators have recognized that some homeless persons live elsewhere, but there are few empirical studies of the non-skid-row homeless man. Frequently social isolates who do not live on skid row have been excluded from the category of homeless persons by definitions which limit the phenomenon to participants in skid-row subculture. As a result, there is a distinct lack of information about the homeless population as a whole.

Levinson (1963:597) has compared the homeless men on skid row to the visible part of an "iceberg" of homelessness. The dimensions of the "submerged bulk" of the homeless population in one area may be inferred from Nash's (1964) estimate that in Manhattan alone there were 30, 000 homeless men in addition to the 7, 500 residents of the Bowery.

Definitions of Homelessness

The definitions of homelessness underlying most studies can be roughly grouped into two classes. One of these is the "spatial" or "ecological" view, in which residents of a particular area in a city are defined as homeless. According to the other perspective, homeless men are the "unattached" and "isolated," regardless of their economic status or area of residence. Sometimes both orientations are blended in a single work which defines homelessness in the latter sense but limits research to homelessness as spatially defined.

In one of the earliest large-scale studies of homelessness, Solenberger (1911: 3-4) recognized that not all homeless men visit charitable institutions and live on skid rows. She pointed out that the term "homeless" applied to men who had left one family group and had not yet identified themselves with another, and stressed that her work did not apply to the entire population of homeless men, but merely to those "who live in cheap lodging houses in the congested part of any large city." Her sample consisted of men who applied for assistance at the Chicago Bureau of Charities between 1900 and 1903.

The homeless man described in Anderson's The Hobo (1923: ix, 87, 89) is the "migratory casual worker." Neither his description of homeless men as "the men who inhabit Hobohemia" nor his classification of types of homelessness alludes to the existence of homeless men outside the ranks of lower-class casual workers and non-workers. The focus of Sutherland and Locke (1936) is even more limited: throughout their work "homeless man" is synonymous with "shelter man."

Dunham (1953: 14) is among those who identify homeless men in terms of their skid-row habitat while defining them in terms of personal characteristics or "situational factors." He approaches a formal definition of homelessness in his characterization of the homeless as those who have a high probability of being incompletely socialized and who are socially isolated to a high degree.

Clients of skid-row agencies have been subjects in Levinson's studies of homelessness (Levinson: 1947; 1957; 1958; 1966), but his definition of homelessness includes not only skid-row men but all persons who have learned a "fundamental detachment from life" and a "nonacceptance of the values of our society." The men on skid row who have attracted attention because they are socially troublesome are only a small part of an "invisible mountain of homelessness" (Levinson, 1963: 596-597).

The title of one of the Chicago reports, The Homeless Man on Skid Row (Tenants' Relocation Bureau,1961),
implies that there may be homeless men elsewhere, but
the reports give exclusive attention to the skid-row man.
Bogue (1963:5) recognizes a broad category of homeless
individuals, "civilian persons living outside of regular
households but not in institutions," but is concerned only
with the portion of this population that resides on skid
row.

Recently Wallace (1968) has documented the diversity in researchers' definitions of homeless and skid -
row men, listing five attributes by which the unattached
have been identified in the past. He combines these
characteristics in a property space, subsuming them
all under the term "skid - rower." His choice of the
latter term is somewhat unfortunate because half of the
cells in his table refer to persons who do not live on
skid row, and several of the works he cites to support
the contention that researchers differ in their definitions
of "skid-rower" were not defining skid-row men at all,
but rather, chronic police case inebriates (Pittman and
Gordon, 1958) or transients (Minehan, 1934). Wallace
correctly perceives a common, unifying element in the
multiplicity of definitions but to label that element
"skid-rower" is to divert attention from the majority of
the homeless, the transient, and the poor.

What the five characteristics have in common is
that they all are related to "detachment from society
characterized by the absence or attentuation of the affiliative bonds that link settled persons to a network
of interconnected social structures" (Caplow et al.,
1968:494). Thus, transience tends to prevent one from
establishing stable social bonds, residence on skid row
and involvement in its institutions places one in a stigmatized minority of outcasts without providing the bonds
of solidarity and interpersonal responsibility common
to many other out-groups, chronic inebriety disrupts
social bonds as well as physiological balance, extreme
poverty prevents one from performing customary roles
in society, and living without kin removes one from the
social context prescribed as most intense and suppor-

tive as well as from those roles to which the interpersonal responsibility of greatest scope tends to be attached. In short, these elements utilized by various writers to describe the homeless or skid-row population all have to do with the weakening or absence of affiliations.

The unifying element in the diverse definitions of homeless or skid-row persons, social affiliation, also provides a tie to one of the major theoretical perspectives of modern sociology, Merton's anomie theory, according to which one responds to the strains generated by disjuncture between societally prescribed goals and available means for achieving those goals by rebellion, innovation, ritualism, or retreatism. Merton (1957: 153) has identified tramps and vagrants as retreatists, but there has been a notable lack of research on the dimensions and consequences of retreatism. A clarification of the relation between disaffiliation and retreatism seems in order.

Retreatism and Disaffiliation

The terms "withdrawal" and "retreatism" are closely linked, and perhaps an attempt at delimiting retreatism might begin with a consideration of their meanings. As a transitive verb, to withdraw means to take back or away; as an intransitive verb, it means to retire, retreat, or go away. In either sense, there is motion from one place or state to another.

Retreat may be defined as retirement or withdrawal from what is difficult, dangerous, or disagreeable, and may also denote a place of seclusion, privacy, safety, or refuge. The term focuses on the act of leaving the difficult or disagreeable situation, but retreat from something necessarily is retreat to something. Like the fleeing general who is merely "advancing in a different direction," one moves from one place or state to another. Like "retirement," retreat connotes a coming out of circulation, a step from activity into inactivity or from active into passive service.

The parallel between spatial and social withdrawal makes it apparent that there are absolute and relative degrees of retreat and that one cannot retreat from where he has never been. Thus, certain fairly inert segments of the population can never manifest much retreat. They may be "outsiders," but since they have never been affiliated to any great extent, retreat is impossible for them.

The critical problem in the sociology of retreat is the extreme difficulty of separating retreatist behavior from the normal processes of making choices between more or less agreeable alternatives. All men are retreatists in the sense that they tend to retire from what is disagreeable and embrace the agreeable. When is withdrawal retreat, and when is it merely change?

Just as all members of society may engage in illegal behavior without thereby being considered criminal, so may they all manifest some degree of withdrawal from social involvement (retreatist behavior) without thereby qualifying for the label "retreatist." As with the term "criminal," the status "retreatist" might be reserved for those who bear the stigma of identification with particular societal institutions such as public shelters. Another possibility, preferable in the present theoretical context, is simply to reserve the term for those who manifest a high degree of retreatist behavior.

If retreatism is conceptualized as extensive social disaffiliation, the problems of operationalization are greatly simplified. Any measure of social involvement or energy outlay might serve, and, unlike the usual ecological definition (e.g., residents of skid row are retreatists), the concept is culture-free. Whatever form social affiliation happens to take, retreatism denotes withdrawal from that involvement into a state of near non-affiliation.

Incidentally, this usage is congruent with Merton's (1964: 219) conception of retreatist behavior as almost universal:

There is a streak of the innovator, of the ritual-
ist, retreatist, and rebel in most of us. Whether
these will find open expression and then become
recurrent depends, in the aggregate of cases, at
least as much on the responses of associates as
on our character and personality.

In summary, all men may be retreatists to some degree;
some retreatism is a consequence of adaptation   to
anomie, and some is attributable to other processes, including the responses of associates. Moreover, this type
of conceptualization allows the researcher to distinguish
the retreatist from the person who simply has chosen a
pattern of life that happens to be compatible with retreatism.

According to anomie theory, retreatism represents
one of several deviant adaptations to the goals - means
disjuncture. The emphasis in the theory is on "adaptation" and the retreatist is identifiable only in terms of
that process and its terminus in social withdrawal.   In
contrast, the present discussion has paid little attention
to the factors that lead to retreatism. Instead, the aim
has been to conceptualize the state of retreatism in a way
that would permit identification of the retreatist without
regard to the process producing the retreat.

However, now that retreatists have been identified
as a subclass of the population of disaffiliates,the relation
of retreatism to other forms of disaffiliation may be considered briefly. In this connection some attention necessarily will be given to the process of becoming homeless
or disaffiliated.

At least three major "paths to disaffiliation" may
be distinguished. First, "external" changes may leave
an individual with few affiliations. For example, family
and friends may die, one's occupation may become obso-
lete, or biological changes in the individual (disease or
senility) may make him incapable for forming or maintaining new organizational ties; at the same time social change or "natural causes" may remove the   old
organizations. In these cases society may be seen as

"withdrawing" from the individual: his world has disappeared, and he remains alone and unattached, a stranger
from another time or place.

A second possibility is that the individual with-
draws from society.   That is, he may find himself estranged from organizations to which he formerly belonged;
for numerous reasons he may voluntarily cut himself
adrift.   "The man without a country" is a classic example of this type of withdrawal. In some cases, society
may expel the individual, or the cost of his remaining in
society may be so great that he feels constrained to leave.
Exiles and outlaws are examples of this type, as are persons who adapt to anomie by retreating.

A third avenue to unattachment is lifetime isolation.   Some persons are outsiders from their youth, and
have never been affiliated to any degree.   Such persons
may be considered "undersocialized" in the sense that ,
for one reason or another, they have not had the experience and opportunities which serve to provide most people with ties to several kinds of organizations.

Disaffiliation is one of the fundamental processes
of social life.   Organizational ties constantly are being
made and dissolved. From the standpoint of a particular
group, a disaffiliate is one who terminates his member -
ship in the group. Factors contributing to that termination
and the disaffiliate's subsequent career may or may not
be of interest to the remaining members of the organization.   It is possible that his disaffiliation from the one
organization precedes more intense and extensive affiliations.   Nevertheless, from the standpoint of the original
organization, disaffiliation has occurred. Thus, what
is retreatist behavior from one point of view may be in-
terpretable as affiliative from another.

The formation, cessation, and attenuation of ties
being a predictable aspect of ongoing social life, organizations establish norms for recruiting, reactivating, and
replacing role-incumbents. Moreover, not only do organizations have established procedures for dealing with
new members, the disaffected and the marginal members, but they have modes of inter-organizational sanc-

tion whereby to some degree even a former member is "available" for sanction, provided he is a participant in another organization that is part of the same societal system. Therefore, although from the standpoint of particular organizations considerable disaffiliation may occur, from a wider, societal perspective all may proceed relatively smoothly. The role incumbents change, but the roles continue to be played and those who play them remain under the control of the larger system via the sanctions of specific organizations.

The stability of the larger system is threatened not by the continual forming and dissolution of bonds, but by the dissolution of bonds without the formation of new ones. The disaffiliate who does not reaffiliate moves beyond the power of particular organizations, and hence beyond that of society. He poses a threat because he has moved beyond the reward system; he is a man out of control. Being functionally if not actually devoid of significant others, property, and substantial responsibility, he is not subject to the usual social constraints. It is no threat to the fully disaffiliated man to threaten the forfeiture of his property, the imprisonment of his family, or the loss of his job. He has none of these. Perhaps the only sanction remaining is corporeal punishment, and in a system where the use of such punishments is minimized there is no way to control the retreatist _predictably_. He may go along with the rules, but there is no guarantee that he will do so, and because he is not part of the team, not privy to the conspiracy, he has no stake of any size in the continuance of the facade. He cannot be trusted.

Although total disaffiliation puts one beyond the power of the society, in another sense the retreatist is the most powerless of men. Where most men have numerous organizations through which they can multiply their influence, he has only his own resources to command. Social power comes through social organization, and one who has or is willing to cut all ties is at once both powerless and extremely powerful, being a law unto himself.

A Social Psychological Approach

The conception of retreatism described above permits the researcher to identify the retreatist in terms of his behavior (e. g., the number of his memberships) but does not take into account his perceptions or expectations. An alternative approach based upon the individual's conceptions of what is "normal" or "socially expected" will be considered briefly.

If the essence of retreatism is social withdrawal, a measure involving the subject's perceptions of the extent of his own withdrawal would seem justified. The advantage of a social psychological definition of this kind is that it requires no assumption that all retreatists have the same opportunities for affiliation or the same understanding of social expectations. In effect, each man provides his own standard, and the extent of his retreatism is measured against that standard. According to this approach, retreatism might be defined numerically as that proportion of all activities perceived by the individual as expected of him which he actually performs. Thus, it would take into account the extent to which he is affiliated, either quantitatively or qualitatively, in comparison with his perceptions of the level of affiliation expected of him.

By this definition, a person who did not measure up to society's expectations as he perceived them might be a retreatist in his own eyes and yet elicit no societal sanction. In contrast, the definition of retreatism as extreme disaffiliation involves behavior of higher visibility and a greater likelihood of negative sanction. The degree to which retreatists in the latter sense (extreme disaffiliates) also perceive themselves as having withdrawn from those activities expected of them is an empirical question deserving research.

---

[1] I have profited from reading an unpublished paper by John R. Dugan in which he proposes a social psychological definition of retreatism and a procedure for operationalizing the elements of the "retreatist equation."

Summary

The aim of the present discussion has been to specify more clearly the nexus between homelessness and retreatism in a way that would increase the theoretical relevance of the sizable body of research about homelessness and skid row. A review of researchers' definitions of homeless or skid-row men led to the isolation of a common element, low social attachment or disaffiliation. Since Merton and others have identified the activities of vagrants and hobos as illustrative of what they mean by retreatism, it seemed probable that the essence of retreatism was disaffiliation. Although specification of an operational threshold distinguishing the retreatist from the person who experiences more normal disaffiliation is best left to the empirical researcher, the general conceptualization is unambiguous. Skid row, like any other area of the city, may include affiliated men as well as disaffiliates. Among the population of disaffiliates, some may be identified as retreatists, depending on the extent of their current and former affiliations. In the framework offered, all retreatists are disaffiliates, but not all disaffiliates are retreatists.

REFERENCES

Anderson, Nels.
  1923 The Hobo: The Sociology of the Homeless Man.
        Chicago: University of Chicago Press.
Bogue, Donald J.
  1963 Skid Row in American Cities. Chicago: Community & Family Study Center, University of
        Chicago.
Caplow, Theodore, Howard M. Bahr and David Sternberg.
  1968 "Homelessness." International Encyclopedia
        of the Social Sciences 6: 494-499.
Dunham, H. Warren.
  1953 Homeless Men and Their Habitats: A Research
        Planning Report. Detroit: Wayne University.

Levinson, Boris M.
1947   "A Comparative Study of Certain Homeless
       and Unattached Domiciled Men, " New York
       University, unpublished doctoral dissertation.
1957   "The Socioeconomic Status, Intelligence, and
       Psychometric Pattern of Native-Born White
       Homeless Men," Journal of Genetic Psychology
       91 (December): 205-211.
1958   "Some Aspects of the Personality of the Native-
       Born White Homeless Man as Revealed by the
       Rorschach." Psychiatric   Quarterly Supple-
       ment 32 (Part 2): 278-286.
1963   "The Homeless Man: A Psychological Enig-
       ma, " Mental Hygiene 47 (October): 590-601 .
1966   "Subcultural Studies of Homeless Men." Trans-
       actions of the New York Academy of Sciences
       29 (December): 165-182
Merton, Robert K.
1957   Social Theory and Social Structure. Glencoe:
       Free Press.
1964   "Anomie, Anomia, and Social   Interaction :
       Contexts of Deviant Behavior. " Pp. 213 - 242
       in Marshall Clinard (ed.), Anomie and Deviant
       Behavior. New York: Free Press.
Minehan, Thomas.
1934   Boy and Girl Tramps of America. New York:
       Farrar & Rinehard.
Nash, George.
1964   The Habitats of Homeless Men in Manhattan.
       New York: Columbia University , Bureau of
       Applied Social Research.
Pittman, David J. and Wayne T. Gordon
1958   Revolving Door: A Study of the Chronic Police
       Case Inebriate. Glencoe: Free Press.
Solenberger, Alice Willard.
1911   One Thousand Homeless Men: A Study of Orig-
       inal Records. New York: Russell Sage Foun-
       dation.

Sutherland, Edwin H. and Harvey J. Locke.
  1936   Twenty Thousand Homeless Men. Chicago: J. B.
          Lippincott.
Tenants' Relocation Bureau.
  1961   The Homeless Man on Skid Row. Chicago: Ten-
          ants' Relocation Bureau.
Wallace, Samuel E.
  1968   "The Road to Skid Row." Social Problems 16
          (Summer): 92- 105.

SURVIVORSHIP AND SOCIAL ISOLATION: THE CASE OF THE AGED WIDOWER

Felix M. Berardo

The rapid social change which has characterized American society since the late nineteenth century has been accompanied by significant modifications in family organization and structure, with important implications for aged family members. Unfortunately, however, scholars are not agreed about the consequences of these changes. For example, the changes alleged to have brought about the isolation of older persons from their children and the development of feelings of neglect and loneliness among them are also cited as having produced closer affective ties between the older person and his children (Brown, 1960:170). Research concerning the relationship between the social isolation of the aged and their personal adjustment has similarly resulted in contradictory interpretations. Thus, while the findings of some investigators indicate that a decrease in contacts with friends accompanies deteriorating social adjustment, others have found no relationship between adjustment and the frequency of interaction with friends, relatives, and children (Morrison and Kristjanson, 1958).

One of the reasons suggested for the discrepancies in research findings and interpretations in this area is the tendency for investigators to treat "the aged" as a homogeneous population. Thus,

> . . . data on the aged often are not distinguished with respect to widowhood status; consequently exact information concerning the widowed becomes difficult to ascertain. Moreover, in most of the research that has been done, differences in levels of functioning as well as differences in backgrounds and experiences are overlooked or ignored; social class and cultural values are typically not differ-

Adapted from The Family Coordinator 19 (January, 1970).

entiated nor considered; and a host of important socio-economic variables are submerged under the all-inclusive homogeneous category of "the aged." (Berardo, 1968:199)

In order to illustrate the heterogeneous character of the older population and to provide insight into the nature of their adaptations to a changing status, this paper concentrates upon one segment of that population, namely, the aged survivor. More specifically, it seeks to examine the environmental conditions surrounding the aged male survivor and to assess his accommodation to widowhood status. As such, this paper forms a companion piece to an earlier work by the author dealing with the social adaptation of female survivors (Berardo, 1968).

WIDOWHOOD STATUS AND AGING

That widowhood status[1] presents rather serious problems for both individuals and families has long been recognized. This fact is perhaps most dramatically illustrated by periodic demographic analyses and other research which have consistently demonstrated that widows and widowers exhibit higher rates of mortality, mental disorder, and suicide than married persons of the same age (Berardo, 1968). These findings are particularly relevant to the older population, who experience more disruption of marital status through death of spouse than any other age group. The aged person in American society finds himself in a phase of the life-cycle which requires certain economic and sociological adaptations if he is to execute successfully an acceptable pattern of daily living which is not detrimental to his self-concept. For the aged married, the requirements for accomplishing this transition are eased by a variety of circumstances, including the benefits of mutual planning and sharing, reciprocal

------

[1]Unless otherwise specified, the term widowhood as used in this paper will have reference to male survivors only.

socio-emotional support, and the psycho-social buttress of a lengthy and continuous period of paired interaction and activity. On the other hand, for the aged widowed the problems of adaptation are compounded by the absence of a significant role partner. Both the social and psychological supports necessary for maintaining a balanced existence are frequently diminished and, in some instances, almost totally absent. [2]

Widowhood: A Neglected Aspect of the Family Life-Cycle

It would seem that the large and growing population of elderly people, a significant proportion of whom are widowed, would provoke systematic study of the problems and individual-familial modes of adaptation to survivorship. However, a recent review of the literature reveals that for a variety of reasons the special problems that confront the widowed both at the time of bereavement and later have received little attention from social scientists. Moreover, with respect to those investigations which have been carried out:

> . . . researchers have generally concentrated on the bereavement processes, per se. Consequently, they have approached their subject matter primarily, if not exclusively, from a psychological (including social-psychological and psychoanalytical) frame of reference. The personal, intrapsychic reactions to the shock of "dismemberment" have been particularly stressed. Within this context, case history analyses of individual conflict and adjustment to annihilation--with specific emphasis on the phenomena of grief, sorrow, and other components of the mental-emotional mourn-

---

[2]Most sociologists would no doubt agree with Bogue that: "few events in the life-cycle require more extensive changes in activities, responsibilities, and living habits (or cause greater alterations in attitudes, reranking of values, and alterations of outlook on life) than does a change from one marital status to another." (Bogue, 1959:212)

ing process--predominate. (Berardo, 1968:198)

It has been noted that this type of orientation is characterized by a general lack of concern with the social life of the widowed and their long-term adjustments (Gorer, 1965:150). Apparently, very few investigators have attempted to develop the sociological implications of widowhood status or to discover the social and environmental factors associated with the adaptive behavior of the bereaved. [3] Indeed, it appears that the majority of sociological research on widowhood has focused on individual reactions to the immediate crisis event, with little attention given to the adaptation of survivor families over time (Berardo, 1968:198).

Widowhood must be viewed as a social and emotional crisis situation[4] involving increasing numbers of older people and their families. It requires the development of alternative patterns of behavior if the individual is to maintain satisfactory relations with his family, kin groups, and the community, and if the survivor is to sustain a minimum level of personal equilibrium. Sociologically, widowhood status requires the reintegration of

---

[3]As Hilton (1967:182) reminds us: "Intra-psychic events, whatever their explanation, do not pursue their course regardless of current happenings in the world about. Mourning is enacted in society. The bereaved will receive some comfort and help from others. After the loss of a person, new patterns must be established with the family and with friends and in a wider society that expects individuals to show a balance of personal dependence and independence. Mourning cannot be complete unless the bereaved succeed in making an adequate worldly adjustment without the one they have lost."

[4]In recent decades, social scientists and caseworkers have shown increasing interest in examing family crisis and exploring various modes of crisis intervention. For a review and elaboration of both the clinical and social definitions of the crisis concept as it applys to widowhood, see Hill (1958), Parad and Caplan (1960), Miller and Iscoe (1963), Parad (1965), and Mackey (1968).

roles suitable to a new status. The diverse ways in which this is accomplished and the extent to which the aged male survivor is able to make a satisfactory transition will be considered in the remainder of this paper.

Male Survivorship More Problematic

Some sociologists have suggested that, from an individual as well as familial standpoint, the problems of a surviving husband are more serious than those which confront a surviving wife. It has been noted, for example, that a large proportion of aged widows are capable of living alone and taking care of themselves, whereas an aged widower is more likely to need someone to prepare his meals and provide him with other kinds of general care. "Moreover, the aged mother is more likely to be invited to live in the family of a son or daughter because she can be very useful in the household and pay her way in services rendered in the home." (Smith, 1955:267-269)The point is that the female survivor is more numerous (widows currently outnumber widowers by more than four to one), her economic problems perhaps more difficult, and she is more likely than the aged widower to be welcomed into the home of her adult married offspring and to find a useful place there.

In this connection, the lot of the aged widower has been graphically portrayed as follows:

> The elderly widower is less numerous in the population than is the widow. He may be as acutely stricken by his wife's death as the widow by that of her husband. A lifetime of close association with a woman whose complementary activities form the basis of a home now requires the most basic revision for which the widower may be wholly unprepared. If the wife was the homemaker-housekeeper, all those things upon which he depended and could anticipate in the management and upkeep of their mutual affairs devolve wholly upon him. The economy of convergent interests, the mutual resolution of each other's basic needs, the

reciprocity of activities establishing well-ordered
roles which is a bulwark of marriage are supplant-
ed by a solitary and often disjointed independence.
The viniculum that is marriage is disengaged by
death and the widower may find himself incapable
of remaking his life into an integrated whole.
(Kutner, et al., 1956:63)

Thompson and Streib (1961:177-211) similarly contend
that for the widow, unlike the widower, housekeeping
tasks usually do not represent any marked change of patterns and problems of adjustment.   For a large proportion of widows who live alone daily household tasks are
important and meaningful activity, and "ability to maintain certain standards of good housekeeping often represents' a challenge and a test of the degree to which the
older woman is avoiding 'getting old.'" In this same connection it has been suggested that the role of grandfather
probably includes a much narrower range of meaningful
activities than the role of grandmother, and on this account may be another important factor in the life adjustment of the elderly male survivor (Cavan,1967:526-536).
An additional factor favoring the female is her preference
for the type of recreation that can be engaged in during
old age, such as knitting and hobby crafts; in contrast,
the elderly male is often not vigorous enough to carry on
his former outdoor activities (Landis, 1942:607; Berardo,
1967b:19-20.

On the other hand, there are sociologists who suggest that it is the woman and not the man who faces the
greatest difficulty in returning to the single status.   Bell
(1963:412−416),for example, feels that the role of the
widow may be socially and psychologically more difficult
than the role of the widower for a variety of reasons.
He argues that in American society: 1) marriage is generally more important for the woman than the man and,
therefore, when it is terminated by death she loses a
more basic role than may be the case for the surviving
husband; 2) the widow is more apt to be forced to "go it
alone" because, in comparison to the widower she receives less encouragement from family and friends to

remarry; 3) the widow faces much more difficulty in providing and caring for herself and her children because her financial resources usually are considerably less than those of a widower; and 4) because there are far greater numbers of widows than widowers, and because the majority of them are widowed at advanced ages, it is much more difficult for a surviving wife than for a surviving husband to change her status through remarriage.

Actually, there is little consistent evidence that survivorship status demands more drastic role changes for either sex. The following examination of the available comparative evidence concerning their relative adaptive patterns may be a step toward illuminating the problem.

SOCIAL ADAPTATION OF THE AGED WIDOWED

Some recent empirical information concerning the status of the aged widower comes from a study conducted in Thurston County, Washington (Berardo, 1967b). This study focused on the critical problems confronting the aged married and widowed population and involved a comparative sociological analysis of the ways in which these problems were resolved. The most isolated subjects in the Thurston County sample were the aged widowers. This was especially true among those respondents who were older, relatively uneducated, and living in a rural environment. Another factor that led to social isolation was poor health, which sometimes caused a widower to be confined to his home and consequently limited his social contacts. [5] In addition, it was noted that, in compari-

---

[5] A comment by Rose (Rose and Peterson, 1965:10) is relevant here: "good health is sufficiently rare, and becoming rarer with advancing age, so that old people make much of it and exhibit a special admiration for those who remain healthy. A sickly old man who cannot take care of himself has little status among the elderly (or among any in the society, except perhaps his family) even if he is wealthy, whereas a vigorous old man with keen senses will be accorded high status among his compeers even though he lives exclusively on a modest pension."

son with other marital statuses, widowers were least likely 1) to be living with children, 2) to have a high degree of kin interaction or be satisfied with extended family relationships, 3) to receive from or give to children various forms of assistance, or 4) to have friends either in or outside of the community or to be satisfied with their opportunities to be with close friends. Further, they were least apt to be church members or to attend church services, or to belong to and participate in formal organizations or groups. Apparently, the overall consequences of all this is an insufficient amount of stimulating and rewarding social interaction.

There are, however, less easily identifiable factors which may be associated with the social isolation of the aged widower in American society. Such factors are cultural in nature and have to do with sex-role definitions and expectations. We have already noted the consensus among some sociologists that the role of the female remains relatively unchanged upon the death of her spouse. The assumption is that a woman will continue to perform her household duties, such as cleaning and cooking and other tasks, in much the same way as when her husband was alive. Consequently, many aged widows can maintain separate living quarters and care for themselves. The aged widower, on the other hand, is confronted with a series of practical problems as a result of the death of his wife. He finds himself faced with accomplishing additional and traditionally female tasks, such as keeping house. Consequently, he is likely to need someone to prepare his meals, maintain the household, and provide him with general care. At the same time, however, there is a general societal expectation that males should fend for themselves and avoid taking on a dependency status. This is an expectation which the aged widower is not always able to live up to. But his awareness of that expectation may lead to a certain hesitation or reluctance to seek assistance. In fact, in certain instances this awareness may make the widower feel compelled to sustain a public image of self-sufficiency in the face of a burdensome existence. It is quite possible that the isolation and loneliness of some widowers are the consequences of this reluctance to admit an inability to maintain a rewarding independent existence.

Other findings from the Thurston County study are informative. The rather low degree of social participation observed on the part of the widowers was not due to a lack of available free time. On the contrary, widowers in the sample generally had a greater surplus of leisure hours than persons in other marital statuses. Nevertheless, they had much more difficulty in occupying themselves with meaningful activity.

The lower degree of kinship interaction among aged widowers is partially explained by the central role assigned to females in maintaining kinship obligations. In American society, the female has assumed responsibility for integrating the kindred, whether through direct contact or via other communicative processes (Berardo, 1967a). Thus, women generally exhibit a much greater involvement in the kinship system than men (Farber, 1964: 206-214). Moreover, it has been observed that the greater participation of females in the performance of duties imposed by kinship provides them with many opportunities for exhibiting a preference for the maternal side of the family: "In those activities with relatives which are not clearly obligatory, a woman is able to express her preference for her own blood relatives, and in doing so increase their contact with her children as compared with her husband's relatives' contact." (Robins and Tomanec, 1962:340- 346)The consequences of this emphasis on the maternal line are eventually reflected in widowhood. Thus, in some recent research on extended family relations it was found that when the surviving parent was the mother kinship interaction remained almost as high as when both parents were alive. On the other hand, when the surviving parent was the father, the frequency of interaction with extended family members was nearly as low as when both parents were deceased (Berardo, 1965:107). [6]

---

[6]It should be noted that interaction with kin on the part of the husband need not necessarily be decreased as a result of the death of the wife. In principle there is nothing

SOCIAL CONSEQUENCES OF WIDOWHOOD STATUS

In examining the changes in status and age identification (i.e., conceptions people have of themselves as being young, middle-aged, or old) that occur over the life-span, Blau (1956) analyzed data gathered from a representative sample of respondents 60 years of age or older residing in Elmira, New York. She notes that although the loss of one social status is generally accompanied by entry into another, in the case of retirement or widowhood such transitions are particularly difficult. Both of these transitions are major status changes which typically occur in old age and which denote the permanent loss of two crucially important social roles as well as the activities and relationships that define them

It was hypothesized that such changes in social status among the aged would be associated with shifts in their age identification. However, analysis revealed only partial confirmation of this hypothesis. Although retirees of each age level considered themselves old more frequently than those who were still employed, this was less true of the widowed. At each age level, the widowed considered themselves old only slightly more often than those who were still married. This differential effect of retirement and widowhood on age identification was explained in terms of the differential perceptions and consequences of the two statuses. More specifically:

> Retirement is a social pattern which implies an invidious judgment on the part of others in the society about the lack of fitness of old people to perform a culturally significant role, whereas the death of the marital partner, being a natural event, and not a socially induced one, does not have such implications in our culture. Thus, the retired in-

---

to prevent the surviving husband from initiating and promoting extended family interaction. He may, for example, write letters and make telephone calls, as well as actually visit with married offspring and other relatives.

dividual, but not the widowed one has reason to believe that he is socially defined as old. (Blau, 1956:200)

Moreover, retirement abruptly removes a person from his occupational peer group and either drastically reduces or completely eliminates his participation in those informal but meaningful social relations developed on the job. The death of a spouse, on the other hand, eliminates only a single crucial social relationship. Blau concluded that perhaps "loss of membership in a peer group has more pronounced effects on the self-image of older people than the loss of an intimate interpersonal relationship, and that this helps to explain the differential effect of retirement and widowhood on age identification." (Blau, 1956:200)

Widowhood and Friendship Patterns

There is evidence that major shifts in social status which occur as a result of widowhood and retirement significantly affect friendship patterns. Blau (1961) found that the maintenance of friendship ties was an important mechanism of adjustment among older people following either retirement or widowhood, and that while the extent of friendship participation generally declined with age, changes in marital status or employment status tended to have an adverse effect on friendships.[7] A closer examination of the data, however, revealed that the consequences of widowhood on the individual's social participation varied by age. For persons seventy years of age and older, widowhood had no detrimental effects on their

---

[7]It will be recalled that the Thurston County study also revealed that married persons had more friendship ties than widowed persons. Moreover, widowers were most likely to have no friends at all. In addition, the widowed were more likely than the married to prefer friends of their own age group, and widowers were most likely to state such a preference (Berardo, 1967b:25-26).

social participation, whereas the friendships of those still in their sixties were adversely affected. This finding is explained in terms of the greater number of widowed persons available at the older age levels:

> Widowhood appears to have an adverse effect on social participation only when it places an individual in a position different from that of most of his age and sex peers. People tend to form friendships with others in their own age group, and to the extent that this occurs, the widowed person under seventy is likely to be an "odd" person at social gatherings, since most of his associates are probably still married and participate with their spouse in social activities. This difference in his marital position may very well have a detrimental effect on his participation. But after seventy, married couples who continue to participate jointly in social activities become the deviants, since most of their friends in this age group are likely to be widowed. (Blau, 1961:431)

In terms of sex differences, analysis showed that among older persons under seventy, the loss of a spouse had a more adverse effect on the social participation of widowers than on that of widows. Again, a structural explanation is offered to account for these differences. In the age group under seventy there was a much larger proportion of female survivors (43 percent) than male survivors (13 percent). Given this imbalance with reference to his age and sex group, the aged male widower occupies a more deviant position than his female counterpart. This means that most of the friends of the male widower in his sixties are still married. Although widowhood status is likely to decrease an older woman's social participation with married friends, the over-all decrease will not be as great as that observed among widowers, since widows under seventy are more likely to have associates who also are widowed.

In the age group over seventy, however, the proportion of widowers increases substantially with the result that the earlier differences observed between married and widowed men practically disappear. At that point widowhood status ceases to have an isolating effect upon aged male survivors. When a widower enters his seventies, he discovers that many more of his friends have also lost their wives. In short, he encounters a larger pool of male survivors with whom he can interact in terms of social companionship. These and other findings led to the conclusion that "widowhood tends to exert a detrimental effect on friendships in those structural contexts where it is relatively rare but not in those where it becomes more prevalent." (Blau, 1961:433)

Loss of Occupational Role and Social Isolation of Widowers

The evidence seems fairly clear that the adjustment of older males to widowhood status is rather directly linked to two major factors, namely, their health and occupational status, with the latter playing the more dominant role (Kutner, et al., 1956:66-67). During most of his working life, the American husband engages in roles sharply differentiated from those of the wife. From a sociological point of view, it is primarily by virtue of his significance in the occupational sphere and attendant social role of family breadwinner that the husband manages to develop and sustain a satisfactory self-image and status both in society and in the home (Lipman, 1962:475-485).

However, with the onset of retirement traditional sex-differentiated roles and the self-concepts which derive from them frequently undergo various degrees of strain and alteration, especially in the case of males. Whereas many wives of retirement families are able to satisfactorily continue their traditional role as homemaker, a similar pattern of role continuity is denied the husband: "the role of wage earner, which he had conceived as his primary role, is suddenly withdrawn; structurally he is isolated from the occupational system, and this shock often has grave effects upon his entire existence." (Lipman, 1962:476) Thus, if an older man becomes unemployed through retirement, suffers ill health, and loses his wife as well, it would no doubt be gross understatement to suggest that the groundwork is laid for some rather damaging consequences. [8] For example, Kutner and his associates (1956:67) found that while the morale of widowers remained fairly high, it was severely affected by the subsequent losses of employment and good health. However, the onset of poor health was not as detrimental to morale as was retirement or unemployment. Interestingly, when married and widowed men who were employed and in good health were compared, no differences in morale were observed.

WIDOWHOOD, MORTALITY, AND SOCIAL ISOLATION

Townsend's (1957) analysis of social isolation among the aged in London led him to conclude that while it was generally difficult for older persons to adapt to new situations, those forced to adjust their lives following the death of a spouse faced particular difficulties. In this connection, he was impressed by the expressions of loneliness voiced by the widowed respondents in his sample. [9] This led him to hypothesize that the aged widowed were likely to exhibit higher mortality rates than married or single persons, including their age peers who had been widowed when younger (Townsend, 1957:178). While Townsend was unable to obtain systematic data about the influence of bereavement upon death rates, he did examine mortality rates by age and marital status for England and

---

[8]Sociologists have stated this as a more general principle: "The more life disruptions a person had had, the greater the probability that he would have a low morale." (Montgomery,1965:41)

[9]Of importance here is the useful conceptual distinction between isolates and desolates in old age. Townsend suggests that isolates are persons who have become secluded from their families and from society, whereas desolates are persons who have been recently deprived of the company of a loved one (Townsend, 1957:182). It is his contention that desolation rather than isolation is the major reason for loneliness in old age.

Wales. His analysis showed higher death rates among
older widowed people than others, with the highest death
rates occurring among the aged widowers. Townsend
noted that the higher mortality of males, and widowers
in particular, could not be explained entirely by biological
and physiological differences. Instead, "the social and
especially the family circumstances of individuals are a
major determinant of the rate of decline in the power of
self-adjustment and self-defense in later life." (Townsend, 1957:181-182) On the basis of evidence from his
own study Townsend suggests that socially isolated or
desolated aged persons will not survive as long as older
persons who continue to function within a secure family
system.

Analyses of national vital statistics and census data
for the United States by Kraus and Lilienfeld (1959) revealed that the widowed have significantly higher mortality rates than married persons of the same age, and
that mortality rates are particularly high among young
widowed people. [10] They suggest three possible explanations for the higher death rates among the widowed:
1) individuals with a short survival potential tend to
choose mates like themselves; 2) the widowed and his deceased spouse share the unfavorable environmental factors which led to the death of the first spouse; and finally,
3) the grief, new worries, responsibilities, and alterations in daily routine that follow bereavement have a damaging effect upon the surviving spouse.

Young, Benjamin, and Wallis (1963) similarly suggest that the shock of widowhood might weaken the re-
sistence to other causes of death. In order to test this
notion, they examined the "duration effect" of being widowed, that is, how long people had been widowed when

---

[10]The mortality differential is greatest for white males
between the ages of 25 and 34. A male widower of this
cohort is 4.3 times as likely to die as his married counterpart. Among the age groups beyond 34 the preponderance of the death rates of the widowed over those of
the married decreases steadily with age.

they died. Their analysis of the "duration effect" of widowhood on the mortality of 4,486 widowers aged 55 and over showed that widowhood increased the mortality rates of these male survivors by about 40 percent in the first six months following bereavement. This initial increase in widower mortality was eventually followed by a return to the level for married men in general.

Additional investigations in the United States as well as abroad have supported the general finding regarding the higher mortality of the widowed and, in particular, the widower. Moreover, recent research by Rees and Lutkins (1967) has provided rather dramatic statistical confirmation of the long-standing hypothesis that a death in the family produces an increased post-bereavement mortality rate among close relatives, with the greatest increase in mortality occurring among surviving spouses. During the first year following bereavement deaths among the bereaved close relatives were seven times as frequent as among a control group. The mortality rate for male relatives was significantly greater than that for female relatives, and the rate for widowers was considerably higher than that of widows. [11]

At present, precise knowledge is lacking concerning the primary causative agents underlying this association between bereavement and mortality. Homogamy (the tendency for the fit to marry the fit and the unfit to marry the unfit), common infection (both spouses dying from the same disease), joint unfavorable environment (unfavorable environmental circumstances that cause one spouse to die also cause the other to die), loss of care (i. e., care formerly provided by the deceased spouse), have all been suggested as possible influences (Young,

---

[11]Rees and Lutkins' analysis suggests that young and middle-aged men whose wives died outside of the home are particularly vulnerable. For the total sample, there was five times the risk if the original death occurred some place other than home or hospital, probably because deaths at "other sites" were invariably sudden and the shock to relatives presumably greater.

Benjamin and Wallis, 1963). Another frequently cited factor is the so-called "broken heart" syndrome. Relevant to this syndrome are British studies indicating that the great increase in mortality among widowers is largely attributable to death from coronary thrombosis and arteriosclerotic heart disease (Parkes and Benjamin, 1967: 232).

Finally, a number of researchers have suggested that the emotional stress associated with grief may lower physical resistance to disease and even a person's "will to live." In this connection, several investigators have asserted that western culture is more stressful to males, since it permits women to express their emotions overtly but encourages men to suppress similar feelings. Thus, for example, Tunstall (1966:153) suggests that aged male survivors are more apt to be affected by the demise of their wives because "the psychological position is very different for men, since widely accepted norms of emotional and social behavior in our society make it more acceptable for women to weep, to express grief and to receive comforting and consolation--but less acceptable for men."

WIDOWHOOD AND SUICIDE

Durkheim was the first well-known sociologist to stress the connection between widowhood and suicide. He argued that suicides which occurred at the crisis of widowhood were

> . . . really due to domestic anomy resulting from the death of husband or wife. A family catastrophe occurs which affects the survivor. He is not adapted to the new situation in which he finds himself and accordingly offers less resistance to suicide. (Durkheim, 1951:259)

Numerous investigators have since demonstrated that within a given age group the suicide rates of the widowed are consistently higher than for the married, and the rate of completed suicides is significantly higher for males. A recent review of these studies indicates that

suicide--whether attempted or successful--frequently
tends to be preceded by the disruption of significant social interaction and reciprocal role relationships through
the loss of a mate (Rushing, 1968). Moreover, these
studies further reveal that the death of one or both parents
in childhood is common among attempted and actual suicide victims and that the incidence of suicide among such
persons when they attain adulthood is much greater than
for comparable groups in the general population.

Although a great deal of research has been conducted on the etiology and social correlates of suicide,
investigators frequently ignore or fail to report the details concerning the differential rates of widows and widowers. Durkheim (1951:171-216) was exceptional in his
attempts to specify the conditions under which widowhood
would be more disastrous for males or females. Among
other things, he showed that widowers with children were
more prone to self destruction than widowers without
children. It was Durkheim's contention that the presence
of children tends to intensify the crisis through which
the widower is passing. Forced to shoulder a double burden
and to perform a variety of maternal functions for which
he is unprepared, the male survivor with children finds
his life acutely disrupted. "It is not because his mar-
rage is ended but because the family which he heads is
disorganized. The departure, not of the wife but of the
mother, causes the disaster." (Durkheim, 1951:188)
Thus, in a more recent study of the adjustment of children in motherless homes (Wargotz, 1968) it was found
that widowers generally were unable to communicate effectively with their children in a manner that led to the
smooth operation of the family from both an emotional
and a practical viewpoint. The basic reason for this was
the father's inability to understand and compensate for the
deceased mother's functions.

WIDOWHOOD AND MENTAL ILLNESS

That a high correlation exists between marital status
and mental illness has been repeatedly noted in the scientific literature. While considerable professional con-

troversy prevails over identification of the exact sequence
of the antecedent-consequent conditions which predispose
individuals toward various forms of organic and psychogenic disorders, the evidence is quite consistent that
widowed persons experience a substantially higher rate
of mental disorders than the still married, particularly
among the older populations. Widowed males are particularly susceptible (Adler, 1953).

The association between marital status and mental
disorders has been shown to be a function of several intervening factors, including age, socio-economic status,
physical condition, and the degree and duration of social
isolation (Adler, 1953; Bellen and Hardt, 1958; Lowenthal, 1964, 1965). Problems of social isolation, often
accompanied by distressing loneliness, are especially
germane to the personal adjustment of aged survivors,
a very high proportion of whom are residing alone as
occupants of one-person households (Belcher, 1967).

A large-scale assessment of the mental health of
the American public (Gurin, et al., 1960:236-238) included a comparison of widows, widowers, and persons
in other marital statuses. Among the findings: 1) the
widowed said they worried "all the time" more frequently than any other group except the divorced and separated
women (female survivors reported extreme worrying
more often than widowers); 2) again with the exception
of divorced or separated women, the widowed were unusually low in their reported feelings of present happiness (this was especially true of male survivors); and
3) widows and widowers were most pessimistic, with
more anticipation of unhappiness and death in the near
future than any other group (widowers were more pessimistic than widows). The researchers concluded:

> The picture of the widowed status is a bleak one;
> with divorce, it seems to be the solitary status
> which holds the greatest threat to positive adjust-
> ment . . . the widowed group--the only clearly
> non-voluntary solitary status--reports particu-
> larly intense feelings of distress, both in the pre-
> sent and in anticipation of the future. (Gurin, et
> al., 1960:238)

A number of studies have found higher gross rates of psychiatric impairment among the widowed (as well as the separated, divorced, and single) than among the married (Bellin and Hardt, 1958). However, the relationship between widowhood status and mental disorder often appears to be contingent upon other variables. For example, Lowenthal and Berkman's (1967) study of the mental health of the aged in San Francisco showed that the relationship between widowhood and psychiatric impairment was conditional upon the pattern of socio-economic status, physical condition, and other factors. Among aged respondents in good physical condition the differences between the widowed and married in rate of psychiatric impairment were either small or nonexistent, regardless of socio-economic status. On the other hand, for subjects of high socio-economic status and in poor physical condition, psychiatric impairment was much more frequent among the widowed than the married. These and other findings led the investigators to suggest that "poor physical condition is more closely related to mental disorder among the aged than is socio-economic status; for regardless of socio-economic status, the highest impairment rates . . . occur in conjunction with poor physical condition." (Lowenthal and Berkman, 1967: 74-75)

The conditional relationship of marital status (widowhood in particular) and psychiatric difficulties was further demonstrated when rates of impairment were compared with reference to respondents' sex and age, deprivation (measured by poor physical condition, low social activity, and complaints about living arrangements), and marital status. This comparison showed little difference in rate of psychiatric impairment between married and widowed respondents who were "relatively nondeprived," but a pronounced difference in favor of the married among those respondents exhibiting high deprivation. The investigators concluded that the "vulnerability to the stresses of widowhood is especially contingent on the incidence of other deprivations present; the greater the latter, the fewer would be the resources

to withstand the additional stresses of widowhood."
(Lowenthal and Berkman, 1967:75)

CONCLUDING REMARKS

The transition from agrarian to urban and industrial society in America was accompanied by the emergence of
a conception of the aged which stressed the involuntary
structural isolation of older couples from their children
and relatives (Parsons, 1959). In this perspective the
young were seen as giving priority and allegiance to the
norms of occupational achievement and this, along with
the high mobility of the labor force, was said to isolate
older people from their families. Consequently, there
developed a view of the aged family as rejected, lonely,
and a liability. To a considerable extent, this stereotype
continues to prevail in both the popular mass media and
scientific literature. As one gerontologist has commented: "most theories of aging are couched in the
language of despair." (Kutner, 1962:6)
   In recent decades, however, empirical evidence
has accumulated which casts considerable doubt upon
what Shanas (1963) has termed this "myth of alienation."
Her analysis of national census data on persons 65 years
and older showed that the majority of the noninstitution-
alized aged in the United States who had children were
in close proximity to at least one of them, and saw them
often (Shanas, 1961). Cross-cultural comparisons
(World Health Organization, 1959; Shanas, 1967) reveal
that a similar pattern prevails in Britain, Denmark, the
United States, and other industrialized societies.
   Within the above context, the situation of the aged
widower in America would appear to represent an anomalous case. The evidence presented in the preceding pages
strongly suggests that the aged male survivor encounters
rather severe difficulties in his efforts to adapt to the
single status, and that these difficulties differ in kind
from those experienced by his female counterpart.
   In addition to the practical necessity of becoming
proficient in domestic roles, the widower must find an

adequate substitute for the intimacy of that primary relationship once provided by his wife, and this is perhaps the most difficult task of all. For some, remarriage provides a partial solution, but in American society the courtship opportunities of the aged are limited. Even if an older male is successful in locating a potential second mate he may still have to overcome certain obstacles related to an apparent cultural bias against such unions. McKain (1969:6) has commented recently on the social sanctions against marriages of older persons:

> One solution for the widowed person who wishes to live in a family environment is to remarry and have a home of his own. The older person, independent and financially secure, vigorous and in good health, needing and appreciating companionship, is in a good position to remarry. However, at this point a barrier has been erected between what he wishes to do and what society expects him to do. His friends, his children and the community at large rise up and condemn his remarriage. He is regarded as "too old for that." The wagging fingers, the knowing smiles, the raised eyebrows and the cruel tongues are set in motion. Marriage is for the young in age, not the young in heart. Our ideas of marriage have lagged behind important changes in the family as a social institution. Attitudes have not kept pace with practices. Social conventions are not consistent with social realities.

McKain contends that such conditions have prevented older persons from marrying and have forced many elderly couples to marry in secret. Apparently, many such couples who desire to marry in spite of family and community pressures do so by crossing state lines in order to avoid public opinion and public censure (McKain, 1969:6-7).

We have seen that the widower's problems of adjustment are further compounded by the loss of his occupational role. For most of his adult life his work has been a principle source of his identity and self-conception. Retirement severs that identity, often abruptly, and removes the male survivor from meaningful contact with friends and co-workers. The combined retiree-widower status places him in a position of structural isolation, leading to reduced communication and interaction with significant others. The culture provides little in the way of guidelines concerning the steps that must be taken if he is to reorganize his life successfully and avoid succumbing to the process of alienation.

Finally, it should be noted that in American society separation and isolation are intimately associated with death. For example, prevailing funeral customs tend to dramatize the separation process; the activities and religious ceremonies surrounding the burial often serve to emphasize the loss. Moreover, there is an emphasis on the nuclear family and on a narrow circle of significant others which may produce an exaggerated sense of social isolation and generate considerable anxiety among the bereaved.

> . . . most individuals live within a tight security circle, relying upon only a few people for emotional gratification. This tends to produce intense, rather than diffuse affective relationships, rendering separation from only a few people a potentially critical emotional experience. The possibility of finding adequate substitutes for significant others is remote. As a consequence, the whole self-image of an individual is under maximum risk when he is faced with separation. (Howard and Scott, 1966:163)

Indeed, it has been argued that in American society separation from significant others is tantamount to social isolation. [12] The analysis presented in this paper would

---

[12] Howard and Scott (1966:164) also comment on the reciprocal relationship between death and social isolation, noting that persons who are undergoing the process of becoming socially isolated frequently in turn become overly concerned about death: "the individual experiencing sep-

lead one to conclude that, at least in the case of the aged male survivor, such an argument has considerable validity.

REFERENCES

Adler, Leta M.
  1953   "The Relationship of Marital Status to Incidence and Recovery from Mental Illness." Social Forces 32 (December):185-194.
Belcher, John C.
  1967   "The One-Person Household: A Consequence of The Isolated Nuclear Family?" Journal of Marriage and the Family 29 (August):534-540.
Bell, Robert R.
  1963   Marriage and Family Interaction. Homewood, Illinois: Dorsey.
Bellin, Seymour S. and Robert H. Hardt.
  1958   "Marital Status and Mental Disorders Among the Aged." American Sociological Review 23 (April):155-162.
Berardo, Felix M.
  1967a   'Kinship Interaction and Communications Among Space-Age Migrants." Journal of Marriage and the Family 29 (August):541-554.
  1967b   Social Adaption to Widowhood Among a Rural-Urban Aged Population. Washington Agricultural Experiment Station Bulletin 689, College of Agriculture, Washington State University.

aration from others may become obsessed with the idea of death. Ordinary values, those previously associated with primary groups or with society in general, may pale into insignificance when they are no longer shared with significant others. As these values lose their saliency, behavior patterns once structured by culturally shared imperatives may come to be based upon only the grossest considerations of life and death. As a result, the fear of death may come to outweigh the fear of dying, and the person may be motivated toward ego-destructive behavior."

1968   "Widowhood Status in the United States: Perspective on a Neglected Aspect of the Family
Life Cycle." Family Coordinator 17 (July):
191-203.
1969   Death, Bereavement, and Widowhood: A Selective Bibliography. Department of Sociology,
Washington State University (mimeographed).
Bernard, Jessie.
1956   Remarriage: A Study of Marriage. New York:
Dryden.
Blau, Zena S.
1956   "Changes in Status and Age Identification."
American Sociological Review 21 (April):198-
203.
1961   "Structural Constraints on Friendship in Old
Age." American Sociological Review 26 (June):
429-439.
Bogue, Donald T.
1959   The Population of the United States. Glencoe,
Illinois: Free Press.
Brown, Robert G.
1960   "Family Structure and Social Isolation of Older
Persons." Journal of Gerontology 15 (April):
170-174.
Cavan, Ruth S.
1962   "Self and Role Adjustment During Old Age."
Pp. 526-528 in Arnold M. Rose (ed.), Human
Behavior and Social Processes: An Interaction-
ist Approach. Boston: Houghton-Mifflin.
Durkheim, Emile.
1951   Suicide: A Study in Sociology. Glencoe, Illinois:
Free Press.
Farber, Bernard.
1964   Family: Organization and Interaction. San
Francisco: Chandler.
Freud, Sigmund.
1924   "Mourning and Melancholia." Pp. 152-170 in
Collected Papers of Sigmund Freud. Vol. IV.
London: The   International   Psychoanalytic
Press (1949).

Gorer, Geoffrey.
    1965   Death, Grief, and Mourning. Garden City,
            New York: Doubleday.
Gurin, Gerald, Joseph Veroff, and Sheila Feld.
    1960   Americans View Their Mental Health. New
            York: Basic Books.
Havighurst, Robert J. and Ruth Albrecht.
    1953   Older People. New York: Longmans, Green.
Herzog, Elizabeth and Cecelia E. Sudia.
    1968   "Fatherless Homes." Children 15 (September-
            October):177-182.
Hill, Reuben.
    1958   "Social Stresses on the Family." Journal of
            Social Casework 39 (February):139-150.
Hilton, John.
    1967   Dying. Baltimore: Penguin Books.
Howard, Alan and Robert A. Scott.
    1965   "Cultural Values and Attitudes Toward Death."
            Journal of Existentialism 6 (Winter):161-174.
Kraus, Arthur S. and Abraham Lilienfeld.
    1959   "Some Epidemiological Aspects of the High
            Mortality in the Young Widowed Group." Jour-
            nal of Chronic Diseases 10 (September):207-217.
Kutner, Bernard, David Fanshel, Alice M. Togo and
            Thomas S. Langner.
    1956   Five-Hundred Over Sixty. New York: Russell
            Sage.
Krupp, George R. and Bernard Kligfeld.
    1962   "The Bereavement Reaction: A Cross-Cultural
            Evaluation," Journal of Religion and Health 1
            (April):222-246.
Landis, Judson T.
    1942   "Hobbies and Happiness in Old Age." Recrea-
            tion 35 (January):607, 641-642.
Langner, Thomas S. and Stanley T. Michael.
    1963   Life Stress and Mental Health. New York:
            Free Press.
Lindemann, Erich.
    1944   "Symptomatology and Management of Acute
            Grief." American Journal of Psychiatry 101
            (July):141-148.

Lipman, Aaron.
1962   "Role Conceptions of Couples in Retirement."
        Pp. 475-485 in Mark Tibbetts and Wilma Dona-
        hue (eds.), Social and Psychological Aspects of
        Aging. New York: Columbia University Press.
Lowenthal, Marjorie F.
1964   "Social Isolation and Mental Illness in Old Age."
        American Sociological Review 29 (February):
        54-70.
1965   "Antecedants of Isolation and Mental Illness in
        Old Age." Archives of General Psychiatry 12
        (March):245-254.
Lowenthal, Marjorie F. and Paul L. Berkman.
1967   Aging and Mental Disorder in San Francisco.
        San Francisco: Jossey-Bass.
McKain, Walter.
1969   Retirement Marriage. Agricultural Experiment
        Station Monograph 3, University of Connecticut.
Mackey, Richard A.
1968   "Crisis Theory: Its Development and Relevance
        to Social Casework Practices." Family Life
        Coordinator 17 (July):165-173.
Miller, Kent and Ira Iscoe.
1963   "The Concept of Crisis: Current Status and
        Mental Health Implications." Human Organi-
        zation 22 (Fall):195-201.
Montgomery, James E.
1965   Social Characteristics of the Aged in a Small
        Pennsylvania Community. College of Home
        Economics Research Publication 233, Pennsyl-
        vania State University.
Morrison, Denton E. and G. Albert Kristjanson.
1958   Personal Adjustment Among Older Persons.
        Agricultural Experiment Station Technical Bul-
        letin 21. South Dakota State College of Agricul-
        ture and Mechanical Arts.
Parad, Howard J. (ed.)
1965   Crisis Intervention: Selected Reading. New
        York: Family Service Association of America.
Parad, Howard J. and G. Caplan.
1960   "A Framework for Studying Families in Crisis."
        Social Work 5 (July):5-15.

Parkes, C. Murray and Bernard Benjamin.
 1967 "Bereavement," British Medical Journal 3
       (July-September):232-233.
Parsons, Talcott.
 1959 "The Social Structure of the Family." Pp. 241-
       274 in Ruth N. Anshem (ed.), The Family: Its
       Function and Destiny. New York: Harper.
 1962 "The Aging in American Society." Law and
       Contemporary Problems 27 (Spring):22-35.
Phillips, Bernard S.
 1957 "A Role Theory Approach to Adjustment in Old
       Age." American Sociological Review 22 (April):
       212-217.
Rees, W. Dewi and Sylvia G. Lutkins.
 1967 "Mortality of Bereavement." British Medical
       Journal 4 (October-December):13-16.
Robins, Lee N. and Miroda Tomanec.
 1962 "Closeness to Blood Relatives Outside The
       Immediate Family." Marriage and Family Liv-
       ing 24 (November):340-346.
Rose, Arnold and Warren A. Peterson (eds.)
 1965 Older People and Their Social World. Philadel-
       phia: Davis.
Rushing, William.
 1968 "Individual Behavior and Suicide," Pp. 96-121
       in Jack P. Gibbs (ed.), Suicide. New York:
       Harper and Row.
 1969 "Deviance, Interpersonal Relations, and Sui-
       cide." Human Relations 22 (February):61-76.
Shanas, Ethel.
 1961 "Living Arrangements of Older People in the
       United States." The Gerontologist 1 (March):
       27-29.
 1963 "The Unmarried Old Person in the United States:
       Living Arrangements and Care in Illness, Myth,
       and Fact," Unpublished paper prepared for the
       International Social Science Research Seminar
       in Gerontology, Makaryd, Sweden.
 1967 "Family Help Patterns and Social Class in Three
       Countries." Journal of Marriage and the Fam-
       ily 29 (May):257-266.

Smith, T. Lynn.
1955 Social Problems. New York: Crowell.
Srole, Leo, Thomas L. Langner, Stanley T. Michael,
Marvin K. Opler, and Thomas A.C. Rennie.
1961 Mental Health in the Metropolis. New York:
McGraw-Hill.
Strub, Holger R.
1966 "Family Structure and the Social Consequences
of Death" Pp. 191-200 in Jeanette R. Forta and
Edith S. Deck (eds.), A Sociological Framework
for Patient Care. New York: Wiley.
Thompson, Wayne E. and Gordon F. Streib.
1961 "Meaningful Activity in a Family Context," Pp.
177-211 in Robert W. Kleemier (ed.), Aging
and Leisure: A Perspective into The Meaningful Use of Time. New York: Oxford University
Press.
Townsend, Peter.
1957 The Family Life of Old People. Glencoe, Illinois: Free Press.
Tunstall, Jeremy.
1966 Old and Alone: A Sociological Study of Old People. London: Routledge and Kegan Paul.
Wargotz, Helen.
1968 "The Adjustment of Children in Motherless
Homes," The Single Parent 11 (May-June):4-10.
World Health Organization.
1959 Mental Health Problems of the Aging and the
Aged, Technical Report, Series No. 171. Geneva: World Health Organization.
Young, Michael, Bernard Benjamin and Chris Wallis.
1963 "The Mortality of Widowers," The Lancet 2
(August):454-456.

DIMENSIONS OF
RELIGIOUS DEFECTION

Armand L. Mauss

It is probably indicative of a bias in social science that religious commitment is considered a research problem, but religious defection is not, or so it would seem from the paucity of available research literature on the subject of religious defection. A recently published and very comprehensive bibliography of social science literature in the field of religion (Berkowitz and Johnson, 1967) not only has no topical section on defection, but does not list even a single book or article devoted to that topic. An extensive search on my own part through various important works in the sociology and psychology of religion failed to uncover more than an occasional oblique mention of religious defection in connection with some other topic, but not even a paragraph on defection per se. [1]

   The most explicit and direct references that I found in the literature on this general topic were Fichter (1954), Moberg (1962), and Marty (1964). Fichter introduces a typology of parish members, including the categories "marginal," "dormant," and "dead;" these would seem collectively to correspond somewhat to what I am here calling "defected" or "disinvolved," although Fichter stops at the descriptive level and attempts no analytical elaboration upon his categories.

   Adapted from Review of Religious Research, 10 (Spring, 1969), pp. 128-135, by permission of the author and publisher.
[1] Among the works consulted were: Allport (1950), Glock and Stark (1965), Glock et al., (1967), James (1902), Lenski (1961), O'Dea (1966), Joachim Wach (1944), and Weber (1964). Also consulted were all the volumes of the Journal for the Scientific Study of Religion, and all articles in the American Journal of Sociology and the American Sociological Review whose titles seemed relevant.

Moberg is concerned mainly with the question of conversion experience. Marty's focus is largely theological rather than sociological, and is more upon subjective, personal experiences of unbelief, whereas my focus is more upon certain objective concomitants of disinvolvement.

There is, of course, no scientific reason that religious defection should be any less interesting or important than, say, political defection or, for that matter, dropping out of school. Religious "drop-outs" may not present the kind of critical societal problem that school "drop-outs" do, or the kind of interesting political problem presented by the "switchers" and "cop-outs" from various political movements, but as a scientific problem, religious defection offers at least as much potential yield as these other kinds. For one thing, the incidence and the variety of religious defection might give us clues as to the nature and consequences of change within religious cultures and organizations; and defectors may provide an important source of recruits to various new social and religious movements, cults, and sects. Moreover, from the point of view of the religionist there is the additional potential gain of an insight into the causes and types of religious defection that can lead to effective programs of prevention and reactivation.

It should be made clear at the outset that the term "defection" will be used herein to refer to the withdrawal from fellowship or activity by church members who have had some history of regular attendance and involvement in the church, not merely nominal affiliation; nor will the term refer to the simple "denominational switching" that is sometimes associated with mixed marriages, social mobility, and the like (although, of course, "defectors" might join other denominations subsequent to their defection). The term "defection," as I use it, will be more or less synonymous with "disaffection" (or, more colloquially, "dropping-out").[2] It might

---

[2]It has been suggested to me that my definition of "defector" might not take due account of what might be

also be termed "disinvolvement, " to indicate that it is an opposite or counterpart to the concept of religious "involvement. " It may be noted that the concept of social "disinvolvement" or "defection" in the context of institutional religion is rather akin to the "disengagement" theory of aging (Cumming and Henry, 1961), a perspective that focuses on the social genesis of the role-withdrawal of the aged.

THE THREE DIMENSIONS OF
RELIGIOUS DEFECTION

The identification of religious defection as a general phenomenon is only the beginning of a study of this topic, for we must expect to find different dimensions of religious disinvolvement, just as we find different dimensions of involvement. Glock and Stark (1965) have discussed five theoretical dimensions of involvement, and recently Morton King (1967) used a very elaborate empirical process to identify nine such dimensions. We should probably not expect religious disinvolvement to be any less complex.

One dimension of disinvolvement or defection that is perhaps best known to academicians is what we might call the intellectual dimension (this would be the negative counterpart of Glock's "ideological dimension" of involvement). This dimension refers to the kind of disinvolvement that is based upon disbelief of certain central tenets of a religion accompanied, presumably, by a belief in rival secular doctrines. Atheism and agnosticism are perhaps the most common expressions of this dimension of disinvolvement, although there are

_____

called the "de facto defector, " who may have ceased to believe, but who continues to participate for some reason or another. Though I recognize that such church members may indeed exist, I do not include them in the definition, mainly because of the difficulty in identifying them empirically.

many possible indicators, some of which would be unique to certain denominations. Indicators for this dimension that might be used with some degree of success in a survey instrument would be: expression of disbelief in any kind of God, or in the literal divinity of Jesus; a belief in evolution of the species; a belief in the merely palliative function of religion; or reading habits that center on books and journals of secular "high culture, " rather than on religious literature. We might expect intellectuals and academics to be particularly exemplary of the intellectual dimension of defection, since there is evidence (though not conclusive) that higher education in many academic fields, especially in the social sciences and humanities, is generally incompatible with religious commitment. Stark (1963) suggests that this incompatibility is inherent in the differences between religion and these secular fields in approach, method, and premises; Greeley (1965) claims that the relatively low level of religiosity among academicians is only the result of selective recruitment to academic life; and Thalheimer (1965) presents evidence that intellectual defection from religion begins to take place well before the college years. In any case, it seems well established, both from research and from common experience, that the intellectual dimension is one dimension of defection that can be quite readily identified.

It should be added here in passing that one need not be an academician, or even highly educated, to experience this kind of defection; and conversely, that there are, of course, such things as religious intellectuals and academicians. In fact, there may well be another expression of intellectual defection altogether, besides that seen in the rejection of traditional theological concepts; that is the intellectual (or ideological) defection that occurs because of a perceived lack of metaphysical or other worldly orientation or theology in some of the more liberal denominations.

Turning from matters of belief, let us consider religious disinvolvement on the strictly social dimension. The importance of the various social functions of religious involvement is stressed in the classical studies of the sociology of religion and is central to the thought of early theorists such as Durkheim (1961). More recently, Lenski (1961) has identified two varieties of social involvement in religion, a "communal" or primary group involvement, and an "associational" or secondary group involvement. Glock and his associates (1967) have shown the importance of various social factors for religious involvement, and he has hypothesized that "social deprivation" in the secular world is one of the determinants of involvement in religious organization. Other research (Photiadis, 1965) indicates that involvement or participation in the church on the social level functions to produce overt conformity to church norms, independently of the intellectual (or belief) dimension. Finally, it is reported (Hagburg, 1966) that the level of participation in an organization is dependent upon the primary group satisfactions which members receive from participating, and it is suggested that churches, labor unions, and other organizations are functional counterparts or equivalents in offering such satisfactions to their members.

If, as this literature suggests, social ties and social integration of the individual are so important in producing religious involvement, then we might plausibly infer that disinvolvement or defection can occur as a consequence of either the disintegration of social bonds, unsatisfying social experiences, or the formation of strong social ties outside the church. Empirical indicators of disinvolvement on the social dimension might be: loss (or lack) of close friends in the church; relatively low social status compared to the congregation generally; personal acquaintance with few, if any, church workers, lay leaders, or clergy; marriage to a devout member of another faith; and perceptions of "coolness" or "cliques" among members of the congregation.

Anyone who has discussed religion with very many defectors, however, has heard expressions of disaffection that have little to do with lack of social ties, or with conscientious intellectual problems: charges that regular church-goers are hypocrites, that the churches are interested only in money, and that religion was forced on one as a child are among the most common cliches heard in the company of the defected. Given the human capacity for rationalization and other ego defense mechanisms, one wonders whether to take such charges at face value as the "real reasons" for the defection. The experiences upon which such charges are based surely have occurred in the lives of many who have not defected, so there is nothing automatic about the defector's reaction to such experiences. It is proposed here that charges of this kind might be considered symptoms of the kind of defection that occurs on the emotional dimension, which is the third of our three dimensions of defection, and which religionists might prefer to call the spiritual dimension.[3] There are some passing references to this kind of dimension in psychological literature.

Gordon Allport (1950:32-33, 103) discusses briefly the common phenomenon of youthful rebellion against parental religion and points out that many youngsters drift away from religion ". . . not because of intellectual doubts, but because of a gnawing sense of guilt and shame, due perhaps to sex conflicts." He also identifies a kind of "acute negativism" toward religion that he regards as "emotionally over-determined," perhaps as a reaction to some kind of earlier trauma (such as when religion seemed ineffectual in the face of unhappiness or tragedy), or perhaps as a symptom of repressed animosity toward one's father, in accordance with the Freudian theory. Writing in a somewhat similar vein, Richard McCann (1967:210) sees the "seed for future agnosticism" sown in unhappy, unsatisfying, emotionally deprived, or rigid family environments, especially in the more fundamentalist homes.

The purport of such observations is not to suggest that the emotional problems that people have with religion are not real problems, but only that they are more deep-seated than would be apparent from the rationalizations offered by the emotionally defected. Such ra-

---

[3]For a defense of the use of such concepts as "spiritual" by social scientists, see Moberg (1967).

tionalizations can be regarded, however, as perhaps the most readily available empirical indicators of emotional defection. It would be premature at this stage of the work to attempt a comprehensive catalogue of all the emotional conditions and symptoms that are related to the emotional dimension of defection. This dimension is perhaps the most elusive and subjective of the three, in the sense that objective empirical indicators of it are much harder to identify than is the case with the intellectual and social dimensions. The assistance of psychologists would be very helpful at this point. Perhaps what has been offered above, however, is sufficient prima facie evidence for the existence of this emotional dimension.

THE TYPOLOGY DERIVING FROM
THE THREE DIMENSIONS

Having identified, hopefully, three discrete dimensions which appear among religious defectors, I hasten to make the obvious but necessary observation that not all defection is unidimensional. The three dimensions may be combined into a typology which will reflect the various combinations of types of defection. The result is the eight-celled typology represented in Figure 1. Cell a would contain the "total defectors," those who are high on all three dimensions of defection. Individuals in cell b might be called "psychological defectors," since their defection is both intellectual and emotional, but not social. The "cultural defectors" of cell c are high on both the social and intellectual dimensions. Cell d has the purely "intellectual defectors." In cell e are the "alienated defectors" who may not have intellectual problems, but who are both socially uninte-grated and emotionally distressed. Cell f contains the purely "emotional defectors," and cell g the purely "social defectors." Cell h is a residual category representing those who have become disinvolved in church for reasons associated with other possible dimensions. Such people are not offended or disaffected about anything; they are simply taken away from church activities by such

FIGURE 1. AN ATTRIBUTE SPACE FOR RELIGIOUS DEFECTION

| | High Emotional Defection | | Low Emotional Defection | |
| | Social Defection | | Social Defection | |
	High	Low	High	Low
High Intellectual Defection	Total Defectors a	Psychological Defectors b	Cultural Defectors c	Intellectual Defectors d
Low Intellectual Defection	Alienated Defectors e	Emotional Defectors f	Social Defectors g	Circumstantial Defectors h

circumstances as going away to military service and have not yet overcome the inertia and become reinvolved. These I call "circumstantial defectors." All such terminology is, of course, tentative at this point, and the suggested eight names for these cells might have more poetic than empirical value. Nevertheless, by whatever names, these eight types of religious defection are logically derivative from the three dimensions, and they comprise a taxonomy that we can regard as heuristic and useful, if not exhaustive.

CONCLUSION

What is offered here is typology of types of defectors from organized religion derived from a combination of three dimensions of religious defection. Though a hypothetical construct, it is based upon many years of participant observation in church reactivation programs. Presumably the typology is generalizable and adaptable to studies of defectors from any organized religion, although the relative weights of the three dimensions probably vary from one denomination to another.

From a scientific point of view, a typology of the kind proposed here might have considerable heuristic value, not only for its more obvious taxonomic function, but also as a guide in the study of change. For example, comparisons of the relative proportions of the different types of defectors from various denominations at different points in time may indicate the direction of changes taking place in the relations between those denominations and secular social institutions. While the typology does not tie directly into an existing body of scientific theory, it has many indirect ties to much of the work on religious commitment or involvement, since it involves negative counterparts to several ideas that have been advanced on the subject of commitment, as indicated throughout the preceding discussion.

From the point of view of ecclesiastical policy, the typology indicates the need for designing church reactivation programs that will take account of the fact that there are different forms and styles of defection,

just as there are different forms and styles of commitment or conversion. All too often religious leaders
tend to see their presumptive flocks as comprising only
two types, "good" (active) members and "bad" (inactive)
members. Once it is realized that the latter category,
as well as the former, is a complex one, the foundation
will have been laid for varied and flexible reactivation
programs that can employ an intellectual approach to
the intellectual dimension of defection, a comprehensive
fellowshipping program for the social dimension, and,
for the emotional dimension, perhaps a series of informal counseling and group therapy sessions, with combinations of such approaches being employed for defectors of the types that involve more than one of the three
dimensions.

REFERENCES

Allport, Gordon.
    1950   The Individual and His Religion.   New York:
            Macmillan.
Berkowitz, Morris I., and Edmund Johnson.
    1967   Social Scientific Studies of Religion: A Bibli-
            ography. Pittsburgh : University of Pittsburgh
            Press.
Cumming, Elaine, and William E. Henry.
    1961   Growing Old: The Process of Disengagement.
            New York: Basic Books.
Durkheim, Emile.
    1961   The Elementary Forms of Religious Life. New
            York: Collier Books.
Fichter, Joseph H.
    1954   Social Relations in the Urban Parish. Chicago:
            University of Chicago Press.
Glock, Charles Y., and Rodney Stark.
    1965   Religion and Society in Tension. Chicago:
            Rand McNally.
Glock, Charles Y., Benjamin B. Ringer and Earl R.
        Babbie.
    1967   To Comfort and to Challenge. Berkeley: Uni-
            versity of California Press.

Greeley, Andrew.
   1965   "The Religious Behavior of Graduate Students."
         Journal for the Scientific Study of Religion 1
         (Fall):34-40.
Hagburg, Eugene C.
   1966   "Correlates of Organizational Participation."
         Pacific Sociological Review 9 (Spring):15-21.
James, William.
   1902   The Varieties of Religious Experience. New
         York: Modern Library.
King, Morton.
   1967   "Measuring the Religious Variable: Nine Pro-
         posed Dimensions." Journal for the Scientific
         Study of Religion 6 (Fall):173-185.
Lenski, Gerhard.
   1961   The Religious Factor. New York: Doubleday.
Marty, Martin E.
   1964   Varieties of Unbelief. New York: Holt, Rine-
         hart, Winston.
McCann, Richard.
   1967   "Developmental Factors in the Growth of Ma-
         ture Faith." Pp. 204-211 in Richard D. Knudten
         (ed.), The Sociology of Religion. New York:
         Appleton-Century-Crofts.
Moberg, David O.
   1962   The Church as a Social Institution. Englewood
         Cliffs: Prentice-Hall.
   1967   "The Encounter of Scientific and Religious Val-
         ues Pertinent to Man's Spiritual Nature." Socio-
         logical Analysis 28 (Spring):22-33.
O'Dea, Thomas F.
   1966   The Sociology of Religion. Englewood Cliffs:
         Prentice-Hall.
Photiadis, John D.
   1965   "Overt Conformity to Church Teaching as a
         Function of Religious Belief and Group Partici-
         pation." American Journal of Sociology 70
         (January):423-428.
Stark, Rodney.
   1963   "On the Incompatability of Religion and Science:
         A Survey of American Graduate Students."

Journal for the Scientific Study of Religion 3 (Fall):3-20.

Thalheimer, Fred.
1965   "Continuity and Change in Religiosity: A Study of Academicians." Pacific Sociological Review 8 (Fall):101-108.

Wach, Joachim.
1944   Sociology of Religion. Chicago: University of Chicago Press.

Weber, Max.
1964   The Sociology of Religion. Boston: Beacon Press.

ANNOTATED BIBLIOGRAPHY

SKID ROW AND ITS MEN

BOOKS

Anderson, Nels. The Hobo: The Sociology of the Homeless Man. Chicago: University of Chicago Press, 1923. Pp. 302.
The author spent much time "on the road" previous to his studies and wrote this classic under the supervision of urban ecologists at the University of Chicago. His description of Chicago's hobohemia, based on his own observations supplemented by 400 interviews and numerous case histories, depicts the habitats of the homeless, types of hoboes, their health, sex, and political groups, and the mission and welfare institutions they use.

Anderson, Nels. Men on the Move. Chicago: University of Chicago Press, 1940. Pp. 357.
Turning from what he describes as the romantic account of his earlier thesis (The Hobo), Anderson attempts to describe the total scope of migrancy, from its beneficial function of balancing employment needs to the less attractive aspects of poverty and suffering. This excellent review of the literature on migration includes consideration of the broader implications of industrialism as a system. The author argues that, given the national scope of migration, the federal government should play an initiating and coordinating role to enable the nation to meet rationally both the problems and opportunities afforded by extensive migration.

Bendiner, Elmer. The Bowery Man. New York: Thomas Nelson & Sons, 1961. Pp. 187.
A history of the Bowery is followed by a depiction of its present general atmosphere and accounts of the author's experiences with homeless men. The book is aimed at the popular rather than the professional audience. There is an extended case history of one Bowery man, but no footnotes or bibliography.

Bogue, Donald J. Skid Row in American Cities. Chicago: Community & Family Study Center, University of Chicago, 1963. Pp. 251.
Findings from the National Opinion Research Center's 1957-58 survey of Chicago's skid rows are summarized. The sample of 613 men included residents in cubicle-type hotels, rooming houses, and missions on Chicago's five main skid rows; men arrested in the skid-row precinct; county hospital patients with skid-row addresses; and a quota sample of men sleeping outside. Data are provided on respondents' daily activities, attitudes toward skid row, illness, death, transiency, recreation, drinking behavior, social and occupational mobility, family background, and personality structure. The interpretation is strongly oriented toward rehabilitation. Census data on other skid rows, interviews with resource persons, and a chapter on present Chicago services to the homeless are included.

Dees, Jesse Walter, Jr. Flophouse: An Authentic Undercover Study of "Flophouses," "Cage Hotels" Including Missions, Shelters and Institutions Serving Un-Attached (Homeless) Men. Francestown, N.H. : Marshall Jones, 1948. Pp. 170.
Public relief policies in England from the reign of James I are briefly reviewed. Mass relief policies in 11 American cities are described and compared in the light of the British experience. The history of shelters for the homeless in Chicago is delineated and contemporary conditions of relief institutions in Chicago are described in great detail. The author's qualifications include a period of participant observation when he disguised himself as a homeless man. The influence of shelters and lodging houses on their clientele is described, and there are recommendations for increasing the pressures that push homeless men toward reintegration.

Elman, Richard M. The Poorhouse State: The American Way of Life on Public Assistance. New York: Pantheon, 1966. Pp. 305.
Elman reviews the difficulties confronting anyone who

attempts to receive Home Relief in New York City. He claims that the needy are not informed and are often misinformed by investigators, and that the City forces the applicants to play a frustrating game in a circle of referrals. One chapter discusses the homeless man in New York City and his problems of establishing indigence in order to obtain relief. The homeless person may not submit to inquiries into his past or to rehabilitation and therefore often is declared ineligible for assistance. There is a long case history about a dependent man seeking help and unwilling to use the channels of the present welfare system.

Gilmore, Harlan W. The Beggar. Chapel Hill: University of North Carolina Press, 1940. Pp. 252.
Justification for this study of mendicancy in modern urbanized Western society is the author's opinion that control of begging can best be achieved if its causation is understood. After discussing "our mendicant heritage," various types of beggars and their "art" are described. One chapter is entitled "The Natural History of a Failure." There are also chapters on why people continue to give to beggars and on control of begging. Finally, there is an extensive bibliography.

Gray, Frank. The Tramp: His Meaning and Being. London: J. M. Dent & Sons, 1931. Pp. 268.
Like many others who wrote about tramps, this author lived for some time among them, but his work is not simply descriptive. It quickly leaves the descriptive stage to discuss the history of tramps in England and to make policy recommendations. It is argued that the existence of tramps must be recognized as a national rather than a local problem. Finally, there is a plea for greater research and public surveillance of vagrants and a greater concern for rehabilitation, particularly for young vagrants.

Harrington, Michael. The Other America. Baltimore: Penquin Books, 1963. Pp. 203.
As part of a discussion of poverty in the U.S., Harring-

ton describes his experiences as a member of the Catholic Worker group in New York's Bowery during 1951 and 1952. His personal encounters with the alcoholic derelict are reported, and the brutal self-abasement of the Bowery is vividly described. He criticizes the public for their apathy but notes that even more tragic than the ponderous bureaucratic charity are the alcoholic's self-protective indifference and his callous failure to understand why anyone might want to help him.

Hunter, Robert. Poverty. New York: Macmillan, 1904. Pp. 382.
This work includes a chapter on vagrancy which discusses skid row and its denizens. Vagrants are classified as either indigent and infirm, professional and voluntary, or accidental and involuntary. Each type of vagrancy is viewed within the matrix of the skid-row environment common to all. The vice and degeneracy of skid row and its tendency to pervert morality are stressed. A competitive industrial system which requires a surplus of labor available for casual employment is seen as the cause of vagrancy. A possible solution to the problems of vagrancy is "social dredging" (removal of vagrants from skid row to self-supporting agricultural or industrial colonies).

Jones, Howard. Alcoholic Addiction: A Psycho-Social Approach to Abnormal Drinking. London: Tavistock, 1963. Pp. 209.
A life history study of 72 male alcoholics imprisoned for public drunkenness or under treatment at the Ontario Alcoholism Research Foundation's clinic revealed that a person's history of "social advantages" determined differences in drinking behavior and social adaptation. Compulsive drinking is interpreted as a means of reducing stress deriving from dependency, deprivation and social insecurity, and apparently insoluble personal problems. Problems of prevention and treatment are discussed.

Lahaye, Nicole.   Aspects Actuels du Vagabondage en Belgique.   Bruxelles: Centre National de Criminologie, 1967. Pp. 150.
Although the number of vagrants in Belgium has decreased since 1914, the population has reached numerical stability and still poses a problem. The ramifications of an 1891 law repressing vagrancy and mendicancy are explained. A discussion of more current (up to 1963) legislation and statistics on institutions, and of the use of shelters, missions and other establishments is presented as background to an empirical study. Questionnaires were administered to a sample of 993 men and 39 women charged with vagrancy and institutionalized in 1963. Regional and linguistic distribution, demographic and mobility data, and data on alcoholism and criminal recidivism are included. The study is considered a general work preliminary to research in greater depth. The concluding section of the book discusses the social, economic and legal aspects of the problem and makes recommendations for the prevention and rehabilitation of vagrants.

Nascher, I. L.   The Wretches of Povertyville: A Sociological Study of the Bowery.   Chicago: Joseph J. Lanzit, 1909. Pp. 298.
This account written between 1903 and 1906 describes the institutions of the Bowery area and illustrates with case histories the various types of persons found there. Nascher's account tends toward the lurid aspects of Bowery society: gambling, thieving, prostitution, and opium use. In discussing possible solutions to these conditions, he stresses the importance of rehabilitation through vocational guidance.

National Assistance Board. Homeless Single Persons. London: Her Majesty's Stationery Office, 1966. Pp. 308. Increased public concern over the problems of social misfits and drifters in society led the National Assistance Board to expend their regular survey of reception centres to include, in addition to those persons using the reception centres, persons "sleeping rough" (outside),

using lodging houses, hostels, or shelters, and persons
seeking financial help from the Board. The first part
of the survey consisted of collecting information about
establishments used by homeless persons, and about
the places where people were known or were thought to
be "sleeping rough." Data were obtained from 567 establishments throughout the country, most of them privately operated. Counts of persons sleeping rough were
obtained by consulting police, social workers, and other
informants for a list of places used, and then counting
all men in these places on a particular night.   Information was obtained by interview from 81 percent
of those found sleeping rough. The second part of the
study included a survey of lodgers in the lodging houses
and reception centres, a summary of statistics on national assistance paid, a compiling of medical statistics
on men using a reception centre, and a survey of applicants for local assistance. Final results of the survey are contrasted with findings from previous surveys .
It is demonstrated that enough accommodations were
available. However, there is a need for further detailed
studies of persons sleeping rough, medical conditions
among homeless men, relations between imprisonment
and homelessness, and possible improvements in the
available lodging.

Phelps, Harold A. Contemporary Social Problems .
New York: Prentice-Hall, 1932. Pp. 783.
A lengthy section on economic sources of social disorganization and an entire chapter devoted to homelessness are included in this text on social problems. A
general definition of homelessness is followed by a description of types of homelessness and characteristics
of homeless persons, including their occupations, age
and nativity, marital status, education, intelligence ,
and health. The work contains useful discussions of
transient families, of the relation between business conditions and homelessness, and of homelessness as an
urban problem. Rehabilitative and preventive programs
for the country and for the urban communities are proposed.

Pittman, David J. and Gordon, T. Wayne. Revolving Door: A Study of the Chronic Police Case Inebriate. Glencoe: Free Press, 1958. Pp. 154.
Detailed case histories were obtained from 187 inebriates incarcerated in Monroe County Penitentiary, Rochester, New York, during 1953 and 1954. The sample was randomly chosen from all inebriates admitted to the penitentiary during that year. The authors view the career pattern of the chronic inebriate as having three dependency phases: preconditioning for dependency, formation, and confirmed dependency. According to their "undersocialization" hypothesis, police case inebriates are insufficiently socialized and hence are unprepared to meet the demands society places upon adults. "Undersocialization" includes the experience of broken parental homes and serious emotional handicaps due to "stress" in family of orientation. Excessive drinking is seen as a secondary rather than a primary cause of homelessness and chronic inebriety (maladjustments lead to the drinking which then leads to homelessness). Two career patterns of public intoxication are distinguished, the "early skid" and the "late skid." Several case histories are summarized.

Queen, Stuart Alfred and Mann, Delbert Martin. Social Pathology. New York: Thomas Y. Crowell, 1925. Pp. 662.
A chapter entitled "Homeless Men" gives three illustrative case studies: 1) a seasonal laborer, 2) migratory nonworkers or "bums," and 3) a disabled, elderly homeless man. Distinctions are based on the degree of attachment to social norms revealed by the men under consideration. Among the factors causing men to detach themselves from society and either to drift from town to town or to become rooted in skid-row areas are economic disabilities, personal demoralization, and alcoholism. Constructive programs toward eliminating skid row are listed.

Riis, Jacob A. How the Other Half Lives. New York: Hill and Wang, 1957. Pp. 231.

This classic is a description of living conditions on New York's Lower East Side in 1890. The history of tenement housing in New York City is outlined and there is a descriptive inventory of tenement areas according to prevalent ethnicity. Included is a depiction of the Bowery and the life style of its homeless men. Riis' general thesis is that tenement life-style and environment reinforce already existing conditions of physical and moral decay. His observations are based on personal experience as a police reporter on the Lower East Side, statistics of the Police Department, and census data.

Riviere, Louis. Mendicants et Vagabonds. Paris: Librarie Victor Lecoffre, 1902. Pp. 239.
Despite technological and medical advances, mendicancy and vagrancy still exist. The author traces the history of the vagabond in France from the Middle Ages, with special reference to gypsies, literary accounts of vagabondage, and institutions and legislation dealing with the indigent, the orphaned, and the criminal. Mendicancy and vagrancy in other European countries receive some attention. Preventative and rehabilitative measures are discussed.

Solenberger, Alice Willard. One Thousand Homeless Men: A Study of Original Records. New York: Russell Sage Foundation, 1911. Pp. 374.
This study of the types, characteristics, and origins of homeless men is based on social and demographic data collected from the case records of 1,000 men who applied for public assistance at the Chicago Bureau of Charities between 1901 and 1903. Included are selected case histories and appendices of supplementary data such as descriptions of the lodging house.

Sutherland, Edwin H. and Locke, Harvey J. Twenty Thousand Homeless Men. Chicago: J. B. Lippincott, 1936. Pp. 207.
This is the report of a team of six Chicago sociologists who passed as clients in the Chicago shelters for homeless men of the Illinois Emergency Relief Commission in 1934 and 1935. Among the topics considered are

the daily routine of the shelters, types of interaction
among the clients, attitudes (mainly negative) toward
the shelters, socialization, and backgrounds of the clients. Many clients had become dependent only since
the Depression. The report adopts the orientation of the
clients in emphasizing the inefficiencies and injustices
in the management of the shelters. Concluding chapters
summarize the history of homelessness and discuss public policy.

Valdovinos, Carlos. La Vagancia, La Mendicidad y
Demas Estados de Desvalimiento. Santiago: la accion
del Patronato Nacional de los Desvalidos en el estudio
de este problema, 1942. Pp. 96.
El Patronato Nacional de los Devalidos was founded to
study destitution in Chile and to propose the necessary
solutions. The present report of causes and consequences of destitution covers 1) poverty and disability, 2)
male, female and child beggars,   3) homeless waifs
and abandoned adolescents living in the streets; and 4)
old people who are a burden to their families. The
main recommendations are for the establishment of
shelters and rehabilitation programs for people in
penury and for dentention homes for vagrants and beggars.

Vexliard, Alexandre. Le Clochard: Etude de Psychol-
ogie Sociale. Bruges: Desclee de Brouwer, 1957.
Pp. 317.
Based on Vexliard's doctoral dissertation at the Sor-
bonne, this work contains individual analyses of 61 male
and female tramps in Paris and in the provinces. He
considers three broad categories which identify the
main causes of vagrancy: "conditions sociales," "pro-
blimes individuels," and "insuffisances psychologigue."
The author seems to see "conditions sociales," in particular private property and individualism, as primary
background factors. He develops this thesis further in
another book, La Sociologie du Vagabondage. Case
histories and descriptions of the life style of the tramp
are given in much detail. His conclusions describe in

a very general way the most fruitful solutions to the problem and reaffirm the complicity of social institutions
in the proliferation of vagrancy.   There is a good bibliography of 245 items, mostly French publications .

Vexliard, Alexandre.   Introduction a la Sociologie du
Vagabondage.   Paris: Marcel Riviere, 1956. Pp. 244.
Throughout history there have always been vagabonds,
"forgotten men, " excluded from normal social life. At
different times, different conditions have caused vagabondage, but each new group comes from the permanent
base of the old, sick, and mentally deficient, and from
persons excluded from social organization because of
war or transformations in society. In antiquity, political
changes caused vagabondage, slavery playing an important role. The Middle Ages produced religious outcasts.
Since the 14th century economic problems have been the
major producers of vagabonds.   Under the capitalist,
industrialist, individualist system, the dispossessed
person finds himself at the mercy of impersonal socio-
economic forces.   In the last hundred years, modern
technology has drawn people into the city; but the city
has been unable to absorb everyone into industry and unemployment and vagabondage have resulted, especially
in the United States and Great Britain.   Those who condemn vagabondage believe that the vice and laziness of the
individual cause vagabondage, that charity causes pauperism, and conclude that repressive laws are the solution .
Others argue that social conditions have produced unemployment and vagabondage, and assert that part of the
Judeo-Christian ethic is the responsibility for providing
aid to the unfortunate victims of civilization. The existence of vagabondage indicates that certain individuals are
unable to integrate themselves into society. Criminolo-
gists, taking a psychological point of view, tend to believe
that certain types of individuals are destined to become
vagabonds; but according to the sociological point of view
different kinds of people find themselves on the fringes of
society at different times. Western society is characterized by its tendency to live day by day, and its dependence
on "natural laws" even in its social organization. Natural

selection in the course of society means that those who cannot make it are left behind. Recently society has begun to recognize the right of every man to life within the existing social institutions. The necessary reforms and greater institutional flexibility will bring about social integration and thus eliminate vagabondage.

Wallace, Samuel E. Skid Row as a Way of Life. Totowa, New Jersey: Bedminister Press, 1965. Pp. 219.
Wallace's treatment of skid-row subculture includes a history of skid rows in general and the development of the U.S. skid row. The main elements of skid-row life (sleeping quarters, charity, bars, jobs, the law) are investigated, and the process whereby one becomes a skid-row man is outlined. Employment history, financial background, personality characteristics, and exposure to skid row are important factors in socialization into skid-row life. Skid row is conceived as a distinctive culture with its own values and status system.

Webb, John N. The Migratory Casual Worker. Washington, D. C. : Works Progress Administration, Division of Social Research, 1937. Pp. 128.
This book draws principally from interviews conducted by the Federal Emergency Relief Program with 500 casual workers in 13 cities. It is stressed that migratory casual workers were only a small proportion of all transient relief recipients. Migration and work patterns, types of work, earnings, and personal histories of migratory workers are described. Transient agricultural laborers were found to be relatively less mobile than transients in industrial jobs. It is concluded that national employment offices, unemployment insurance and public works projects are likely to be the most acceptable governmental programs for migratory casual laborers. A chapter on case histories includes three examples of wanderlust as a motivation for transiency.

Webb, John N. The Transient Unemployed. Washington, D. C.: Works Progress Administration, 1935. Pp. 132.

This well organized report brings together the results of a series of studies conducted in the Division of Research, Statistics and Finance of the Federal Emergency Relief Administration and presents an exhaustive analysis of the characteristics of the transient population, their movements and reasons for migration, and the problems involved in their reabsorption into private industrial employment. The general conclusion, drawn in terms of unemployment and the function of relief, is that "the dissolution of the transient population will proceed only as rapidly as business and industry can provide the employment essential to stability." The sample of transients, drawn from the relief rolls of 13 cities, included about 25, 000 unattached transients and 1, 900 transient family groups. An appendix includes supplementary tables and abstracts of case histories.

Zorbaugh, Harvey W.   The Gold Coast and the Slum: A Sociological Study of Chicago's Near North Side. Chicago: University of Chicago Press, 1929. Pp. 287. Zorbaugh's study is a heavily documented sociological description of Chicago's complex Near North Side, from about 1865 when it was an elite residential section to 1929 when several areas had deteriorated into slums or symptomatic bohemias and the sense of community was notably absent. Sections on homeless men include a discussion of slum derelicts and alcoholics and of the dilemma facing the young worker or student in the anonymous rooming house world. The study is documented with material from such sources as the case history of a young girl pursuing a musical career and the diary of a dope addict.

ARTICLES

Allen, William H.   "The Vagrant: Social Parasite or Social Product," Proceedings of the Thirtieth National Conference of Charities and Corrections, (1903), pp. 379-386. Viewing the problem historically, there has been little

progress either in the theory or the practice of the
treatment of vagrancy. It is suggested that the vagrant is not himself diseased but rather is a symptom
of an inadequacy or shortcoming in the social body. The
author contends further that "attempts to commit the
public to a belief in his total depravity, criminality, and
half-heartedness will continue to be generally ineffective
because such belief is contrary to everyday experience
and observations." Following accusations of those who
fall victim to panhandlers as merely egocentric, self-
styled messiahs, Allen states that private charities organized around the idea of rehabilitation would serve
the vagrant far better than a handout, which he characterizes as an abdication of conscience and "vagrancy
of intellect and sympathy." Measures toward the establishment of comprehensive relief agencies are suggested.

Anderson, Nels. "Highlights of the Migrant Problem
Today," Proceedings of the National Conference of
Social Work, 67 (1940), pp. 109-117.
The "knight of the road" and the depression migrant are
contrasted in terms of economic milieu and reasons for
vagrancy. Statistics from studies of the hobo are mar-
shalled to demonstrate the demographic differences between that group and the depression migrants, and the
thesis that such migrancy is the result of the labor surplus is supported. The continuation and, if necessary,
expansion of federal work programs for the unemployed
is urged so as to limit the number of depression migrants.

Bahr, Howard M. "Drinking, Interaction, and Identification: Notes on Socialization into Skid Row," Journal
of Health and Social Behavior, 8 (December, 1967),
pp. 272-285.
This paper focuses on aspects of adult socialization into the deviant community of skid row. Residence on
skid row is defined as a stigma, and extent of acceptance
of the stigma and identification with skid row are viewed
as varying with drinking behavior, interaction with other

skid-row men, and interaction with people who do not live on skid row. These ideas are tested in a secondary analysis of data gathered in a 1964 survey of 92 skid-row men selected at random from the registers of four Bowery lodging houses. The findings suggest that adult socialization into a stigmatized subculture and socialization into "normal" groups operate according to the same general principles. Certain social implications of these findings are discussed.

Bahr, Howard M. "The Gradual Disappearance of Skid Row," Social Problems, 15 (Summer, 1967), pp. 41-45. Annual enumerations of the Bowery, Manhattan's skid-row area, have shown a consistent decline in population. Inquiries were sent to commissioners of welfare in 40 U.S. cities to determine if the declining skid-row population is a local or national phenomenon. Results indicate that in most cities the skid-row population is declining. Apparently, this decline is not due to a decrease in the absolute size of the homeless population, but rather to several factors which have operated to disperse homeless men from the traditional skid row to other parts of the city.

Bahr, Howard M. "Worklife Mobility Among Bowery Men," Southwestern Social Science Quarterly, 49(June, 1968), pp. 128-141. Occupational mobility patterns of 66 men living on New York City's Bowery are analyzed in a study of worklife mobility among the unskilled. Detailed occupational histories were obtained from a random sample of lodgers in Bowery hotels. Respondents' lifetime mobility profiles were compared in a replication of Bogue's research about worklife mobility patterns among skid-row men. Mobility histories of Bowery men are quite similar to those of men on Chicago's skid row. However, Bowery men tend to have more stable worklives, and the "typical" skid-row patterns described by Bogue do not fit any sizable proportion of them. In general, the Bowery respondents have not "skidded" very far; most have spent their entire worklives in low status employment. Among those men who have been downwardly mobile, personal problems such as illness, family dissolution, or drinking are associated with their loss of status.

Bahr, Howard M. and Caplow, Theodore. "Homelessness, Affiliation, and Occupational Mobility," Social Forces, 47 (September, 1968), pp. 28-33.
Extensive affiliation and employment histories were obtained from a sample of 203 Bowery men and a control sample of 125 residents of a low income metropolitan census tract. Compared with the control sample, Bowery men had long histories of low affiliation, both before and after their arrival on skid row. The two samples did not differ much in occupational mobility, but their affiliative patterns had been quite different. The association between downward mobility and affiliation loss was weaker than anticipated. In the light of these findings, the homelessness of Bowery men is not attributable to their downward mobility.

Bahr, Howard M. and Langfur, Stephen J. "Social Attachment and Drinking in Skid-Row Life Histories," Social Problems, 14 (Spring, 1967), pp. 464-472.
Information from life history interviews with residents of lodging houses on New York City's Bowery is used in an examination of the relation between extent of current drinking and lifetime affiliation with organizations. Although Bowery residents may maintain throughout life relatively low extent of social attachment, the life histories of heavy drinkers on the Bowery are characterized by higher degrees of attachment to society than are those of abstainers and moderate drinkers. The heavy drinker is especially liable to severe losses of affiliation during adulthood. In contrast, the abstainer on skid row is often a man who never was "attached" to the social order, and his arrival on skid row is merely a further step in a career of nonattachment.

Caplow, Theodore. "Transiency as a Cultural Pattern," American Sociological Review, 5 (October, 1940), pp. 731-739.
For many Americans transiency has become a normal phase of life and may represent social mobility rather than social pathology. The context of American tran-

siency has changed markedly since the onset of the Depression produced unusual temporary conditions such as high rates of transiency among children and women. The present situation is reviewed in light of Caplow's personal experience "on the road" in 1939. Most transients are young men. There is an absence of formal organization among hoboes, but there is an extensive informal network. Previous status hierarchies have disappeared. Transients manifest little conflict or racial prejudice in social relations among themselves, but they are antagonistic toward the agencies that aid (or persecute) them. Traditionally vagrants have been stigmatized as criminals; as "the road" becomes a definite, recognized American pattern both the traditional institutional procedures and antisocial behavior of transients may be modified.

Caplow, Theodore, Bahr, Howard M. and Sternberg, David. "Homelessness," International Encyclopedia of the Social Sciences, 1968, 6, pp. 494-499.
Homelessness may take many forms, from permanent wandering to skid-row dereliction. Characteristic of all of them is a detachment or attenuation of affiliative bonds that link the settled individual to the social structure. Homelessness as a religious ideal characterizes Christian, Muslim, and Buddhist history. Dominant forms of contemporary homelessness seem to arise from industrialization, urbanization, and social change. Three of these--the refugee, the migratory farm laborer, and the skid-row man--are considered in detail.

Culver, Benjamin F. "Transient Unemployed Men," Sociology and Social Research, 17 (July-August, 1933), pp. 519-535.
Interviews were conducted with 136 clients of the Shelter for Transient Men at Palo Alto, California. Frequency distributions are given for state of origin, age, education, marital status, occupation, health, causes of unemployment (subjective), and nationality. These data are the basis for generalizations about an "average unemployed transient man" and a discussion of his attitude toward poverty and unemployment.

Docter, Richard F. "Drinking Practices of Skid Row Alcoholics," Quarterly Journal of Studies on Alcohol, 28 (December, 1967), pp. 700-708.
Interviews with 172 male alcoholics (drawn from sheriff's office rehabilitation units, Salvation Army centers, and out-patient clinics in southern California) were conducted in 1965 to determine 1) what type of beverage was drunk at a particular phase in the drinking history, 2) why a particular beverage was preferred, 3) the effects of moderate intoxication, and 4) what subjects thought about their ability to control their drinking. At the onset of the drinking history beer was the favorite beverage; later less beer was drunk, and whisky became more important; at the end nearly all subjects preferred wine. Stated reason for their preference changed from "taste" at the initial phase to "price" for the wine phase.

Feeney, F. E., Mindlin, D. F., Minear, V. H.,and Short, E. E. "The Challenge of the Skid Row Alcoholic: A Social, Psychological and Psychiatric Comparison of Chronically Jailed Alcoholics and Cooperative Alcoholic Clinic Patients," Quarterly Journal of Studies on Alcohol, 16 (December, 1955), pp. 645-667.
Fifty male workhouse cases referred to an alcoholic clinic in Washington, D. C., by the "Drunk Court" were compared with the 50 male clinic patients who had attended the largest number of therapy sessions. Comparisons were made for age, race, marital status, sibling status, intelligence, education, work history, and drinking history. The workhouse group, though relatively lacking in education, orderly career, resources, and family affiliations, proved to have fewer serious alcoholic reactions.

Kellner, Florence. "Public Intoxication in Rochester," Quarterly Journal of Studies on Alcohol, 26 (March, 1965), p. 117.
Kellner, in this brief critique of an earlier study of public intoxication in Rochester by Zax, Gardner, and Hart, questions the finding that homeless alcoholics do not

seek arrest so that they may find shelter in the jail, noting that the finding stems from statistics on arrests of all publicly intoxicated persons, not just homeless men. Further, she notes that the rate of incarceration is not distinguished from the arrest rate.

Jackson, Joan K. and Conner, Ralph. "The Skid Road Alcoholic," Quarterly Journal of Studies on Alcohol, 14 (September, 1953), pp. 468-486.
A discussion of the informal organizations among skid-row men for getting and drinking wine considers how these groups impede successful treatment of alcoholism. Among skid-row men, the "lushes" are identified as having the most prestige. They form many small groups, some of which cohere for a long time. The groups sustain mutual survival, provide emotional support, and seem to meet the alcoholic's dependency needs without forcing him to recognize the fact that he is dependent. There is a depiction of the process of joining a "lush" group and of its structure and norms.

Locke, Harvey J. "Unemployed Men in Chicago Shelters, " Sociology and Social Research, 19 (May-June, 1935) , pp. 420-428.
Researchers worked and lived among clients of Chicago shelters for unemployed men to determine the characteristics of the clientele and the effects of shelter life. Other data include a statistical analysis of 8,000 occupational schedules, an ecological study of 3,000 clients, and 1,000 life histories. Men who live in shelters are divided into five categories: 1) casual laborers, 2) steady unskilled workers, 3) bums and beggars, 4) skilled tradesmen, and 5) white-collar workers. Effects of shelter living varied by type of client. Casual laborers expressed satisfaction with the shelter and had little interest in getting out, while most of the steady unskilled workers voiced despair and deteriorated to the "bum level." Most bums and beggars were content with the level of living but also (the beggars, particularly) resented regimentation of shelter life, preferring to remain outside until conditions curtailed their activities there. The

last two groups, the skilled and white-collar workers, revealed more severe psychological disorders, losing self-respect and becoming demoralized by what they regarded as a begging situation. However, a majority of the white-collar workers appeared to be in better mental condition than the rest of the men, expressing optimism and focused intentions.

Levinson, Boris M. "The 'Beat' Phenomenon in Wechsler Tests," Journal of Clinical Psychology, 20 (January, 1964), pp. 118-120.
In a report on administration of the Wechsler test to a sample of 182 single skid-row men residing in New York, the author attempts to determine to what extent the feeling of hopelessness ("beat") common to culturally disadvantaged persons might affect performance. Verbal IQ was found to be higher than Performance IQ. This failure in performance seems to reflect the internalization of the feeling of unworthiness or uselessness. It is concluded that the Wechsler tests are useful instruments for the study of social pathology.

Levinson, Boris M. "A Comparative Study of Northern and Southern Negro Homeless Men," The Journal of Negro Education, 35 (Spring, 1966), pp. 144-150.
Twenty-four pairs of northern and southern homeless Negro men on the Bowery were matched for full scale WAIS IQ tests; respondents were selected from waiting lines before the New York City Department of Welfare Men's Shelter in 1962 and 1963. In terms of occupational levels and marital status, significant differences were found between these northern and southern homeless Negro men. It is suggested that school experiences have been overrated and life experiences underrated in the scoring on IQ tests. The meaning of life on skid row varies; life there does not represent a decline for all men. There is some discussion of migration patterns and comparisons of survey findings with New York City Department of Welfare statistics.

Levinson, Boris M. "A Comparative Study of the WAIS Performance of Native-Born Negro and White Homeless," Journal of Genetic Psychology, 105 (December, 1964), pp. 211-218.
This article attempts to demonstrate that homeless men, regardless of background, have aversive learning experiences in common and that from these experiences certain personality traits develop which ultimately lead to homelessness. The WAIS test was administered to a random sample of 32 cases; findings are contrasted with known results from a group of white homeless persons. The two groups are found to have similar psychometric patterns.

Levinson, Boris M. "The Homeless Man," Psychological Reports, 17 (October, 1965), pp. 391-394.
This review of research on homelessness identifies major themes in the recent literature, including the idea that homeless men are an unfortunate "waste product" of industrialization. Social security and unemployment compensation are seen as changing the composition of skid row in that they reduce the number of men living there for economic reasons alone. Problems of defining homelessness are discussed. The author's main interest is in identifying the parameters of the "homeless personality," a personality type he assumes to exist in all cultures.

Levinson, Boris M. "The Homeless Man: A Psychological Enigma," Mental Hygiene, 47 (October, 1963), pp. 590-601.
The personality structure of the homeless man is distinguished from that of the alcoholic. The personality of the homeless man is seen as a consequence of aversive learning experiences and of the internalization of indifference and detachment from life. There is need for an interdisciplinary analysis (including clinical psychologists, urban sociologists, and students of alcoholism) of the origin and problems of the homeless man.

Levinson, Boris M. "The Intelligence of Middle-Aged White Homeless Men in Receipt of Public Assistance," Psychological Reports, 1 (March, 1955), pp. 35-36.

An intelligence test (the Wechsler-Bellevue Form 1) was administered to 50 men selected randomly from a total population of 369 white homeless men, aged 40-59, living in a municipal shelter of a large eastern city. It was found that the sample fell into the normal intelligence range. Accordingly, the causes of homelessness must be sought in factors other than level of intelligence.

Levinson, Boris M. "Note on the Intelligence and WAIS Pattern of White First-Time Applicants for Shelter Care," Psychological Reports, 16 (April, 1965), p. 524. Because a base line is needed for interpreting psychological test findings of homeless men, the author administered the WAIS to 41 consecutive white first-time applicants for shelter care. The results show that the intelligence of these homeless men falls within normal limits. In interpreting test data of skid-row men, however, it must be remembered that psychologically healthy men respond differently to skid row than do the psychologically deteriorated.

Levinson, Boris M. "The Socio-economic Status, Intelligence, and Personality Traits of Jewish Homeless Men," YIVO Annual of Jewish Social Science, 11 (1956-57), pp. 122-141.
This article is a by-product of a large-scale study on the intelligence, psychometric patterns, personality patterns, and personality traits of native-born white homeless men conducted at the Men's Shelter of the New York City Department of Welfare in 1955. Jews constituted a very small proportion of the sample group (8 of 1,350). Background variables were nativity, family status, reasons for dependency, age, employment and health. Intelligence was measured by the Wechsler Adult Intelligence Scale. To ascertain personality structure the following tests were administered: Rorschach, Thematic Apperception Test, Rosenzweig, Picture Frustration Study, and Draw-A-Person. Qualitative summaries of the results are presented for the Jewish respondents. Socio-cultural forces which affect homelessness and withdrawal are illustrated in three case histories.

Levinson, Boris M. "The Socioeconomic Status, Intelligence, and Psychometric Pattern of Native-Born White Homeless Men," Journal of Genetic Psychology, 91 (December, 1957), pp. 205-211.

Fifty white, native-born men selected randomly from the line of applicants at the Men's Shelter during the summer of 1955 were given the Wechsler Adult Intelligence Scale by Levinson and his students. Information was also obtained about their socio-economic backgrounds. These men had higher occupational status, better education and were much older than the average homeless man. Their relatively high scores on vocabulary tests may indicate that at one time they had above average intelligence. In other respects, their verbal ability did not differ significantly from that of the general population. However, in tests of "performance" they were subnormal.

Levinson, Boris M. "Some Aspects of the Personality of the Native-Born White Homeless Man as Revealed by the Rorschach," Psychiatric Quarterly Supplement, 32 (Part 2, 1958), pp. 278-286.

In 1955 Levinson administered the Rorschach to 49 men at the Men's Shelter. Of the 49 only 40 tests were suitable for analysis. He comments that following the administration of the test the inquiry with the men was "singularly unrevealing" and "rarely productive of new concepts." On the basis of the 40 Rorschachs the personality structure of homeless men is assessed. They are emotionally immature, depressed, lack drive or definite goals, are not adaptable, have feelings of despair and worthlessness, have few interests, are passive, and feel insecure. Also, their social contacts are at a very low level, they have difficulty understanding themselves and others, they show intellectual inefficiency and they have thinking disorders. Levinson suggests that the condition of homelessness has only intensified emotional problems which date far back in the individual's life history and concludes that homelessness is a natural outcome of "latent personality trends."

Levinson, Boris M. "Subcultural Studies of Homeless Men," Transactions of the New York Academy of Sciences, 29(December, 1966), pp. 165-182.
This article is a summary of studies of homeless men who received assistance from the New York City Department of Welfare, the Men's Shelter, or private shelters. It is maintained that as welfare programs eliminate the purely economic causes of homelessness, it becomes necessary to investigate personality traits and patterns of personality disorder among homeless men. Regardless of the subcultural context the homeless person exhibits patterns of withdrawal and an incapacity to act in the culturally defined male and female roles.

Levinson, Boris M. and Baron, Samuel. "Responses of Homeless Men to Baron M-Limits Blots," Psychological Reports, 2 (December, 1956), p. 431.
This is a report of administration of a personality test (the Baron M-Limits Blots) to 50 native-born white homeless men. Responses indicate extreme anxiety, depression and ego-impoverishment among them.

Lewis, Orlando F. "The Tramp Problem," Annals of the American Academy of Political and Social Science, 40 (March, 1912), pp. 217-227.
Lewis seeks the establishment of a national committee to study transients and their problems, and to aid them in finding employment. Inebriety and vagrancy are the principal problems needing attention. Three aspects of the employment problem are considered: some transients do not want to work, others are physically unable to work, and a third group seeks work but cannot find it.

McCook, John J. "A Tramp Census and Its Revelations," Forum, 15 (August, 1893), pp. 753-766.
This report of a census of 1,349 residents of municipal shelters in U.S. cities presents statistics on employment, age, health, length of vagrancy, reasons for vagrancy, nativity, marital status, alcohol consumption, criminal records, and religion. These data are compared to the results of a similar study of 841 residents

of English casual wards. Tramps manifest a disease which the author labels "moral taint;" he asserts that it is both contagious and hereditary. The article's conclusion lists suggestions for the elimination of mendicancy.

Morris, Albert. "Some Social and Mental Aspects of Mendicancy," Social Forces, 5 (June, 1927), pp. 605-613.
Morris examines the various "tricks" employed by beggars to create sympathy, the social causes leading to mendicancy, and the motives which prompt people to give to beggars. The factors leading men to mendicancy include failure to hold a job, old age, alcohol and drugs, industrial accidents and physical weakness. People give to beggars out of shame in not giving, pity, and a feeling of social responsibility.

Nichols, Malcolm S. "Homeless Persons," Social Work Yearbook, 1933. New York: Russell Sage Foundation, 1933, pp. 215-217.
This brief article describes changing patterns of the homeless man's life, particularly the increased mobility afforded by the automobile and other advances in transportation. The author notes the considerable variation in the quality of lodging houses and believes that government supervision will lead to improvement of these facilities as well as to a general upgrading in the quality of social services available to homeless men. The Depression's effect on these men--increasing their number and making their plight more desperate--has led to greater public awareness of the need for expansion of services to the homeless and greater coordination of efforts by private and public groups.

Nimkoff, Meyer F. "Personality-Problems of Beggars," Sociology and Social Research, 12 (May-June, 1928), pp. 431-442.
Quoting at length from comments of beggars he has observed, the writer maintains that rehabilitation depends on developing and correcting the personality structure of beggars. Some are seen to bear grudges against humanity and have an obsessive desire to get even, while

others, aware of a chance for easy money and charmed by the opportunity for exhibition, take up begging simply to avoid competing in the mainstream of society. The author concludes that begging presents a dangerous cycle for these men, because their personality problems multiply with their begging experience.

Nylander, Towne. "The Migratory Population of the United States," American Journal of Sociology, 30 (September, 1924), pp. 129-153.
A consideration of the types of migrants in the United States and the reasons for their existence as migrants includes suggestions for control of the migrant problem. Typification of vagrants and causes of vagrancy are based on a scanty review of participant-observer literature, a neo-romantic work ethic, and a collection of tales in the vernacular of "the road."

Ottenberg, Donald J. "TB on Skid Row," National Tuberculosis Association Bulletin, 42 (June, 1956), pp. 85-86.
During a six-week period, 1,750 persons from Philadelphia's skid-row precincts were given chest x-rays. The yield of active disease was eighteen times that of the population at large. Tuberculosis is viewed as a disease inherent in the skid-row life-style and it is suggested that the solution to the problem of tuberculosis on skid row lies in the treatment of that way of life as well as in medical treatment.

Pangborn, Major. "Discussion of Vagrancy," Proceedings of the Thirty-Fourth National Conference of Charities and Correction, (1907), pp. 73-74.
A railroad executive estimates the number of vagrants in the United States (430,000) and their cost to the railroads ($18,500,000 annually). Official reports of persons killed and injured on the railroads form the basis for his estimates.

Park, Robert E. "The Mind of the Hobo: Reflections Upon the Relation Between Mentality and Locomotion," pp. 156-160 in Park, Robert E., Burgess, Ernest W., and McKenzie, Roderick D., The City, Chicago: University of Chicago Press, 1925.

Park addresses the question which the hobo poses to Mead's ideas about the development of mind and society: if "mind is an incident of locomotion," and social organization develops "in locomotion," then why does the highly mobile hobo have so few associations? He concludes that the hobo has no destination; his movement is expressive, not instrumental. "All forms of association among human beings rest finally upon locality and local association."

Pascal, G. R. and Jenkins, W. O. "A Study of the Early Environment of Workhouse Inmate Alcoholics and its Relationship to Adult Behavior," Quarterly Journal of Studies on Alcohol, 21 (March, 1960), pp. 40-50. The relationship between behavior of significant adults during the subjects' first ten years of life and the later adult behavior of the subjects was investigated in two experiments with alcoholic inmates and matched non-alcoholic controls. Total number of subjects (both experiments) was 38. Alcoholics and controls differ significantly in behavior of parents and siblings during the first 10 years of the subject's life. Results indicate that alcoholics experienced deprivation during childhood. Findings are consistent with studies of early stimulus deprivation among animals.

Peterson, W. Jack and Maxwell, Milton A. "The Skid Road 'Wino,'" Social Problems, 5 (Spring, 1958), pp. 308-316.
Interviews with 33 winos in Spokane and Seattle are the basis for this discussion of differences among skid-row men and the degree of which their life is group centered and subject to normative control. The "wino" way of life is described, and the relationship of winos to other skid-row alcoholics is analyzed. The authors conclude that winos are not isolates, but rather "live as social beings in a society of their fellows" and help each other solve problems of procuring food, drink, shelter, protection, and companionship. This article is largely based on Peterson's M.A. thesis, "The Culture of the Skid Road 'Wino'."

Potter, Ellen C. "The Problem of the Transient, " Annals of the American Academy of Political and Social Science, 176 (November, 1934), pp. 66-73.
This brief history of transiency in the U. S. includes a rationale for the sudden increase in homeless men following the panic of 1929. The findings of two censuses of homeless men undertaken by the Committee on the Care of the Transient and Homeless early in 1933 are reviewed. Census data are used to illustrate the scope of the transient problem, and various governmental programs are evaluated.

Rice, Stuart A. "Contagious Bias in the Interview, " American Journal of Sociology, 35 (November, 1929), pp. 420-423.
Rice's discussion of interviewer bias and its quantitative measurement derives from interviews with 2, 000 skid-row men about the reasons for their homelessness.

Rice, Stuart A. "The Homeless, " Annals of the American Academy of Political Science, 77 (May, 1918), pp. 140-153.
Homelessness is considered a function of job status and employment. Rice constructs a typology of homelessness including four types: the self-supporting, the temporarily dependent, the chronically dependent, and the parasitic. General characteristics of each type are described. The discussion is based on the author's personal experience with Bowery men; in 1916-1917 he visited the Bowery disguised as an itinerant, and later he was superintendent of the New York Municipal Lodging House.

Rooney, James F. "Effects of Imported Mexican Farm Labor in a California County, " The American Journal of Economics and Sociology, 20 (October, 1961), pp. 513-521.
Rooney deals with problems caused by the importation of Mexican nationals as farm laborers in a California county. Their presence keeps farm wages at a low level which causes native workers to seek jobs in industry, making further importation necessary. The local farm labor force, composed of persons unable to hold

or qualify for industrial jobs, consists largely of vagabonds and alcoholics. The difficulty in employing reliable
work crews leads farmers to use contractors, who take
a percentage of the laborers' wages and transport the
men daily from the local metropolitan center to the
farms. That this practice augments the skid-row population is confirmed by increases in the number of arrests
for drunkenness.

Rooney, James F. "Group Processes Among Skid Row
Winos: A Reevaluation of the Undersocialization Hypothesis," Quarterly Journal of Studies on Alcohol, 22
(September, 1961), pp. 444-460.
As a participant observer on three California skid rows
the author observed that skid-row men take deliberate
steps to structure social relationships around the activity of purchasing and drinking wine in groups. These
relationships have both a "socio-group function"--to get
more alcohol for one's money--and a "psyche-group
function"--to satisfy emotional needs for personal contact. Rooney describes the role of the initiator in forming a group, in holding funds, and in serving as host,
and also touches on the long- and short-term behavior
expected of group members. His evidence fails to support either the "undersocialization" hypothesis or the
conception that skid-row men are especially lacking in
social (inter-personal) skills.

Rosenman, Stanley. "The Skid-Row Alcoholic and the
Negative Ego Image," Quarterly Journal of Studies on
Alcohol, 16 (September, 1955), pp. 447-473.
Most of this article is a detailed psychoanalytic case
history of a single skid-row alcoholic, aged 27, unmarried, of Scandinavian background. He is an only child,
his mother died during his adolescence, and the relationship with his father was hostile. He had a high IQ
but only completed one year of high school, and began
drinking heavily during his teens. The report analyzes
his ego image as extremely unworthy, degraded, and
repellent, and shows how this image functions in determining his behavior. The role of the "skid-row bum"

image as it operated in the personalities of two non-alcoholic patients (college students) is also described.

Rubington, Earl. "The Bottle Gang," Quarterly Journal of Studies on Alcohol, 29 (December, 1968), pp. 943-955. "Bottle gangs" are groups of men who meet for the purpose of buying and consuming alcoholic beverages. Informants, direct observation, and participation were used in a study of social structure and control among bottle gangs in an "East Coast" city of 150,000. A definite pattern of salutation, negotiation, procurement, consumption, affirmation, and dispersal was found; each stage has a particular function and manifests certain formalities and rules which are much talked about, but often broken and little enforced. In contrast to West Coast bottle gangs, eastern gangs are characterized by simpler rules and greater variability in conformity and sanctions on deviance; West Coast bottle gangs are more organized, stable, and externally controlled. These differences may be explained by differences in the ecology and social organization of neighborhoods wherein the bottle gang occurs.

Rubington, Earl. "'Failure' as a Heavy Drinker: The Case of the Chronic-Drunkenness Offender on Skid Row," pp. 146-153 in Pittman, David J. and Snyder, Charles R., Society, Culture and Drinking Patterns. New York: John Wiley & Sons, 1962.
In this discussion of the social values, social hierarchies and social mobility among skid-row drinkers, Rubington maintains that heavy drinkers form "bottle gangs" or planned drinking episodes and that social relationships are established between "givers" (usually heavy drinkers who are able to work regularly or are casual workers) and "takers." A main concern among these drinkers is the avoidance of social punishment, i.e., arrest, which marks them in the area and limits their mobility. After being arrested, such a social drinker often will migrate to another skid row hoping to conceal his identity from police. Skid-row drinkers maintain rank differences as much as possible and must face the problem of denying their failure.

Sorenson, Karen and Fagan, Ronald J. "Who's on Skid Row: The Hospitalized Skid Row Alcoholic," Nursing Forum, 2 (Spring, 1963), pp. 86-112.
The article focuses on the chronically ill skid-row man whose personality adjustment techniques involve pathological drinking and skid-row habitation. The dynamics of the relationship of patient to hospital staff members are described. There is an account of the general process of social and physical debilitation which ends in dereliction for the alcoholic. This process is related to patient-staff interaction during the period of hospitalization.

Stearns, M. E. "Correlation Between Lodgings of Homeless Men and Employment in New York City," American Statistical Association Proceedings, 1929, 24 (Number 165A, 1929), pp. 182-190.
The author attempts to explain the variation in number of homeless men seeking shelter at the Municipal Lodging House in New York City between 1896 and 1928. In general, the proportion of men seeking shelter has increased in cycles. The effects of increased population or seasonal conditions are discounted as primary causal factors. The fluctuations in number of homeless men are attributed to variations in factory employment in New York State. The inverted curve of the index of factory employment in New York, 1919-1927, matches almost exactly the curve representing the number of men lodged in the Municipal Lodging House.

Straus, Robert. "Alcohol and the Homeless Man," Quarterly Journal of Studies on Alcohol, 7 (December, 1946), pp. 360-404.
Two hundred and three clients of the Salvation Army Men's Social Service Center in 1946 were interviewed in a study of the relationship between alcoholism and homelessness. Typical patterns of alcoholism and homelessness are illustrated in four case histories. Findings are presented on marital history, sexual outlets, relation to parental homes, nationality, religion, mobility, education, and occupation. Results support

the undersocialization theory with respect to both alcoholism and homelessness.

Straus, Robert. "Some Sociological Concomitants of Excessive Drinking as Revealed in the Life-History of an Itinerant Inebriate," Quarterly Journal of Studies on Alcohol, 9 (June, 1948), pp. 1-52.
The life history of an itinerant inebriate, reviewed here in considerable detail, supplements an earlier study by Straus of a group of homeless men. From earliest childhood the subject had been deprived of opportunities to participate in normal social activities and to share social experience. His present situation and society's current expense in supporting him at a state hospital are traceable to these past deprivations. Thus, this life history illustrates the broad sociological concept of undersocialization.

Straus, Robert and McCarthy, Raymond G. "Nonaddictive Pathological Drinking Patterns of Homeless Men," Quarterly Journal of Studies on Alcohol, 12 (December, 1951), pp. 601-611.
The majority of 444 men using a daytime shelter on the Bowery were found to have considerable control over their drinking and over the amounts they spent on alcohol. The authors explore differences in the patterns of "controlled" and "uncontrolled" drinkers, motives for nonaddictive drinking, and attitudes of the respondents toward their drinking. It is noted that the respondents have sought a way of life marked by minimal responsibility.

Swenson, Clifford and Davis, Hugh C. "Types of Workhouse Inmate Alcoholics," Quarterly Journal of Studies on Alcohol, 20 (December, 1959), pp. 757-766.
The authors attempt to distinguish types of skid-row alcoholics among 20 male inmates arrestees for public drunkenness in the Knox County (Tennessee) Workhouse. Analysis of psychological tests and extensive case histories produced five types: 1) isolates who drink nonbeverage alcohol and had strict mothers, 2) same as type 1 except that these had possessive mothers, 3) iso-

lates who do not drink nonbeverage alcohol, 4) same as type 3 and manifesting paranoid schizophrenic character- istics, and 5) sporadic or "spree drinkers." Drinking behavior is seen as a function of the relationship with father, while other psychopathological symptoms derive from the mother-son relationship.

Terry, James, Lolli, Giorgio and Golder, Grace. "Choice of Alcoholic Beverage Among 531 Alcoholics in California," Quarterly Journal of Studies on Alcohol, 18 (September, 1957), pp. 417-428.
This study of alcoholics' beverage preferences was con- ducted among 491 male and 40 female alcoholics at the Santa Rita Rehabilitation Center, Alameda County, Cal- ifornia. Respondents manifested low educational and employment levels and poor marital adjustment. Early drinking preferences were for, first, distilled spirits, second, beer, and third, wine. Analysis of the wine drinkers showed that a majority would prefer spirits other than wine and that consumption of it reflected lim- ited funds rather than a specific addiction to wine. With- in particular drinking sprees, the percentage of wine consumption relative to other alcoholic beverages was noted to increase over the duration of the spree.

Wallace, Samuel E. "The Road to Skid Row," Social Problems, 16 (Summer, 1968), pp. 92-105.
The variety of researchers' definitions of the "skid row- er" are reviewed and combined into an attribute space. Variables included are 1) place of residence, 2) degree of residential mobility, 3) participation in skid-row institu- tions, 4) lack of family ties, and 5) low income and low rent. Inconsistencies among research findings are at- tributed to differences in the way the skid rower has been defined. Recruitment into skid row manifests four phases: dislocation from the rest of society, exposure to skid row subculture, regular participation in skid-row insti- tutions, and integration into the skid-row community. Drinking and being drunk on skid row is the expected pat- tern and is dictated by groups norms. Alcoholics on skid row have lower status than drunks because their drinking

is for individual gratification rather than a group activity. In addition to the drunk and the alcoholic there are
other distinct skid-row statuses, including hobos, beggars, tour directors and mission stiffs. The gradual
disappearance of skid row is noted.

Wilson, Robert S. "Transient Families," The Family,
11 (December, 1930), pp. 243-251.
Problems of transient families are analyzed with reference to depression unemployment, attitudes of the transients, and options for control (mainly in the area of
public health) open to social welfare agencies and the
community. A typology of transient families is based
on the process of social disaffiliation which accounts for
their present life style.

Zax, Melvin, Gardner, Elmer A. and Hart, William T.
"Public Intoxication in Rochester: A Survey of Individuals
Charged During 1961," Quarterly Journal of Studies on
Alcohol, 25 (December, 1964), pp. 660-678.
The authors studied 5,524 arrests for public intoxication in Rochester during 1961. Public intoxication accounted for 59 percent of the criminal court load.
The arrests involved 3,185 people, including 115 who had
more than five arrests in the year. At all ages, nonwhite men had higher arrest rates than white men. Education and family income were negatively related to
arrest rates, and arrest rates were higher in the central
business district and in areas with a high proportion of
one-room dwelling units (the skid-row areas) than in other
sections of the city. More arrests occurred in warm
months.

OTHER WORKS

Advisory Social Service Committee of the Municipal
Lodging House, The Men We Lodge: A Report to the
Commissioner of Public Charities. New York Advisory
Social Service Committee, 1915. Pp. 42.
In March, 1914, approximately 2,000 male residents of
the Municipal Lodging House were surveyed with particular attention to job histories and employability. Use

of alcohol and personality problems also were noted. Most respondents were unemployed primarily because of the current economic recession. Ten percent were unable to work. The activities and facilities of the Municipal Lodging House are described and its immediate needs are estimated. A number of brief case histories are included.

Anderson, Nels. Homeless in New York City. New York: Board of Charity, 1934. Pp. 470.
This work is a comprehensive description of homeless persons in New York City and of the agencies that serve them. There is a history of the Bowery, an account of the operating procedures of the various mission, shelter, and welfare agencies, and a description of types of homeless persons (boys, old men, women and children, Negroes, Jews, and Irishmen) and of their personal characteristics and attitudes. Also there are discussions of police practices and vagrancy, earnings and work experiences of homeless men, health and sanitation among them, and a report of a neuropsychiatric examination of 900 men. Problems of enumerating the homeless and of the seasonal variation in their population are outlined. The manuscript concludes with an appraisal of the services available to homeless persons in New York.

Anderson, Nels. Report on the Municipal Lodging House of New York City. New York: Welfare Council of New York City, Research Bureau, 1932. Pp. 180.
Including a history and description of the Municipal Lodging House's organization and services, this report deals principally with a June, 1931, medical and psychiatric study of 1,000 homeless men at the lodging house. Not only were personal, social and employment histories obtained, but Wasserman test results from 425 men are also reported. Other sources of data include municipal records, annual reports of the lodging house, previous studies, and observations by the author and co-workers. A principal conclusion is that these homeless men would have been better served if the municipal lodging house

had cooperated more closely with other agencies and if the men had received more individual attention.

Bahr, Howard M. Homelessness and Disaffiliation. New York: Columbia University, Bureau of Applied Social Research, 1968. Pp. 437.
A three-year program (1965-67) of research on causes and consequences of homelessness included interviews with two samples of skid-row men (203 Bowery men and 199 clients at Camp LaGuardia, an institution for aged and infirm skid-row men) and two control samples drawn from lower- (N=125) and upper-income (N=104) metropolitan census tracts. The report discusses respondents' social characteristics and backgrounds, compares findings with previous skid-row surveys, and evaluates nine theoretical orientations to the etiology of homelessness (undersocialization, anomie, "demon rum," habituation to dependency, family structure, generational retreat, economic marginality, social marginality, and multiple factor approaches). Several chapters compare affiliation profiles for the various samples and subsamples; family, employment, and voluntary affiliations are considered separately. Skid-row men are shown to be much less affiliated than the control respondents, and their relative disaffiliation extends back over much of the life history. A section on occupational mobility includes illustrative case histories.

Bain, Howard George. "A Sociological Analysis of the Chicago Skid-Row Lifeway," unpublished master's thesis, University of Chicago, 1950. Pp. 175.
Bain attempts to provide a complete sociological analysis of every type of person residing in the skid-row community. A number of personal interviews are recorded, demonstrating different reasons for and degrees of involvement with skid row. The main hypothesis is that in order to exist a community must satisfy the needs of its members. The isolationism, irresponsible living, and use of alcohol to repress anxiety are seen as the primary modes of need satisfaction offered to citizens of skid row.

Baker, Michael A. An Estimate of the Population of Homeless Men in the Bowery Area. New York: Columbia University, Bureau of Applied Social Research, 1965. Pp. 35.
The census of the Bowery described in this report is the second in a series of annual enumerations completed as part of the research program of the Homelessness Project. Between 1964 and 1965 the population declined by about five percent. In addition to describing procedures and results of the census there is a summary of enumerations of the Bowery population by earlier investigators.

Bassett, Lucy A. Transient and Homeless Persons: A Bibliography, Jacksonville: Florida Emergency Relief Administration, 1934. Pp. 87.
Over 400 titles are classified into categories of general background, state and federal transient programs, types of transient programs, types of transients and homeless persons, casework techniques, and legislation, both existing and proposed.

Blumberg, Leonard, et al. The Men on Skid Row. Philadelphia: Department of Psychiatry, Temple University School of Medicine, 1960. Pp. 273.
A study of Philadelphia's skid row was conducted by Temple University School of Medicine under authorization from the Greater Philadelphia Movement and the Redevelopment Authority of the City of Philadelphia. One weekend in February, 1960, 200 white-frocked junior and senior medical students descended on skid row and interviewed 2,249 men (about 80 percent of the resident population). Two interview forms were used: a "short form" was given to 80 percent of the respondents, and a "long form" to the others. Most of the data obtained have to do with the men's current drinking patterns, living accommodations, health, and perceptions of themselves and their neighborhood. Some information about personal and family histories, work histories, and education was also obtained.

Bowery Project. Summary Report of A Study Undertaken Under Contract Approved by the Board of Estimate,
Calendar No. 14, December 19, 1963. New York: Columbia University, Bureau of Applied Social Research,
1965. Pp. 49.
Under a grant from the City of New York the Bowery
Project: 1) estimated the numbers of homeless men
throughout Manhattan; 2) estimated the population of the
Bowery in 1964 and in previous years; 3) located
habitats of homeless men outside the Bowery; 4)
described procedures by which homeless men are
arrested and arraigned, and the frequency with which
this occurs; 5) calculated death and hospital utilization
rates for Bowery men, and investigated illness and
cause of death among them; 6) compiled special reports
on facilities catering to the homeless, on Bowery land
values, and on previous accounts of skid row and homelessness; and 7) secured federal funds for a three-year
study of the etiology and consequences of homelessness.

Brantner, John Paterson. "Homeless Men: A Psychological and Medical Survey," unpublished doctoral dissertation, University of Minnesota, 1958. Pp. 205.
This dissertation is an analysis of the case records of
1,622 consecutive admissions to the Minneapolis Salvation Army Men's Social Service Center. Minnesota
Multiphasic Personality Inventories were administered
to 296 of the men; results showed that most of them were
sociopathic (asocial, amoral, and psychopathic). In addition, the case record data revealed that most were
transients, dropped out of school earlier than the rest
of the male population, were divorced or had never
married, and had criminal records. They drank excessively, but in a pathological, non-addictive way. Many
were physically ill but most were well enough to work.

Caplow, Theodore, Lovald, Keith A. and Wallace, Sam-
uel E. A General Report on the Problem of Relocating
the Population of the Lower Loop Redevelopment Area.
Minneapolis: Minneapolis Housing and Redevelopment
Authority, 1958. Pp. 217.
With the assistance of the U.S. Bureau of the Census a

special enumeration was conducted in Minneapolis' skid row, and more intensive interviews were completed with a random sample of 280 residents of the area. This final report specifies the demographic characteristics of the skid-row population, considers some of the problems faced by the men (bad health, excessive drinking, poor housing), and discusses the availability of housing for relocation purposes. A description of the basic institutions of skid row includes private establishments (restaurants, bars, hotels and lodging houses, missions, second-hand stores, liquor stores, movie theaters, and a barber college) as well as public facilities (streets, parks, employment agencies, hospital, library, and courthouse). Proposals for action include the recommendation that before redevelopment of the area begins, new single-room housing units be constructed near the center of the city. Rentals in these new facilities would be comparable to those currently paid on skid row, and a municipal agency would be established to assist the men in relocating.

Cook County Service Bureau for Men. Characteristics of Unattached Men on Relief. Chicago: Illinois Emergency Relief Commission, 1935. Pp. 32.
The characteristics of men aided by the Relief Commission facilities and programs are described.

Cross, Dorothy E. A Behavior Study of Abraham Bernstein, One of 123 So-Called Homeless Men Who Were Interviewed at the Chicago Municipal Lodging House in 1924. Chicago: Chicago Employment Bureau, 1924. Pp. 39.
This work is a curiously ambivalent study of a homeless man interviewed at the Chicago Municipal Lodging House. Simple repression as a means for handling homeless men is abjured explicitly, but lack of sympathy for the homeless man is evident throughout. Bernstein, described as "a typical black sheep from a respectable family," allegedly was chosen because his history was easy to corroborate: it is suggested that he does not differ appreciably from others interviewed by the author. Fol-

lowing exhaustive description and case history, the author, in a chapter entitled "The Abraham Bernstein Technique, " cynically assesses the behavior of the homeless man vis-a-vis the interviewer, finally convicting him of various sycophantic techniques aimed at evoking pity. Such behavior is seen as typical; unfortunately, the reader cannot determine whether the image of the homeless man as an unfeeling exploiter of the public-at-large is the author's premise or conclusion. "Bernstein's history and experience are like a burning fagot among a score of social agencies, silhouetting one against another. With a persistence and a waywardness that are provoking, he tests out their capacity for handling cases like his and shows up the need of closer coordination in the administration of social agencies dealing with the homeless man. "

Demone, Harold W. and Blacker, Edward.   The Unattached and Socially Isolated Resident on Skid Row. Boston: Boston Community Development Program, 1961 . Pp. 84.
This planning report describes the dimensions of the skid-row problem and the major resources (or the lack of them) available for dealing with the problem.   Prepared as groundwork for Boston's urban renewal plan, the report reaches a major conclusion: unless the skid-row men are enrolled in a planned community program, they inevitably contribute to new skid rows developing in marginal areas.   A number of recommendations are made, all of which call for greater public concern for the skid-row man and the community in which he lives .

Departamento de Accion Educativa, Beneficencia publica del d.f., La Mendicidad en Mexico.   Report submitted to Lic.   Ramon Betata, Chief of the Departamento de Accio Educativa, Efficiencia y Catastros Sociales, October 13, 1930.   Pp. 134.
This study of mendicancy in Mexico City considers general and specific aspects, causes and origins, past legislation, illustrative case histories, and recommendations for action.   Also reviewed are mendicancy as an insti-

tution, and the relationship between mendicancy and Catholicism, public health, alcoholism, and disorganization in the family. Public institutions for mendicants are described.

Dunham, H. Warren. Homeless Men and Their Habitats: A Research Planning Report. Detroit: Wayne University, 1953. Pp. 55.
A research proposal and community action program follow a review of the literature on the skid-row community. The usual background of the homeless man includes little education, broken home, institutional living, and wandering. Alcohol is not a major cause of homelessness, but is an adjustment mechanism for coping with skid row.

Freund, Roger Henry. "Begging in Chicago," unpublished master's thesis, University of Chicago, 1925. Pp. 117.
Freund interviewed 61 chronic beggars and visited the homes of 15 of them. Thirty persons who gave alms to beggars, 48 storekeepers, and workers in 12 organizations dealing with beggars were also interviewed to determine the nature and extent of begging. Many case histories are presented.

Heller Committee for Research in Social Economics . The Dependent Aged in San Francisco. University of California Publications in Economics, 5 (No. 1, 1926). Pp. 127.
This report of a 1925 survey of 846 dependent aged persons and of 18 institutions and relief agencies in San Francisco is one of the earliest large-scale surveys of homeless and dependent persons. A chapter on homeless old men in San Francisco, based on 100 interviews with drifters lodged by the Salvation Army and the Volunteers of America, treats the causes of their drifting and describes how San Francisco aids homeless men. Statistics are presented for age, sex, nativity, literacy, citizenship status, length of residence in the nation, state and city, age when dependency began and length

of dependency, education, occupation, physical disability, marital and parental status. Perhaps the most
striking difference between the dependent aged and other
elderly people is their lack of family ties. "Those aged
are dependents because they are alone in the world. In
major part they are persons who never married or
whose family ties have been broken." Many brief case
histories are included. There is also a description of
the programs for aged dependents of San Francisco and
Alameda County. The study concludes with a summary
of the costs of supporting the dependent aged and an
estimate of the probable costs of a state pension.

Kean, George Gabriel. "A Comparative Study of Negro
and White Homeless Men," unpublished doctoral dissertation, Yeshiva University, 1965. Pp. 264.
The method consisted of comparing three groups of thirty male subjects: 30 homeless Negroes whose selection
to homelessness was largely ascribed to sociological
forces; 30 homeless whites among whom psychological
factors were presumed most important in routing them
to homelessness; and a control group of 30 "domiciled"
Negroes. Subjects were clients of the New York City
Municipal Men's Shelter or Welfare Center clients. The
groups were compared in terms of social background
and with reference to results from various psychological
tests. Observed differences between groups were small.
It is concluded that sociopathological and psychopathological forces operated interdependently to cause homelessness, although in particular cases forces of either
kind may predominate.

Laubach, Frank Charles. "Why There are Vagrants: A
Study Based Upon an Examination of One Hundred Men,"
unpublished doctoral dissertation, Columbia University,
1916. Pp. 128.
One hundred men who applied for work at a woodyard
operated by the Charity Organization Society of New
York City were interviewed, and data were obtained on
their age, race, health, ethnicity, marital status, employment histories, and alcoholism. The author distin-

guishes between individual and social factors leading to
vagrancy. The study is weakened by the author's obvious
religious biases, e.g., "if family ideals are impure
and low, vagrancy will result." The general conclusion
is that drunkenness ("intemperance") is the greatest
cause of vagrancy. Policies for the elimination of vagrancy are recommended.

Levinson, Boris M., A Comparative Study of Certain
Homeless and Unattached Domiciled Men, unpublished
doctoral dissertation, New York University, 1947.
Pp. 284.
Levinson compares random samples of 50 "domiciled"
white unattached men receiving public assistance at the
New York City Welfare Center and 50 white "homeless"
men receiving shelter care at the municipal lodging
house in an attempt to determine whether unattached
domiciled men differ from homeless men. Variables
considered include relief history, medical history,
criminal record, family background and home environment, social and sexual adjustment, intelligence, and
personality patterns. Both samples tend to be ill and
unemployable. Although there are certain differences
between the samples (e.g., domiciled men are more
likely to be foreign-born, homeless men are more likely to have experienced downward mobility and are more
apt to show mental deterioration) the samples are not
different enough to merit the differential treatment giv-
en by the Department of Welfare. Suggestions are made
for improving welfare care of unattached men. There
are several illustrative case histories.

Lovald, Keith Arthur. "From Hobohemia to Skid Row:
The Changing Community of the Homeless Man," unpublished doctoral dissertation, University of Minnesota,
1960. Pp. 502.
Both hobohemia and its later form, skid row, are specialized "status communities" wherein economic, social, and political circumstances combine in a distinctive
manner. A comparison of the hobohemia of the period
between the world wars and Minneapolis' skid row in

1958-59 reveals many changes. Data for the comparison are drawn from the large-scale survey of Minneapolis' skid-row area directed by Theodore Caplow and historical and sociological descriptions of hobohemia, especially the work of Nels Anderson. Formerly most hobohemians were short-term laborers; now a large proportion of the skid-row population lives on public financial assistance or retirement income. Hobohemians were highly mobile and often were arrested for vagrancy. Skid row men are more settled, and tend to be arrested for drunkenness rather than vagrancy. The institutions for homeless men have changed also; occupational institutions, formerly most important, have been displaced by certain leisure and recreational institutions.

McKinsey, John Paul. "Transient Men in Missouri," unpublished doctoral dissertation, University of Missouri, 1940. Pp. 310.
The author draws upon an analysis of 6,000 case records of transient men and six years personal experience as an administrator in the federal transient program in this investigation of transients and of the agencies that deal with them. Historical statistics on transiency (1900 to 1940) are given, and transients' behavior and demographic characteristics are described. Three chapters deal with the operation of the Works Progress Administration and the Federal Transient Bureau. As a class transients tend to be indistinguishable from unemployed persons (except for their lack of a stable address). Many of them tend to be temporary transients, and they demonstrate egocentric, unstable, and apathetic behavior. The federal programs have provided adequate relief to transients but their efforts at preventing transiency have met with limited success.

Minneapolis Study, Department of Sociology, University of Minnesota. "Participant Observation Journal." Minneapolis: unpublished research reports of the Department of Sociology, 1958. Pp. 1,215. (Typewritten)
The experiences and observations of participant observers on skid row in Minneapolis are recorded.

Nash, George. The Habitats of Homeless Men in Manhattan. New York: Columbia University, Bureau of Applied Social Research, 1964. Pp. 174.

Not all homeless men live on skid row. Researchers combed Manhattan to discover places where other homeless men lived. Various sites were discovered, including trucks, abandoned buildings, and sewer pipes. The estimation of a non-Bowery homeless population presupposed a definition of homelessness that did not depend on skid-row residence. Men aged 21 and over who lived without kin, spent less than 30 dollars per month on living quarters, and were not employed in a high-status occupation were defined as homeless. Most men buried at city expense met these criteria. Death certificates for 511 city burials were examined. About one-fifth of the city burials were Bowery men. Characteristics of city burials from outside the Bowery (marital status, age at death, cause of death) were similar to those of Bowery men. The ratio of Bowery to non-Bowery city burials and the enumerated population of the Bowery were used to estimate the number of homeless men in all of Manhattan (38,500). Areas of concentration of homeless men are identified, and their demographic characteristics examined. Factors that influence the location of the habitats of homeless men include nonresidential facilities they patronize, services provided for them, and police practices.

Nash, George and Nash, Patricia. A Preliminary Estimate of the Population and Housing of the Bowery in New York City. New York: Columbia University, Bureau of Applied Social Research, 1964. Pp. 29.

Records of commercial lodging houses, municipal shelters, missions, rooming houses, and hotels in the area were examined in an enumeration of the Bowery population. Inspection of older records made it possible to estimate the population of the area in 1949, and hence to consider population trends. Some units in the area (apartments, private homes, tenements) house non-homeless persons. Total population of the Bowery Study Area in 1964 was 10,572; 55 percent were homeless men.

Peterson, William Jack. "The Culture of the Skid Road Wino," unpublished master's thesis, State College of Washington, 1955. Pp. 119.
Twenty-four winos were interviewed in an attempt to discover the culture and social organization of skid-row men. Six respondents were inmates of the Spokane city jail, six were members of Alcoholics Anonymous in Spokane and Seattle, and 12 were inmates of the Seattle Police Rehabilitation Farm. Following a discussion of the winos' characteristics (family background, occupational history, drinking history) Peterson considers their distinctive roles and the institutions that impinge upon them. Distinct roles in the temporary bottle gangs ("wine-procuring organizations") are the "promoter" and the "runner." Skid-row role patterns, in descending status, are the "worker," the "wino" (who will work when he has to), the "chiseler" (who will not work under any circumstances), and the "dehorn" or "rubby-dub" (who drinks non-beverage alcohol). The language and taboos of winos are briefly treated.

Rooney, James F. "Perception of Social Relations and Work Orientation on Skid Row," unpublished master's thesis, University of California, 1959. Pp. 219.
A TAT was administered to 120 skid-row men in seven cities from coast to coast by the author who posed and worked as a migratory worker. A life history was gathered from each subject. Thematic analysis indicated an extreme passive orientation, i.e., the sustaining of social relationships is done by others.

Russell Sage Foundation Library. Bulletin No. 74: Vagrancy. New York: Russell Sage Foundation, 1925. Pp. 4.
There are 56 items in this selected annotated bibliography.

Schaaf, Albert H. The Economic Importance and Necessity for Unification of the Labor Market Located in Sacramento Redevelopment Area Number One. Sacramento: Redevelopment Agency of the City of Sacramento, 1957. Pp. 13.

The economic importance of the labor force of the Sacramento Redevelopment Area No. 1 is evaluated with
reference to the regional economy and a proposal that a
unified labor market and housing center be provided
for relocating the occupants of this area. Relying on
a 1957 Real Estate Research Corporation survey of 396
hotel and dormitory residents of the Labor Market Area
(8 percent of the universe) and upon local, county and
state data, the author concludes that the Redevelopment
Area residents are of little economic importance in
either the agricultural or nonagricultural sectors. Regarding the idea of unified hiring, employment, and living facilities, it is concluded that economic factors do
not support the concept of a unified relocation center.

Schubert, Herman J. P. Twenty Thousand Transients:
A One Year's Sample of Those Who Apply for Aid in a
Northern City.   Buffalo: Emergency Relief Bureau,
1935.   Pp. 150.
Data were collected for the various intake divisions of
the Transient Center in Buffalo, New York. Three
major groups were differentiated: homeless men, seamen, and families. Each group is described by age,
race, ethnicity, length of time on the road, occupational
status, marital status, and subjective reasons for transience. Causal deductions are offhand and unsystematic;
there are generalizations about treatment and control.

Shulimson, Bert and Clair, Kate. A Social Survey of
the Federal-Anderson Project Area. Pittsburgh: Department of City Planning, 1965. Pp. 35.
The Federal-Anderson Project Area, Pittsburgh's skid
row, is studied as a preliminary step in the formulation
of redevelopment plans. Sources of data include the
census, court and public assistance records, and 1965
estimates by the Department of City Planning. The history of the area and characteristics of its present population are outlined. Most residents of Federal-Anderson
are either 1) families and single persons too poor to
move elsewhere   or who have other personal reasons
for staying, or 2) men who are disorganized and have a
drinking problem. The report also contains a descrip-

tion of commercial activity in the area.

Trice, Andrew H. Present and Future Requirements for Agricultural Labor from the Sacramento Labor Market Area. Sacramento: Redevelopment Agency of the City of Sacramento, 1958. Pp. 50.
The report focuses on two problems: the importance of Sacramento's skid-row labor to surrounding farmers, and the need for job recruitment for relocated skid-row men.   Trice reviewed relevant literature, conducted interviews with 20 farmers and questioned members of growers' associations and public employment personnel. He concludes that the farm labor supplied by residents of the Sacramento Labor Market Area is less important than in previous years, but that plans for reconstructing a labor market and recruitment area are still valuable because 1) significant numbers of men continue to seek farm labor, and 2) such a reconstruction is of psychological value to laborers and the unemployed.

Tenants' Relocation Bureau. The Homeless Man on Skid Row. Chicago: Tenants' Relocation Bureau, 1961. Pp. 109.
This report is based on research conducted by the National Opinion Research Center in cooperation with the Chicago Community Inventory.   Donald Bogue's Skid Row in American Cities draws from the same body of data. A review of the historical background is followed by a description of the functions of skid row (low cost of living, labor market, locus of welfare activities, and neighborhood of anonymity, tolerance and companionship) and of the classes of its residents (elderly or physically disabled men, semi-settled or settled working men, migratory workers, transient "bums," criminals, and chronic alcoholics).   There are separate chapters on characteristics of the skid-row residents as a whole, problem drinking and alcoholic dereliction, the handicapped and ill, the workingmen, the old men and pensioners, migration and mobility, death on skid row, and selected attitudes of the residents. It is concluded that the economic functions of skid row are minor and that its

elimination is possible. A program for the redevelopment of skid row and the relocation and rehabilitation of its residents is proposed; its success depends on increased cooperation and coordination among planning, housing, redevelopment and welfare agencies. There are excellent photographs, maps, and a bibliography of 122 items.

United States Library of Congress. Select List of References: Vagrancy. Washington, D.C.: United States Library of Congress, Division of Bibliography, Nos. 127-159, 1916. Pp. 230.
"Vagrancy," No. 127, is three pages long, and contains 33 items.

Wallace, Samuel E. Skid Row and Its Inhabitants. New York: Columbia University, Bureau of Applied Social Research, 1965. Pp. 133.
After a brief history of vagabondage and the emergence of skid row, Wallace reviews the major theoretical orientations to the etiology of homelessness. Psychological theories of alcoholism and sociological theories of undersocialization, anomie and retreat, interrupted socialization, and isolation are described as inadequate to explain why one becomes a skid-row resident. Wallace's theory focuses on processes of recruitment and socialization: the individual is dislocated from the wider society and exposed to skid-row subculture, his participation there interrupts his normal socialization and substitutes for it progressive integration into the skid-row community. Implications of the theory for research, welfare, and rehabilitation are discussed. There is an extensive annotated bibliography (240 items).

Weinberg, Samuael Kirson. "A Study of Isolation Among Chicago Shelter-Home Men," unpublished master's thesis, University of Chicago, 1935. Pp. 71.
Carried out under the direction of Edwin Sutherland and based on data similar to that used by Sutherland and Locke in Twenty Thousand Homeless Men, this thesis analyzes pre-shelter experiences of 92 homeless men. The withdrawal of homeless men from participation in

all types of primary groups is emphasized.

Weltman, Robert E. "A Comparative Study of Institutionalized and Non-Institutionalized Homeless Men," unpublished doctoral dissertation, Yeshiva University, 1964. Pp. 151.
This study is a comparison of transient and permanent clients at Camp LaGuardia, a custodial institution for homeless men run by the New York City Welfare Department. A sample of 39 native white, middle-aged, healthy permanent residents with important camp jobs was compared to a group of 29 men who had left the camp. The former were found to be more often married, more middle-class in background, more moderate in drinking, and more intelligent. The study is marred by sampling deficiencies but contains interesting comments on the homeless personality.

Western Real Estate Research. Analysis of the Sacramento Labor Market Area. Sacramento: Redevelopment Agency of the City of Sacramento, 1957. Pp. 133.
Western Real Estate Research contracted to prepare an analysis of the characteristics and needs of the single male population of the Labor Market Area. Data were obtained from preliminary inventories of land use and population, intensive surveys of residents, hotels, and businesses in the area, and from interviews with leaders of public and community agencies. A survey of pedestrians provided information about the importance of nonresidents to the economy of the area and the visitors' reasons for coming. The population of unattached persons in the Labor Market Area was about 4,800. Estensive tabulations of population characteristics are based on interviews with all residents in a random sample of hotels and lodging houses (N=511). Managers of hotels and lodging houses in the sample also were interviewed. Most (97 percent) residents were male, over 80 percent reported no dependents, median age was 54 years, most had resided there a year or more, over 30 percent were unemployed and almost half had no friends in the area.

Wilson, John Madison. "A Sociological Investigation and Comparative Analysis of Patterns of Beliefs of Negro and White Male Alcoholic Offenders Regarding the Use of Alcoholic Beverages," unpublished doctoral dissertation, University of Maryland, 1965. Pp. 253. A questionnaire concerning attitudes about alcohol use was administered to a sample of 150 Negro and white male alcoholic offender inmates of the jail and workhouse in Washington, D.C. Findings support a hypothesized difference between Negro and white offenders; as expected, the Negro offenders tend to express more permissive beliefs. Interracial differences are shown to exist in beliefs about seven specific areas of alcohol use, including quantity of consumption, social pressures relative to drinking and incarceration, public intoxication, familial drinking, social ceremonial drinking, and definitions of alcoholism.

Vanderkooi, Ronald C. Skid Row and Its Men: An Exploration of Social Structure, Behavior and Attitudes, Kalamazoo: Technical Bulletin B-39, Michigan State University Institute for Community Development and Services, 1963. Pp. 30.
After several days as a participant observer the author interviewed 71 residents of Chicago's skid row. He describes the respondents' social characteristics, voting, leisure time activity, and reasons for coming to skid row. There is also an analysis of their patterns of alienation as indicated by an abbreviated version of the Dean Alienation Scale. Responses reflecting powerlessness, social isolation, and normlessness are discussed separately.

TAVERNS AND BARS

BOOKS

Cavan, Sherri. Liquor License: An Ethnography of Bar Behavior. Chicago: Aldine, 1966. Pp. 246. Data were obtained through participant-observation in approximately 100 bars in San Francisco. The bar is seen as a setting for social interaction having its own peculiar normative standards. Drinking places are differentiated in terms of functions they ostensibly perform for their patrons. It is concluded that the characteristic feature of the bar setting is that it grants the freedom to be indifferent about matters which would otherwise demand concern, at least concern over the social consequences of indifference.

Firebaugh, W. C. The Inns of Greece and Rome. Chicago: Pascal Covici, 1928. Pp. 271. Drawing from Herodotus, Homer, Vergil and others, the author describes the role of inns and taverns for the Assyrians, Babylonians, Greeks and Romans. The function and status of inns is seen as an index of national character and societal values. Many situations are described--for example, the taverns of Athens are said to have been filled by the lower class, the sailors and watermen, idlers and vagrants, rioters, and abandoned women. The author's aim is to give a complete picture of the meaning of hospitality and the role of the inns with respect to all levels of society.

Firebaugh, W. C. The Inns of the Middle Ages. Chicago: Pascal Covici, 1924. Pp. 274. This attempt to describe the quality of life during the Middle Ages in Europe focuses on inns, taverns, and alehouses. Life styles of high society, vagabonds and serfs, and those between these two extremes are sketched. The overall theme is hospitality. Numerous examples of laws, codes, traditions, local lore and poetry are given. Descriptions of vagabonds, drunkards and serfs are often vivid. There is no bibliography and few citations of sources.

Mass-Observation. The Pub and the People: A Worktown Study. London: Victor Gollancz, 1943. Pp. 350. "Worktown, " an industrial city (pop. 180, 000) in northern England, was studied by "Mass Observation, " a sociological research group. Observers spent two years studying the town informally. From a depth analysis of pub life in Worktown, the observers draw conclusions about pub life in general. The drinking establishments, clientele, beverages, diversions, and related societies and institutions are discussed. The pub was found not to be an escape from home life into better surroundings, but rather a psychological retreat from responsibility, family, and mill life. The pub-going community constituted 15 percent of the Worktown population. Members of the lower class were found to be greatest pub-goers; most middle-class people drank at home, and the upper classes drank at clubs. Pub-going is seen as a beneficial physiological and psychological change from routine. There is an extensive bibliography.

ARTICLES

Clark, Walter, "Demographic Characteristics of Tavern Patrons in San Francisco, " Quarterly Journal of Studies on Alcohol, 27 (June 1966), pp. 316-327.
In 1962 interviews about drinking practices were conducted with an area probability sample of 1, 268 adult residents of San Francisco.Respondents were questioned about patronage of bars, taverns, and cocktail lounges; forty percent patronized a tavern at least occasionally. Segments of the population over-represented among tavern patrons include heavy drinkers, men, younger people, and the unmarried. Amount of drinking is related to tavern patronage, but most patrons are not heavy drinkers. Income is positively related to tavern use, occupational status is not. Married, divorced, separated,

and widowed persons use taverns less frequently than single persons. The tavern is a place where ritualistic expressions of sentiment occur; it provides entertainment and relaxation, and is a public gathering place wherein people are relatively "open" to one another.

Clinard, Marshal B. "The Public Drinking House and Society," pp. 270-292 in Pittman, David J. and Synder, Charles R. (eds.), Society, Culture and Drinking Patterns. New York: John Wiley & Sons, 1962.
After a summary of laws dealing with the sale and consumption of alcohol within taverns, the chief functions of the tavern (apart from drinking) are discussed. The tavern functions as 1) a meeting place, 2) a place of recreation, and 3) a place to talk over personal problems. These three aspects are more important in defining a tavern than its obvious characteristic as a dispensary of alcohol. There is no significant evidence that taverns promote either alcoholism or juvenile delinquency.

Gottlieb, David. "The Neighborhood Tavern and the Cocktail Lounge: A Study of Class Differences," American Journal of Sociology, 62 (May, 1957), pp. 559-562.
Interviews held in 24 taverns (60 respondents) and 22 cocktail lounges (48 respondents) in Chicago provided the data for this study. The author contrasts taverns and lounges, pointing out that the former are more likely to provide a basis for social interaction. Both types of establishments are faced with problems as the predominant social make-up of the neighborhood changes, but in different degree. The lounge generally caters to a higher class clientele, for the most part transient. It is the tavern that mirrors the changing neighborhood context. Usually the pattern of change is a period of resistance followed by gradual acquiescence. The proprietor is faced with the decision of serving the new clientele and losing his old customers, or selling. In the study of community change the tavern is the community in microcosm.

Macrary, Boyd. "The Tavern and the Community, " Quarterly Journal of Studies on Alcohol, 13 (December, 1952), pp. 609-637.
Three principal themes are presented regarding taverns in America, 1) conflicting attitudes toward taverns, 2) types of taverns, and 3) functions of taverns. Drawing upon 1, 441 questionnaires from respondents in Dane County, Wisconsin, the author describes a wide range of attitudes and discusses the views of patrons in order to identify the function that taverns serve. Five types of drinking establishments are discussed: the skid-row bar, the downtown bar, the drinking and dining tavern, the night-club, and the neighborhood bar. The taverns fill a social need, often serving more persons than churches or theaters. It is suggested that these needs are related to certain characteristics of urban-industrial society.

Melendy, Royal L. "The Saloon in Chicago, " American Journal of Sociology, 6 (November, 1900 and January, 1901), pp. 289-306, 433-464.
This study was sponsored by the Ethical Subcommittee of the Committee of Fifty to gather information about the "liquor problem. " Observations were made at the Chicago Commons, a social settlement in the center of the industrial district. Melendy describes the style of life of the men drawn to the saloons and the various services the saloons provide: they function as informal employment bureaus, entertainment centers, business centers, and family recreation centers, depending on the type of neighborhood they serve. Other organizations may also provide these services and thus serve as substitutes for the saloon. Fraternal organizations, singing societies, trade unions, boys' clubs, pleasure clubs, church societies, social settlements, amusement enterprises, billiard halls, and other organizations are considered as such functional equivalents. The author concludes that the "present evil may be removed," i.e., a substitute for the saloon provided, via 1) improved lodging facilities, 2) better and cheaper food, 3) public

upkeep of public conveniences, 4) more places for recreation and amusement, and 5) better education.

Moore, E. C. "Social Value of the Saloon, "American
Journal of Sociology, 3 (July, 1897), pp. 1-12.
This paper stems from an investigation of the saloons in
Chicago's 19th ward in 1896. The author visited saloons
and made observations under the assumption that the saloons met some social need. He concludes that they
meet the primal needs for food, and for social stimulation and gratification. Although sympathetic to the ideals
of reformers and prohibitionists, he argues that their
efforts are too miniscule and that they fail to direct
themselves to the needs of the working men. There are
interesting observations about the role of the saloon keeper and the effects of alcohol.

Popham, Robert E., "The Urban Tavern: Some Preliminary Remarks," Addictions, 9 (Autumn, 1962),
pp. 16-24.
An understanding of social relationships in the tavern
setting is a necessary step toward understanding drinking behavior in general. A brief account is given of the
principal findings of a six-year exploratory study of
tavern behavior, based in part on field work in Canadian taverns. Opposition to the tavern has a long history,
and manifestly has dealt with the role of alcohol in
creating social problems. Opposition is concentrated in
certain groups that lack first hand knowledge of taverns
and are threatened by social change. Although an investigation (1900) showed little correlation between
taverns and major social problems, opposition persisted
and seemed to be grounded in its "social role" as a
meeting place. Both the coffee house and the tavern have
been instrumental in revolutions and trade union movements and both have been targets for opposition. Popham presents figures showing little correlation between
drunkenness and tavern frequency. Moreover, statistics
from Ontario and Manitoba suggest that there is no direct relationship between liberality of liquor laws and
arrests for drunkenness.

OTHER WORKS

Dumont, Matthew P. "Tavern Culture: The Sustenance
of Homeless Men." Boston: Laboratory of Community
Psychiatry, Department of Psychiatry, Harvard Medical
School (no date; ca. 1966). Pp. 11.
This discussion of the tavern as a social system draws
on the author's periodic observations at the Star Tavern
in Boston. Drinking habits, eating habits, and daily
social patterns of tavern habitues are reported. A description of the tavern as a social system leads to the
suggestion that the tavern be viewed as a possible extension of governmental health agencies.

THE LAW

ARTICLES

Bacon, Seldon D. "Alcohol, Alcoholism, and Crime," Crime and Delinquency, 9 (January, 1963), pp. 1-14. Alcoholics and criminals are types who deviate from social norms by deviating from drinking customs or from those customs codified in law. This paper's concern is whether the use of alcohol is directly related to the social deviance of committing a crime. Since overuse of alcohol results in a temporary case of extreme desocialization which allows a person to commit an extraordinary act, alcohol might directly influence a criminal act. But this type of desocialization and the acts resulting from it cannot properly be assessed unless they be compared to the actor's normal behavior.

Beck, Stanley M., and Parker, Graham E. "The Intoxicated Offender--A Problem of Responsibility," Canadian Bar Review. 44 (September, 1966), pp. 563-609. The current controversy between individual responsibility and criminal law is reviewed. The authors consider the history of intoxication in criminal law, the intoxicated offender in court, the effects of alcohol, and the effectiveness of present methods of dealing with the intoxicated offenders.

Bittner, Egon. "The Police on Skid Row: A Study of Peace Keeping," American Sociological Review, 32 (October, 1967), pp. 699-715. This article is based on a year's field work in police departments of two unidentified cities located west of the Mississippi. Skid row is seen as a context where peace-keeping aspects of police work predominate over law enforcement, and the problems and practices of peace-keeping on skid row are described. The patrolman's definition of skid row includes a feeling that trust is irrelevant, that the past has little relevance for the present, and that present situations have minimal implications for the future. The skid-row man tends to lack the statuses that permit identification and accountability in the rest of society, hence skid row has an atmosphere of "objective irresponsibility." The major elements of skid-row policeman's peace-keeping are his detailed knowledge of people and places in the area, subordination of strict legal culpability as grounds for sanction, and use of coercive interventions as determined by the immediate situation and with little regard for their long-range consequences for the person involved. Skid-row patrolmen operate under wide discretionary freedom and hence are subject to a virtual absence of disciplinary control.

Borkenstein, Robert F. "Alcoholism and Law Enforcement," Crime and Delinquency, 9 (January, 1963), pp. 84-88.
The author points to four categories of law dealing with alcohol: 1) laws dealing directly with public safety; 2) laws reflecting moral attitudes; 3) laws reflecting attitudes of minorities; and 4) laws governing licensing, revenues, and problems of sale and purchase. Direct police action is necessary only in the first category, e. g., arrest of a drunken driver, while other categories are under the jurisdiction of special boards or offices. It is recommended that a clear definition of intoxication be used by police in dealings with laws of the first category.

Chambliss, William J. "A Sociological Analysis of the Law of Vagrancy," Social Problems, 12 (Summer, 1964), pp. 67-77.
There are few analyses of the relationship between laws and the social setting in which they emerge. Chambliss examines the emergence of vagrancy from 1349 to 1743, noting a shift in the definition of vagrants and the purpose of the laws. The earlier laws were aimed at control of the undesirable and the criminal. It is suggested that the vagrancy laws reflected important "vested interest" groups, initially the powerful landowners, later the merchants. There is a very brief treatment of vagrancy laws in the United States.

Driver, Richard J. "The United State Supreme Court
and the Chronic Drunkenness Offender," Quarterly
Journal of Studies on Alcohol, 30 (March, 1969), pp.
165-172.
Despite 1966 rulings by lower courts that alcoholic chronic drunkenness offenders could not be criminally convicted of public intoxication, in 1967 in Powell v. Texas
the Supreme Court did not reverse the Texas Court
and find the state public drunkenness statute unconstitutional. Powell raised the question of whether the public
drunkenness statute provided "cruel and unusual punishment" and thus violated the Eighth Amendment. The majority decision to affirm the conviction seems a result
of the "utterly inadequate" testimony presented for
Powell, and a majority of the Court indicated that if the
arguments presented (as opposed to the inadequate record) were correct then criminal punishment of alcoholics for public intoxication is unconstitutional.

Dubin, Gary V. and Robinson, Richard H. "The Vagrancy Concept Reconsidered: Problems and Abuses of Status Criminality," New York University Law Review,
37 (January, 1962), pp. 102-136.
The concept of vagrancy as it is embodied in United
States legal statutes is reviewed. The evolution of English vagrancy law and its incorporation into American
legal tradition is examined, and the authors argue for
legal reform. As presently written and enforced vagrancy laws are unconstitutional. Further, legal acceptance
of status criminality impedes crime prevention.

Foote, Caleb, "Vagrancy-Type Law and Its Administration," University of Pennsylvania Law Review, 104
(March, 1956), pp. 603-650.
The history, theory and purposes of vagrancy-type laws
and their administration in Philadelphia, Pennsylvania
are reviewed. Data on current administration are derived from observations of trials, interviews with
convicted vagrants, and police and House of Correction records. Problems such as inadequate definitions of vagrancy, drunkenness, and disorderly
conduct, assumption of guilt, and lack of con-

cern for illness (physical or mental) are illustrated.
There are three proposals for immediate action: 1) the
Voluntary Defender system should be extended to magistrates' courts, 2) vagrancy-type cases should be transferred to municipal courts, and 3) closer cooperation of
the court and social welfare services should be encouraged. The extension of procedural safeguards to vagrancy-type cases guarantees not only the individual's rights
but in the long run also serves the well-being of society.

Greenland, Cyril. "Habitual Drunkards in Scotland,
1879-1918. A Historical Note," Quarterly Journal of
Studies on Alcohol, 21 (March, 1960), pp. 135-139.
This paper is a description of governmental attempts to
deal with the problem of alcoholism ("dipsomania" or
"oinomania") in Scotland in the late nineteenth and early
twentieth century. The provisions of specific legislative
acts, e. g., the Inebriates Act of 1898, and the recommendations of legislative committees, e. g., the Royal
Lunacy Committee, are examined in the light of their
evolution and institutionalization. Administrative processes in the institutions and sanitaria sanctioned or
established by legislative action are discussed in connection with definitions of the alcoholic, the mentally ill,
and the criminal, and the continuing problem of differentiation of the three categories.

Hall, Jerome. "Drunkenness as a Criminal Offense,"
Quarterly Journal of Studies on Alcohol, 1 (March, 1941),
pp. 751-766.
Hall discusses the difficulties involved in establishing
whether a man is drunk or sober. Only in a few cases
(e. g., driving while intoxicated) is a person punished
for intoxication. In cases such as murder committed
while intoxicated, murder is the charge, not intoxication.
The present objective standard of sobriety is precarious
at best, and when the nature of the case permits, the
question of sobriety is avoided.

Johnson, A. W. "Poor Man's Law in Manitoba," Canadian Bar Review, 25 (May, 1967), pp. 478-486.
The Poor Law in Manitoba was developed so that a needy

person could apply for a lawyer's services without having
to pay his fees. Certificates of need are issued by the
Needy Person's Committee, which in turn receives support from the Manitoba Bar. Although the work is limited
by its local nature, it has provided a necessary service,
and similar legal aid centers are needed in other provinces.

Lacey, Forrest W. "Vagrancy and Other Crimes of Personal Condition, " Harvard Law Review, 66 (May, 1953),
pp. 1203-1226.
Crimes of condition differ from other crimes in that
they are crimes of being rather than acting or failing to
act. Lacey reviews statutes dealing with crimes of condition, particularly vagrancy, and points out various
difficulties in assessing these crimes. Vagrancy arrests
provide police with a means for crime control rather
than crime prevention. Skid-row habitues, hoboes, and
tramps, although vagrants, are not dealt with by provisions in vagrancy statutes; these types cannot really be
classed as criminals, and punitive measures are useless
against them.

Lisle, John. "Vagrancy Law: Its Faults and Their
Remedy, " Journal of Criminal Law and Criminology,
5 (1914-1915), pp. 498-513.
Defining vagrancy is difficult because vagrancy laws do
not distinguish between three types of poor persons:
the impotent, the able who will work, and the able who
will not work. In reforming the laws, there is no need
to create new classifications, but rather a need to recognize the divisions that exist. Historical treatment of
the able who will not work is discussed. A central farm
colony is recommended as the best possible form of detention for vagrants, and since reformation is the eventual goal, an indefinite term of commitment should be
established for the vagrant.

Millis, Harry A. "The Law Affecting Immigrants and
Tramps, " Conference of Charities and Corrections,
(1896), pp. 355-361.
Current legislation affecting the poor and the vagrant

and the means of enforcing such legislation are described. The article is nothing more than a catalogue of the measures enacted by state and local governments against paupers and tramps.

Murtagh, John M. "Alcohol and the Law," pp. 229-241 in Lucia, Salvatore P. (ed.), Alcohol and Civilization. New York: McGraw-Hill, 1963.
This article by a criminal court judge stresses the need to view the problem of drunkenness arrests from a philosophical standpoint; human law should not be confused with moral law. Most arrestees are not pathological alcoholics, but in a condition of human degradation. Chronic drunkenness is a problem of public health, not of crime. The law has the right to incarcerate an individual only if his actions interfere substantially with the other members of society. Passive drunkenness should not be a criminal offense. Wholesale arrests of drunkenness offenders are based on ignorance and merely demonstrate that society is reluctant to grapple with the real problem.

Murtagh, John M. "The Law in Relation to Problem Drinking and Alcoholism," New York State Journal of Medicine, 58 (March, 1958), pp. 727-729.
From the premise that problems related to alcohol consumption cannot be solved through penal legislation, it is argued that the most fruitful possibilities for action lie in the area of public health. The welfare program of New York City and the history of penal legislation on alcohol in New York are used to substantiate this contention.

Reid, R. F. "Alcohol: Problems and Recent Legislation," University of Toronto Law Journal, 18 (January, 1968), pp. 87-97.
A 1966 amendment to the statutes of British Columbia provides a comprehensive attempt to treat alcoholism. Problems inherent in the assumptions of the amendment are outlined. Defining alcoholism is left to the magistrate; the legislation is leveled at the chronic public drunk; there is an assumption that reclamation is possible through a process which is publicly humiliating, and specific treatment is not described. The rising problem,

historical remedies, and a need for legislation dealing with the non-public alcoholic are discussed. Necessary changes in treatment and facilities are outlined, and there is a summary of the requirements dealt with by the President's Commission of Law Enforcement and Administration of Justice.

Rosenheim, Margaret K. "Vagrancy Concepts in Welfare Law, " pp. 187-242 in TenBroek, Jacobus (ed.), The Law of the Poor. San Francisco: Chandler, 1966.
The author marshals evidence in support of tenBroek's contention that vagrancy concepts have established a hold on the welfare system, and have become less important in the criminal law. Historically the wandering stranger was seen as a potential criminal, and laws were made to curtail his activity. The eventual establishment of the welfare system and the recognition of different kinds of vagrancy led to a differentiation between criminal vagrancy and other forms of vagrancy. In the United States the crime of vagrancy seems to have been eliminated, and those who formerly would have been labeled vagrants are taken care of by welfare programs. Individual programs (Aid to Families with Dependent Children, Old-Age Insurance, training programs) are evaluated and related to vagrancy concepts. Rosenheim suggests that vagrancy concepts within the welfare system (e. g., making distinctions between the able-bodied and other dependents) have prevented certain individuals from receiving needed assistance.

Rubington, Earl. "The 'Revolving Door' Game, " Crime and Delinquency, 12 (October, 1966), pp. 332-338.
Public and police indifference toward the possible rehabilitation of alcoholics has created the endless cycle of arrest, lock-up, discharge, and future arrest that plagues so many chronic alcoholics. Alcoholics Anonymous, doctors, and public health officials have entered into this futile game as "spoilsports, " changed the rules somewhat, and reduced the number of players by having alcoholics sent to clinics instead of jails. The game will be over when it is finally decided that public drunkenness is not a misdemeanor but an indication of illness.

Scott, Woodrow W. "Recorded Inebriety in Wisconsin:
An Analysis of Arrested Inebriates in Two Wisconsin
Counties," Sociology and Social Research, 39 (November-
December, 1954), pp. 96-102.
Arrests for inebriety in 1940 in Wisconsin's Dane and
Douglas counties are analyzed. The former, with a
primarily agricultural population of 169, 000, had 2, 237
arrests of 1, 506 persons; the latter had 1, 771 such
arrests of 1, 175 persons in a population of 43, 500. In
both counties, first arrests accounted for about one-
half of the cases. Dane County arrests were 42 percent nonresidents, twice the Douglas County rate for
nonresident arrests. Douglas had a larger proportion
of teen-age arrests for inebriety. Both counties' arrests
were predominately male and urban, and manual laborers, Negroes, and Indians were overrepresented in the
arrested population.

Utah State Board on Alcoholism and University of Utah
Graduate School of Social Work. "A Study of Arrests
for Drunkenness in Salt Lake City," Quarterly Journal
of Studies on Alcohol, 11 (December, 1950), pp. 695-
701.
A sample of 580 chronic drunkenness offenders were
studied to determine the effects of arrest, fine, and confinement. Statistics on age, residence, race, criminal
record, and other factors are presented. There is a
detailed analysis of the cost to the state of the present
penal procedures.

OTHER WORKS

Markel, Nan. A Preliminary Study of New York's Legal
Agencies and Their Effects on Homeless Men and the
Bowery. New York: Columbia University, Bureau of
Applied Social Research, 1964. Pp. 45.
The substance of penal legislation as it is used with
reference to homeless men, and police and court procedures in their arraignment are reviewed. In 1963
arrests for drunkenness and disorderly conduct accounted for one-fourth of all arrests in New York City. Ninety

percent of those arrested were given suspended sentences. Analysis of arrest rates by type of offense demonstrated that serious crimes were no more frequent on
the Bowery than in other sections of the city.

U.S. Department of Health, Education, and Welfare.
The Court and the Chronic Inebriate: Conference Proceedings. Washington, D.C.: U.S. Government Printing Office, 1965.
This conference is described by Lyndon Johnson as "an
important first step toward considering the removal from
the court and penal system of those chronic alcoholics
who might be treated more effectively by health and social
agencies." David Pittman discusses sociocultural and
socialization determinants of inebriety, alcohol as an
adjustive mechanism in the life career, and possible
methods of changing the patterns of care for public intoxication cases. A physician discusses "Medical and
Psychiatric Aspects," a corrections expert reviews
"Correction and the Alcoholic," two municipal judges
outline court programs and standards for handling chronic
inebriate offenders, and there are statements on the roles
of official and voluntary social agencies in dealing with
the problems of the chronic offender. Of particular interest is Judge William Burnett's outline of an innova-
tive program of standards for handling drunk offenders
in the Denver County Court. The program includes
release of offenders when sober on personal recogni-
zance, fines for early offenders, payment of fines in
lieu of court appearance, and voluntary enrollment in a
"Court Honor Class" or Alcoholics Anonymous in lieu of
the fine. Pp. 43.

TREATMENT, PUNISHMENT, REHABILITATION: HOMELESSNESS

BOOKS

Cross, William T. and Cross, Dorothy E. Newcomers and Nomads in California. Stanford: Stanford University Press, 1937. Pp. 149.
An administrative view of the vagrancy problem is presented by officials of a government agency. William Cross was an administrator for the State Emergency Relief Administration in 1933 and conducted field observations among itinerants traveling by railroad and highway and a one-day census of the migrant population of California. In the present volume he summarizes the federal emergency legislation that aided transients and describes the nature of the transients and the California experience with destitute homeless people. A chapter on "Beginnings of Rehabilitation Work" describes shelters and rehabilitation programs for transient individuals and families. Policy implications of the California experience are considered. The traditional attitude toward westward migrants and pioneer settlers will no longer suffice; organized assistance is now necessary. There is an excellent bibliography (230 items).

Dawson, William Harbutt. The Vagrancy Problem. London: P. S. King & Son, 1910. Pp. 270.
Vagrants are differentiated into four categories on the basis of life style. The history of the Poor Law since its revision in 1834 is reviewed in the light of data from casual wards which show the number of vagrants to be increasing. According to Dawson, society must stamp out the "social parasite," both for the good of society and that of the vagrant. Methods for the control of vagrancy in Germany and Belgium are discussed in detail, and the author concludes that similar approaches (detention camps and labor colonies) ought to be instituted in England.

Fergusson, Robert Menzies. The Vagrant: What to Do with Him. London: James Nisbet, 1911. Pp. 62. Drawing upon the findings of the Commissioners on the Poor Laws and Relief of Distress and of The Departmental Committee on Vagrancy, Fergusson argues for police control of vagrants and for increasing efforts at rehabilitation. Rehabilitation is essential because the typical vagrant is one whose "mainspring came into the world broken; his reproductive instinct, however, remains intact." The proposed solution is the creation of labor colonies. Even if rehabilitative hopes are not achieved, a program of labor colonies keeps vagrants off the streets. Labor colonies in foreign lands are described and the need for different types of colonies (e. g., special ones for epileptics) is discussed.

Illinois, State of. Biennial Report of the Illinois Emergency Relief Commission: Covering the Period July 1, 1934 through June 30, 1936. Chicago: State of Illinois, 1937. Pp. 233. See following item.

Illinois, State of. Biennial Report of the Illinois Emergency Relief Commission: Covering the Period July 1, 1936 through June 30, 1938. Chicago: State of Illinois, 1939. Pp. 250. Following two previous reports, entitled the First and Second Annual Reports of the Illinois Emergency Relief Commission, these volumes describe the organization and scope of the Commission's relief program and present a statistical breakdown on the characteristics of the relief population. There is also a survey of public and private relief programs in other localities. These reports would be particularly valuable to one studying either the Commission itself or the details of the problems it faced. Each volume is indexed and includes a listing of the Commission's publications.

Johnson, Alexander (ed.) A Guide to the Study of Charities and Corrections. Boston: Executive Committee of the Conference of Charities and Corrections, 1908. Pp. 353.

This work is a reference source and index of the proceedings of the National Conference of Charities and
Corrections for the years 1874 to 1907. Within each
topical subdivision (e. g. , statistics, blind and deaf education, medical charities) are cited various papers, reports, and studies. Usually there is a brief annotation.

Johnson, Glenn H. Relief and Health Problems of a
Selected Group of Non-Family Men. Chicago: University of Chicago Press, 1937. Pp. 81.
The report of a 1936-37 study (by the School of Social
Service Administration of the University of Chicago) of
144 resident non-family men who were under the care
of the Cook County Relief Administration presents numerous statistics regarding work histories, education,
and employability as well as samples and summaries of
more subjective data derived from interviews.   Chicago's program of care for homeless men is reviewed.
It is concluded that the problem of homelessness can
best be confronted by 1) seeing it as a part of the larger
problem of poverty and 2) integrating or more closely
coordinating the several professions and disciplines
concerned.

Kelly, Edmond. The Elimination of the Tramp. New
York: G. P. Putnam's Sons, 1908. Pp. 111.
A program is offered for the elimination of vagrancy
problems in the United States. Kelly advocates the
establishment of labor colonies after the example of
Switzerland and Holland. His version of the ideal labor
colony, largely modeled on the free colony at Tannenhof,
Switzerland, would have the following characteristics:
1) self-support, 2) some provision to encourage reform,
specifically in teaching vocational skills, and 3) orientation toward agriculture since so few vagrants have
particular skills and because competition with existing
industries must be avoided. Also included is a chapter,
"Indiscriminate Almsgiving," in which Kelly maintains
that private charities provide reinforcement for vagrancy. Appendicies include a classification scheme
(tramps, hoboes, and bums) and a list of the rules and
regulations of the Nusshof colony.

Kelly, Edmond. The Unemployables. London: P. S.
King & Son, 1907. Pp. 60.
Kelly discusses various categories of vagrants and the
labor colonies of continental Europe, with particular
attention to the Swiss system. He is interested in applying the labor colony concept to the British situation, although this brief work does not attempt to resolve some
of the problems of such application, e. g. , the necessary
modification of Britain's workhouse system. The problem of finding a balance between rehabilitative and custodial programs for the unemployed is considered.

Niebanck, Paul L. The Elderly in Older Urban Areas:
Problems of Adaptation and the Effects of Relocation.
Philadelphia: University of Pennsylvania, Institute of
Environmental Studies, 1965. Pp. 174.
Niebanck presents a comprehensive description of the
elderly urbanites who are forced to relocate, using data
from the census, records of various urban renewal programs, and other relevant records and studies. The
economic dimensions are considered (e. g., income
ranges, housing costs, moving costs) and an argument
is made for giving greater consideration to the social-
psychological costs of relocation for the elderly. The
author argues that relocation should be seen in the larger
context of improving the quality of city life, rather than
simply as the removal of residents from the areas subject to urban renewal. There is a good bibliography.

Paulian, Louis. Paris qui mendie: mal et remede.
Paris: Ollendorf, 1893. Pp. 302.
The resources and methods of distribution of public and
private welfare agencies in Paris are described. It is
argued that fakers and confidence men siphon off much
of the money that is meant for the truly poor. Paulian
lived as a "faux pauvre" and describes the various means
available for getting relief while not really deserving it.
He advocates distribution of charity only to those who
cannot work and the forcible suppression of mendicancy.
He proposes a poverty test based on the proposition that
all beggars are lazy and if their representations were
true, they would work. Forced labor will thus unmask

"tous ces voleurs de pauvres." Reorganization of public welfare and centralization of private welfare are advocated.

Special Consular Reports. Volume 9: Vagrancy and Public Charities in Foreign Countries. Washington, D. C. :
Government Printing Office, 1893. Pp. 372.
The nature of the "tramp problem" and methods for dealing with it in more than 20 different nations are summarized by the United States Consulates in those nations .
Discussion is directed to six basic areas: the definition
and regulation of the tramp, efforts at punishment or
suppression, organization of almsgiving, attempts at rehabilitation, effects of decentralized distribution of charities, and the regulation of the intermarriages of paupers .
Reports from consulates in Germany and England are
particularly detailed.

Senate Committee on Manufactures. "Seventy-second
Congress, second session, on S. 5121. Relief for Unemployed Transients." Washington, D. C. : U. S. Government Printing Office, 1933.
These subcommittee hearings included the testimony of
sociologists, heads of state labor camps, heads of children's aid societies, railroad special agents, Travellers'
Aid Society personnel, and unemployed transients. Also,
there are summaries of letters received from mayors of
500 selected municipalities answering the question "How
are you meeting the problem of the transient?" Among
those testifying was Nels Anderson.

ARTICLES

Anderson, Harriet E. "Centralized Care of the Homeless," The Family, 11 (February, 1931), pp. 318-319 .
It is recommended that municipal welfare departments
differentiate types of homeless people so as to better
cope with the problem of homelessness and vagrancy.
The basis of the proposal derives from an assessment
of subjective opinions of a small number of randomly
encountered homeless people and the success of a Louis-
ville, Kentucky, welfare system.

Anderson, Harriet E. "Travelers and Non-Residents,"
The Family, 9 (May, 1928), pp. 75-79.
A recommendation for greater administrative organization among existing welfare groups is combined with terse
descriptions of some national and local relief agencies.

Barbour, Levi L. "Vagrancy," Proceedings of the Eighth
Annual Conference of Charities and Correction, (1881),
pp. 131-138.
The author distinguishes between the simple poverty
arising from unforeseen, uncontrollable circumstances
and pauperism, which connotes street begging and prey-
ing on the public. He is here concerned with pauperism,
and favors a "tough" approach similar to a program
adopted in Detroit which emphasized compulsory labor
for vagrants.

Binder, Rudolph M. "The Treatment of Beggars and
Vagabonds in Belgium," Journal of Criminal Law and
Criminology, 6 (March, 1916), pp. 835-848.
The article deals with legislation designed to suppress
begging and vagabondage, the administration of poor-
houses and workhouses set up by the legislation, the type
of inmate in the institutions, and a general discussion of
the conditions and regulations of life for the inmates.
There are data on recidivism, age of inmates and trends
in numbers of admissions. The ultimate solution to the
problem of vagrancy and unemployment is seen in a more
rational appraisal of the nature of the unfit. Society
must prevent the propagation of the unfit by segregation
of the sexes or sterilization.

Blumberg, Leonard, Shipley, Thomas E., Jr., Shandler,
Irving W., and Niebuhr, Herman. "The Development,
Major Goals and Strategies of a Skid Row Program:
Philadelphia," Quarterly Journal of Studies on Alcohol,
27 (June, 1966), pp. 242-258.
The Philadelphia program to relocate and rehabilitate
skid rowers without creating a new skid row was begun
in 1952. The initial phase was preparation of a set of
recommendations for a casework-oriented program.
Census data and interviews with 2,249 skid-row men

were collected and a diagnostic and relocation center was established. The growth of this center into a full scale operation is the final phase of the program. Its purpose is to aid skid-row men to know about and use opportunities in the wider community. The authors introduce the notion of "limited optimal discrepancy" that provides a theoretical orientation and rationale for approaching skid-row problems.

Cross, William T. "The Poor Migrant in California," Social Forces, 15 (March, 1937), pp. 423-427.
California has experienced phenomenal immigration, part of which has been homeless persons and destitute migrant workers. State and federal efforts to deal with the migrants are described.

Dawson, William Harbutt. "German Tramp Prison," Fortnightly Review, 87 (February, 1907), pp. 282-291.
The workhouse at Benninghausen operates on the theory that sloth is the cause of vagrancy and correction can be attained by occupying the men's time with work. A rough idea of the system's effectiveness may be obtained by considering recidivism rates. About half of the inmates have been in prison before and are likely to return again.

Devine, Edward. "The Shifting and Floating City Population." Annals of the American Academy of Political and Social Science, 10 (September, 1897), pp. 149-164. This plea for "remedial measures" to eradicate the beggar problem cites as particularly worthwhile a program initiated in Bismarck's Germany. It included such measures as the formation of anti-begging societies, centralized control of national shelters, labor colonies, and the imprisonment of beggars and those who aid them. The feasibility of such a program in New York City is discussed.

Edmison, J. Alex, "Civil Rehabilitation," Canadian Bar Review, 27 (November, 1949), pp. 1091-1110.
The problems of the discharged prisoner include personality problems arising from long confinement, physical needs, employment, and social adjustment. Present

rehabilitation programs and agencies are discussed; the functions of civil rehabilitation agencies are seen to be crime prevention, penal reform, and rehabilitation. The need for more trained sociologists and social workers in the field of criminology is stressed.

Fike, Norma, "Social Treatment of Long-Term Dependency, " Social Work, 2 (October, 1957), pp. 51-56. There are individuals and families who seem incapable of independent functioning for more than brief periods . They keep returning to social agencies for help, often maintaining contact with more than one agency at a time. They may have physical ailments as well as social or psychological problems. It is natural for the social worker to become discouraged about the chronically maladjusted client, to believe his case hopeless and not worth continued effort and further depletion of community resources. The social worker needs to be aware of such changes in his own attitudes as well as of the difficulties sometimes present in distinguishing between the apparent and the actual problem of the client.

Gillin, John L. "Vagrancy and Begging, " American Journal of Sociology, 35 (November, 1929), pp. 424-432.
The historical development of and social responses to vagrancy and begging are described. The institutions of slavery, prostitution, and vassalage limit the number of vagrants. Charitable and governmental responses to vagrancy are reviewed. Labor colonies are cited as fruitful mechanisms of control which have been particularly successful in Belgium and Switzerland.

Gilmore, Harlan W. "Social Control of Begging, " The Family, (October, 1929), pp. 179-181.
The public must be educated to give their alms to social agencies which specialize in dealing with beggars, rather than to the beggars themselves. The latter practice only encourages begging and aggravates the problem. Also it is necessary that the police departments follow the letter of the law in arresting beggars. Begging will

continue as long as the public gives money directly to beggars and the police take a sympathetic stand on arresting them.

Goldsborough, Ernest W. and Hobbs, Wilbur E. "The Petty Offender, " The Prison Journal, 36 (April, 1956), pp. 3-26.
This article describes a study conducted in Philadelphia from October, 1954, through December, 1955. Subjects were 35 males released from the House of Correction. The goal was to make them self-sustaining citizens through project guidance and use of follow-up agencies. Homeless men are characterized by at least one of the following: 1) lack of assets, 2) family difficulties, 3) lack of trade or special skills, 4) physical, emotional or mental illness, and 5) criminal record. It was nec-essary to confront all of these problems. The project had 20 percent success, with seven men achieving self-sufficiency. The authors note a need for additional community resources, particularly the development of half-way houses, and remark on the inadequacy of clin-ics in keeping track of patients. Brief case histories are included.

Guild, June Purcell. "Transient in a New Guise, " Social Forces, 17 (March, 1939), pp. 366-372.
The role of social casework in aiding transients is eval-uated in an analysis of case records of 858 transient men aided in 1938 by the Travelers Aid Society in Virginia . Usual case work procedures (registering, clearing, in-terviewing, verifying, and recording) are shown to have little effect on transients. Case workers had only brief contact with their clients. Individual transients often had several incomplete, overlapping, and/or conflicting records with the agency. It is suggested that agencies fingerprint all of their cases to assure proper identifi-cation. This need not violate a man's confidence and it would facilitate the obtaining of background information on the cases from FBI records. Some were "criminal and social recidivists of long standing. " Fingerprinting is a simple, cheap, and infallible method of identifica-tion, and its use in transient programs is recommended .

The social worker has a responsibility to safeguard the public interest and to protect and treat the individual client. Centralization of facilities and case records would make it easier to study and   treat the transient .

Hallwachs, G. M. "Decentralized Care of the Homeless in a Crisis," The Family, 11 (February, 1931), pp. 314-317.
Decentralization of relief agencies in time of economic depression and unemployment results in demoralization and duplication with injury to the detached man, the agency, and the community, and actually accentuates the problem by attracting more vagrants. Decentralized care is equated with the establishment of bread lines and soup kitchens by private charitable groups. Data are from a study of bread lines in which 155 men were interviewed (only 4. 5 percent qualified as legal residents of New York City) and records of municipal relief agencies.

Hoy, Walter R. "Care of the Homeless in St. Louis," The Family, 9 (October, 1928), pp. 209-219.
Facilities aiding homeless residents of St. Louis are discussed and several proposals are made toward the improvement of these facilities (e. g., adequate free employment service, additional working-men's hotels, and separation of relief-giving and religious programs).

Jackson, Jason F. "The Rural Tramp," Proceedings of the Thirtieth National Conference of Charities and Correction, (1903), pp. 401-404.
The specialized forms of charity and rehabilitation offered by the city ought to be adopted in the rural areas. Too often the rural communities contribute to a man's vagrancy by feeding him and sending him on. Instead, he must be induced to stop and either work or go to prison. Either alternative decreases the tramp population.

Jones, D. Caradog. "The Social Problem Group," Canadian Bar Review, 23 (March, 1945), pp. 183-225 .
The first part of this article defines economic poverty, tracing original definitions through more modern con-

siderations, and giving data on costs of living for various items, such as food, housing, and clothing. Based on this subsistence level a "poverty line" is drawn, and the question of whether the standard of living will rise is considered. The second part of the article considers "mental poverty, " discussing the influences of heredity and environment, the measurement of intelligence, and the definitions of mental and moral poverty. The so-called "social problem group" is that stratum of society having the highest rates of insanity, pauperism, criminality, unemployment, prostitution, alcoholism, and similar conditions. It is recommended that periodic community surveys be instituted to permit determination of whether the "quality" of the people is getting better or worse, and to what extent the various social problems are contributing to the trend.

Lilliefors, Manfred. "Social Casework and the Homeless Man, " The Family, 9 (January, 1928), pp. 291-294 . Most homeless men are migrant workers, and shelters are recommended for their care when unemployed. Other homeless types are beggars, thieves, and petty criminals. Vagrants of these latter categories have more varied class origins than do migrant workmen. Rehabilitation through personal counseling by social workers is suggested.

Marsh, Benjamin C. "Causes of Vagrancy and Methods of Eradication, " Annals of the American Academy of Political and Social Science, 23 (1904), pp. 445-456. The author spent several weeks as a tramp and beggar in London and Philadelphia and interviewed 118 men at the Wayfarers' Lodge of the Philadelphia Society for Organizing Charity. His observations and findings are the basis of a typology of vagrancy and a discussion of its causes and possible modes of correction. An appendix summarizes the data obtained in the Philadelphia interviews.

Marsh, Benjamin C. "Methods Employed by American Cities to Eradicate Vagrancy, " Proceedings of the Thirtieth National Conference of Charities and Correction, (1903), pp. 414-415.

Between these two pages is an excellent fold-out chart giving the following information for 29 major American cities: 1900 population, legal status of begging and vagrancy, penalties and enforcement procedures, and statistics on arrests, sustenance provided, and rehabilitation facilities. Marsh concludes that state laws are more efficacious than municipal ordinances. Boston is shown to have the best treatment program for transients.

Marsh, Benjamin C. and Keller, Frances A. "Bibliography on Methods of Dealing with Tramps and Vagrants," Proceedings of the Thirtieth National Conference of Charities and Correction, (1903), pp. 411-414.
Fifty-four entries for the period 1890-1902 are divided into four categories. In addition to the "methods" section, there are subdivisions on mendicancy, unemployment, and vagrancy.

McCook, John J. "The Tramp Problem: What It Is and What to Do with It," Proceedings of the Twenty-Second National Conference of Charities and Correction, (1895), pp. 288-301.
Statistics on tramps in public lodging houses in Massachusetts for the period 1870-1895 and national estimates for 1890 and 1895 demonstrate that the number of tramps is increasing, and that significant increases occur during industrial depressions. Drinkers and single men are the first to be laid off, the last to be hired, and once they learn to live without working many of them never seek steady work again. Proposed solutions include a rigorous labor test for charity, enforcement of long and indeterminate prison sentences to insure the reformation of tramps, public support of railroads to prevent train-jumping, and remorseless repression of hobo camps lest they attract the interest of children and win potential converts to vagrancy.

Mills, C. Wright. "The Professional Ideology of Social Pathologists," The American Journal of Sociology, 49 (September, 1943), pp. 165-180.
Mills analyzes textbooks on social pathology to discover the typical perspectives and concepts which constitute a

professional ideology. Many texts consist of a series of fragmented facts with disregard for the broader social structure. This is due to similiarities in backgrounds of the authors and to the uniform nature of sources used in preparation of the books. A basic "ideology" emphasizing practical problems as deviations from norms standard for the society overlooks changes in the nature of the normative structure itself. The texts view pathology in terms of lack of socialization or biological theories. The situational approach and the case approach have obscured the linkage between individual and structure by stressing the individual. The adjustment view of immigration and the impact of Cooley's concept of society as processual have retarded the possibility of social action. When structural totality is considered, it is conceived as harmonious primary groups, normatively superior to the individual. One view of pathology involves transgressions of "humanitarian ideals." Another, using notions of cultural lag and evolving technology, sees problems and stress on community welfare as the byproducts of urbanization. A third evaluates social change as continuous balance among societal elements stressing maladjustment as pathology. In all the texts "normality" either is not identified or is equated with goals and norms of the middle-class, Protestant ideals of the small towns of America. None of the books consider the possibility of changing basic institutions.

Plunkert, William J. "Is Skid Row Necessary?" Canadian Journal of Corrections, 2 (April, 1960), pp. 200-208.
The author describes the most common characteristics of skid row and its men. These men are generally inadequately prepared for competitive labor in an industrial society. Varying degrees of hostility and problems of interpersonal relations are noted. Mission workers, urban planners and other groups have long considered the problems of skid row, but basic data are still missing. A psycho-socio-economic study of about 3,000 representative cases is recommended in order to provide a base for developing programs to eliminate and prevent skid row.

Plunkert, William J. "Public Responsibility for Transients," Social Service Review, 8 (September, 1934), pp. 484-491.
Facilities of the Federal Emergency Relief Administration for the care of transients are outlined. The population affected by FERA programs as of March, 1934, is set at 130, 000, and tabulations by race, age, and sex are presented. General comments on the rehabilitation process are offered with the conclusion that federal funds for longer-range rehabilitation programs are unlikely to be forthcoming; hence, organization on the state level is advocated.

Plunkert, William J. "Skid Row Can Be Eliminated," Federal Probation, 25 (June, 1961), pp. 41-44.
It is maintained that skid row is allowed to exist because of the antiquated idea that it is a necessary and dynamic subculture important for industrial expansion. Current treatment, based on English Poor Laws, is mainly punitive, and it is not widely recognized that the habitues of skid row form a stable population. The work of several outstanding treatment centers (Detroit, Chicago, Boston, and Seattle) is described. There is need for a comprehensive community plan for rehabilitation which would include internal medicine, psychiatry, psychology, sociology, and religion.

Poole, Ernest. "A Clearing-House for Tramps, "Everybody's Magazine, 18 (May, 1908), pp. 649-659.
The purposes and practices of the lodging house are described in an account of an interview with "Cap" Mullenbach, the head of the Chicago Free Municipal Lodging House. Various tramp tales are related. Mullenbach stresses the problems of finding work for tramps and advocates the establishment of a national employment bureau.

Rice, Stuart A. "The Failure of the Municipal Lodging House," National Municipal Review, 11 (November 1922), pp. 358-362.
Rice was superintendent of the Mills Hotel, a privately owned facility for lodging homeless men. He compares

the New York City Municipal Lodging House and the Mills Hotel and concludes that the latter was a more efficient facility both economically and from the clients' standpoint. In addition to its "wholesale" methods, the failure of the Municipal Center is due to the absence of clear-cut organization and defined responsibilities. The viability of the "shelter concept" depends on gearing welfare institutions to the needs of the client population.

Rolleston, Charles. "Mischievous Charity," West-minster Review, 163 (February, 1905), pp. 148-155. The author contends that a large percentage of the mendicant class in Britain are in that condition because of a preference not to work, rather than inability to do so. Reference is made to a survey of 2,000 mendicants of which 500 gave definite answers indicating that they preferred to live off gratuities and alms or relatives rather than work. Rolleston considers valid only that kind of charity which "helps a man to help himself." As a possible remedy he suggests establishing a Central Labor Bureau which would assign the able-bodied unemployed to jobs in areas which have a labor shortage.

Rolleston, Charles. "Social Parasites," Westminster Review, 162 (December, 1904), pp. 623-632. The practice in England of "indiscriminate and misguided" almsgiving increases pauperism by removing the incentive to work. England's benevolent associations and government relief programs encourage a lack of thrift in the lower classes. In some cases it is more profitable for a mendicant to continue begging   than to work at manual labor. A labor test rather than relief in the form of money or food would eliminate the social parasites.

Sigal, Nan M. "The Unchanging Area in Transition," Land Economics, 43 (August, 1967), pp. 284-293. Although still much used, the concept of the area in transition is unsuitable for describing blight in the centers of cities. Four deteriorated subsections of Manhattan were examined, including the Bowery. None had changed appreciably in value in decades. Speculation was not common, nor were buildings generally cheap compared to the value of the land. An alternate description is proposed which attributes blight to the complexities of organizing improvement and redevelopment and suggests that the term "dead land" is a more accurate description of these areas.

Willard, Alice C. "Reinstatement of Vagrants Through Municipal Lodging Houses," Proceedings of the National Conference of Charities and Correction, (1903), pp. 404-411.
The author's observations of the lodging house population of Chicago are the basis for a typology of vagrants, including the unemployed but honest laborer, the unfortunate down-and-out, and the "social parasite." Public and private facilities for the care of the homeless are reviewed, and recommendations are made that each of these types of vagrants be treated at the municipal lodging house, where each type can be segregated and receive rehabilitative care appropriate to its particular needs and situation.

Willard, Eugene Bertram. "Psychopathic Vagrancy," Welfare Magazine, 19 (May, 1928), pp. 565-573.
The burden of this paper is toward a mobilization of social forces to cope with derelicts and to segregate them from society. The author recounts personal observations of four derelicts and assesses their behavior as degenerate. It is maintained that bread lines are an incentive to vagrancy and that vocational aid is ineffective in removing vagrants from the streets. A suggested solution is that psychiatry should unite with policing in such matters, the implication being that force and confinement are the answers to the problem.

Wood, Samuel E. "Municipal Shelter Camps for California Migrants," Sociology and Social Research, 23 (January-February, 1939), pp. 222-227.
Fresno Shelter Camp is a program of the city of Fresno, California designed to accommodate would-be vagrants, particularly during the winter months when jobs are scarce. Although transients normally are limited to one-

day stays in the shelter, the author sees the program as beneficial in terms of reducing petty crime and in meeting the transients' needs. Both of these goals are attained at minimal social expense. Similar shelter programs should be developed in other California communities.

OTHER WORKS

Adams, Frank Dawson. The Day Shelter for Unemployed Men, Montreal: A Social Experiment. Montreal: McGill University, 1932. Pp. 23.
This shelter for unemployed single men operated from October 27, 1931, through April 29, 1932. Because some men were served many times, it is not known how many different men were helped; the author estimates a monthly average of 5, 000. Activities of the Shelter are described , and the cooperation of private groups, businesses and public agencies in supporting the shelter is acknowledged . There are examples of letters to shelter staff   members and several illustration.

Bauer, Catherine and McEntire, Davis.   Redevelopment in Sacramento's West End, Report #5: Relocation Study, Single Male Population.   Sacramento: Redevelopment Agency of the City of Sacramento, 1953. Pp . 18 . The subjects of this relocation plan are the 4, 500 skid-row men who reside in Redevelopment Area #1. As many as two-thirds of these men are transients who find low-skill employment in both agriculture and industry.   They are a heterogeneous group in terms of age, nationality , and other demographic characteristics. Little emphasis is put on training programs; rather, the   focus   is on relocation without destroying ties which are valuable to the men, insuring job availability, and providing services that are within the men's economic and psychological reach.   In addition to several suggestions about administration, financing and programming, this report sets various parameters so that more detailed cost-benefit analyses can be made and various financial reservoirs tapped.

Beasley, Robert W. "Care of Destitute Men in Chicago,"
unpublished master's thesis, University of Chicago,
1933. Pp. 138.
Chicago's relief and shelter policies and practices since
1900 are reviewed. Much identical information is to be
found in the report of the Illinois Emergency Relief
Commission. Data obtained from a survey of 6,009 men
receiving shelter care also are reported.

Boston Overseers of the Poor. Street Begging. Boston: J. E. Farwell, 1865. Pp. 25.
This special report summarizes the history of governmental regulation of mendicancy and the scope of the
current problem. There are suggestions for new methods of control.

Boxerman, William I. "Sheltering Activities of the He-
brew Sheltering and Immigrant Aid Society of New York
City, 1919-1935, unpublished master's thesis, School
for Jewish Social Work," 1938. Pp. 474.
A review of the problems of homeless men in general
and Jewish homeless in particular includes a lengthy
analysis of the case histories of several Jewish homeless men.

Buffalo Emergency Relief Board. Thirty-Three Thousand on Relief. Buffalo: Emergency Relief Board,
1937. Pp. 18.
This June, 1937 statistical study of 10,658 cases
(33,081 persons) on the Buffalo Emergency Relief Bureau
rolls includes 3,922 single or unattached persons, of
whom 2,347 were single males. Common forms and
causes of homelessness are noted, and it is indicated
that the prognosis for homeless men is slow rehabilitation and long-term relief status.

Committee on Care of Transient and Homeless. After
Five Years: The Unresolved Problem of Transient Unemployed, 1932-1937. New York: Committee on Care
of Transient and Homeless, 1937. Pp. 12.
Meeting in Philadelphia in 1932, a number of social
workers of the National Conference of Social Work had

resolved to attack transiency and homelessness more vigorously and systematically. This paper is a summary of the years 1932-1937. Various programs are cited, principally the Federal Transient Program which was designed to provide both a comprehensive national program and to stimulate activity by the states. The committee concludes that conditions are still bad; vigorous governmental aid and public education are needed to provide for the transient.

Committee on Homelessness, Annual Report of the Committee on Homelessness. New York: Jewish Social Service Association of New York and the United Jewish Aid Societies of Brooklyn, 1930. Pp. 15.
The 640 homeless men under the Committee's care in 1929 are described. The Committee's purpose is seen as threefold: to direct social services, to coordinate programs and refer men to available facilities, and to create greater public awareness of the problem of homelessness.

Holtz, Dorothy O. A Report on the Relocation of Residents, Business and Institutions from the Gateway Center Project Area. Minneapolis: Minneapolis Housing and Redevelopment Authority, 1963. Pp. 21.
About 2, 400 unattached residents of the Gateway Center Project Area were to be relocated. A special research program established the characteristics of the area's residents. The proposed building of new low-rent single-room occupancy buildings by the city was rejected; the accepted alternative was the establishment of an office of relocation designed to help homeless men find facilities within the existing housing market. About 80 percent of the unattached men moved into other parts of the city. Effects of the relocation on businesses and missions are summarized.

Illinois Emergency Relief Commission. Men in the Crucible. Chicago: Illinois Emergency Relief Commission, 1932. Pp. 77.
The work of the Illinois Emergency Relief Commission and a collection of 6, 009 life histories of men receiving

shelter care are described. The report focuses on the services and programs of the shelters. Numerous statistics on homeless men are given.

Independent Cooperators' Committee. Rehabilitation and Redevelopment: A Plan to Rehabilitate the Homeless Men on the Cooper Square (Robert Owen) Site Through Urban Renewal. New York: The Independent Cooperators' Committee for the Renewal of Cooper Square (Robert Owen) Cooperative Housing, 1961. Pp. 36. A plan for rehabilitation in the Cooper Square area in New York City is summarized. Background data on homeless men in that neighborhood are drawn from various local organizations (NYC Department of Welfare, Salvation Army) and from Bowery hotels. Other sources are studies on skid row and urban renewal in Chicago, Minneapolis, Philadelphia and Sacramento, and the committee's observations on the Cooper Square site. Proposals for immediate action include establishment of a diagnostic and rehabilitation referral center, a halfway house program for chronic alcoholics, psychiatric treatment and training centers, and low-rent apartments for the aged. The committee foresees extension of their proposed program to the entire Bowery area.

The Industrial Christian Alliance. Helping Men to Help Themselves. New York: The Industrial Christian Alliance, c. 1903. Pp. 30.
The Industrial Christian Alliance and its efforts to enable men whose lives have been "distorted by sin" to return to the labor market are described in this illustrated brochure. The Alliance began its work in 1891 and has established facilities for housing, eating, washing, reading, carpentry and chair-caning. Private donations and services in support of the Alliance are encouraged.

Leonard, Howard B. Final Relocation Report on Project No. UR Calif. 5-1--Capitol Mall. Sacramento: Redevelopment Agency of the City of Sacramento, 1963. Pp. 29.
The Capitol Mall Project Area covered fifteen blocks, contained 1.7 percent of Sacramento's population, and

was the source of 40 percent of the police calls, 40 percent of relief funds spent, and 70 percent of all tuberculosis cases. The Project Area was not an integrated community; few ties bound the people together. After an initial survey of housing needs, attempts were made to relocate everyone in suitable housing meeting Agency standards. Cooperation was obtained through the help of a Citizens' Advisory Committee, private and public organizations, and neighborhood council meetings. Over a four-year period, 408 families, 725 individuals, 350 businesses, and 22 institutions were relocated.

Leonard, Howard B. and Herren, Marguerite. Relocation Profile; The Final Relocation Report on Project No. Calif. R-18--Capitol Mall Extension. Sacramento: Redevelopment Agency of the City of Sacramento, 1964. Pp. 41.
The Capitol Mall Extension Project was the second of a three-phase redevelopment program to rebuild Sacramento's West End. This report summarizes the process of relocation. Before relocation was begun, an informational brochure was sent to each resident in the area. In addition the Redevelopment Agency operated a speaking program and worked with local newspapers and public and private agencies. Housing resources were found through newspapers, private citizens, FHA, VA, and the Housing Authority. In all, 91 families, 804 individuals and 445 businesses and nonprofit organizations were relocated. Ninety percent of the displaced individuals lived in skid-row type hotels, and the great majority of them planned to continue living in such hotels in other sections of the city. The Agency assisted businesses by finding new locations, obtaining loans, and giving advice. The process of relocation is illustrated in two case histories, one of a family and the other of a small business. Tables and exhibits show maps of the area, number and types of families, businesses, and individuals, and copies of the informational brochure and letters which were sent.

Lewis, Orlando F. Vagrancy in the United States. New York: printed privately, 1907. Pp. 74.
Contemporary methods of dealing with vagrancy are critically reviewed and reforms suggested. These include prison labor camps, cumulative sentencing, centralization of welfare agencies, and the creation of a special police force. In the appendix are reprints of current vagrancy laws, descriptions of the organization of selected municipal lodging houses, and fragmentary data on the inmates of labor colonies in Europe.

McEntire, Davis. Redevelopment in Sacramento's West End, Report #2: Survey of Population and Employment. Sacramento: Redevelopment Agency of the City of Sacramento, c. 1951. Pp. 46.
This report summarizes data obtained from interviews with over 500 randomly selected hotel residents and household heads in a redevelopment area. The results indicate diversity of race and nationality, a preponderance of manual and low-skilled workers, and the presence of both older sedentary residents and younger migratory residents. The area is shown to be a large casual labor market for both the agricultural and non-agricultural sectors.

Reed, Ellery F. Federal Transient Program: An Evaluative Survey, May to July, 1934. New York: The Committee on Care of Transient and Homeless, 1934. Pp. 143.
This three-month study conducted during the first year of the Transient Program of the Federal Emergency Relief Administration is based on the administrative files of the FERA. It is better characterized as evaluative and descriptive than as statistical or analytical. Conclusions include recommendations for stricter enforcement of health codes and greater attention to food programs.

Roseman, Alvin. Shelter Care and the Local Homeless Man. Chicago: Public Welfare Association, 1935. Pp. 56.
A   description of the functions and operation of the

Chicago Service Bureau for Men includes a brief history of the organization of public welfare in the United States and a description of living conditions in shelters. Social case work in the Chicago shelters is reviewed, and recommendations are made for improvement of the welfare system in general on the basis of the Chicago experience. A section of the report is devoted to alcoholic therapy in the shelter situation.

Seamen's Aid Society. Annual Reports. Boston: Seamen's Aid Society. 1833-1850.
Wives of prominent Bostonians formed a charitable group which sought to "improve the condition and character of seamen and their families." The annual reports describe the collection and distribution of charities and the operation of a clothing store which sold goods made by wives and widows of seamen. There is a liberal sprinkling of Biblical thoughts on charity.

Shandler, Irving W. Philadelphia's Skid Row: A Demonstration in Human Renewal. Philadelphia: Redevelopment Authority of the City of Philadelphia, 1965, Pp. 30. The activities of the first 16 months of the Diagnostic and Relocation Center on Philadelphia's skid row are reported. Supportive services of the Center include a "doorstep interview," intake interview, medical, dental, and podiatric evaluation, psychological screening, psychiatric evaluation, staff determination of a workable relocation plan, and follow-up interviews after relocation. Interim conclusions are drawn about the nature and effectiveness of each service. Activities of the Center include contacting a random sample of skid-row men and trying to get them to come to the Center. Almost half of the entire random sample agreed. There is a statistical summary of the Center's activities from May, 1963, to September, 1964. It is reported that the Center's experience indicates that skid row can be controlled, given proper organizational facilities.

Society For the Suppression of Mendicity. The First Report of the Society Established in London. London: J. W. Whiteley, 1819. Pp. 61.

The administrative report of this new society contains its constitution, membership and other organizational details.

Society for the Suppression of Mendicity. Third Annual Report. London: J. F. Dove, 1821. Pp. 42.
Statistics are presented on the 4,546 cases registered at the Society's office in 1821, including information on nativity, "alleged causes of distress," and place of residence. The Society's methods of almsgiving are described, and several case histories are produced as illustrations. The criteria for qualifying for aid (being industrious and of good character) are stressed.

Thomas, Logan L. Report on the Greater New York Gospel Mission. New York: Welfare Council of New York City, 1931. Pp. 95.
The Greater New York Gospel Mission was founded in 1929 and located in Greenwich Village, near the Bowery, as a Christian refuge for the morally, physically, and spiritually deprived man. This report includes a brief history of public and private welfare services in New York City, but the major portion is devoted to a thorough description of the physical setting, organization and programs of the mission. Four principal types of activities are described: feeding, providing shelter, treatment directed toward rehabilitation, and conversion. Examples of case histories and sermons are often colorful. The author concludes that the shelter and food programs are excellent, and that the personal approach toward treatment is a sound basis for further expansion.

Vanderkooi, Ronald C. Relocating West Madison "Skid Row" Residents: A Study of the Problem, with Recommendations. Chicago: Chicago Department of Urban Renewal, 1967. Pp. 44.
Interviews with 210 residents of Chicago's West Madison skid row are the basis for this report on the problems of skid-row men as they perceive them in the context of impending urban renewal. Also, there is a discussion of public attitudes toward skid row based on 45 questionnaires completed by college students and their parents.

The development of a "half-way community" is advocated; relocated skid-row men would be concentrated in an area where greatly upgraded versions of all functional facilities available on skid row would be offered.

Whiting, William Alberti. What the City of New York Provides for the Homeless. New York: Department of Public Charities, 1915. Pp. 15.
Services and the usual routine of the Municipal Lodging House are described.

Wilson, Robert S. Community Planning for Homeless Men and Boys. New York: Family Welfare Association of America, 1931. Pp. 144.
The experiences of fourteen cities and two rural counties in meeting problems of care for homeless men and boys during the winter of 1930-31 are appraised. For each locality there is a brief history of the problem of transience, an analysis of the needs and resources for care of the homeless, and a description of existing welfare agencies' plans for the immediate future. The study is aimed at the short-term consequences of the Depression for unskilled workers. A general program for the care and rehabilitation of the homeless is outlined.

TREATMENT, PUNISHMENT,
REHABILITATION: ALCOHOLISM

BOOKS

Apple, Dorrian (ed.) Sociological Studies of Health and
Sickness: A Source Book for the Health Professions.
New York: McGraw-Hill, 1960. Pp. 350.
Problems of patient care are illustrated in this collection
of articles on medical sociology. Topics considered include the recognition of need for health care, the patient's
point of view, psychosocial processes in illness, and the
organization of hospitals. Particularly relevant to the
study of disaffiliation are "Alcoholism and Tuberculosis"
by Jackson and Holmes, "Observations on Dissociation
as Social Participation" by Stanton and Schwartz, and
Bales' article on cultural differences in alcoholism rates.

Block, Marvin A. Alcoholism: Its Facets and Phases.
New York: John Day, 1965. Pp. 320.
A layman's guide to every aspect of alcoholism, this
work has chapters on definition, legal aspects, types of
medical treatment, and the various types of personalities
that may use alcohol to smooth over their disorders. Dr.
Block sees alcoholism as only a segment of a larger
mental health problem and maintains that, should a person possess the physiological affinities that lead to dependence on alcohol, then alcoholism serves as a term
which may define his personality disorder. A chapter
on skid-row alcoholism describes the various methods
of rehabilitation, such as inhospital service, outpatient
clinics, halfway houses, and foster homes.

Gerard, Donald L. and Saenger, Gerhart. Out-Patient
Treatment of Alcoholism, Toronto: University of Toronto Press, 1966. Pp. 249.
A pilot study estimated the type, variety and scope of
the data that could be obtained from clinic records, and
devised intake, treatment, and follow-up records for

systematic data collection. Approximately 100 patients from each of four clinics were included in the sample. At intake patients' social involvement was meager (less than half were employed); their participation in treatment was brief; follow-up interviews (one year after treatment) were completed with about three-fourths of the patients. Between intake and follow-up many of the patients changed in health, social stability, work status, and extent of interpersonal relationships, but the proportion of patients improving was about the same as the proportion manifesting deterioration. Various patient and treatment characteristics are evaluated as predictors of outcome. A number of case histories are presented, including some of skid-row men.

Jones, Howard. Alcoholic Addiction: A Psychosocial Approach to Abnormal Drinking. London: Tavistock, 1963. Pp. 209.
Life histories were obtained from 72 male alcoholics in Toronto, half of whom were in prison and half under the care of a residential treatment unit. Salient characteristics of the alcoholics include dependence, insecurity, ego-needs, and sexual problems, including homosexual tendencies and oedipal fixations. Jail-clinic differentials in occupational history, self-insight, marital status and other variables seem to indicate that clinic patients are more likely to be rehabilitated, and that clinical-therapeutic methods are more successful than jailing. Treatment must take into account both psychological factors and the social environment in which the person functions.

King, Arthur (pseud.) Seven Sinners. New York: Harcourt, Brace and World, 1961. Pp. 295.
For ten years, beginning in 1950, the author worked with 30 alcoholics (27 men and 3 women) all of whom had above average intelligence. They served both as subjects and co-investigators. The author at the time was a Columbia University student in psychotherapy. The subjects participated for various lengths of time in nine principal activities: physical training, educative counseling, reading, organization, vocational guidance, socialization,

aesthetics, religious investigations and experimentation. All subjects were successfully rehabilitated. The author emphasizes his belief that directed reading was a critical part of the therapy in that it activated subjects' creativity. Seven case histories are presented in detail. A bibliography lists the books used by the author and his subjects. This book is based on the author's doctoral dissertation. See Cain, Arthur.

Marriage, Adrian. The Police Court Drunkenness Offender: A Study of the Police Court Drunkenness Offender and Survey of Contemporary Methods of Care. Vancouver: Alcoholism Foundation of British Columbia, 195.7. Pp. 173.
This study, undertaken to provide information for a committee considering the establishment of a Jail Farm for chronic drunkenness offenders, includes a review of previous research on alcoholism. The chronic offender is described as an undersocialized person, homeless and without the ability to maintain employment. Results of a survey of nineteen treatment programs in North America are reported. The programs studied manifest considerable diversity in history, structure, and method, but almost all are concerned with alcoholism as only one aspect of the over-all problem of homeless persons. Since the majority of alcoholics are not found on skid row, it seems that community organization rather than penal reform is required. Recommendations are made that the Foundation work closely with existing social agencies.

Schmidt, Wolfgang, Smart, Reginald G. and Moss, Marcia K. Social Class and the Treatment of Alcoholism: An Investigation of Social Class as a Determinant of Diagnosis, Prognosis, and Therapy. Toronto: University of Toronto Press, 1968. Pp. 111.
This monograph summarizes an analysis of records of the Toronto clinic of the Alcoholism and Drug Addiction Research Foundation for a sample of 248 patients first admitted during the years 1958-60. The researchers examined class differentials in sources of referral to the

clinic, diagnosis, and treatment, and present evidence that clinical practice favors patients from the higher classes. Distinct class lines were found in the clinicians' descriptions of patients, diagnoses, and recommendations for therapy or treatment. Lower-class patients tended to be excluded from certain treatments and some of the treatments recommended for them are incompatible with lower-class life organization. It is suggested that differential treatment by social class may reflect clinicians' lack of understanding of lower-class values and consequent difficulty in establishing intimate relationships with lower-class patients.

Sparer, Phineas (ed.) Personality, Stress, and Tuberculosis. New York: International Universities Press, 1956. Pp. 629.
This volume contains an array of articles on the clinical, medical, psychiatric, psychological, and psychosomatic aspects of tuberculosis. The importance of the psychologist and psychiatrist in the treatment of hospitalized tuberculosis patients is emphasized, with special stress on recalcitrant patients, including those suffering from alcoholism. Relevant articles include "The Problem of Alcoholic Tuberculous Patients" and "Some Aspects of the Sanatorium Adjustment Difficulties of White Male Skid Row Alcoholic Tuberculous Patients."

ARTICLES

Anant, Santokh S. "Former Alcoholics and Social Drinking: An Unexpected Finding," The Canadian Psychologist, 9 (January, 1968), p. 35.
In a follow-up of alcoholic patients treated by verbal aversion techniques a patient was found who had been able to return to social drinking and still maintained control of his drinking.

Anant, Santokh S. "The Treatment of Alcoholics by a Verbal Aversion Technique: A Case Report" MANAS: A Journal of Scientific Psychology, 13 (December, 1966), pp. 79-86.
This article presents the case and treatment history of

a 43-year-old single male, formerly a merchant seaman and a confirmed alcoholic who had participated in Alcoholic Anonymous without success. Treatment, including relaxation and unpleasant auditory stimulation, is described in some detail. At time of writing, more than a year after treatment, subject was still living without alcohol. Verbal aversion techniques are said to be more convenient and effective than chemical or electrical techniques.

Armstrong, John D. and Gibbins, Robert J. "A Psychotherapeutic Technique with Large Groups in the Treatment of Alcoholics," Quarterly Journal of Studies on Alcohol, 17 (September, 1956), pp. 461-478.
During a twelve-month period, the authors observed a group therapy session of alcoholics, consisting of 32 "core" members and others who came irregularly. Results showed that group therapy has certain advantages over individual therapy. The group can be self-directing and self-managing, flexible, but under the control of the therapist.

Asher, Robert W. "Supervision of the Problem Drinker on Probation, "Quarterly Journal of Studies on Alcohol, 17 (March, 1956), pp. 73-88.
A method of alcoholic rehabilitation through personal counseling is described, and the importance of the attitudes of counselors toward alcoholics is emphasized. Five case histories illustrate the uses of the proposed method. A probation office setting may serve an important and productive function in the redirection of alcoholics.

Bacon, Selden D. and Miller, Dudley P. "The Connecticut Commission on Alcoholism, " Connecticut State Medical Journal, 11 (September, 1947), pp. 742-747.
The passage of an act by the 1945 session of the Connecticut State Legislature to establish the Connecticut Commission on Alcoholism is attributed to a statewide concern for mental hygiene, the presence of a vast reserve labor force in prisons (70 percent are incarcerated inebriates) during a period of severe manpower shortage,

and the activities of Alcoholics Anonymous and a group of Yale researchers. The content of the legislation and the activities, policies, and problems of the Commission are discussed.

Bell, R. Gordon. "Alcohol and Loneliness," Journal of Social Therapy, 2 (Third Quarter, 1956), pp. 171-181.
Persons who have not learned normal interaction skills during childhood may come to use alcohol as an alternative to interaction. Treatment of alcoholism should be aimed at shifting dependence from chemicals to people.

Blacker, Edward and Kantor, David. "Half-Way Houses for Problem Drinkers," Federal Probation, 24 (June, 1960). pp. 18-23.
Data from a 1958 survey of halfway houses in 49 states and all Canadian provinces are used in constructing an ideal halfway house. There are four basic assumptions: 1) number of individuals served is kept small; 2) individuals are required to maintain sobriety; 3) through employment aids, all individuals are eventually expected to pay their ways; and 4) therapeutic environment is maintained, involving group therapy, religious and vocational counseling and Alcoholics Anonymous meetings.

Blake, George B. "A Follow-up of Alcoholics Treated by Behavior Therapy," Behavior Research and Therapy, 5 (May, 1967), pp. 89-94.
Two samples of alcoholics treated by behavior therapy were compared at six and twelve months after release. The control group (N=25) had electrical aversion conditioning only; the experimental group (N=37) had relaxation-aversion treatment. Patients treated with the relaxation approach showed greater improvement. Plans are being made for similar cross-cultural studies.

Block, Marvin A. "A Program for the Homeless Alcoholic," Quarterly Journal of Studies on Alcohol, 23 (December, 1962), pp. 664-649.
In-Hospital service, outpatient clinics, foster homes,

halfway houses, rehabilitation centers, permanent supervision, and state hospitals for alcoholics are considered. The primary focus of therapy is to provoke initiative toward rehabilitation. Decent, congenial living arrangements should be developed for patients who could pay their way. Those needing therapy but fearing social pressure might respond to this approach.

Boggs, Marjorie. "The Role of Social Work in the Treatment of Inebriates," Quarterly Journal of Studies on Alcohol, 4 (March, 1944), pp. 557-567.
The primary problem in rehabilitation is seen as a need for a change in attitudes, not only of the alcoholic, but of other members of his family. An alcoholic with abilities and special skills is often employed in menial jobs because he is unwilling to face the responsibility of a better, skilled job. The alcoholic's wife may express desires to be loved and provided for, but her own immaturity often weakens the emotional security of her husband. Both spouses need to achieve emotional maturity. Three case histories are given.

Bourne, Peter G., Alfor, James A. and Bowcock, James Z. "Treatment of Skid-Row Alcoholics with Disulfiram," Quarterly Journal of Studies on Alcohol, 27 (March, 1966), pp. 42-48.
Sixty-four volunteer alcoholics and 132 involuntary (the alternative was incarceration for drunkenness) subjects in Atlanta, Georgia were given daily doses of disulfiram. All of these persons are described as drunkenness repeaters in poor health. Thirty-two of the volunteers and 61 of the compulsory patients were still taking the drug at the end of the nine-month study. The authors suggest that the relative success of this experiment and the low incidence of harmful side effects point to a possible means of breaking the traditional alcoholic cycle. Negro subjects were significantly more responsive than whites to treatment, which is seen as evidence that their drinking patterns differ.

Brillinger, Roy, "The Role of the Probation Officer with the Alcoholic," Canadian Journal of Corrections, 5 (April, 1963), pp. 73-85.
The alcoholic may go to a probation officer voluntarily, or be referred by the court. In either case, each person's needs must be considered individually in deciding what further resources should be drawn upon. Some of the resources which may be available in the community are Alcoholics Anonymous, a physician, a clergyman, or a private clinic or hospital. The decision to refer a client to a treatment clinic must be based on several factors, including the client's motivation, a court recommendation, physiological effects, a history of mental illness, or need for psychiatric care. The probation officer may elect to undertake the case himself; if so he must try to obtain and maintain an honest, warm relationship with the client while trying to help him. Additional work with the family, wife, or parents may be needed. The probation officer should always keep in mind the goals of the treatment, and be realistic and practical.

Brown, Reginald F. "An Aftercare Program for Alcoholics," Crime and Delinquency, 9 (January, 1963), pp. 77-83.
The experience of an Alcoholics Anonymous group established to furnish aftercare (parole) for the alcoholic offender released from penal institutions in Ontario, Canada is evaluated. The sample consists of 40 men divided into five classifications on the basis of their drinking status as revealed in a four-year follow-up. Group I includes 15 men who returned neither to drinking nor to prison and who have undergone a fundamental change toward socialization. Group II consists of four men who, although suffering relapses to alcohol, have finally become successfully rehabilitated. Group III contains seven men who, although showing no personality change and continued to drink excessively, appear to have become socially rehabilitated. Group IV consists of one man who, although completely changed in personality concerning drinking, attempted armed rob-

bery and was reincarcerated. Group V includes the remaining 13 men who were unaffected by the AA program. The author maintains that to be rehabilitated an alcoholic must be converted and that such conversions are more frequent in AA than in other programs.

Cook, Stan, "The Pattern of Recovery of the Alcohol Addict," Canadian Journal of Connections, 1 (January, 1959), pp. 29-37.
Post-treatment drinking behavior of 1,199 alcohol addicts released from an Ontario reform institution was examined. Data were the reports of four "Rehabilitation Officers" about their respective ex-patients. Results indicate that the recovery pattern of the first year following treatment is prognostic of subsequent drinking behavior. Implications for rehabilitation include the suggestion that post-treatment care need not extend beyond the first year.

Chaves, Aaron D., Robins, Arthur B. and Abeles, Hans. "Tuberculosis Case Finding Among Homeless Men in New York City," American Review of Respiratory Diseases, 74 (December, 1961), pp. 900-901.
During 1960, personnel of the New York City Health Department tested 9,000 men at the Men's Shelter for signs of active tuberculosis and found 144 new cases (a "phenomenally high" rate of 16 per 1,000) and a total of 307 active cases new and old. Of 107 men with previously known and registered active tuberculosis, almost all had left a hospital against medical advice. All active cases were referred to a hospital; about 20 percent disappeared before being admitted, and another 30 percent left the hospital against advice within four months.

Daly, Emmet. "A Report on the Pilot Plan Alcoholism Rehabilitation Clinic at San Francisco," Quarterly Journal of Studies on Alcohol, 1 (June, 1952), pp. 345-355.
Following a study which revealed a significant incidence of repeaters among those arrested for drunkenness, an inpatient clinic was established in the San Francisco Jail. Persons convicted for drunkenness were given the option of going to the clinic, which involved a 90-day

sentence (approximately 23 days in the clinic and the rest of the time under its supervision). A group of 40 patients included 20 classified as passive dependent persons, 17 as psychoneurotic and 3 as psychopathic. The author concludes that skid-row inhabitants are not illiterate social misfits, and are not unreceptive to sympathetic and conscientious personal aid. The cooperative efforts of Alcoholics Anonymous are illustrated and commended.

Deutscher, Irwin. "The Petty Offender: Society's Orphan," Federal Probation, 19 (June, 1955), pp. 12-18. Denizens of skid row with long arrest records for public drunkenness are said to account for over half of all arrests in the United States. Having retreated from society, they are not sufficiently helped to return to normal life by Alcoholics Anonymous, missions, and similar organizations. It is recommended that social workers serve as adjuncts to courts, that provisions for employment be improved, that specialized courts be set up, and that rehabilitation programs by social agencies be geared to reintegrating the petty offender into society.

Diethelm, Oskar. "Some Fundamental Considerations in the Treatment of Chronic Alcoholism," pp. 191-198 in Himwick, Harold E. (ed.), Alcoholism. Washington D. C.: American Association for the Advancement of Science, 1957.
Aspects of the treatment of the chronic alcoholic other than the regulation of alcohol intake are described. The whole personality must be adjusted if the patient is to cope successfully with other people and outside pressures when his emotions are not dulled by the use of alcohol. The success of a patient's recovery must be judged in terms of his total life adjustment rather than merely his attitude toward alcohol.

Drucker, Lewis. "Screening Inebriates in Municipal Courts," Quarterly Journal of Studies on Alcohol, 6 (September, 1945), pp. 209-212.
Since the chronic inebriate is so often at the mercy of municipal court judges, a logical starting point for re-

habilitation and control efforts would be at this level. The author draws on his experience as judge of the Municipal Court in Cleveland in demonstrating that from the standpoint of rehabilitation customary judicial procedures are inefficient at best.

Fergus, Emily B. and Jackson, Joan K. "The Tuberculous Alcoholic Before and During Hospitalization, "American Review of Tuberculosis and Pulmonary Diseases, 79 (May, 1959), pp. 659-662.
Reaffirming the relatively high incidence of tuberculosis among skid-row alcoholics, the author argues that treatment of both tuberculosis and alcoholism must be conducted with consideration of the personality structure of the skid-row man, for he often drinks to identify with his culture. Staff members of tuberculosis hospitals also should provide treatment for alcoholism and be more aware of the general problems of alcoholism.

Finlay, Donald G. "Effect of Role Network Pressure on an Alcoholic's Approach to Treatment, " Social Work, 11 (October, 1966), pp. 71-77.
In a study of 57 patients from the Alcoholism and Drug Addiction Research Foundation, the various factors that might impel an alcoholic to seek and accept help are examined. The general proposition suggested by the findings is that an alcoholic's approach to treatment is influenced by the degree and durability of his role network pressure. Among alcoholics the primary therapeutic task is the creation, enhancement, and maintenance of a high level of personal concern.

Floch, Maurice. "Imprisoned Abnormal Drinkers: Application of the Bowman-Jellinek Classification Schedule to an Institutional Sample: Part I. Review and Analysis of Data. Part II. Illustrative Case Histories and Conclusions." Quarterly Journal of Studies on Alcohol, 7 (March, 1947), pp. 518-566, and 8 (June, 1947), pp. 61-120.
Part I consists of a review of works prior to 1940 dealing with types of alcoholics and with improvement in classification due to the Bowman-Jellinek system. This sys-

tem is described and its application to a sample of 276 male alcoholics in the Detroit House of Correction is discussed. Data on age, convictions, race and nationality, marital status and physical condition of respondents are included. Problems of administering the classification schedule are considered. Part II presents 16 case histories and their classification by the Bowman-Jellinek method. Applicability and utility of this method are evaluated. It is suggested that an expansion of public mental-hygiene programs could prove valuable in controlling alcoholism.

Gibbins, Robert J. and Armstrong, John D. "Effects of Clinical Treatment on Behavior of Alcoholic Patients," Quarterly Journal of Studies on Alcohol. 18 (September, 1957), pp. 429-450.
Researchers followed up a sample of 102 alcoholics who had been hospitalized for at least six days and had subsequently visited an outpatient clinic three or more times. During treatment comprehensive drinking histories obtained. Post-treatment behavior was recorded in follow-up interviews. Duration of follow-up ranged from 9 to 55 months. Data sufficient to permit calculation of months of abstinence were obtained from 69 respondents. Evaluation of effects of clinical treatment was limited to changes in drinking behavior following admission. Extent of change is measured by comparing number of months of pre-admission abstinence to months of post-admission abstinence. Significant changes in drinking patterns followed treatment at the clinic. These changes were related to respondents' social stability, use of disulfirum, and payment for treatment, but were unrelated to age, number of years of excessive drinking, and duration of outpatient contact. The limited utility in evaluative research of value-laden terms like "success" and "improvement" is noted.

Gill, Howard B. "The Alcoholic in the Penal Institutions," Quarterly Journal of Studies on Alcohol, 6 (September, 1945), pp. 233-238.
Gill, general superintendent of penal institutions in the

District of Columbia, recognizes that alcoholism is a disease (or a symptom of disease) but indicates that alcoholics may be handled effectively within the penal institutions. He suggests that jail personnel attend meetings of Alcoholics Anonymous and confer with local police and health authorities in an attempt to place harmless alcoholics in facilities where they can be treated. Eventually alcoholics, like the insane, will be removed to separate institutions. In the meantime the staff of penal institutions must be trained to recognize and deal with the alcoholics' special problems.

Glatt, M. M. and Whitely, J. Stuart. "Problems of Alcoholics at Different Social Levels," Monatsschrift fur Psychiatrie and Neurlogie, 132 (June, 1956), pp. 1-12.
This comparison of two groups of homeless men (N's= 130, 84) and a group of alcoholics in a mental hospital (N=121) in terms of age, age at which breaksown first occurred, suicidal attempts, antisocial behavior, marital discord, and use of alcohol is basically a psychological demography of the three groups. It also includes observations of occupational mobility based on case histories with attempts to characterize mobility in psychological terms. A discussion of the relevance of group therapy concludes that while major problems and therefore preferred therapeutic approaches may differ for different groups, therapy and Alcoholics Anonymous would be useful at all social levels.

Griffin, P. J. "The Revolving Door: A Functional Interpretation," Canadian Review of Sociology and Anthropology, 3 (August, 1966), pp. 154-166.
Interviews, questionnaires, and observation techniques were used in a study of chronic drunkenness offenders in Ontario. Findings suggest that the criminal stigma attached to alcoholism, the addiction effects, and the personal isolation of the alcoholic make him particularly susceptible to the "revolving door" of intoxication, arrest, trial, jail, release, and intoxication. The legal structure allows the alcoholic to continue his addiction, adds to his tension, and provides little professional help.

Gunner, Morris. "The Rehabilitation Program at Camp LaGuardia," Social Service Review, 40 (September, 1946), pp. 426-429.
Camp LaGuardia is an institution near Chester, New York to which homeless and alcoholic skid-row men in New York City are voluntarily committed. The origin and facilities of Camp LaGuardia are briefly described, and rehabilitation techniques are illustrated in two case histories. The Camp is viewed as a model for rehabilitative agencies in other cities.

Haberman, Paul W. "Factors Related to Increased Sobriety in Group Psychotherapy with Alcoholics," Journal of Clinical Psychology, 22 (April, 1966), pp. 229-235.
Alcoholic patients who showed increased sobriety after a period of group psychotherapy are compared to those who showed no change or decreased sobriety. Those who did not improve were more often college educated, had more severe alcoholism, and went to fewer therapy sessions.

Hart, William T., Gardner, Elmer A. and Zax, Melvin. "Community Facilities for Alcoholics in Rochester, New York," Quarterly Journal of Studies on Alcohol, 25 (December, 1964), pp. 747-753.
Facilities dealing with alcoholics in Monroe County are summarized in an attempt to establish a framework for future studies. The jail, the court, the Alcoholism Center, Alcoholics Anonymous, the Salvation Army and business establishments are described with respect to their approach to alcoholism. Future studies will analyze statistical findings to determine the relationships among the agencies in contact with the alcoholic.

Hawkins, Norman G. "Skid Road--A Health Challenge," The Journal-Lancet, 77 (May, 1957), pp. 153-156.
Hawkins reports a study of 153 skid-row men afflicted with tuberculosis admitted to the Firland Sanitorium in Seattle, Washington between January 1953 and June 1955. Forty-seven percent of the sample were alcoholics, and 44 percent were from jail. Sixty-seven of the subjects, about one-third of whom were alcoholics, left the sani-

torium against medical advice ("irregular discharge").
The irregular discharge rate of the skid-row men was
significantly higher, while the alcoholics' irregular discharge rate was lower, compared to all persons admitted
to the sanitorium during the period under study. The
comparatively low rate of irregular discharge among
alcoholics raises questions about earlier findings which
show higher positive correlations between alcoholism
and irregular discharge rates.

Jackson, Joan K. "The Problem of Alcoholic Tuberculous Patients," pp. 504-538 in Phineas J. Sparer
(ed.), Personality, Stress, and Tuberculosis. New
York: International Universities Press, 1956.
The findings of a research project dealing with the
psychosocial aspects of tuberculosis, with special reference to tubercular alcoholics, are presented. The
study compares tubercular alcoholics, non-tubercular
alcoholics, and tubercular non-alcoholics with respect
to several social and personal background variables,
such as number of environmental changes and occurence
of personal crises. Subjects were 34 non-tubercular
alcoholics confined to the Seattle Police Rehabilitation
Projects, and 55 tubercular patients at Firland Sanitorium, some of whom were also alcoholics. Respondents originally derived from similar environments in
downtown Seattle, including the "Skid-Road" section.
Tuberculosis and alcoholism are treated as consequences of social stress, and it is concluded that neither
alcoholism nor tuberculosis occur as isolated single
events. Rather, both tend to be preceded by signs that
the person is having difficulties in maintaining or
achieving "a personally satisfying and stabilizing life
adjustment."

Jackson, Joan K. "Some Aspects of the Sanitorium
Adjustment Difficulties of White Male Skid Road Alco-
holics," pp. 539-572 in Phineas J. Sparer (ed.),
Personality, Stress, and Tuberculosis. New York:
International Universities Press, 1956.
Some of the social and psychological factors that contri-

bute to the difficulties of "Skid Road" alcoholics in adjusting to sanitorium life are considered. Aspects of
life on skid row that are relevant to patients' adjustment
in the hospital are described and typical problems which
arise during the course of hospitalization and which are
attributable to the skid-row life pattern are delineated.
A general conclusion is that the skid-row culture deter-
mines the behavior of most of the alcoholics. Adjustment difficulties occur when skid-row and hospital modes
of behavior clash, as they do in the sanitorium setting.
Suggestions for resolution and minimization of adjustment difficulties are offered.

Jackson, Joan K., Fagan, Ronald J. and Burr, Roscoe
C. "The Seattle Police Department Rehabilitation Project for Chronic Alcoholics," Federal Probation, 22
(June, 1958), pp. 36-41.
The Seattle Police Department set up a temporary rehabilitation center in the industrial district where alcoholics serving sentences were admitted on a voluntary
basis. At the center the patient was given a job under
a supervisor. Visitors were encouraged and the reestablishment of family contacts was emphasized.
Alcoholics Anonymous services and various forms of
recreation were available. The ultimate aim was to
release the patient with clothes, job, housing, and some
pocket money, but community attitudes made this difficult. A follow-up study of 95 patients showed a definite
decrease in the number of arrests and time spent in jail
during the six months following release from the center.

Jackson, Joan K. and Holmes, Thomas H. "Alcoholism
and Tuberculosis," Human Organization, 17 (Spring,
1958), pp. 41-43.
The problems of treating alcoholic tubercular patients
are illustrated in this study of 100 tubercular alcoholics
and 50 non-tubercular alcoholics. Pride at being unlike "respectable" people is fostered by skid-row culture.
This pride leads to defiance of authorities in TB clinics
and withdrawal from the mainstream of society. Psychological depression and guilt lower the resistance of
alcoholics to TB. Reversion to skid-row life is common upon release or escape from the TB clinic, and a

return for more extended treatment often is necessary.

Jones, Herbert W., Roberts, Jean and Brantner, John.
"Incidence of Tuberculosis among Homeless Men," Journal of the American Medical Association, 155 (July 31,
1954), pp. 1222-1223.
Four hundred and five men who visited the Salvation Army
Men's Social Service Center in Minneapolis between October, 1952 and August, 1953 were given chest roentgeno-
grams. Distribution by age and point of origin is noted.
The rate of new cases in this group was found to be 55.5
times as great as the rate over a similar period for the
general population. The skid-row life-style is identified
as the prime cause of the differential. Implications for
public health programs are noted.

Jones, Howard. "Alcohol and Corrections," Canadian
Journal of Corrections, 1 (October, 1959), pp. 29-33.
Drunkenness seems linked with impulsive crimes, hence
to limit such crime the emphasis must focus on the drunkenness rather than the violence. But recent research
suggests that inebriety and crime may be functional equivalents, in that with increased age drinking may replace
crime as a mode of psychological need satisfaction, or
because a person cannot achieve success as a criminal.
In Canada there are more convictions for drunkenness
than for any other type of offense, except for municipal
traffic offenses. It is recommended that drunkenness
offenders be excluded from prisons and instead be established in some kind of half-way house or hotel. Moreover, sentencing of inebriates might be left to treatment
authorities such as social workers and psychiatrists.

Katz, Lawrence. "The Salvation Army Men's Social
Service Center. II: Results," Quarterly Journal of
Studies on Alcohol, 27 (March, 1966), pp. 636-647.
The nature of the population served by San Francisco
and Lytton centers and results of rehabilitation programs
are examined. In many respects, service center clients
are like other homeless and jailed alcoholics, but they
are better educated and have held better jobs. Among
program participants, rate of abstinence increases by

two-thirds, employment by 40 percent, and mobility shows a marked decrease. Extent of a client's improvement is determined largely by the length of his participation in the program. A varied program is essential.

Katz, Lawrence. "The Salvation Army Men's Social Service Center," Quarterly Journal of Studies on Alcohol, 25 (June, 1964), pp. 324-332.
Salvation Army Centers for rehabilitation of alcoholics are described. The program of these centers is to rehabilitate and/or spiritually regenerate unattached and homeless men. The ultimate aim is to reintegrate alcoholics into society and make them productive and useful members. Admission is based on identifiable and treatable handicaps and willingness to take part in the therapy programs. Individual group psychotherapy, vocational counseling and other such services are offered. The San Francisco and Lytton centers are cited as examples and considered in detail.

Klein, Eva. "The Treatment of Alcoholism," American Journal of Psychotherapy, 3 (January, 1949), pp. 74-85. The case history of a male alcoholic, aged 52, describes his life, childhood, and family situation.

Knight, Robert P. "The Dynamics and Treatment of Chronic Alcohol Addiction," Bulletin of the Menninger Clinic, 1 (September, 1937), pp. 233-250.
Etiological factors are illustrated in the case histories of ten male alcoholic patients. The orientation is psychoanalytic.

Kraft, T. and Al-Issa, I. "Alcoholism Treated by Desensitization: a Case Report," Behavior Research and Therapy, 5 (February, 1967), pp. 69-70.
The case is that of a 20-year-old single male whose drinking started at the age of 16. The patient had a childhood history of difficulty in verbal communication; desensitization, with relaxation produced by hypnosis, focused on getting him to imagine himself talking with a variety of groups and types of people. After the nineteenth treatment alcohol consumption was considerably

reduced but the patient had to be desensitized from the therapist, on whom he had developed a strong dependence . Desensitization is based on the assumption that use of alcohol is a method of dealing with anxiety, tensions, or frustrations. The treatment was considered a success in this case.

Krimmel, Herman E. and Falkey, Bruce D. "Short-term Treatment of Alcoholics," Social Work, 7 (July, 1962), pp. 102-107.
The long-term treatment plan is discouraging for the alcoholic who wants to be cured. The authors have had experience with fewer interviews per person and have a 30 to 40 percent success in treatment. They say "treat the symptom" and present several case studies to illustrate the success of this procedure. Short-term therapy, although not successful in all cases, offers a good chance of reaching more alcoholics at a lower cost.

Lee, John Park. "Alcoholics Anonymous as a Community Resource," Social Work, 5 (October, 1960), pp. 20-26 . Alcoholics Anonymous has been able to succeed in helping alcoholics where other methods have failed because it meets the basic needs of the alcoholic at the time he is confronted with the program. These needs are hope, acceptance by others, realization that alcoholism is his problem, and self-acceptance. It is important for social workers to understand the basis of A.A.'s success, which includes its methods, its reliance on spiritual guidance (although it is religiously unaffiliated), and the needs it fills for the alcoholic. Social workers must be prepared to let members of A.A. work in their own way.

Lerner, Arthur. "Considerations of Content Material of Group Counseling Sessions with Jailed Alcoholics," Quarterly Journal of Studies on Alcohol, 15 (September, 1955), pp. 432-452.
Verbatim accounts are presented of two teaching-counseling sessions attended by male alcoholic inmates at the Los Angeles City Jail. On the basis of a study of numerous sessions including those reported, the content of the sessions is divided into five categories: 1) problems

associated with incarceration, 2) definitions of alcoholism, 3) behavior, 4) facing the problem of giving up
drinking, and 5) methods of adjustment in the life of the
alcoholic.

Lerner, Arthur. "Interaction among Male Alcoholic Inmates, " Sociology and Social Research, 38 (May-June ,
1954), pp. 313-319.
Interaction among male alcoholic inmates is illustrated
in this description of four teaching-counseling groups at
the Los Angeles County Jail. In all, 78 men participated;
they were divided into groups of about 20. Each group
had its own teacher-counselor and convened for three
hours once a week for four weeks. There appeared to be
a decrease of expressed verbal hostility during the final
session as compared to the first three meetings. The
interacting process followed a trend from a "testing" and
orientation period through a less tense experience to
an attitude of "what do we do now?" The interaction reflected the inmates' attitudes about themselves, their
peers, authority figures, the jail, and other factors. The
primary value of the sessions seemed to be that the inmates experienced a form of release through verbaliza-
tion, interchange of ideas, and the arousal of a feeling
of personal worth without fear of reprisal.

Lerner, Arthur. "Self-Evaluation in Group Counseling
with Male Alcoholic Inmates, " International Journal of
Group Psychotherapy, 5 (July, 1955), pp. 286-298.
Seventy-eight alcoholic inmates of the Los Angeles County
Jail participated in an experimental program consisting
of a series of four three-hour group therapy sessions
each attended by about 20 men. The first two sessions
were marked by hostility, distrust, and "testing" of the
counselor, but the last two showed an increase in mutual
trust and cooperation among the men.

Malzberg, Benjamin. "First Admissions with Alcoholic
Psychoses in New York State, Year Ended March 31 ,
1948. With a Note on First Admission for Alcoholism
without Psychosis, " Quarterly Journal of Studies on
Alcohol, 10 (December, 1949), pp. 461-470.

Malzberg demonstrates that there is a relation between the number of new cases of alcoholism in civil hospitals and the occurrence of war, with first admissions declining during a war and rising in number at its termination. Most cases considered were of less than a year's duration; females accounted for most of those lasting more than a year. A comparison of alcoholics with and without psychoses showed those without psychoses to be younger, better educated, and of higher economic status .

Malzburg, Benjamin. "A Study of First Admissions with Alcoholic Psychoses in New York State, 1943-44 ," Quarterly Journal of Studies on Alcohol, 8 (September, 1947), pp. 274-295.
Admissions of alcoholic psychotics to New York State hospitals for mental disease during the fiscal year 1944 are compared to selected previous years. Analytical categories include age, sex, race, national origin, economic and marital status and the rural-urban dichotomy. Rates of admission declined during both world wars and increased in the interwar period. Negroes, Irish, and urban-dwellers have high rates of admission for alcoholic psychoses.

Marshall, William E. and Griggs, D. G. "A Study of Patients at the Alex G. Brown Memorial Clinic, Mimico, " Canadian Journal of Corrections, 6 (April, 1964), pp. 225-235.
The purpose of the study was to provide a systematic description of the patient population at the Clinic between 1952 and 1961. History of the facility, the general characteristics of the patients and the degree of successful adjustment of patients in the year following their discharge are reviewed. All patients at the Clinic are serving sentences for some breach of the law. They can be referred by the court or self-referred at the end of their sentence. Treatment is by the use of drugs, discussions, education, counseling, religious services, and build-up of physical health. A rehabilitation officer handles the release of the patient and his connections with society. There is an intensive follow-up service, with

many sources of information about the discharged patient.   In this study,   complete abstinence was not a
necessary criterion of satisfactory adjustment.   Between 1952 and 1961 the proportion of satisfactory adjustments declined. In part, this decline may reflect the
following: patients were harder to locate in 1961; a
higher proportion of cases referred directly by the court;
the ratio of staff to patients had decreased; and patients
tended to be younger than before.

Martinson,   Robert.   "The California Recovery House:
A Sanctuary for Alcoholics, " Mental Hygiene, 48 (July,
1964), pp. 432-438.
In California there are approximately 50 independently
owned and operated recovery houses that serve over
4, 000 residents a year at almost no cost to the public .
Most clients are of middle or lower-middle class origin.   They are expected to pay room and board if at
all possible,   and are required to perform household
chores and keep their quarters clean.   As part of the
therapy, most of the houses require the resident to get
an outside job.   Even in the church-sponsored houses
the influence of Alcoholics Anonymous is strong, and
staff members often are ex-alcoholics.   The usual stay
is about three months.   The house provides a secure
base from which the alcoholic can take his first steps
back into society.

Mayer, Joseph, Needham, Merrill A. and Myerson,
David J.   "Contact and Initial Attendance at an Alcoholism Clinic, " Quarterly Journal of Studies on Alcohol ,
26 (March, 1965), pp. 480-485.
Boston's Peter Bent Brigham Hospital Alcoholism Clinic for outpatient service had 193 patients contacted and
accepted for intake appointments in 1962. In this study,
patients who appeared for the intake appointment are
compared with those who did not.   An analysis of intake
information, e. g., sex, age, marital status, income,
employment status, and source of referral, did not differentiate between the two groups.   However, there was
an inverse relation between length of time between con-

tact and scheduled appointment and the probability that the appointment would be kept. This relationship is discussed with reference to the crisis needs of alcoholics and their inability to delay satisfaction of needs.

McCollough, William E. "A Two-Year Survey of Alcoholic Patients in a California State Hospital, " Quarterly Journal of Studies on Alcohol, 13 (June, 1952), pp. 240-253.
During 1947 and 1948 approximately 3, 200 persons were patients in California state hospitals under commitments as alcoholics. Of the newly committed, 769 (601 males and 168 females) were included in the survey. Data consisted of material normally available in case records. The average age at commitment was 48 for men and 38 for women. Both men and women specified emotional reasons for excessive drinking. There was a relatively high turnover in the alcoholic patient population, with 5. 2 months the median length of committment. Group psychotherapy is judged to be the most hopeful and practical type of medical treatment for state hospital programs.

MacCormick, Austin H. "Correctional Views on Alcohol, Alcoholism and Crime, " Crime and Delinquency, 9 (January, 1963), pp. 15-28.
The "revolving door jails" and "street cleaning" measures to which most alcoholic offenders are subjected are archaic and disgraceful. Except for programs sponsored by Alcoholics Anonymous few correctional institutions provide any means for treatment or rehabilitation of problem drinkers. The success of Alcoholics Anonymous in such ventures and the corollary to this success--increased public understanding of alcoholism--should provoke increased efforts toward rehabilitation. Programs for crime prevention and control should take into account that many non-alcoholic prisoners who have other behavioral problems are responsive to A. A. programs.

Mendelsohn, Jack H. and Chafetz, Morris E. "Alcoholism as an Emergency Ward Problem," Quarterly Journal of Studies on Alcohol, 20 (June, 1959), pp. 270-275.

A study of alcoholic patients seeking emergency ward aid in Detroit indicates that a wide range of medical problems are encountered in these patients and that they vary greatly in age and socio-economic status. Findings also suggest that the emergency ward may be useful in directing future rehabilitation and therapy.

Mills, Robert B. and Hetrick, Emery S. "Treating the Unmotivated Alcoholic: A Coordinated Program in a Municipal Court," Crime and Delinquency, 9 (January, 1963), pp. 46-59.

A program conducted by the Cincinnati Municipal Court and the Alcoholism Clinic at the Cincinnati General Hospital attempts to treat the so called "untreatable" or "unmotivated." Alcoholics referred by the judge to a psychiatric team are screened for acceptance on the following criteria: ego strength, degree of shame, response to authority or conscience, and willingness to accept treatment. The Clinic provides individual and group psychotherapy and collateral counseling with spouses. Working in liason with probation officers the psychiatrists provide patients with ego support and aid them in dealing with daily problems. In five years, the court psychiatric clinic referred 280 persons to the alcoholism clinic of whom 185 entered treatment. As the efficiency of the method was demonstrated the court made entrance into the clinic a condition for probation.

Mindlin, Dorothee F. "The Characteristics of Alcoholics as Related to Prediction of Therapeutic Outcome," Quarterly Journal of Studies on Alcohol, 20 (September, 1959), pp. 604-619.

Characteristics of the individual alcoholic which might assist in predicting therapeutic possibilities in psychiatrically oriented out-patient treatment are sought in a comparison of five different groups of alcoholics. The groups varied in size from 29 to 68 persons. Eight

characteristics differentiate success and failure groups:
marital status, present economic status, occupation,
criminal record, motivation, intelligence, diagnostic
category, and Rorschach signs.

McMahon, Colonel J. F. "Programs and Policy of the
Volunteers of America with Respect to the Treatment of
Alcoholics," Quarterly Journal of Studies on Alcohol,
13 (June, 1962), pp. 356-359.
Services provided by this organization include: 1) sustenance and shelter, 2) programs of employment in scrap
and clothing salvage in 63 cities (50 percent of those
employed are alcoholics), and 3) religious and psychological counseling.   Rehabilitation takes from a few
weeks to two years.   Total abstinence is demanded.
Less than 15 percent of the clients are totally cured,
but the extending of periods of sobriety is viewed as a
beneficial effect.

Moore, Merrill and Gray, M. Geneva.   "Alcoholism at
Boston City Hospital.   I.   Admission of Alcoholic Patients to Haymarket Square Relief Station, with Estimate
of the Cost of Their Care, 1927-1937," New England
Journal of Medicine, 221 (July 13, 1939), pp. 45-49.
Approximately 40, 000 case records of patients admitted
from 1927-1937 were examined to learn the incidence
of alcoholism among all admissions to the Haymarket
Square Relief Station.   About one quarter were found to
be alcoholic.   Routine treatment for acute alcoholic patients fails to lower incidence or expenditures.   It is
suggested that the symptomatic and emergency care of
alcoholism is insufficient.   Social and psychotherapeutic
techniques are recommended.

Moore, Merrill and Gray, M. Geneva.   "The Management of the Alcoholic Probationer," Journal of Criminal
Psychopathology, 3 (January, 1942), pp. 465-476.
A large proportion of the inmates of houses of correction are alcoholics, and they are likely to appear as
probationers.   The probation officer should recognize
that alcoholism is a symptom rather than a disease, and
must help the probationer to solve his problems without

alcohol, or refer him to a doctor. There is a list of 35 "musts and mustn'ts" for the probationer who is trying to stay sober.

Munt, Janet Staples. "Fear of Dependency: A Factor in Casework with Alcoholics," Social Work, 5 (January, 1960), pp. 27-32.
The thesis that the resistance of alcoholics to social case-workers is based on "an intense fear of the dependency for which the alcoholic longs" is illustrated in two case histories. The caseworker must reconcile the wish-fear paradox of dependency of alcoholics in terms of the ex-perience of the individual patient.

Myerson, David J. "An Active Therapeutic Method of Interrupting the Dependency Relationship of Certain Male Alcoholics," Quarterly Journal of Studies on Alcohol, 14 (September, 1953), pp. 419-426.
This paper describes attempts by psychiatrists at New Hampshire Alcoholism Clinic to solve the problem cre-ated by a person in a patient's social context who per-petuates the patient's drinking by protecting him. Three cases illustrate the problem: background, therapeutic approach, and results are given. The general roots of the problem include the insatiable demands, omnipotent feelings and unreasonableness of the patient, and the psychological problems of the protector. Psychotherapy for both patient and protector is suggested as a solution.

Myerson, David J. "An Approach to 'Skid Row' Prob-lem in Boston," New England Journal of Medicine, 249 (October 15, 1953), pp. 646-649.
Description of a rehabilitation program for derelict alco-holics includes a discussion of demographic character-istics and personality traits of approximately 300 alcoholic patients from skid-row areas in Boston's Long Island Hospital. The rehabilitation program is illustrated in a case history. The characteristics of a group of 119 alcoholics who followed the Long Island program and its effect on them are discussed. On the basis of these findings, it is asserted that the Long Island plan of pro-tective environment and working parole offers an oppor-

tunity for alcoholic patients to eliminate or substantially reduce alcoholic intake. Strengths and weaknesses of the program are considered.

Myerson, David J. "Clinical Observations on a Group of Alcoholic Prisoners with Special Reference to Women," Quarterly Journal of Studies on Alcohol, 20 (September, 1959), pp. 555-572.
This discussion of the life patterns of female alcoholic prisoners is drawn from clinical material accumulated during a decade of experience with alcoholics at the Long Island Hospital and the Massachusetts Correctional Institute. Alcoholism is seen as a mechanism for adjusting to isolation, the need for which may be traced to the structure of family relations during childhood. Isolation during and after adolescence reinforces a preexisting looseness of family ties and represents a culmination of deprivation. Both homosexual and heterosexual attempts to resolve the isolation tend to end in failure. The prison is seen as a good context for therapy because of its enforced isolation and control.

Myerson, David J. "The 'Skid Row' Problem. Further Observation on a Group of Alcoholic Patients, with Emphasis on Interpersonal Relations and the Therapeutic Approach," New England Journal of Medicine, 254 (June 21, 1956), pp. 1168-1173.
A second report on the skid-row population of a Boston hospital includes an analysis of 101 men in terms of nationality, religion, extent of education, duration of drinking history, and nature of separation from families. Their dependent relationships with bartenders, policemen, and employers are explored. The therapeutic approach is to create a group spirit among the men, leading them to attempt reestablishment of ties with their families. Partial success was achieved with 54 men, 12 of whom returned to their families and were considered total successes.

Myerson, David J. and Mayer, Joseph. "Origins, Treatment, and Destiny of Skid-Row Alcoholic Men," New England Journal of Medicine, 275 (August 25, 1966), pp. 419-425.

The rehabilitation of 101 indigent alcoholic patients in a Boston hospital who volunteered for a work-oriented halfway house program in 1952 is evaluated ten years later. A control group of 108 skid-row alcoholics who never applied for the halfway house is also evaluated. In addition to hospital data, information on subjects' contacts with agencies of public welfare enabled investigators to obtain two- or three-generation histories of the skid-row alcoholics. In comparison with the control group the treatment group showed less frequent parental contact with public welfare agencies, higher occupational attainment, and lower frequencies of arrests prior to hospital admission. Successful rehabilitation occurred for 22 percent of the treatment group, partial rehabilitation for 24 percent, and failure for 54 percent. Evaluation of background variables for both treatment and control groups leads to the conclusion that the better-educated, occupationally skilled married men with backgrounds of more self-sufficiency tended to enter the treatment program, and success in that program was associated with high rankings on these same characteristics. Subjects in both groups had poorly organized childhoods. Recommendations include a plea that coordinated community therapeutic services be made more readily available at an earlier age. For example, the police and courts should direct young drunkenness offenders to treatment centers rather than to jail or the streets.

New York City Welfare and Health Council, Committee on Alcoholism, Board of Visitors of Hart Island. "The Hart Island Program for Alcoholics in New York City," Quarterly Journal of Studies on Alcohol, 14 (March, 1953), pp. 140-146.
New York City Department of Welfare Center for Alcoholic rehabilitation on Hart Island is discussed. The program attempts to reorient alcoholics to society, providing shelter and jobs during an average stay of about ten weeks. To date, 2,300 men have been treated. The program should be expanded and a halfway house established.

Pinardi, Norman J. "Helping Alcoholic Criminals: A Pilot Study, " Crime and Delinquency, 9 (January, 1963), pp. 71-76.
Thirty alcoholics currently on probation or parole are compared with a control group of regular alcoholic patients at the Florida Alcoholism Rehabilitation Program. The alcoholic criminals generally are younger, healthier, less educated, and from a lower social stratum. They also show a higher incidence of parental alcoholism and divorce rates. They display anti-social behavior in addition to the alcoholism. The higher social status of the control group is thought to account for most of the differences.

Plaut, Thomas F.A. "Alcoholism and Community Caretakers: Programs and Policies, " Social Work, 12 (July, 1967), pp. 42-50.
Problem drinkers constitute a large proportion of the clientele of community helping agencies, few of which have taken responsibility for providing adequate treatment for them. The impact of alcoholics on the various services is demonstrated, and lay and professional attitudes toward problem drinkers are described. Requirements for adequate services are outlined.

Popham, Robert E., de Lint, Jan E. E., and Schmidt, Wolfgang. "Some Comments on Pittman's 'Rush to Combine, '" British Journal of Addictions, 63 (1968), pp. 25-27.
Pittman has argued against combining treatment programs for alcoholism with those for other addictions. The authors question Pittman's position, noting that while there are dissimilarities between alcohol and other addictions, there are also important historical and practical similarities. A combined program should not mislead researchers and clinicians since a) mixed addiction is often encountered in alcoholic patients; b) psychoactive drugs are being used to treat alcoholism; c) there is a trend toward a "total person" approach to treatment, and bringing all addictions within the scope of a single agency is consistent with this trend; and d) comparisons of different types of addicts within a clinical population

may reveal important etiological clues about addiction to particular drugs.

Quirk, Douglas A. "Former Alcoholics and Social Drinking: An Additional Observation, " The Canadian Psychologist, 9 (October, 1968), pp. 498-499.
Brief case reports on two alcoholics indicate that under certain conditions alcoholics may return to social drinking following treatment for alcoholism without reverting to uncontrolled drinking.

Rhodes, Robert J. and Hudson, Richard M. "A Follow-up Study of Tuberculous Skid Row Alcoholics, " Quarterly Journal of Studies on Alcohol, 30 (March, 1969), pp. 119-128.
It has long been recognized that skid row contributes disproportionately to the incidence of tuberculosis in the U.S., but few studies have been made to determine the long-term effects of treatment. A sample of 28 white male alcoholic and tuberculosis patients discharged from Firland Sanitorium in Seattle were sought for follow-up interviews within a year of discharge. The skid-row patients were extremely difficult to locate; only 15 of the 28 were located and interviewed. Although their physical health was objectively better than when admitted to the sanitorium, the respondents' over-all functioning and level of striving for self-sufficiency were lower. It is concluded that the "good, dependent patient" role adopted during long-term hospitalization is maintained upon return to the community. Rather than rehabilitating, the stay in the sanitorium confirms these subjects in their chronic dependency.

Rubington, Earl. "Alcoholic Control on Skid Row, " Crime and Delinquency, 13 (October, 1967), pp. 531-537.
It is proposed that an Alcoholic Control Unit staffed by paid skid-row alcoholics patrol streets and remove drunks and derelicts to a skid-row hospital unit. The proposal is based on the proposition that the influx of new elements into skid row is breaking up the established "moral order." Although homeless alcoholics are indifferent to public disorder, establishment of the proposed unit may

reorganize community interest and build solidarity. As a corollary, it is suggested that employment at the unit may initiate patterns of total abstinence for a small but influential group of men.

Rubington, Earl. "The Chronic Drunkenness Offender," Annals of the American Academy of Political and Social Science, 315 (January, 1958), pp. 65-72.
The man arrested three or more times a year often belongs to the skid-row drinking subculture, and can be rehabilitated through a halfway house association which changes his social relations. The halfway house is valuable because its methods are less traumatic for the participant than other programs. As more data are collected about various programs and participation in them, the author hopes to find new approaches to rehabilitation which are more valuable to the individual and the community.

Rubington, Earl. "Grady 'Breaks Out': A Case Study of an Alcoholic's Relapse," Social Problems, 11 (Spring, 1964), pp. 374-380.
"Grady" is a "loner" chronic drunkenness offender who became a shelter house member, a mission resident, and finally a mission employee. After 29 months of abstinence he got drunk. Grady's relapse is assessed in terms of folk and scientific interpretations of alcoholic relapse. Rubington concludes that "those social settings in which alcoholics seek to practice abstinence can be characterized by degree of social strain and by presence or absence of umpires. Given low strain and personality change, abstinence seems rather likely. Without personality change, abstinence seems likely only under two social conditions: when strains are minimal, or when strains are maximal and umpires are present." The significant question in this case may be why Grady remained sober as long as he did rather than why the relapse occurred.

Rubington, Earl. "Organizational Strains and Key Roles," Administrative Science Quarterly, 9 (March, 1965), pp. 350-369.
"Shelter House" is a halfway house for alcoholics run

by a director and four counselors, all members of Alcoholics Anonymous. In dealing with clients, counselors assume one of several key roles (controller, confidant, crony, or convert). Each role involves certain responsibilities: the controller focuses his attention toward discipline at Shelter House; the confidant is concerned with the members, interacting with them and providing support; the crony is oriented to maintaining his own sobriety, moving freely among members; the convert is even more self-oriented than the crony. Although these roles provide a structure for smoother relations with members, they are apt to cause difficulties among the counselors themselves by placing them in competition with one another.

Shepherd, Ernest A. (ed.) "Seattle Police Department Establishes Rehabilitation Center for Alcoholics," Quarterly Journal of Studies on Alcohol, 11 (March, 1950), pp. 167-170.
An experimental rehabilitation center established by the Seattle Police Department is described. The center is staffed by police personnel and operated on a semi-military basis. After careful screening, patients are admitted from the jail. Regular hours, work, and good food are emphasized. A great effort is made to find jobs for men leaving the center, as this is an important factor in keeping them out of further trouble. Local labor unions and other agencies have assisted in the program.

Storm, Thomas and Smart, Reginald G. "Dissociation: A Possible Explanation of Some Features of Alcoholism, and Implication for its Treatment," Quarterly Journal of Studies on Alcohol, 26 (March, 1965), pp. 111-115.
Recent studies indicate that habits acquired while under the influence of drugs, including alcohol, are not transferred to a non-drugged condition, and vice versa. It is suggested that a possible method of treatment of alcoholics would be to condition the drugged alcoholic not to take drinks. He would then respond to cues of increased intoxication by not drinking.

Thieman, Joseph. "Part-time Protective Environment and Working Parole as an Adjuvant in Treatment of Alcoholics," New England Journal of Medicine, 231 (July, 1944), pp., 9-11.
Maladjusted alcoholics may be rehabilitated through a program of living in a hospital and holding an outside job. Recommended duration of this program is one year. Three case histories are chosen to illustrate this thesis.

Thomas, Robert E., Gillam, James H., and Walher, Dollie R. "Casework Services for Alcoholics in a Magistrate's Court," Social Work, 5 (January, 1960), pp. 33-38.
An experiment in a Maryland magistrate's court wherein problem drinkers could opt for professional help is described. The sample consisted of 80 males, each of whom received the care of a caseworker. Records of these subjects over a three-year period were evaluated using an adapted version of a schedule devised by the State Division of Mental Health to assess its county rehabilitation clinics. Recidivism in the sample population was reduced substantially. The experimental procedure should be incorporated into the standard processes of magistrates' courts.

Treger, Harvey. "How You Can Help the Alcoholic Offender," Federal Probation, 22 (March, 1958), pp. 25-30.
These instructions to the beginning probation officer cover how to recognize an alcoholic, how to gain his respect and trust, how to get him to accept responsibility, and how to spot some of the more common attitudes and difficulties.

Trice, Harrison M. "The Affiliation Motive and Readiness to Join Alcoholics Anonymous," Quarterly Journal of Studies on Alcohol, 20 (June, 1959), pp. 313-320.
Thirty-seven alcoholics who readily joined Alcoholics Anonymous are found to differ slightly in affiliation motive from 37 others who were repeatedly exposed but did not join. The major difference between the two groups is in occupational status; the affiliates have histories of higher status jobs.

Wattenberg, William W. and Moir, John B. "Factors Linked to Success in Counseling Homeless Alcoholics," Quarterly Journal of Studies on Alcohol, 15 (December, 1954), pp. 587-594.

Previously studied skid-row alcoholics in Detroit (N = 770) were followed up to determine which cases had made successful adjustment after counseling and to what facts or processes, if any, successful adjustment could be attributed. Criteria of success were sobriety and employment for at least six months, with no arrests for public intoxication during that time. All but 70 of the subjects showed unsuccessful adjustment: they were still drinking and still on skid row. Factors linked to successful adjustment in the remaining 70 cases were the same as have been found related to adjustment of alcoholics at higher social levels, e. g., marriage, skilled occupation, church attendance, and recognition that one is an alcoholic. The men most likely to benefit from counseling are those who have not fully accepted skid-row life style.

Weil, Thomas P. and Price, Charles P. "Alcoholism in a Metropolis," Crime and Delinquency, 9 (January, 1963), pp. 60-70.

Studies of the municipal jail population in Baltimore, Maryland revealed that one-third of all prisoners were charged with drunkenness, disorderly conduct, and vagrancy. Almost all of these (98 percent) are caught up in the "revolving door" cycle of arrest, sobering up, release, and re-arrest. Selected statistics on the prisoners are given; they generally are young, single, fairly healthy, and unskilled. Programs for treatment and rehabilitation of alcoholics in 14 of Baltimore's 17 general hospitals are reviewed and compared with alcoholism prevention and control programs (out-patient clinics, halfway houses, farm programs, foster homes) in other cities. The review of alcoholism programs supports recommendations that a comprehensive rehabilitation center for alcoholics should have a socio-medical therapeutic approach and be administered by the city department of health, social welfare, or hospitals rather than the department of corrections. It should be located near personnel and ancillary community facilities and should contain an emergency room, intensive in-patient unit, multiphasic screening clinic, rehabilitation unit, custodial section, "day and night" center, and outpatient department. Finally, the rehabilitation center needs a well-respected spokesman and promoter.

Whalen, Robert P. and Lyons, John A. "Medical Problems of 500 Prisoners on Admission to a County Jail," Public Health Report, 77 (June, 1962), pp. 497-502.
In September, 1960, one-half of 500 prisoners kept for longer than 48 hours in Albany County Jail were alcoholics. Characteristics usually attributed to vagrant alcoholic males were observed.

Wilbur, Barbara M., Salkin, David and Birnbaum, Harold. "The Response of Tuberculous Alcoholics to a Therapeutic Community," Quarterly Journal of Studies on Alcohol, 27 (December, 1966), pp. 620-635.
The hypothesis that alcoholics with tuberculosis would remain longer in a hospital for treatment if involved in a "therapeutic community" (a special ward of others like themselves engaged in a program of activity including formal meetings, open communication between staff and patients, free expression of feelings, shared responsibility for ward administration, and an atmosphere of self-inquiry) rather than being treated under conventional ward management is tested on an experimental group of 120 skid-row alcoholics at the Veterans Administration Hospital in San Fernando, California. A control group of 141 skid-row alcoholics received conventional treatment. The hypothesis was refuted: the therapeutic community had an adverse effect on subjects who had arrest histories and little demonstrable effect on non-arrested subjects. It is concluded that high maturity (non-arrested) subjects respond best to treatment-oriented supervision while low maturity subjects require a custody-oriented program.

Zappala, Anthony and Ketcham, Frank S. "Toward Sensible Rehabilitation of the Alcoholic," Public Health Reports, 69 (December, 1954), pp. 1187-1196.

Cultural (stereotypical) and clinical theories of alcoholism are briefly summarized. The impact of each
theory on the penal and public health institutions in
Washington, D. C. is systematically reviewed. Modern
clinical and psychotherapeutic treatment of alcoholics
is the most efficient and humane way to attack the problem.

OTHER WORKS

Bailey, Margaret B. New York Alcoholism Vocational
Rehabilitation Project: The Inclusion of Vocational
Counseling in an Alcoholism Rehabilitation Program.
New York: The National Council on Alcoholism, 1963.
Pp. 52.
This is a report of an experimental program for the
treatment of alcoholism conducted by the National Council on Alcoholism in New York City between December,
1958 and November, 1962. Data were collected from
235 persons (136 men, 99 women) seeking help. Vocational disability is one of the alcoholic's problems. In
this study vocational counseling was the experimental
variable; it was offered to half of the patients. Six
groups were formed: three received group psychotherapy, group vocational counseling, and individual vocational counseling; the remaining three groups received
group psychotherapy only. Among patients receiving
vocational counseling marked improvement of work
performance was noted. The author recommends intensive vocational counseling as part of future alcoholic rehabilitation programs.

Bateman, Nils Ivan. "Selected Factors as Related to
Outcome of Treatment for Hospitalized Alcoholics,"
unpublished doctoral dissertation, Florida State University, 1965. Pp. 133.
Factors associated with completion of treatment for alcoholism and success of that treatment are investigated
in a study of male alcoholic patients who had received
treatment at a state alcoholism hospital. Factors
associated with completion of 25 or more days of a 28-

day prescribed stay at the hospital included high social status and church membership. Successful treatment was more frequent among the older respondents, those who had abstained prior to hospitalization, and those who had previously attended Alcoholics Anonymous meetings regularly.

Brook, Rupert Ramsay. "Personality Correlates Associated with Differential Success of Affiliation with Alcoholics Anonymous," unpublished doctoral dissertation, University of Colorado, 1962. Pp. 124.
Predictions concerning the outcome of affiliation with Alcoholics Anonymous were derived from a theory of conceptual systems and personality organization. Subjects were 30 former members of A. A. hospitalized for alcoholism and 30 active members who had been sober a year or more. Data were obtained by interview; the schedule included information about personal background, experience with A. A., and items designed to measure mental age, stage of conceptual functioning, and priority given to various needs. Findings corroborate the hypotheses; affiliates and exaffiliates (and subgroups of both) may be differentiated according to the predicted personality correlates.

Cain, Arthur Homer. "Philosophical Psychology of the Socially Estranged Alcoholic," unpublished doctoral dissertation, Columbia University, 1960. Pp. 463.
Over a ten-year period the author worked with a group of thirty alcoholics using a program of physical training, educative counseling, reading, social reorganization, vocational guidance, esthetic training, experimentation, religious investigation, and social participation. All were successfully rehabilitated. Seven case studies are presented. Reading activity is seen as a critical component of the rehabilitation process. Cain suggests that there are more varieties of alcoholics than are generally recognized, and criticizes Alcoholics Anonymous and general psychotherapy for taking a narrow view that ignores important aspects of the "total human organism." The dissertation was later published as Seven Sinners under the pseudonym "Arthur King."

Carpenter, Edward Milton.   "Treatment at a Rehabilitation Center and the Subsequent Adjustment of Chronic
Drunkenness Offenders, " unpublished doctoral   dissertation,   University of California,   Berkeley,   1964.   Pp.
198.
A sample of 179 men was drawn from a population of
1, 420 at the Single Men's Rehabilitation Center in San
Francisco and subsequently divided into four groups on
the basis of whether they had experienced a group activity begun by the social worker there and whether they
had been admitted to the Center once or several times.
Data were obtained from case records and interviews
with staff members.   Group treatment was found to be
significantly related to improved adjustment patterns.

Clinebell, Howard John, Jr. "Some Religious Approaches to the Problem of Alcoholism," unpublished doctoral
dissertation, Columbia University, 1954. Pp. 562.
The history, working philosophy, psychodynamics, conceptual adequacy and effectiveness of five religious approaches to alcoholism are described   and   evaluated.
The specific approaches are 1) Bowery Mission("straight
evangelistic"), 2) Salvation Army ("modified straight
evangelistic"), 3) Oxford Group Movement ("streamlined,
upper-middle class adaptation of the evangelistic technique"), 4) Alcoholics Anonymous ("radical modification of the Oxford Group theory and technique"),   and
5) Emmanuel Movement ("outside the evangelistic tradition").   An effective religious approach to alcoholism
is outlined. Clinebell interviewed 79 alcoholics; illustrative case material is included in the appendices.

Detroit Mayor's Rehabilitation Committee on Skid Row
Problems and the Michigan State Board of Alcoholism .
The Homeless Alcoholic: Report of the First Annual
International Institute on the Homeless Alcoholic.   Lan-
sing: Michigan State Board of Alcoholism, 1955. Pp. 69 .
The institute was sponsored to allow presentation of
experimental material for use of similar institutes and
programs for alcoholic rehabilitation in other cities .
One article deals with the problem of the homeless man
in general and the   other papers describe Detroit's

approach to the rehabilitation of homeless men. Each article is summarized briefly below.

Straus, Robert. "The Homeless Alcoholic, Who He Is, His Locale, His Personality, the Approach to His Rehabilitation," pp. 7-14.
The author attributes greater public awareness of the distinction between alcoholics and homeless men (derelicts) to the work done by Alcoholics Anonymous and the growth of community outpatient clinics. Clinical studies and statistics on marital status, employment, and residential patterns illustrate that although homeless men tend to be alcoholics, many alcoholics are not homeless. Among many homeless men the basic problem is dependency, not alcohol. Differences among homeless men must be clarified and taken into account by those who develop treatment programs.

Schwartz, Alan. "The Committee," pp. 15-18. The establishment in 1951 of the Mayor's Rehabilitation Committee and its efforts to establish an outpatient clinic for alcoholics are described. The Detroit clinic has broad community support, and it is hoped that it will be a model for similar programs in other cities.

Shoults, Sanford. "The Program," pp. 18-22. The history and achievements of the outpatient clinic in Detroit are related. The voluntary nature of the program and its emphasis upon counseling and on referring clients to other specialized programs within the community are stressed.

Dunham, H. Warren. "A Closer Look at the Homeless Alcoholic," pp. 23-31.
Dunham discusses the homeless man on skid row and the professional hobo. The skid-row alcoholic is defined as a man possessing a curable neurosis. Much of the text is historical, autobiographical and anecdotal.

Zappala, Anthony. "The Challenge of the Skid Row Alcoholic," pp. 32-44.
History and methods of the District of Columbia out-patient clinic for alcoholics are summarized. Clinic patients are compared to workhouse inmates, and differences in rehabilitation methods and aims of the two institutions are described. An attempt is made to illustrate

the importance and intercorrelation of medical, psychiatric, social and legal considerations. Basic to the rehabilitation of the homeless man is his establishment of "meaningful relatedness" to some other person.

Stine, Arthur. "Rehabilitation of the alcoholic and What it Means to the Taxpayer," pp. 45-55.
The author, a public accountant and a recovered alcoholic, contrasts the costs of the alcoholic to the community with the economic contributions the recovered alcoholics can make. The treatment of alcoholics must include harnessing their "useful assets" rather than merely keeping them out of circulation. The alcoholism problems of Indians in New Mexico are described, as are the successful methods of rehabilitation centers in Utah. Clinics are not enough, neither are criticism, preaching, or psychologizing. Two important aspects of successful treatment are the establishment of meaningful personal ties and the availability of other people who have successfully recovered from alcoholism.

Daniel, Ralph W. "Michigan's Alcoholism Rehabilitation Program," pp. 56-60.
Homelessness is a consequence of a lifetime of inadequate experience, and rehabilitation must attempt to make up for incomplete socialization. Rehabilitation of the homeless alcoholic requires an understanding of both homelessness and alcoholism, two distinct problems. A general approach must coordinate various facilities and community agencies. In the Michigan program the general hospital is a focal point in such coordination.

Division of Alcoholic Rehabilitation, Skid Row and Alcoholism: An Annotated Bibliography. "Berkeley: State of California Department of Public Health, 1961. Pp. 21.
In 1960 a state senate committee held hearings on the skid-row problem in California. This bibliography was compiled in connection with those hearings. It consists of an introductory summary of the literature on skid row and its men, the drinking problem, and rehabilitation programs, followed by 32 annotated references. The annotations are detailed and well-written.

Fifth and Sixth Annual Institutes on the Homeless and Institutional Alcoholic. New York: National Council on Alcoholism, 1961. Pp. 28.
The papers of the Fifth Annual Institute deal with rehabilitation of skid-row men and the planning necessary to coordinate urban renewal and rehabilitation. There are two papers, Myerson's description of a hospital rehabilitation program for homeless alcoholics, and Mackelmann's treatment of skid row and urban relocation. The three papers of the Sixth Annual Institute deal with the law and drunkenness, the treatment of chronic drunks, and community approaches.

Myerson, David J. "The Boston Long Island Hospital Rehabilitation Program for the Homeless Alcoholic," pp. 1-5.
Based on three years experience with the Boston Long Island Hospital Rehabilitation Program, which sought to reintegrate the homeless alcoholic through institutional hospital support, Myerson argues that the critical quality of skid row is the lack of family ties and family structure, both of which reflect severe characterological disorders. He argues that alcoholics can be taught to improve themselves, thereby easing their dependence upon society.

Mackelmann, D. E. "Skid-Rows--A Modern Concern of Planning and Redevelopment Agencies," pp. 6-12.
Relocation programs as they have developed with expanded urban renewal are discussed in the light of the 1957-58 study of Chicago's skid rows. Examples of continual relocation of the same people support the contention that a concerted effort at rehabilitation is needed to eliminate this costly repetition. Long-term planning is necessary, and the public must not expect instant rehabilitation.

Ketcham, Frank. "Legal Interpretation of the Alcoholic's Responsibility for Criminal Acts while Intoxicated," pp. 13-15.
Alcoholism reduces criminal responsibility in two ways: 1) alcoholics may be offered insanity commitment; 2) alcoholism may serve either a) to remove responsibility from the person or b) to mitigate responsibility on the

grounds of no intent. The history and problems of balancing three major purposes of the courts--retribution, deterrence, and rehabilitation--are summarized.

LoCicero, Victor J. "A Multidisciplined Approach to the Skid Row Habitues, " pp. 16-24.
Philadelphia's interdisciplinary appro ach to skid row includes collection of skid-row data, psychiatric treatment, rehabilitative treatment, follow-up studies, and orientations to future programs and needs. The author concludes that those involved with the Philadelphia efforts have provided a gross view of the problems and potential answers, but more data and ideas are needed.

Robertson, Frances. "Houston's Integrated Attack on a Metropolitan Skid Row Problem, " pp. 25-28.
The Houston Council on Alcoholism serves as a public education body, as a coordinator of agencies and information, and as an agency for evaluating progress. Positive response to skid-row problems will eventually prove successful.

Fourth Annual Institute on the Homeless and Institutional Alcoholic. New York: National Council on Alcoholism, 1959. Pp. 66.
Organizers of the Fourth Annual Institute attempted to widen the Institute's perspective and achieve relevance to the "sick alcoholic" population rather than being limited to the problems of skid row. There are five papers on various aspects of "community treat - ment" and three concerned wtih "skid row and urban renewal. "

Duplain, George W. "The Utilization of Community Resources by a Salvation Army Program," pp. 1-7.
The manager of the San Francisco Men's Social Service Center describes the facilities, aims, and practices of his Center. Clients are admitted on two-week probation. Full participants in the program may remain as long as two years. The rehabilitation process includes careful screening, reorientation classes, personal counseling, group and individual psychotherapy, recreational activities, and job placement upon "graduation. "

Aikenhead, Robert S. "Rehabilitation and Employment," pp. 8-18.
After describing the typical intake and treatment sequence for clients of the Mayor's Rehabilitation Center (Detroit) the author discusses the rehabilitation problems and prognoses of three types of homeless men, the "reasonably well-motivated" individuals without serious physical or emotional problems, the "semi-institutionalized" who lack some of the assets of the first group, and the "completely institutionalized" who have been totally socialized into skid-row dependency. For the first group the primary goal is rehabilitation ; the second may achieve some improvement of material and social circumstances but chances are that they will always live in the central business district, beyond normal society. For the third group the objective should be improvement rather than recovery. Regardless of the probabilities for recovery, minimum standards for physical surroundings need to be established and maintained.

Hart, Walter C. "A Volunteers of America Research and Demonstration Project," pp. 19-30.
The various approaches to the rehabilitation of homeless men taken by the Volunteers of America since their founding in 1896 are summarized. These include a "congregate approach, "the "individualized approach, " the establishment of a Men's Service Club, and finally , a "multiple approach. " Specific services available under the "multiple approach" are cited. A research and demonstration project sponsored by the federal Office of Vocational Rehabilitation has attempted to evaluate the effects of this treatment program. Variables currently under investigation include motivational and predictive factors and indexes of change. Intake and data research forms are described briefly.

Carlston, J. Robert. "A Program for Rehabilitation and Education of Inmates and Parolees of the Utah State Prison, " pp. 31-37.
The operation of the Alcoholics Anonymous program inside the prison is outlined and justified. Upon release the parolee may be helped by Alcoholic Rehabilitation

Centers or "sponsored" by men who are active A. A. members.

Jackson, Joan K. "The Seattle Police Department Rehabilitation Project, " pp. 38-44.
Facilities and program of the Project are sketched. All patients are male prisoners of the city jail who have requested admission and met Project screening standards. The rehabilitation program emphasizes physical health, a "semimilitary" routine, recreation and visitation, counseling, Alcoholics Anonymous, and religious services. Comparison of patients' arrest rates for the six-month periods preceding arrest and following release shows a significant decrease following treatment. Analysis of factors associated with patient "success" reveals counseling by the staff's A.A. members to be the most significant factor.

Hindman, Wilbert L. "Community Attitudes Toward Reorientation of the Alcoholic into Society, " pp. 45-49.
A quotation from an 1833 Temperance Society publication illustrates that community attitudes toward homelessness and alcoholism have changed little in 125 years. The relationship between the stereotype of the homeless man and his treatment by community agencies is an example of the "self-fulfilling prophecy. " Factors associated with community rejection of the alcoholic are the impact of the temperance tradition, fear, frustration, the stigma of skid row, and institutional rigidities. While the negative stereotype persists, rehabilitation of the homeless alcoholic is unlikely to be very successful.

Dunham, H. Warren. "Skid Rows--Past, Present, and Future, " pp. 50-61.
Public interest in skid row moves in cycles. The current rediscovery is due to concern for urban redevelopment and recent advances in alcoholism research and therapy. Those who work with skid row and its men may take a "collective" (what shall we do about skid row?) or an "individualistic" (who are the men and what are their problems?) perspective. A careful examination of skid row in the light of social change is neces-

sary. Dunham reviews the "Golden Age" of skid row,
its present condition, and its probable future. In the
past skid row was vitalizing, invigorating, and utili-
tarian; today it is apathetic, stagnating, nonutilitarian.
The skid row of the present has existed for about 30
years. Influences which produced it include technological changes in industry which have reduced the size
and mobility of skid-row residents, the social security
program which brought the pensioner to skid row, the
rise of the large industrial unions, increased financial
aids to veterans, and the availability of improved health
facilities.   Skid row cannot be explained in terms of
traits of individual men, but rather in terms of a sociological theory of subcultures. The future of skid row
can be called an "Age of Purposeful Control. " Although
its population will continue to decrease, there will remain "problem" personalities who cannot be fitted into acceptable social roles, and indications are that
there will be little improvement in rates of rehabilitation.

Schwartz, Alan E.   "Plans to Meet the Challenge
under Duress of Current Technological Changes, " pp.
62-66.
Skid row is a city within a city, and mere physical removal will not change its citizens or prevent them from
congregating in other neighborhoods. Community efforts suffer from a lack of valid information about alternatives and consequences. National research
projects and pilot programs are needed.

Gibbins, Robert J."Undersocialization in the Incarcerated Alcohol Addict," unpublished master's thesis,
Queens University, Kingston, Ontario, 1952. Pp. 114.
Gibbins' hypothesis is that because incarcerated alcohol addicts are less socialized than their non-addicted
peers, they will find fewer satisfactions in group participation and will view their environment as hostile.
Further, it is argued that alcohol relieves the tensions
felt by the alcoholic. Comparison of two groups of 26
penitentiary inmates (one of addicts, one of non-addicts)
and a group of 26 Kingston industrial workers showed

that in terms of marital status, occupational and geographic mobility and group affiliation the alcoholic inmates were the least socialized of the three groups.
Interviews, autobiographies and TAT results for 10
alcoholic and 10 non-alcoholic inmates provided additional support for the hypothesis.

Haring, Margery. Out of Community: A Report on the
Homeless People Project. New York: Quaker Project
on Community Conflict, 1967. Pp. 20.
From January 31, 1967 to April 1, 1967, a downtown
New York group of Quakers participated in a Neighbor -
hood Rescue Service which directly approached homeless persons found in the streets. The program was
modest--only 36 persons were directly assisted -- but
it offers a model for a frontal attack upon the   problems of skid row. A community program to approach
the homeless man is proposed, and the need for   a
closer liaison among the   present services and agencies aiding the homeless is noted. The report is illustrated with   extremely good   photographs by Bob
Crawford.

Hart, Walter C. Potential for Rehabilitation of Skid
Row Alcoholic Men. Los Angeles: Volunteers of America, 1961. Pp. 136.
This report summarizes a three-year program to rehabilitate alcoholic residents of Los Angeles' skid rows.
Located in a skid-row building, the project operated an
outpatient facility that provided professional medical,
psychiatric, vocational, religious, and social service
assistance, Rehabilitation was defined as significant increase in abstinence coupled with positive improvement
in employment, earnings, means of financial support,
lodging, or neighborhood of residence. Two   study
groups were evaluated;they differed in that one (N=953)
consisted of persons who merely had to appear at the
center to be treated, while the other (N=175) included
men who were not treated until they had filed a written application and returned for a second visit. Re -
habilitation rates for subjects in these two groups were ,
respectively, 60 and 80 percent.   Researchers at-

tempted to verify follow-up data by taking blood alcohol tests, checking respondents' employment stubs, and attempting to communicate with respondents at their stated addresses. It is recommended that a temporary center for rehabilitation be established in skid row, that homeless alcoholics be treated in general hospitals or all-purpose clinics, and that long-term efforts at greater coordination and integration of therapeutic services be made.

Kantor, David and Blacker, Edward. A Survey of Bridge-water, An Institution for the Chronic Drunkenness Offender. Boston: Office of the Massachusetts Commissioner on Alcoholism, 1958. Pp. 56.
Bridgewater is evaluated in the light of modern correctional and therapeutic approaches to alcoholism, its institutional needs, and the attitudes of its custodial and professional staff, the public at large, and the inmates. A random sample of 52 court-committed inmates is described in terms of demographic characteristics, physical handicaps, employment status, marriage and arrest history, and drinking history. Three basic patterns of alcohol use and skid-row life style are distinguished among the inmates. There are general recommendations for improvement of the institution.

Kelsaw, James William. "A Study of the Problem of Differentiating Alcoholic Criminals," unpublished doctoral dissertation, Washington State University, 1960. Pp. 202.
In an attempt to distinguish alcoholic offenders who are "primarily alcoholics" from those who are "primarily criminals" Kelsaw compared the histories of male alcoholic patients, non-alcoholic prisoners and alcoholic prisoners. Data were obtained by sampling the files of three institutions, the Idaho State Penitentiary (non-alcohol prisoners, N=94), the Shadel Hospital of Seattle (alcoholic patients, N=830), and the Shadel Hospital branch of Idaho (alcoholic convicts, N=76). Intergroup comparisons lead to the conclusion that alcoholic criminals and criminal alcoholics can be distinguished by their mode of adult adaptation to the societal opportunity

structure. The former, primarily criminals, make borderline retreatist-innovationist adaptation, where - as the latter, primarily alcoholics, are retreatists. However, there is passage from one of these statuses to the other, as in the case of the unsuccessful   criminal who retreats in the face of his "double failure"   and becomes primarily an alcoholic.

Mindlin, Dorothee Friendlander. "Group Therapy for Alcoholics: a Study of the Attitude and Behavior Changes in Relation to Perceived Group Norms, " unpublished doctoral dissertation, The American University, 1965. Pp. 166.
Group therapy with alcoholic patients at the District of Columbia Alcoholism Clinic was studied to determine its effectiveness and to measure attitude change. A group of 50 patients in group therapy was compared with a control group of 50 in a lecture series and a "no treatment" group of 19.   Special tests were given and therapist's ratings were obtained before treatment, after 6 and 10 weeks, and after 6 months. Group therapy was   found to improve attitude and behavior, and the lecture group improved as compared to the "no treatment" group. In particular, the group therapy patients showed higher motivation, lower anxiety, better impulse control, and improved attitudes toward alcohol.

National Committee on Alcoholism. Institute on   the Skid Row Alcoholic of the Committee on the   Homeless Alcoholic. New York: Department of Welfare,   1956 . Pp. 94.
On March 29, 1956, a one-day Institute was sponsored by the National Committee on Alcoholism. This report contains a summary statement by William J. Plunkert followed by 11 papers related to rehabilitation programs for homeless alcoholics.   Each paper is   paginated separately.
        Murtagh, John M. "The New York City Program for the Skid Row Alcoholic, " pp. 9.
Murtagh is Chief Magistrate in New York City's Magistrates' Court and Chairman of the Committee on the Homeless Alcoholic. In this address he mentions both

the legal and medical facilities currently available to homeless men in New York City, especially the rehabilitation program at Hart Island. A major problem is public apathy. New legistation reflecting modern conceptions of the skid-row derelict is needed.

Gordon, C. Wayne. "Social Characteristics and Life Career Patterns of the Skid Row Alcoholic, "pp. 13. Gordon reviews findings from an analysis of case histories of 1,046 inmates who had been sentenced at least twice to a penal institution on charges relating to public intoxication in Monroe County Penitentiary during 1954-55. Preconditions and social determinants of the chronic skid-row inebriety include deprivations during childhood and youth, economic marginality and institutionalized living. Types of careers in public intoxication are distinguished ("Early Skid" and "Late Skid") and illustrated with case histories.

Potts, Frank H. "Institutional Treatment for the Alcoholic in Ontario," pp. 5. Treatment available to alcoholic men serving sentences in Ontario is voluntary and involves remaining in a clinic for the last 30 days of the sentence and maintaining contact with the rehabilitation staff for at least a year. Treatment embraces medical, psychological, social and spiritual approaches. The greatest success has been with secondary alcoholics who had been drinking to excess for nine years or less, although some success has been reported with all categories and age groups. Potts is the chief psychologist for the Ontario Department of Reform Institutions.

Hofman, Peter J. "The Salvation Army's Program with Alcoholics," pp. 9. Hofman, a Senior Major in the Salvation Army, describes the "typical" homeless alcoholic and outlines the program of the Harbor-Lights Corps, which provides sleeping, recreational, and counseling facilities for homeless men. Contact with other men in the same condition, or with former residents, is seen as an important part of rehabilitation. Clients are encouraged to join various groups and clubs within the organization. They are expected to pay for room and board as soon

as possible, but are encouraged to stay for two or three
months. If they are not able to compete in regular industry, they may be sent to the Men's Social Service
Center for prolonged treatment. At the Center every-
thing, including clubs and recreation, is provided under
one roof. After rehabilitation, the men are encouraged
to continue membership and to spend time in the recreation rooms at the Center.

     Daniels, James and Spence, L. "The Skid   Row
Alcoholic in New Orleans, " pp. 5.
A new rehabilitation program in New   Orleans utilizes
all the civil and social agencies on a voluntary basis .
Since there is no "voluntary treatment" in New Orleans,
a prospective volunteer is taken before a judge to legal-
ize his stay in the city prison for his 90-day rehabilitation. He can be released early on request of the warden
(Daniels)   or the director of the rehabilitation unit
(Spence). At the end of 30-60 days of day-to-day parole
(days at work, nights at prison) he is ready to help the
new patients; at the end of 90 days he leaves with clothes,
a job, and pocket money, but returns for counseling.
Due to the newness of the program, no statistics are
available, but it appears to be successful.

     Hindman, Wilbert L. "The Utilization of Modern
Techniques in Treating the Skid Row Alcoholic in the
Southwest, " pp. 7.
Hindman, professor of Political Science at U.S.C and
on the Board of Directors of the Volunteers of America
in Los Angeles, describes the rehabilitation of skid-row
alcoholics by the County Welfare Department as well as
the work being done by private organizations. The L.A.
County Welfare Department provides for many in-
digents, gets them jobs, and will place those unfit for
jobs in a camp. After being carefully screened by a
psychologist, a physician, and a police representative,
men are assigned to the new rehabilitation center for
up to 120 days. The center contains a chapter of alcoholics Anonymous, a chaplain, and a vocational training
program. All these programs are underfinanced and
not large enough to take care of the problem. After
rehabilitation at the center, the men are returned to

L. A. with no job or money. A "halfway house" program is badly needed.

Myerson, David J. "Further Observations of a Group of Skid Row Alcoholics With Emphasis on Interpersonal Relationships and the Therapeutic Approach," pp. 16.

Myerson describes a three-year study of 101 destitute and homeless alcoholic skid-row men treated at the Long Island Hospital of Boston. Most of the men were from lower-income backgrounds, and slipped to skid row after the dissolution of family ties. Usually they had been alcoholic for many years. Personality characteristics that kept them from forming normal "give and take" relationships are noted. Over a three-year period 54 out of 101 men improved but only 12 could successfully return to their families and live independently; the rest had to maintain some dependence on the hospital.

Schwartz, Alan E. "The Detroit Program for the Skid Row Alcoholic," pp. 5.

The program of the Detroit Mayor's Rehabilitation Committee consists of several forms of counseling, monetary assistance, and placement on an out-patient basis. There are plans for a special hospital and a halfway house. Potential clients must request acceptance in the program; accepted clients may be referred to Alcoholics Anonymous or some similar organization. Great emphasis is placed on increasing self-respect via job placement. To date over 600 men (out of 4,500) have been rehabilitated. It has been found that some of the best counseling is provided by recovered alcoholics because "they've been there."

Chase, Morris. "The Homeless Woman Alcoholic," pp. 8.

Chase, Director of the Bureau of Institutional Administration in New York City, describes the New York program for rehabilitation of homeless women alcoholics and highlights the dearth of systematic knowledge about this problem. There are fewer avenues of escape from skid row open to women than to men. In New York City there are an estimated 1500 homeless women, of whom about 800 apply to the Department of Welfare each year.   Three hundred of these will be "repeaters, " and almost all of the repeaters are al- coholics. A study of 50 such clients showed an aver- age of two admissions to the Women's Shelter per year; average duration of contact with the shelter was five and a half years. The Women's Shelter program pro- vides three meals a day, clothing, medical care, and job placement.   There are plans for a halfway house and a new shelter in a non-skid-row area.

Wesley I. "Alcoholics Anonymous Views the Skid Row Alcoholic, " pp. 7. A former alcoholic comments on the history and meth- ods of Alcoholics Anonymous. From its inception the program has lacked funds, although now "twelfth-step houses" have been established in some of the larger cities to provide necessities of life for needy alcohol- ics. Those who can pay are expected to do so as part of their learning to accept the responsibilities of life . Some of the larger A. A. centers are described briefly.

Brown,   Chester R.   "A National Review of the Work of Private Agencies With the Skid Row Alcohol- ic, " pp. 5. Brown notes that private agencies were the first to concern themselves with rehabilitating the problem drinker; he welcomes the more recent efforts of pub- lic and state offices, and anticipates greater coordina- tion of public and private programs.

New York State Interdepartmental Health and Hospital Council. "Proposed Program Plan for the Care   and Treatment of Homeless and Severely Debilitated Alco- holics. " Albany: State of New York, 1967. Pp. 49 . The proposed program is based upon a "Report of the Sub-Committee on the Alcoholic Who Comes to the Attention of Law Enforcement Agencies"   (reprinted here) and is aimed at the estimated   30, 000   debili- tated and homeless alcoholics in New York State. Four principal services are suggested: 1) facilities   for detoxification, 2) diagnostic and evaluation centers , 3) congregate living situations combined with rehabilitation, and 4) long-term care facilities for those not able to be rehabilitated. Recommendations include provisions for state financing, linking court procedures and practices to rehabilitation rather than incarceration, and a state-wide central registry.

Rochester Bureau of Municipal Research. Man on the Periphery: A Study of the Monroe County (N. Y.) Penitentiary. Rochester: Bureau of Municipal Research, 1964. Pp. 154.
The background and case histories of prisoners (1, 360 in all) in the Monroe County Penitentiary during the year 1962 are summarized. Following a brief history of the penitentiary is a "profile of the penitentiary prisoner." Prisoners from Monroe County are compared to prisoners from out-of-county. Plans for rehabilitation and treatment and a proposal for a new penitentiary and rehabilitation center complete the report. The "profile of the prisoner" is of interest: alcohol offenders make up 63 percent of the prisoners and 73 percent of total commitments; almost all of the "hard core" prisoners (committed more than six times) are alcohol offenders. The "revolving door" is evident; nearly one-third of all prisoners repeated during the year, and the alcohol offender is the major repeater. The incidence of alcohol offenses is cumulative, their rate increasing with the age of the prisoner. White alcohol offenders are considerably older than Negro alcohol offenders. Alcohol offenders have less education than non-alcohol offenders. Apparently the chronic inebriates in Monroe County may be homeless or wandering, but they are not transient; two-thirds of them had been county residents for a year of more. Non-white offenders were not recent Southern migrants. The penitentiary prisoners are overwhelmingly from the unattached.

Rubington, Earl. What to Do Before Skid Row is Demolished. Philadelphia: The Greater Philadelphia Movement, 1958. Pp. 21.
This proposal for dealing with the social, economic, and political problems of urban renewal of Philadelphia's skid row includes an outline for a temporary diagnostic

and distribution center for skid-row men and suggests that patterns of relocation be based on results from two research surveys, one of "informed persons" and the other of skid-row residents. It summarizes types of skid-row men in terms of their economic affiliation with skid row and the community and suggests survey questions that should be included in the research.

Scott, A. M. "The Chronic Inebriate Offender and the Correctional System," unpublished master's thesis, University of Toronto, 1959. Pp. 130.
Thirty-six chronic inebriate offenders were chosen randomly and interviewed. Data on background, drinking patterns, and psychological attitudes and problems are presented. The seemingly offhand treatment of alcoholics by the courts and jails is discussed and offenders' reactions are recorded (usually resentful towards police and court but not so toward jails). Jails are a source of recognition and a means for satisfying needs. "Regular" prisoners are often at home with guards and routine. Diagnosis and treatment would be more beneficial than incarceration, but facilities are not available.

Second Annual Institute on the Homeless and Institutional Alcoholic. New York: National Council on Alcoholism, 1957. Pp. 71.
The articles in this collection cover two categories: aspects of skid row that should be taken into account (David J. Myerson's "Psychiatric Aspects: The Women of 'Skid Row'" and John M. Murtagh's "Legal Aspects") and skid-row institutions (Thomas M. Downs' "The Hospital," John J. Ford's "The Private Agency," Henry L. McCarthy's "The Public Agency," Joseph D. Lohman's "Law Enforcement, Jails and Prisons," and Clyde Gooderham's "The Utah Program").
        Myerson, David J. "Psychiatric Aspects: The Women of Skid Row," pp. 3-16.
Skid-row women have been dislodged from family life because of alcoholism and/or heterosexual maladjustment. The failures of skid-row women are evident in high rates of divorce, desertion, promiscuity, and prostitution. Several case histories are given. Prob-

lems of rehabilitation include the need for partial protection, individual attention, and access to food so that
patients may satisfy psychological cravings.

Murtagh, John M. "Legal Aspects," pp.17-28.
The use of New York City's welfare programs in keeping arrests of derelicts at a minimum is described.
Murtagh maintains that the application of the penal code
to cases of alcoholism and human degradation is logically and philosophically unsound, and that legislators,
law enforcement agencies, and the general public should
be converted to this view.

Downs, Thomas M. "The Hospital," pp. 29-38.
This report of the Alcoholism Unit in the Philadelphia
General Hospital includes case histories and a summary
of short-term treatment routines. The purpose of the
unit is to "dry out" the person and then to counsel him
about personal problems and introduce him to other
alcoholism rehabilitation programs such as Alcoholics
Anonymous. The program is described as meeting only
a part of the alcoholic's needs.

Ford, John J. "The Private Agency," pp. 40-43.
Ending in an appeal for financial aid, the author discusses experiences of the Volunteers of America in Baltimore and New York City and outlines how the private
agencies save public funds.

McCarthy, Henry L. "The Public Agency," pp.
44-53.
Preventive programs are McCarthy's principle concern
as he introduces the problem of increasing the alcoholic's initiative to work. The major problem is in
finding so-called 'hidden' alcoholics and treating them
before they hit skid row.

Lohman, Joseph D. "Law Enforcement, Jails, and
Prisons," pp. 54-62.
Punitive measures are condemned as a hindrance to rehabilitation. Although it is difficult to reestablish social
interaction after severe isolation, enlightened programs
in jails and prisons should include both physical rehabilitation and opportunities for social interaction.

Gooderham, Clyde. "The Utah Program," pp.
63-69.

Treatment: Alcoholism 239

Gooderham discusses rehabilitation methods in Utah, especially the use of Alcoholics Anonymous and other religious and secular service organizations. There is a brief outline of the homeless alcoholic problem in America as a whole.

Secretary's Committee on Alcoholism, Department of Health, Education, and Welfare. Alcoholism: Activities of the United States Department of Health, Education , and Welfare. Washington, D.C.: U. S. Government Printing Office, 1965. Pp. 59.
This report describes the activities of new agencies concerned with alcoholism and the elements necessary for mobilizing and coordinating programs of control and prevention in the United States. The scope of the program is outlined; community planning, training of personnel, and public education are cited as the Department's principal objectives. Various research and treatment programs funded by the government are listed.

Shay, Earl Russell. "Self Concept Changes Among Alcoholic Patients in Madison (Indiana) State Hospital Resulting from Participation Training in Group Discussion," unpublished doctoral dissertation, Indiana University, 1963. Pp. 219.
Eighteen self-committed males were participants in three-hour group discussion training periods for 12 days following a 12-day control period. Measurement by self-rating and rating by nurses and the investigator occurred at the beginning of the control period and at the beginning and end of the experimental period. Integration of personality occurred during the control (or "drying out") period, but there was a loss of adjustment. Adjustment of personality occurred during the experimental period. Successful therapy requires both integration and adjustment.

Sidlofsky, S. "The Role of the Prison Community in the Behavior of the Chronic Drunkenness Offender," unpublished master's thesis, University of Toronto, 1961 . Pp. 87.

Interviews with 29 chronic drunkenness offenders in
Toronto's Don Jail lead to the conclusion that life in the
jails is not a hardship for these men. Despite the lack
of rehabilitation or resocialization programs in jail ,
chronic drunks find a measure of stability, mutual social
support, and a quasi-familial setting, none of which are
assured on the outside.

Sternberg, David. "The Development of Small-Group,
Short-Term Treatment Centers for Offenders in America, " unpublished master's thesis, New York University,
February, 1964. Pp. 191.
After a discussion of the dysfunctionality of American
penitentiaries, recent experiments to meet the classic
dilemmas of prison organization by small group treatment of delinquents are summarized. Highfields, Start,
and Provo are described at length, from secondary
sources. Later chapters cover Halfway House, criticized
effectively for the short duration of its efforts, and
Synanon, seen as perpetuating dependency in a "protective community. " Legal and psychotherapeutic issues
are outlined.

Third Annual Institute on the Homeless and Institutional
Alcoholic. New York: National Council on Alcoholism,
1958. Pp. 60.
This publication consists of eight essays. Four of the
authors (Murtagh, Greene, Briggs, and McKinney) discuss potentialities for the rehabilitation of alcoholics
through various specific agencies. The others discuss
the treatment of incarcerated alcoholics (Wright, Mac-
Cormick) or consider the more general problems of poverty and skid-row subculture (Rubington, Plunkert).
        Murtagh, John M. "Potentialities for Rehabilita-
tion: Through the Law, " pp. 8-10.
The author, chief Magistrate of New York City and Vice
President of the National Council on Alcoholism, regrets
the traditional public attitudes toward skid row inhabitants and cities these attitudes as the principal reason
that courts do not act in a more sympathetic and en -
lightened way. The approximately one million annual
drunkenness arrests in the U.S. indicate the severity of

the problem. Hopefully the extensive research and educational programs will alter existing negative attitudes.

Briggs, Cecil C. "Potentialities for Rehabilitation: Through the Salvation Army, " pp. 11-14.
The manager of the Salvation Army's Men's Social Service Center of Chicago outlines the clinical, work-therapy and religious aspects of his program. Citing a number of brief case histories, he defends the efficacy and modernity of the Salvation Army's programs and methods. The religious emphasis is seen as a useful element in reaching and maintaining effectual relations with the patients and it is often a valuable support for them.

Greene, Earle. "Potentialities for Rehabilitation: Through the Volunteers of America, " pp. 15-17.
The supervisor of Volunteers of America's Men's Rehabilitation Programs in Baltimore cites his mentor , Major John J. Ford, and field experiences in Baltimore to justify his agency's program of institutional and recreational care for only those who abstain from alcohol, both before admittance to and during participa - tion in the program. Vocational   rehabilitation   is emphasized.

McKinney, George F. "Potentialities for Rehabilitation: Through Alcoholics Anonymous in a   Prison Setting, " pp. 18-23.
A chaplain at New York State's Wallkill Prison traces the origin, operation and necessity of Alcoholics Anonymous groups in his prison and discusses the desirabil - ity of such programs for penal institutions in general . Without citing the comparative recidivism rates of inmates exposed to Alcoholics Anonymous and those not exposed, he argues that inmates who have been involved in prison Alcoholics Anonymous programs are less likely to return to prison. Thus, Alcoholics Anonymous programs in prison reduce state expenditures.

Weight, Roberts J. "A Penitentiary Treatment Program, " pp. 24-31.
The warden of the Westchester County, New York penitentiary outlines the general programs of employment , medical care, counseling and therapy carried on in his prison. He discusses the role of Alcoholics Anonymous ,

particularly the success of the Alcoholics Anonymous meetings conducted on the prison grounds to which persons in   surrounding communities are invited.

Plunkert,   William J.   "The Indigent Man and Alcoholism, " pp. 32-40.
Various urban renewal projects and rehabilitation programs are reviewed in a brief survey of the   general problems of skid row with an   emphasis on alcoholism. The efforts underway and the   program goals are   encouraging, but the magnitude, speed, and comprehensiveness of almost all programs need to be improved.

MacCormick, Austin H. "Penology and Alcoholism," pp. 40-49.
The author surveys the history of penal institutions in Europe and America; American jails generally are very inferior.   However, he is encouraged by programs like the Santa Rita Rehabilitation Center and by the increasing use of Alcoholics Anonymous within prisons.   It is suggested that if alcoholics are to be jailed they should be treated rather than punished or viewed simply as custodial burdens.

Rubington,   Earl.   "The Skid Row Subculture," pp. 50-60.
Seeking the causes of the "revolving   door" process , Rubington suggests that the main cause of recidivism is the skid-row subculture.   Compliance to the norms of the culture by drinking provides at least limited companionship and friendship. The experience of being arrested and jailed simply contributed to alienation and makes the positive aspects of skid row more attractive.

Trice, Harrison Miller.   "A Study of the Process   of Affiliation with Alcoholics Anonymous, "   unpublished doctoral dissertation, University of Wisconsin, 1955 . Pp. 252.
Interviews were conducted with 252 alcoholics,   119 of whom were affiliated with Alcoholics Anonymous. Res - pondents answered questions about their   experiences with A. A. Analysis revealed a three-stage process   of affiliation, including experiences before the first meeting, those at the first meeting, and those   immediately

after the first meeting. Comparisons between the sub-samples reveal distinctive characteristics of the process of successful affiliation with A. A. "Pre-Alcoholics Anonymous" therapy is recommended to enable clinicians to reduce barriers to affiliation.

Viaille, Harold D.   "Prediction of Treatment Outcome of Chronic Alcoholics in a State Hospital," unpublished doctoral dissertation, Texas Technological College , 1963. Pp. 112.
The author attempted to construct prediction tables that would estimate the probability that a patient with particular characteristics would benefit from a treatment program. Criterion measures were whether the patient dropped out of the treatment program, ratings by hospital counselors, and a follow-up study two months after dis - charge. Variables included in the prediction tables were selected in a review of previous research. The research site was a state psychiatric hospital with a treatment program for chronic alcoholics. Subjects were 117 male alcoholics, half of whom were used in the construction of the tables, and half in their validation. Efficiency of prediction ranged from 55 percent to 82 percent.

DRINKING AND ALCOHOLISM: ETIOLOGY AND PATTERNS

BOOKS

Diethelm, Oskar (ed.) Etiology of Chronic Alcoholism. Springfield, Illinois: Thomas, 1955. Pp. 229.
Five essays on various approaches to the etiology and treatment of chronic alcoholism are introduced by a summary of "research on chronic alcoholism" by the editor. A paper on psychopathology and character structure draws from a study of 161 psychiatric case histories to conclude that alcoholism is not a single disease but rather constitutes a symptom which can be located in several disorders, each requiring a different diagnosis and treatment. An article on "Familial and Personal Background of Chronic Alcoholics" by Manfred Bleuler reports an analysis of the life histories of 50 severe alcoholics under treatment at a psychiatric clinic. Other papers in the volume contrast the constitutions of Swiss and American alcoholics, report biochemical experiments on emotions and alcoholism, and explore the cultural factors producing the low rates of alcoholism among the Cantonese in New York City.

Gibbins, Robert J. Chronic Alcoholism and Alcohol Addiction. Toronto: University of Toronto Press, 1953. Pp. 57.
Etiological theories of alcohol addiction and other abnormal drinking patterns are outlined. Variables considered include elements of physiology and heredity, psychopathology, emotional situations, tolerance, mental disorder, drug use, and social and cultural factors. The author rejects the "alcoholic personality" concept but does review studies of the relation between personality variables and alcoholism. There are also reviews and evaluation of current treatment procedures and

special sections describing and evaluating the Yale Plan Clinics, hospital and drug treatment, and Alcoholics Anonymous.

Lucia, Salvatore P. (ed.) Alcohol and Civilization. New York: McGraw-Hill, 1963. Pp. 416.
This book reports the proceedings of a symposium which brought together physicians, sociologists, psychiatrists, psychologists, lawyers, and educators. Positive and negative effects of alcohol on the body, the mind, and society in general are considered.

McCord, William and McCord, Joan. Origins of Alcoholism. Stanford University Press, 1960. Pp. 193.
A longitudinal study of alcoholism is based on a secondary analysis of case histories from the Cambridge-Somerville delinquency study. Intensive data were collected on 255 boys by the Cambridge-Somerville Youth Project. The 29 boys who later became alcoholics are compared to the 226 who did not. After reviewing current theories of alcoholism, the authors analyze "predisposing factors" such as parental conflict and neural disorder. They concentrate on "dependency conflict," a concept referring to the tension in a person between the need to be loved and the strong desire to suppress this need. The alcoholic is likely to have intense dependency needs and to be confused because of inadequate specification of the male role. He develops an "independent facade" during youth which may crumble under adult pressures for independence and masculinity. There follows the collapse of the self-image of independence and the emergence of the repressed dependency trait. The onset of alcoholism may be "triggered" by the presentation of drinking as an attractive way of life, the frustration of dependency urges in childhood, and attacks on the man's self-image of independence.

Pittman, David J. and Snyder, Charles R. (eds.) Society, Culture, and Drinking Patterns. New York: Wiley, 1962. Pp. 616.

Papers about drinking in modern complex societies are arranged in five major sections: drinking in anthropological perspective, observations on the modern setting, social structure and drinking patterns, the genesis and patterning of alcoholism, and responsive movements and systems of control. Several of the papers discuss the characteristics and problems of skid-row men.

Pollmer, E. Alcoholic Personalities. New York: Exposition Press, 1965. Pp. 157.
In this study of alcoholics (including skid-rowers) in Paris, alcoholism is defined as the regular consumption of alcohol in quantities which cause a deterioration of normal adaptive behavior. The alcoholic population is divided into six categories on the basis of sex and level of intelligence. A seventh category consists of "artists." Typical representatives of each category are described. A general conclusion is that alcoholism is brought on by the "subject's suffering from an exceptionally high degree of anxiety, the origin of which is unknown to him, and about which he is consequently unable to do anything."

ARTICLES

Allen, E. B. "Emotional Factors in Alcoholism," New York State Journal of Medicine, 44 (February, 1944), pp. 373-378.
Alcoholics' underlying motives for drinking ("hidden anxieties and strains") are discussed. The three cases whose histories are presented share these characteristics: a sense of inferiority, over-protective or over-emotional mothers, successful fathers, and inadequate heterosexual adjustment.

Armstrong, John D. "The Search for the Alcoholic Personality," Annals of the American Academy of Political and Social Science, 315 (January, 1958), pp. 40-47.
A review of research findings about the "alcoholic personality" leads to the conclusion that the research itself has been methodologically and substantively inadequate.

More rigorous research methods, better theoretical con-
ceptualizations, and co-ordinated research among several academic disciplines are necessary. Future
research will uncover a relationship between alcoholism
and personality.

Bacon, Selden D. "Inebriety, Social Integration, and
Marriage, " Quarterly Journal of Studies on Alcohol, 5
(June and September, 1944), pp. 86-125 and 303-339.
Interviews were conducted with all persons arrested in
eight Connecticut communities during a five-week period
in 1942. The most common charge was inebriety. Over
1, 200 inebriates are compared to various control groups
with reference to marital status, residential mobility,
occupational characteristics, recreation, and education.
Although persons with alcoholic psychoses are a distinct
minority of all inebriates, they have received the bulk
of the research attention. The present study attempts
to focus attention on the more common inebriate. In
general, the inebriate tends to be a nonparticipant in
social organizations. This is particularly true with respect to marriage. Less than half of the inebriates ever
were married and their marital separation and divorce
rates are many times higher than in the general population. In addition, the inebriates have higher residential mobility, more unemployment, hold jobs for
much shorter periods, are under-represented in high
status occupation, are unlikely to engage in recreation
and tend to do so alone or with casual acquaintances.
Non-membership and partial membership are accompanied by a lack of discipline, and excessive drinking is
an apparent shortcut to the pleasures of membership.
Excessive drinking itself leads to further withdrawal
from participation. Reintegration in organized groups
is an essential element in rehabilitation. Lack of marital association is a critical element in inebriety; it is
more significant than the absence of any other form of
affiliation. Inebriety does not cause failure to marry;
rather failure to marry suggests certain personality
trends that also are associated with inebriety. Both for
future research and for therapy, inebriates should be
classified on the basis of marital experience.

Bacon, Selden D. "Alcoholics Do Not Drink," Annals of the American Academy of Political and Social Science, 315 (January, 1958), pp. 55-64.
The title is designed to draw attention to public misconceptions about alcohol, drinking, and alcoholism. Both consumption of alcohol and alcoholism can be described in terms of sets of social norms and behavior. While these norms and behaviors overlap, the general public conception of this overlap is grossly misleading. In some respects drinking and alcoholism are antithetical rather than similar or identical.

Bailey, Margaret B. and Fuchs, Estelle. "Alcoholism and the Social Worker," Social Work, 5 (October, 1960), pp. 14-19.
Members of the New York City Chapter of the National Association of Social Workers responded to a questionnaire containing questions about the concepts of alcoholism and attitudes toward drunkenness. The traditional notion that alcoholism is a problem of "will-power" was not popular; instead the respondents subscribed to the theory that alcoholism is a symptom of underlying emotional disturbance.

Bailey, Margaret B. "Alcoholism and Marriage: A Review of Research and Professional Literature," Quarterly Journal of Studies on Alcohol, 22 (March, 1961), pp. 81-97.
Psychodynamic and sociological research relating to alcoholism and marriage is summarized, with particular stress on the marital status of alcoholics, the spouses of alcoholics, and family adjustment to alcoholism. A major conclusion: "Statistical analyses of marital status have demonstrated that the stereotype of the alcoholic as a marginal undersocialized member of society is no longer tenable. Alcoholics have a high rate of broken marriages, but many are living with their spouses."

Bailey, Margaret B. "Research on Alcoholism and Marriage," pp. 19-30 in National Conference on Social Welfare, Social Work Practice, 1963. New York: Columbia University Press, 1963.

Recent research and professional work on alcoholism and marriage is reviewed with emphasis on the role of the alcoholic's wife. Most of the studies support one of two theories: 1) the wife is a disturbed personality needing an alcoholic mate to dominate, or 2) behavior of the wife reflects changing patterns of interaction within the family rather than a reflection of pre-existing psychopathology. There is no typical pattern for the wives of alcoholics. An integrated psychosocial approach is necessary, and pat generalizations about the wives of alcoholics should be abandoned and particular cases of interaction taken into account.

Bailey, Margaret B., Haberman, Paul and Alksne, Harold. "Outcomes of Alcoholic Marriages: Endurance, Termination or Recovery," Quarterly Journal of Studies on Alcohol, 23 (December, 1962), pp. 610-623.
Wives of alcoholics (N=262) were interviewed in a project undertaken by the National Council on Alcoholism in New York City in 1961. This report used data from 69 interviews divided evenly into three groups: 1) wives with actively drinking husbands, 2) wives whose husbands had achieved sobriety, and 3) wives who had separated from or divorced their husbands. The greatest economic, social and psychological deviance was found in the group of dissolved marriages. Families where the husband achieved sobriety were highest in occupational status and lowest in deviance.

Bailey, Margaret B., Haberman, Paul W. and Sheinberg, Jill. "Identifying Alcoholics in Population Surveys," Quarterly Journal of Studies on Alcohol, 27 (March, 1966), pp. 300-315.
A number of respondents in a survey of the Washington Heights Health District (New York City) were identified as alcoholics. Later interviews with the same population showed that some people previously identified as alcoholics gave no indications of trouble with alcohol, while others not identified in the original survey indicated problem drinking. The original sample consisted of 4,387 households, with wives acting as informants.

Respondents in the second survey were the 99 persons identified as probable alcoholics and a comparable group initially identified as non-alcoholics. One-fourth of the "alcoholics" in the first survey did not admit to drinking problems the second time, and about the same proportion of those who reported problems the second time initially had given no indications of problem drinking. Apparently one's circumstances at the time of the interview influence his willingness to admit problem drinking.

Bartholomew, Allen A. and Kelley, Margaret F. "Incidence of a Criminal Record in 1, 000 Consecutive 'Alcoholics', " British Journal of Criminology, 5 (April, 1965), pp. 143-149.
This study addresses the question, "How often is the alcoholic a criminal?" Examination of clinical files of 1, 000 alcoholics treated at the Alexandra Clinic, an outpatient facility dealing with all socio-economic groups, revealed that about 36 percent have a criminal record. The authors agree with Glatt (1958): "The average alcoholic is not a criminal and does not come into serious trouble with the law." Any trouble connected with alcoholism is usually under the "drunk and disorderly" situation or some minor crime.

Blane, Howard T., Overton, Willis F., Jr., and Chafetz, Morris C. "Social Factors in the Diagnosis of Alcoholism, " Quarterly Journal of Studies on Alcohol, 24 (December, 1963), pp. 640-663.
About half of the 438 male alcoholics admitted to a hospital emergency ward over a ten-month period were assigned to an experimental treatment project. Characteristics of the assigned and those not assigned to the project are compared. Although both groups had a high incidence of unemployment and social isolation, those assigned to the project exhibited more indications of physical disorders, having a higher incidence of previous hospital admissions and medical-surgical complaints. According to the authors, these findings indicate that the medical staff have ambivalent attitudes toward alcoholism as a disease.

Bonney, Merl E. "Parents as the Makers of Social De-
viates," Social Forces, 20 (October, 1941), pp. 77-87.
Five cases of deviant social behavior (a juvenile delinquent, an alcoholic, a homosexual, a political radical,
and a suicide) are introduced and related to particular
patterns of parent-child relationships. A review of
research findings supports the theme that abnormal fam -
ily relationships create subsequent social deviation.

Button, Alan D. "A Rorschach Study of 67 Alcoholics,"
Quarterly Journal of Studies on Alcohol, 17 (March,
1956), pp. 35-52.
This is the first of four articles describing reactions
to the Rorschach and MMPI of 101 alcoholics in the state
hospital at Agnew, California. Only 67 Rorschach pro -
tocols are analyzed. Alcoholism and psychopathy are
seen as reactions to the strains engendered by increased
responsibility in adolescence and by the greater strains
of beginning a career and assuming family responsibilities. Alcoholics and psychopaths have low directivity.
Many alcoholics have much ambition making their in-
capabilities for perseverance particularly hard to bear.

Button, Alan D. "The Genesis and Development of Al -
coholism: An Empirically Based Scheme," Quarterly
Journal of Studies on Alcohol, 17 (December, 1956),
pp. 671-675.
The sample was 101 males hospitalized for alcoholism
in Agnew, California. Factors leading to alcoholism
include a psychologically or physically absent father ,
being the youngest child, feelings of social and sexual
impotence, feelings of hostility, schizoid defenses such
as individualism, withdrawal, and isolation, and depen -
ency "which serves to obviate the patient's and his
family's expectations that he will function as a re-
ponsible adult."

Cappon, Daniel and Tyndel, Milo, "Time Perception in
Alcoholism: A Study of Interval Estimation and Temporal
Orientation in Alcoholic Patients," Quarterly Journal of
Studies on Alcohol, 28 (September, 1967), pp. 430 - 435.

The notion that psychiatric patients exhibit a dysfunction in orientational percepts and have a foreshortened sense of past and future is tested on fifteen alcoholics at the Clinic of the Alcoholism and Drug Addiction Research Foundation (Toronto) and fifteen matched controls. Standard tests of time perception were used (verbal estimate, production and reproduction, future sentence completion tests, and multiple-choice questions regarding past, present, future). No measurable differences between alcoholics and non-alcoholics were found.

Chassell, Joseph. "Family Constellation in the Etiology of Essential Alcoholism," Psychiatry, 1 (November, 1938), pp. 473-503.
A psychoanalytic case history of a young man with an aggressive, hostile mother and mild father illustrates that the attribution of alcoholism to the combination of an indulgent mother and a harsh father needs modification. The neurotic mother and weak father also may foster alcoholism.

Clinebell, Howard J., Jr. "Philosophical - Religious Factors in the Etiology and Treatment of Alcoholism," Quarterly Journal of Studies on Alcohol, 24 (September, 1963), pp. 473-488.
A significant factor in the etiology of alcoholism is the vain attempt to satisfy deep religious needs by means of alcohol. Psychoanalytic, sociological, and philosophical views are presented and interrelated. Religious factors also are important in recovery from alcoholism. The concept of "surrender" receives particular emphasis.

Cranford, V. and Seliger, R. V. "Alcohol Psychopathology in a Family Constellation," Journal of Criminal Psychopathology, 5 (January, 1944), pp. 561-583.
Case histories of four generations of a family prone to alcoholism are presented. The heredity-environment problem is considered briefly. Following treatment, all living family members became abstainers.

De Lint, Jan E. E. "Alcoholism, Birth Order, and Socializing Agents," Journal of Abnormal and Social Psychology, 69 (October, 1964), pp. 456-485.

Interviews conducted with 276 female alcoholics at the time of their admission to the Addiction Research Foundation (1951-1962) are analyzed in a test of the hypothesis that youngest children are prone to alcoholism. The fact that the last-born is more apt to be raised by only one parent than other siblings appears to be more important than birth order as an etiological factor in alcoholism.

Gibbins, Robert J. and Walters, Richard H. "Three Preliminary Studies of a Psychoanalytic Theory of Alcohol Addiction, "Quarterly Journal of Studies on Alcohol, 21 (December, 1960), pp. 618-641.
The hypothesis that alcoholism is linked to repressed homosexuality is investigated in three experiments involving alcoholic patients, overt homosexuals, and normal control subjects. Two of the experiments measured recognition thresholds for words and a third used pairs of pictures, each pair consisting of a male and female symbol. Number of subjects in the experimental and control groups ranged from 10-20. In all three experiments responses of alcoholics were intermediate between those of homosexuals and normal subjects. Although subject to various interpretations, these results suggest that the psychoanalytic theory of alcoholism should not be lightly discarded.

Glatt, M. M. "Alcoholism, Crime and Juvenile Delinquency, " British Journal of Delinquency, 9 (July, 1958), pp. 84-93.
Glatt reviews studies of crime and alcoholism to dispel popular misconceptions about the alcoholic. The average alcoholic is not criminal and does not come into serious trouble with the law. Those alcoholics who commit asocial or antisocial acts do so only after many years of excessive drinking. Continued intemperance has disruptive consequences on family life endangering the personality of children. Complications and reactions to the unhealthy home climate create emotional instability, psychological disturbance, maladjustment and delinquency among the children of alcoholics.

Rehabilitation of the alcoholic is followed by improved relationships within his family. Therapeutic nihilism and defeatism may be due to misconceptions about the connection between alcoholism and psychopathology. The link between parental alcoholism and the child's insecurity is often overlooked; if it were brought to public attention the apathy about the treatment of alcoholics might decrease.

Guze, Samuel B., Tuason, Vicente B., Stewart, Mark A. and Picken, Bruce. "The Drinking History: A Comparison of Reports by Subjects and Their Relatives," Quarterly Journal of Studies on Alcohol, 24 (June,1963), pp. 249-260.
A study of 223 male criminals provided data which enabled researchers to estimate the reliability of the drinking histories obtained by interview. In 90 of the cases a relative was also interviewed, and 39 of these men were identified, by independent means, as alcoholics. A fifteen percent disagreement between relatives and subjects was found for the entire sample, and for the alcoholics the extent of disagreement was 26 percent. About 80 percent of the disagreements were a positive answer from the subject and a negative one from the relative. Using the subject's interview alone, 97 percent of the alcoholics could be identified; using relatives responses alone, only 41 percent could be identified.

Hall, Robert A. "Obsessive-Compulsive Features in a Case of Chronic Alcoholism," Psychoanalytical Review, 37 (January, 1950), pp. 73-78.
The case history of a 33-year-old soldier include detailed analysis of the obsessive-compulsive syndrome.

Harrington, L. Garth and Price, A. Cooper."Alcoholism in a Geriatric Setting," Journal of the American Geriatrics Society, 10 (February, 1962), pp. 197 - 211. Random samples of 56 alcoholics and 56 non-alcoholics at the Veterans Administration Center's domiciliary at Biloxi, Mississippi were compared with reference to 46 background variables, including criminal records, marriage histories, highest annual income, education, job histories, and mental and physical health. For most background variables, there was a significant difference between the alcoholic and non-alcoholic populations .

Henderson, J. P. "Alcoholic Craving From the Subjective Point of View," British Journal of Inebriety, 42 (July, 1944), pp. 44-51.
The autobiography of an ex-alcoholic describes the process of addiction.

Hilgard, J. R. and Newman, M. F. "Parental Loss by Death in Childhood as an Etiological Factor Among Schizophrenic and Alcoholic Patients Compared with a Non-Patient Community Sample," Journal of Nervous and Mental Diseases, 137 (July, 1963), pp. 14-28 . The effects of death of parents during childhood are investigated among patients at Agnew State Hospital (1, 561 schizophrenics and 929 alcoholic patients) and a control sample of 1, 096 residents of San Jose, California. Male alcoholics showed higher rates of loss of both parents than male controls; this finding did not hold for female alcoholics. Many aspects of general personality development are involved with parental loss . Early loss of the mother constitutes the greatest threat to later mental health, but the subject's relationship to the parent substitute is also an important element in his adjustment to adult role expectations.

Hill, Harris E. "The Social Deviant and Initial Addiction to Narcotics and Alcohol," Quarterly Journal of Studies on Alcohol, 23 (December, 1962), pp. 562 - 582. This essay is concerned with 1) conceptualizing social deviance so as to distinguish social pathology from idiosyncratic or personal pathology, 2) applying this formulation to the onset of addiction, and 3) highlighting research needs of the situation, e. g., determination of the desired state of euphoria, or whether initial addiction is to alcohol or drugs.

Hirshberg, Besse. "Alcoholism in the Case Load of the New York City Welfare Department," Quarterly Journal of Studies on Alcohol, 15 (September, 1954), pp. 402-412 .

The incidence of alcoholism among recipients of public assistance and the costs to welfare agencies of caring for alcoholics and their dependents is assessed. Case workers in 14 of 18 Welfare Centers in the New York City Department of Welfare reviewed their cases in an effort to identify alcoholics and problem drinkers. Among 110, 637 families, 533 alcoholics were identified and are described with reference to their age, sex, occupational status, and number of children per family unit. Five of the centers submitted data on each clients' educational status, religious affiliation, ethnicity, and health. Homeless men are not included in these statistics.

Jackson, Joan K. "The Adjustment of the Family to the Crisis of Alcoholism, " Quarterly Journal of Studies on Alcohol, 15 (December, 1954), pp. 562-286.
For three years the author was a member of the Seattle Alcoholics Anonymous Auxiliary, a group of about 50 women whose husbands, most of whom were members of Alcoholics Anonymous, were excessive drinkers. Data for this paper come from notes about the group's discussions of family problems. There are seven critical stages in family adjustment to alcoholism: 1) incidents of excessive drinking strain the husband - wife relationship, and attempts to minimize drinking as a problem lead to the avoidance of other, unrelated problems; 2) excessive drinking isolates the family socially and magnifies the importance of family interaction; 3) attempts to control drinking are abandoned and attempts to relieve tension produce marked emotional disturbances among children; 4) the wife controls the family because the husband no longer can maintain the roles of husband and father, and pity and protective feelings replace the wife's former resentment and hostility toward the husband; 5) having regained self-confidence, the wife separates from the husband; 6) wife and children reorganize the family without the husband and father; and 7) the husband achieves sobriety and family problems center around reinstating him in his former roles.

Jackson, Joan K. "Types of Drinking Patterns of Male Alcoholics," Quarterly Journal of Studies on Alcohol, 19 (June, 1958), pp. 269-302.
A sample of 245 white male alcoholics (clients of various social agencies) classified themselves as to their drinking patterns and companions. Interview data and responses to the Jellinek Drinking History Questionnaire and to psychological tests were analyzed in an attempt to isolate types in terms of duration of heavy drinking, preoccupation with alcohol and psychological involvement, attempts to control drinking and feelings of dis - couragement or helplessness about it, and disturbances in social relationships. The implications for research and treatment are discussed.

Jackson, Joan K. "Alcoholism and the Family," pp. 472-492 in Pittman, David J. and Snyder, Charles R.(eds.), Society, Culture, and Drinking Patterns. New York: John Wiley & Sons, 1962.
The author discusses problems of studying alcoholism in the family setting, reviews recent research on the subject, and outlines her own research which centered on a theory of family crisis. Dealing with alcoholism of the husband-father, the data consist of statements made by wives (N=157) while in group discussions about previous and current behavior of family members. The subjects all participated in Al-Anon Family Group meetings in Seattle from 1951 to about 1961. Family reaction to the crisis of alcoholism is patterned behavior similar to other crisis reaction, and families in which the husband-father is an alcoholic go through several distinct stages.

Jessor, Richard. "Toward a Social Psychology of Ex - cessive Alcohol Use: A Preliminary Report from the Tri-Ethnic Project," pp. 233 - 254 in Lefton, Mark, Skipper, James K., Jr., and McCaghy, Charles H. (eds.), Approaches to Deviance. New York: Appleton-Century-Crofts, 1968.
Neither the sociocultural nor the psychological approach explains behavior adequately. A third alternative, field theory, combines these two into a single comprehensive

approach. Merton's anomie theory is combined with
Rotter's personality theory to produce a theory of
deviant behavior that takes into account both personality substructure and sociocultural substructures .
The research site is a small town in southwestern
Colorado containing three distinct ethnic groups ,
Anglo-Americans, Spanish-Americans, and Indians .
Three separate studies of the community were completed: 1) interviews with a random sample of adults,
2) a survey of all students in the high school, and 3) a
socialization study in which mothers and fathers of high
school students were interviewed. The major research
problem is explaining the relative position of the three
ethnic groups with respect to excessive alcohol use.
Indians are most deviant, with Spanish - Americans in -
termediate between Indians and Anglo - Americans .
The relative positions of the three ethnic groups on
the personality variables are viewed as mediating between sociocultural variables and deviance.

Johnson, F. Gordon and Partington, John T. "Personality Types among Alcoholics, " Quarterly Journal
of Studies on Alcohol, 30 (March, 1969), pp. 21 - 34.
The question of whether there is an "alcoholic personality" was examined through a study of 186 male first
admissions to the Clinic of the Alcoholism and Drug
Research Foundation in London, Canada. Interview
schedules included a test of verbal intelligence and the
Differential Personality Inventory. Interview results
and psychiatric evaluations were used to identify five
personality types. Representatives of these types differ in terms of personal history, current interpersonal orientation, and future potential. It follows that
treatment programs oriented toward the traditional
medical model should be replaced by treatment-research
programs which explore patient interaction and apply
diverse treatment methods.

Keller, Mark. "Alcoholism: Nature and Extent of the Problem, " Annals of the American Academy of Political and Social Science, 315 (January, 1958), pp. 1-11.
This article by the editor of the Publications Division of the Yale Center of Alcohol Studies is the first paper in this volume of The Annals, entitled "Understanding Alcoholism. " The author reviews the basic statistics on alcoholism in the U.S., discusses several of the conceptual and methodological research problems, and summarizes the social correlates of alcoholism.

Keller, Mark and Efron, Vera. "Alcoholism in the Big Cities of the United States," Quarterly Journal of Studies on Alcohol, 17 (March, 1956), pp. 63-72.
Estimates of numbers of alcoholics and rates of alcoholism in cities of 100,000 or more in 1950 are presented.

Lemere, Frederick. "What Happens to Alcoholics, " American Journal of Psychiatry, 109 (March, 1953), pp. 647-676.
Life histories of 500 deceased alcoholics were obtained from members of their families. Findings are presented on the course of alcoholism in the subjects' lives, its effect on their health, and on complications such as suicide, psychosis, and dereliction. Statistical predictions are made as to the path and outcome of alcoholism for any group of alcoholics.

Lemert, Edwin M. "Alcoholism and the Socio-cultural Situation, " Quarterly Journal of Studies on Alcohol, 17 (June, 1956), pp. 306-317.
Theories of intercultural differences in inebriety are summarized and evaluated. Of particular interest is a social isolation theory of alcoholism, based on Durkheim's anomie and expanded by Cheinisse: the argument is that lack of moral consensus and detachment of the individual from the group are causes of alcoholism.

Lemert, Edwin M. "Educational Characteristics of Alcoholics: Some Critical Comments, " Quarterly Journal of Studies on Alcohol, 12 (September, 1951), pp. 475-488.

Data and comparisons that have been cited to support the view that significant educational differences distinguish the alcoholic from the non-alcoholic population are examined with reference to other factors highly correlated with education. It is concluded that the evidence is not convincing: "While this does not sanction the arbitrary statement that alcoholics are not less well educated than social drinkers or abstainers, nevertheless it frees us to entertain just such a hypothesis or even the contrary hypothesis, that alcoholics are drawn from a portion of the population which is better educated than the average."

Lerner, Arthur. "Attitudes of Male Alcoholic Inmates Toward Marriage, Family, and Related Problems," Mental Hygiene, 38 (July, 1954), pp. 468-482.
The sample consisted of 146 male alcoholic inmates in a Los Angeles jail who had histories of extended drinking and multiple arrests. Respondents recognized that their alcohol problems stemmed from a lack of self-confidence and of the respect of other persons. Their attitudes toward family and marriage were similar to those of non-inmate alcoholics. Recommendations are made for an orientation program for male alcoholic inmates. Understanding, love, and tolerance from family members and others are necessary parts of the rehabilitation process.

Lolli, Giorgio. "Alcoholism as a Disorder of the Love Disposition," Quarterly Journal of Studies on Alcohol, 17 (March, 1956), pp. 96-107.
Physiological factors may be involved but primarily alcoholism may be traced to distortions in the mother-child relationships. "It represents the abnormal survival in the adult of a need for the normal infantile experience of uniting pleasure of body and mind. The alcoholic rediscovers this experience in the course of intoxication." Successful treatment must include "restitution of the unattained love."

Mackay, James R. "Clinical Observations on Adolescent Problem Drinkers," Quarterly Journal of Studies on Alcohol, 22 (March, 1961), pp. 124-134.
A survey of 20 adolescent drinkers (12 boys, 8 girls) revealed extreme personal and economic deprivation in family life. Most of their fathers (and some mothers) had been alcoholics, and many fathers had deserted their families. Three illustrative cases are reported in detail.

McCarthy, Raymond G. "Changing Perceptions of Alcoholism," Canadian Journal of Corrections, 6 (April, 1964), pp. 180-197.
The Director of the Summer School of Alcohol Studies of Rutgers University reviews the trends in alcoholism research and treatment since 1940. There is more literature on alcoholism now than ever before, but it is difficult to evaluate the conflicting theories. Alcoholism is still regarded by many as a unique condition rather than an illness. A new emphasis on social psychiatry is needed, leading to the understanding and prevention of certain conditions like alcoholism which presently often are beyond the formal purview of either the medical professions or the agents of social control. Not only the prevention of alcoholism but also means of reducing its virulence should be sought by researchers.

McCord, William and McCord, Joan. "A Longitudinal Study of the Personality of Alcoholics," pp. 413-430 in Pittman, David J. and Snyder, Charles R. (eds.), Society, Culture, and Drinking Patterns. New York: John Wiley & Sons, 1962.
In the Cambridge-Somerville Youth Study, social workers recorded observations of 255 boys and their families. Twenty-nine of the boys later became alcoholics. Of their fathers 83 among 187 were alcoholic. Compared to the non-alcoholics, the alcoholic fathers were more apt to be irregularly employed or unemployed, nonparticipants, affectionate, passive in the family, in conflict with wives, erratically punitive or lax, aggressive, apt to feel "victimized," and most concerned with immediate

enjoyment. The pre-alcoholic boys tended to be unfavorably disposed to their mothers, indifferent to siblings, self-confident without abnormal fears, aggressive, sadistic, and hyper- or moderately active. The difference between pre-alcoholics and the adult alcoholics (fathers) are explained in terms of latent traits suppressed in early life.

Mendelson, Jack, Wexler, Donald, Leiderman, P. Herbert and Solomon, Philip. "A Study of Addiction to Non-Ethyl Alcohols and Other Poisonous Compounds," Quarterly Journal of Studies on Alcohol, 18(December, 1957), pp. 561-587.
Nine case reports of patients addicted to non-ethyl alcohols are presented. The patients were in surprisingly good physical condition. Their behavior during hospitalization for treatment was unusually submissive and compliant. The possible psychodynamics of non-ethyl alcoholism are discussed.

Mizruchi, Ephraim H. and Perrucci, Robert. "Prescription, Proscription and Permissiveness: Aspects of Norms and Deviant Drinking Behavior," pp. 151-167 in Lefton, Mark, Skipper, James K., Jr., and McCaghy, Charles H. (eds.), Approaches to Deviance, New York: Appleton-Century-Crofts, 1968.
Data from three previously published studies of drinking behavior are codified to illustrate how sociological studies can be both specific to immediate problems and useful for the development of general theories. Norms vary in the degree to which the proscriptive or the prescriptive dimension dominates. In addition, the normative order must be distinguished from the factual. Another important aspect is distinguishing the degree of social permissiveness with respect to the behavior. The authors suggest that permissiveness is a condition of unresolved anomie probably characteristic of periods of normative transformation.

Mowrer, Harriet R. and Mowrer, Ernest R. "Ecological and Familial Factors Associated with Inebriety," Quarterly Journal of Studies on Alcohol, 6 (June, 1945), pp. 36-44.

Two areas in Chicago with greatly contrasting inebriety
rates were compared. Inebriety in the Near South Side
was 30 times that of West Ridge. Extensive geographical
mobility, lack of friends, a high divorce rate and lack
of family contact are characteristic of the NSS section.
A consideration of birth order, family size, and other
variables leads to the conclusion that the pattern of the
alcoholic personality is formed by the early family relationship. Social factors subsequently define the basic
pattern but are not the direct causes.

Navratil, L. "On the Etiology of Alcoholism," Quarterly Journal of Studies on Alcohol, 20 (June, 1959) pp.
236-244.
Research on 600 male alcoholics institutionalized in
Austria between 1954 and 1958 is summarized. The relationship of alcoholism to gastric ulcers and surgery is
reviewed, and there are comments on the psychodynamics of alcoholism. Factors which play an important part
in the development of alcoholism include being a last -
child (particularly in sibships of five or more) and dependence on a dominating wife (whom the alcoholic
nevertheless resents). A high proportion of alcoholics
are found to suffer from stomach complaints;a considerable number had developed ulcers prior to their addic-
tive drinking.

Newton, R. R. "Alcoholism as a Neurotic Symptom,"
British Journal of Addiction, 46 (July, 1949), pp. 79-92.
Case histories of a man and a woman are presented.
Both were spoiled in childhood, were hindered in person-
ality development, and manifested hysterical tendencies.

Palola, Ernest G., Dorpat, Theodore L. and Larson,
William R. "Alcoholism and Suicidal Behavior," pp.
511-534 in Pittman, David J. and Snyder, Charles R.
(eds.), Society, Culture, and Drinking Patterns. New
York: John Wiley & Sons, 1962.
The sample is drawn from 121 attempted suicides admitted to King County Hospital (Seattle) and from 73 alcoholics on Seattle's skid row. The hypothesis is that alcohol

provides an alternative type of self-destruction and hence
is a defense against the total self-destruction of suicide.
A comparison of 73 active alcoholics and 50 members
of Alcoholics Anonymous supports the hypothesis. In
the combined sample, 21 (17 percent) had attempted suicide, and 36 (29 percent) had contemplated it. Two-
thirds of the Alcoholics Anonymous members had
attempted or contemplated suicide, compared to only 36
percent of active group. In 39 cases, suicidal thoughts
had occurred before subjects lost control in drinking,
but there were only ten cases of reported suicidal behavior after losing control in drinking. The findings
support the hypothesis that alcoholism may serve as a
substitute for suicide.

Palola, Ernest G., Jackson, Joan K. and Kelleher, D.
"Defensiveness in Alcoholics: Measures Based on the
Minnesota Multiphasic Personality Inventory," Journal
of Health and Human Behavior, 2 (Fall, 1961), pp.185-
189.
Two scales of Minnesota Multiphasic Personality Inventory were used to measure self-protectiveness and defensiveness. Active alcoholics (N=73) from Seattle's
skid row were observed to deny alcoholism while admit-
ting to depression. In contrast, a sample of members
of Alcoholics Anonymous (N=50) admitted alcoholism
but tended to deny their personal unhappiness.

Parker, Frederick B. "A Comparison of the Sex Tem-
perament of Alcoholics and Moderate Drinkers," American Sociological Review, 24 (June, 1959) pp. 366-374.
The Terman-Miles Masculinity-Feminity Test was given
to 50 male inmates of an alcoholic ward and to 50 moderate drinkers. With the exception of an hypothesis
predicting that alcoholics and moderate drinkers with a
preponderance of older male siblings would show higher
masculinity than those with older female siblings (which
was not supported) the results generally confirm the
traditional finding that alcoholics are less "masculine"
than non-alcoholics.

Podolsky, Edward. "The Private Meaning of Time to the Chronic Alcoholic, " Medical Annals of the District of Columbia, 28 (February, 1959), pp. 83-84.
To the alcoholic, time and reality (nearly synonymous) are oppressive. The alcoholic uses alcohol to erase time and to modify his time sense in oblivion.

Podolsky, Edward. "The Sociopathic Alcoholic, Quarterly Journal of Studies on Alcohol, 21 (June, 1960), pp. 292-297.
Six case histories of alcoholic sociopaths are discussed. The author maintains that there is little difference between alcoholic sociopaths and non-alcoholic sociopaths. The sociopath's use of alcohol is seen as 1) an attempt to smooth over guilts and anxieties, and 2) an excuse for antisocial behavior (he would rather be blamed for alcoholism than sociopathy).

Popham, Robert E. "Some Social and Cultural Aspects of Alcoholism, " Canadian   Psychiatric   Association Journal, 4 (October, 1950), pp. 222-229.
Although most therapists tend to be interested in individual alcoholic cases and their backgrounds, the social and cultural aspects are of importance in prevention. Alcoholism, its cause, treatment, and how it is regarded are determined by the particular socio-cultural situation. The psychiatric and psychological approaches to the problem are complementary to the study of mass trends and group differences favored by the social scientists. The Jellinek Vulnerability-Acceptance Hypothesis is a theoretical perspective that may bring together these diverse approaches and account for the differences between nations in prevalence and type of alcoholism .

Robins, Eli, Murphy, George E. , Wilkinson, Robert H. , Jr. , Gassner, Seymour and Kayes, Jack. "Some Clinical Considerations in the Prevention of Suicide Based on a Study of 134 Successful Suicides, " American Journal of Public Health, 49 (July, 1959), pp. 888-899.
In St. Louis City and County in 1956-57, 31 of 134 successful suicides could be also classified as active alco-

holics. Mean duration of alcoholism for the sample was
20 years. Suicide is seen as a possible development of
the later stages of alcoholism.

Roebuck, Julian and Johnson, Ronald. "The Negro Drinker and Assaulter as a Criminal Type, " Crime and De-·
linquency, 8 (January, 1962), pp. 21-33.
This paper establishes a typology based on specific
arrest patterns to be used in the study of crime. Efficacy of the typology is revealed in a comparison of 40
Negroes having an arrest pattern of drunkenness and
assault charges with 360 Negro offenders having a variety
of arrest patterns. The "drunk pattern" group showed
more rigid family background and closer primary group
ties than the other population. Character development
seemed to have been successful to the point that hostility could be manifested only after inhibitions were weakened by alcohol.

Smart, Reginald G. "Alcoholism, Birth Order, and
Family Size, " Journal of Abnormal and Social Psychology, 66 (January, 1963), pp. 17-23.
It was hypothesized that later-borns and persons from
large families would be overrepresented among alcoholics, that the probability of alcoholism increased
with ordinal position, and that first-born alcoholics were
more likely to participate in psychotherapy. Analysis
of family backgrounds of 242 patients in three alcoholism
clinics in Ontario provided support for only one of the
hypothesized relationships, that between family size
and alcoholism.

Smith, Eugenia V. "Field Interviewing of Problem
Drinkers, " Social Work, 4 (October, 1959), pp. 80-86.
Problem drinkers (N = 476) interviewed twice previously
in state hospitals, prison rehabilitation centers or alcoholic outpatient clinics were interviewed in the community, often at the respondent's residence. Aspects of the
survey affecting rapport during the interviewing are discussed. Analysis of interviewing problems suggests
that problem drinkers are not as difficult to interview
as is often assumed. However, the sporadic problem

drinker may be more amenable to an interview at certain stages of his drinking cycle than at other times . Among the problems considered are the   mentally ill respondent, the drunken respondent and the misrepresentation of facts by the respondent. The writer, a social worker, concludes that "social work skills and training are invaluable for field interviewing in research follow-up studies."

Straus, Robert. "Alcoholism," pp.   434-447 in Rose, Arnold M. (ed.), Mental Health and Mental Disorder. New York: Norton, 1955.
Straus outlines briefly the relation between ethnicity and alcoholism, describes the mission of Alcoholics Anonymous, and contrasts homeless alcoholics and   alcoholic clinic patients with reference to their   social backgrounds, drinking habits, and probabilities of recovery .

Strayer, Robert. "A Study of the   Negro Alcoholic," Quarterly Journal of Studies on Alcohol, 22 (March, 1961), pp. 111-123.
Data on 44 Negroes (26 men, 18 women) admitted to the Connecticut Commission on Alcoholism Clinic over a period of nine and one-half years are contrasted to similar data on 1, 264 whites (1, 077 men, 187 women). Features of American Negro subculture are examined for possible significance in the development of patterns leading to excessive drinking, and to motivation for recovery. Negro patients have strong strivings for middle-class status and morality. The matriarchal organization of many Negro families contributes to the development of dependency patterns in Negro men, which in turn may lead to excessive drinking. The matriarchal Negro home places heavy responsibility on the woman and she may drink as a mode of tension reduction. Negro alcoholics , like their white counterparts,   must be treated as individuals and stereotypes must be avoided if therapy is to be effective.

Sutherland, Edwin H., Schroeder, H. G. and Tordella, C. L. "Personality Traits and the Alcoholic," Quarterly Journal of Studies on Alcohol, 11 (December, 1950), pp. 547-561.

Thirty-seven research studies that attempted to differentiate the personality traits of alcoholics from those of non-alcoholics are summarized and evaluated. The general conclusion is that there is no alcoholic personality prior to alcoholism. The basic criticism is that the studies have been inadequate methodologically.

Syme, Leonard. "Personality Characteristics and the Alcoholic," Quarterly Journal of Studies on Alcohol, 18 (June, 1957), pp. 288-302.
Research on personality and alcoholism published between 1949 and 1957 is reviewed in an extension of the work by Sutherland and his associates. There is no empirical basis for the notion that there is an alcoholic personality prior to alcoholism.

Tashivo, Michiko and Lipscomb, Wendell R. "Mortality Experience of Alcoholics," Quarterly Journal of Studies on Alcohol, 24 (June, 1963), pp. 203-212.
Alcoholics (N=1,692) treated in four California treatment facilities between 1954 and 1957 were subjects of periodic follow-up surveys through 1958. Data were obtained by personal interview, and from death certificates of subjects who died. The findings illustrate a high rate of premature deaths among alcoholics.

Ullman, Albert D. "Sociocultural Background of Alcoholism," The Annals of the American Academy of Political and Social Science, 315 (January, 1958), pp. 48-54.
Following a brief review of the literature, the author concludes that physiological and psychological theories of alcoholism often prove inadequate; they may at times be useful for description, but they have little predictive value. The remainder of this essay defends the proposition that alcoholism rates will be low in societies where cultural drinking norms do not conflict with the dominant behavioral drinking patterns. Orthodox Jews, Italians, and Chinese are examples of groups that are well-integrated and have low rates of alcoholism. No original research is reported here; Ullman simply argues that sociocultural, physiological and psychological factors all need to be taken into account.

Vanderpool, James A. "Alcoholism and the Self-Concept, " Quarterly Journal of Studies on Alcohol, 30 (March, 1969), pp. 59-77.
Changes in drinkers' self-concepts under controlled drinking and abstinence conditions were studied in a test of the hypothesis that alcoholics drink to improve their self-concept. One hundred alcoholics under treatment at Downey Veterans Administration Hospital in Downey, Illinois and the Chicago Alcoholic Treatment Center were divided into control and experimental groups of 50 subjects each and given several tests under controlled drinking conditions. Results showed that feelings of confusion and contradiction accompanying drinking contributed to the subjects' poor self-concepts. Feelings of self-esteem, self-confidence, and acceptance, adequacy, social worth, and tolerance to stress and strain were more negative while drinking. It is concluded that alcoholics have a poor self-concept and drink to escape from feelings of inadequacy or loneliness, but the drinking only confirms and aggravates the poor self-concept.

Wahl, C. W. "Some Antecedent Factors in the Family Histories of 109 Alcoholics, " Quarterly Journal of Studies on Alcohol, 17 (December, 1956), pp. 643-654. The effects of five antecedent factors (parental rejection or overprotection, loss of parent by death, divorce or separation, placement in sibling hierarchy, family size and religious affiliation) in the backgrounds of 109 male alcoholics admitted to the Elgin State Hospital (Illinois) in 1948 are evaluated. Findings are: 1) sibling position has no particular effect; 2) alcoholics tend to come from large families, perhaps because of the stresses attending large family membership, such as increased difficulty in identification with parents, intensified sibling rivalry, and economic deprivation; 3) religion has no clear effect; 4) rejection, rather than overprotection, is more frequently encountered in the alcoholic's parental background; 5) 37 percent of the sample lost one or both parents before age 15. Pathological parental attitudes and parental loss seem the most significant factors.

Witken, Herman A., Karp, Stephen A. and Goodenough, Don R. "Dependence In Alcoholics," Quarterly Journal of Studies on Alcohol, 20 (September, 1959), pp. 493-504. Three experiments were designed to compare alcoholics with non-alcoholics in their ability to differentiate their bodies or simple figures from their backgrounds. The three experiments consistently showed alcoholics to be more field dependent than non-alcoholics. Field dependence has also been shown to be high among recovered alcoholics, ulcer patients, obese people, and among ten-year-old boys whose mothers were classed as psychologically "growth constricting."

Wolf, Irving, Chafetz, Morris E., Blane, Howard T. and Hill, Marjorie J. "Social Factors in the Diagnosis of Alcoholism. II: Attitudes of Physicians," Quarterly Journal of Studies on Alcohol, 26 (March, 1965), pp. 72-79.
It is hypothesized that failure to diagnose alcoholism is related to two sets of attitudes, namely 1) the generalized operative presumption that alcoholism occurs primarily among derelicts, and 2) the preference of physicians for a medical diagnosis over one which includes psychological and social factors. Fifteen physicians of the Massachusetts General Hospital were given semistructured interviews; the interview data indicate that the hypothesized attitudes exist. The range and effect of these attitudes are often intertwined with personal and professional perceptions.

Zwerling, Israel. "Psychiatric Findings in an Interdisciplinary Study of Forty-six Alcoholic Patients," Quarterly Journal of Studies on Alcohol, 20 (September, 1959),
A battery of psychological and physiological tests were given to 46 alcoholics, 23 of whom had been "dry" for two years or more. The entire group was found to be schizoid, dependent, depressed, hostile, and sexually immature: ". . . there is a basic sense of estrangement, of separateness from people, or withdrawal from close interpersonal relationships. Even in subjects with the facade of outgoing, sociable behavior, it becomes quickly apparent that not far beneath is this sense of isolation."

OTHER WORKS

Armstrong, Renate Gerboth. "Personality Structure in Alcoholism, " unpublished doctoral dissertation, Uni - versity of Colorado, 1957. Pp. 205.
Hypothetical differences in personality structure between alcoholic males and non-alcoholic males were investi- gated among 50 alcoholic patients from the Colorado State Hospital and 50 non-alcoholic members of various civic groups in Boulder. Each subject rated himself, his mother, father, wife, ideal wife, and ideal self on a standard instrument. In accordance with neo-Freudian theory, alcoholics manifested greater discrepancy than non-alcoholics with respect to self-ideal self, wife-ideal wife, and self-ideal wife. Compared to the non-alco- holics they had more intense but fewer emotional reac- tions, and manifested greater passivity and aggression . Findings not compatible with the hypothesis were that alcoholics tended to describe the father as affectionate and submissive, the mother as dominant and aggres- sive, and did not identify with the mother. Armstrong proposes revision of neo-Freudian theory with respect to parental constellation and alcoholism.

Bailey, Margaret B. , Haberman, Paul W. and Shein- berg, Jill. Distinctive Characteristics of the Alcoholic Family. New York: The National Council on Alcohol- ism, 1965.
This is the final report of a three-year study supported by the Health Research Council of the City of New York. It attempts to identify distinctive interaction patterns of families with alcoholism which otherwise comparable families do not share. The total sample (N=430) con- sisted of three groups: alcoholics, persons with other health problems, and "normals. " Respondents had been interviewed three years previously in a community health research project, making possible some excellent stud- ies of interview reliability. Findings indicate that alco- holics are characterized by lower-class origin and remembrance of childhood as an unhappy period of life . Children of alcoholics revealed behavioral disorders such as stuttering, unfocused fears, temper tantrums , and trouble in school.

Jackson, Joan Katherine. "Social Adjustment Preceding, Accompanying, and Following the Onset of Alcoholism," unpublished doctoral dissertation, University of Washington, 1955. Pp. 360.
The relationship between alcoholism and social adjustment was studied among 56 male alcoholics hospitalized in a Washington sanitarium. The extent of alcoholism was measured by the Jellinek Drinking History and extent of social adjustment was determined from an evaluation of subjects' life histories. Findings are that alcoholism and maladjustment are directly related. The respondents always had had problems relating to peer groups, women, and their parents. Alcoholics tend to have histories of social isolation.

Mueller, Stanley Robert. "The Effects of Alcohol Upon the Alcoholic's Conformity Behavior and Mood State," unpublished doctoral dissertation, Boston University, 1965. Pp. 201.
The hypotheses were that under the influence of alcohol alcoholics would behave more independently and report more positive mood states than non-alcoholics. Thirty male alcoholics and 30 male psychiatric nursing aides from the Veterans Administration Hospital in Brockton, Massachusetts, took alcohol in regulated doses. Conformity decreased among all subjects. It is proposed that alcoholism creates dependency rather than dependency creating alcoholism.

Mulford, Harold A. and Wilson, Ronald W. Identifying Problem Drinkers in a Household Health Survey. National Center for Health Statistics Series 2, No. 16. Washington, D. C.: U. S. Government Printing Office, May, 1966. Pp. 46.
This pamphlet reports a test of the feasibility of using a field survey approach to identify problem drinkers in an urban setting. A cluster sample of the adult population of Cedar Rapids, Iowa, was interviewed. In addition, known alcoholics were added to the sample and this fact was concealed from the interviewers. The Iowa Index of Trouble Due to Drinking and the Iowa Index of Preoccupation with Alcohol were incorporated into the instrument. The study represents an attempt to test validity and general feasibility of using Guttman scaling

procedures to identify alcoholics. The findings confirm that members of the general population will discuss their drinking behavior and are not offended or
disturbed by these inquiries. Results were similar to
previous findings: about three percent of the general
population sample received scores indicating problem
drinking. There was a high degree of agreement among
the indexes used in the study; the Preoccupation scale
and the Trouble with Alcohol index identified three out
of four lower-status known alcoholics, and one out of
three upper-status known alcoholics. The degree of pre-
cision demanded of a measure is a matter of judgment
and ultimately turns upon the question of practical utility. Several guides are suggested for future research
to improve the indicators.

Plunkert, William J. and Holmes, Douglas. New York
City Alcoholism Study: A Report. New York: The National Council on Alcoholism, 1962. Pp. 76.
To identify city needs and resources in preparation for
developing a program for alcoholics, about 14,000 questionnaires were sent to sample populations of physicians,
clergymen, business organizations, labor unions, social
agencies, health agencies, agencies for the homeless,
hospitals, and Alcoholics Anonymous groups serving
residents of New York City. This report summarizes
the responses from informants in each of the nine categories. There seems to be little public interest in alcoholism. It is asserted that more than 80 percent of the
skid-row population suffers from alcoholism and only
about 30 percent of these persons are willing to be
treated. There is need for greater public awareness
about alcoholism, expansion of treatment resources,
and more research.

Popham, Robert E. and Yawney, Carole D. Culture
and Alcohol Use, 2nd ed. Toronto: Addiction Research
Foundation, 1967. Pp. 52.
This bibliography is limited to items with an "essentially anthropological orientation." Although sociological studies of "culturally heterogeneous legal and social

groupings such as chronic drunkenness offenders" were specifically excluded, many of the items are relevant to the study of the relationship between drinking and dis- affiliation (e. g., "The Skid Row Sub-Culture"). The 452 items are divided into four main categories; non- literate peoples, literate peoples, ancient peoples, and theoretical studies.

Sharir, Judith. "Reaction to Failure-Stress in Alco- holics: A Study in Selective Recall, "unpublished doc- toral dissertation, Boston University, 1966. Pp. 127. Thirty male alcoholics who attended outpatient clinics and 30 non-alcoholics were contrasted in their memory of success in experimental tasks, and in performance on subsequent tests after an initial failure. Alcoholics remembered failures while non-alcoholics tended to remember successes. Following failure, alcoholics made more mistakes than non-alcoholics.

Singer, Erwin. "Personality Structure of Chronic Al- coholics, "unpublished doctoral dissertation, New York University, 1949. Pp. 315. Case histories and psychological test performance of 73 chronic alcoholics in a Veterans Administration hospital were compared with various other groups of alcoholics and non-alcoholics. The investigator con- cluded that the chronic alcoholic came from a home where love and guidance were lacking, and as a conse - quence acquired much hostility (which he turned inward upon himself) and low self-esteem accompanied by feel- ings of worthlessness and depression. Alcohol serves as a conscience-relaxer which permits the expression of hostility.

Wellman, Wayne Myron. "The Social and Occupational Stability of Alcoholics--A Study of 830 Male Patients in a Private Sanitarium," unpublished doctoral disser- tation, State College of Washington, 1956. Pp. 84. Wellman analyzes results from narco-psychiatric inter- views (by means of sodium penthothal) with 830 male alcoholic patients at Shadel Sanitarium, Seattle, Wash- ington. Findings refute the idea that alcoholics have low social and occupational stability. A large percentage of the subjects had satisfactory life adjustment. It is concluded that alcoholism is not a "poverty disease" and that the deterioration associated with alcoholism may be limited to only certain segments of the personality; many alcoholics appear to be socially stable and perform their occupational roles adequately.

TRANSIENCY AMONG YOUNG PERSONS

BOOKS

Armstrong, Clairette P. Six Hundred Runaway Boys:
Why Boys Desert Their Homes. Boston: Richard G.
Badger, 1932. Pp. 208.
The causes of running away from home are sought in "a
statistical determination of the comparative frequency of
uncommon and deleterious factors" among 660 delinquent
runaways as contrasted with other groups of delinquent
and nondelinquent boys. Subjects and control samples of
"unlawful entry" and "incorrigible" delinquents were arraigned before the children's court of New York City.
Variables studied include age, intelligence, nationality,
education, economic status, family structure, overcrowd-
ing in the home, family pathology, nervous habits, physical defects, recidivism, experience in institutions, concomitant offender, and companions. In addition to the
statistical analysis, there are 21 pages of case histories.
Family maladjustments are identified as the general cause
of a boy deserting his home, but part of the blame is attributed to the inflexibility of the school system.

Minehan, Thomas. Boy and Girl Tramps of America.
New York: Farrar & Rinehard, 1934. Pp. 267.
The author tramped for two years to collect over 500 case
histories of adolescent transients. This work is an attempt to paint a picture of the lives of these young tramps--
their backgrounds, attitudes, ideas, religious and moral
beliefs, and goals. Included also is a chapter on the history of vagabondage and an argument for national youth
camps and greater public education about homeless youth.
The basic statistical data appear in the appendix. There
is a short glossary of tramp terms.

Outland, George E. Boy Transiency in America: A Com-
pilation of Articles Dealing with Youth Wandering in the
United States. Santa Barbara: Santa Barbara State College, 1939. Pp. 141.

This collection of 20 previously published articles by the author is informally divided into three sections: one dealing with education and educational histories, a second dealing with the work of the Federal Transient Service, and a third having to do with causal factors. Much of the data come from the Central Intake Bureau of the Transient Service of the Federal Emergency Relief Administration in Los Angeles. There is some overlapping and repetition.

Shaw, Clifford R. The Jack-Roller. Chicago: University of Chicago Press, 1930. Pp. 205.
A seventeen-year-old delinquent boy began this life history and added additional sections during the next five years. The material is presented just as he wrote it. Shaw outlines the social and cultural background of the boy and analyzes the life-history data, revealing the boy's point of view, his "social world, "and the sequence and importance of events in the life history. In addition, there is a discussion of the theory and methodology of the life-history approach to social research.

Srivastava, S. S. Juvenile Vagrancy: a Socio-Ecological Study of Juvenile Vagrants in the Cities of Kanpur and Lucknow. London: Asia Publishing House, 1963. Pp. 252.
This study of juvenile vagrancy in India combines a sample survey of 300 juvenile vagrants in the cities of Kanpur and Lucknow with an analysis of the spatial and institutional organization of the cities. Increased vagrancy is seen as a consequence of urbanization. The vagrants' recreational, drinking, and work habits are discussed in a vivid chapter on activities and habit patterns. The author suggests that companionship affiliation is a major factor in juvenile vagrancy. The general background of vagrants is discussed at length. Numerous statistical tables and diagrams are provided.

ARTICLES

Falstein, Eugene I. "Juvenile Alcoholism: A Psychodynamic Case Study of Addiction," American Journal of Orthopsychiatry, 23 (July, 1953), pp. 530-551.

The subject of this detailed case history started drinking at age 12 after the sudden death of his father. He drank alone to get drunk and achieve stupor. Eventually, despite a rejecting mother, he managed a "normal" adjustment.

Nylander, Towne. "Wandering Youth," Sociology and Social Research, 17 (July-August, 1933), pp. 560-568. There are four types of transient boys: 1) the single boy on the road, 2) "road kids" traveling in gangs of from 10 to 100 who work together in large groups, 3) the "gay cat," an "embryonic tramp" or hobo, the single boy who has been on the road for some time and has developed wanderer's characteristics, and 4) the boy who has come under control of a "pervert" and been taught to steal or beg. Boy transiency might be controlled by the establishment of permanent farms throughout the country; these subsistence farms would not produce for market. The ideal farm would be more like a summer camp than a reform school.

Outland, George E. "Determinants Involved in Boy Transiency," Journal of Educational Sociology, 11 (February, 1938), pp. 360-372. Verified information was obtained from social agencies for 3,352 boys (modal age = 18) registered at the Los Angeles Federal Transient Service in 1934-35. Most were native whites with urban backgrounds and were "on the road" for the first time. Major reasons for their leaving home were economic stress, interpersonal stress in the home (over half were from broken homes), and "love of adventure." Despite a decline in the number of transient boys, some type of permanent federal framework for care of migrants of all ages is necessary.

Outland, George E. "The Federal Transient Program for Boys in Southern California," Social Forces, 14 March, 1963), pp. 427-432. From December 12, 1933 to November 21, 1934, Los Angeles attracted at least 10,000 transient boys who registered with the Federal Transient Service. In 1935 southern California was the destination of more wandering boys than any other section of the United States. A unified Social Welfare Department for Boys attempted to reduce transiency and to effect rehabilitation of boys coming to the department. The author describes both the camp program (group treatment) and individual counseling and concludes that the program is relatively successful in its rehabilitation efforts. Continuing federal aid is needed as the problem of wandering boys is national in scope.

Outland, George E. "The Federal Transient Service as a Deterrent of Boy Transiency," Sociology and Social Research, 22 (November-December, 1937), pp. 143-148.
Critics of the Federal Transient Service had suggested that the service and its camps encouraged transiency by providing easy sustenance for transient boys. Outland responds to this argument by demonstrating that the problem of transient boys existed long before the creation of the service. He maintains that a derelict youth is almost always the product of a broken or unstable home and that the establishment of service camps has very little effect in encouraging boys to leave home and take to the road.

Outland, George E. "Should Transient Boys Be Sent Home?" Social Service Review, 9 (September, 1935), pp. 511-519.
Two hundred fifty-one young men who were sent home by the Los Angeles Boys' Welfare Department were studied in a follow-up survey to determine the effectiveness of this approach to boy transiency. Seventy percent were found to be firmly resettled in their home environs. Comments of agency representatives and caseworkers involved are included. Justification is seen for a nationally planned rehabilitation program for the returned transient boy.

Outland, George E. "Sources of Transient Boys," Sociology and Social Research, 19 (May, 1935), pp. 429-434.
Partial results are reported of a study of 10,000 tran-

sient boys who registered in Los Angeles between December 12, 1933, and November 21, 1934. The distribution of transients by state and city of origin is given, and economic disruptions in particular states which might have accounted for their relative contributions of boy transients are noted. California is seen as a positive goal for most of the transient boys.

Youmans, F. Zeta. "Childhood, Inc.: Child Beggars," The Survey, 52 (April-September, 1924), pp. 462-464. The author is concerned with the exploitation of children and discusses the lives and hardships of child beggars, children in street trades, and children on the stage. It is suggested that vigorous public education and community action is needed if child labor is to be reasonably and effectively regulated.

OTHER WORKS

U.S. Department of Labor. Twentieth Annual Report of the Chief of the Children's Bureau. Washington, D.C.: U. S. Government Printing Office, 1932. Pp. 36. Pages 5-9 of this report deal specifically with transient boys. A Children's Bureau survey conducted in March, 1932 obtained data from chiefs of police and social agency heads in 25 United States cities. Data are fragmentary; it is suggested that the survey may underestimate boy transiency. The complicating effect of the Depression is noted, and it is argued that a general shortage of funds and information make federal funding and coordination imperative.

JOURNALISTIC AND LITERARY ACCOUNTS

BOOKS

Alkie (pseud.) An Alcoholic's Story. Cape Town: Miller, 1957. Pp. 157.
A South African physician describes how his social drinking eventually led to alcoholism. After a broken marriage and two unsuccessful attempts at rehabilitation in an institution, he was cured by the Antabuse-Alcoholic treatment and the influence of Alcoholics Anonymous. An appendix includes a synopsis of the symptoms, types, and treatments of alcoholism and an outline of the rehabilitation program of Alcoholics Anonymous.

Allsop, Kenneth. Hard Travellin': The Hobo and His History. New York: New American Library, 1968. Pp. 448.
A British journalist traces the history of the hobo in America, noting changes from the Civil War period through the "peak" of hobo life in the late 1920's and the Depression and on to the hitchhiking era of the present. The political and social attitudes of the hobo are described, including their support for the Populists in the 1890's. A detailed treatment of the hoboes' techniques of survival and their origins is presented. In addition, art, literature and the mass media are reviewed in an assessment of the public image of the hobo. Allsop sees the hobo life as a quest for freedom from mechanization, efficiency, and profits. Hoboes are the last free Americans able to maintain a distance from organized society; the costs of maintaining this distance are noted. In addition to his thorough historical analysis, Allsop obtained primary data by traveling about the United States in search of hoboes. Given the high employment at the time, he was surprised at the relatively large number he found.

Anderson, Dwight. The Other Side of the Bottle. New
York: A. A. Wyn, 1950. Pp. 258.
The author, a member of the Research Council on the
Problems of Alcohol and director of the National Committee on Alcoholism, presents the case for treating
alcoholism as a psychological or physical disorder rather than as a moral problem. Personal experiences are
supplemented by discussion of various past and pro-
jected programs and theoretical approaches to the treatment of alcoholics. The book is directed to the layman.

Anderson, Nels. The Milk and Honey Route: A Handbook
for Hobos. New York: Vanguard, 1931. Pp. 219.
Anderson wrote this volume under a pseudonym (Dean
Stiff). He regrets that so much has been written about
hoboes by men who knew so little about the life of the wandering man, and attempts to correct the situation by
painting a true picture of the hobo life. It is described
as a profession in its own right, demanding of its members particular standards of dress, manners and behavior. There is a extensive glossary of hobo terms.

Augustin, Joseph. The Human Vagabond. London: Hutchinson, 1933. Pp. 256.
This collection of sketches of British tramps and their
habitats is based on the author's personal experience a-
mong them. The style is generally novelistic, and no
theory of homelessness or vagabondage is expounded.

Aydelotte, Frank. Elizabethan Rogues and Vagabonds.
Oxford: Clarendon Press, 1913. Pp. 187.
This literary study of the Elizabethan thief and his methods draws on his characterization in the fictional literature of the time and on a number of anomalous articles
known as rogue pamphlets. The most popular of this
short-lived genre were the works of Robert Greene, a
master rogue who wrote five pamphlets on "conny-catch-
ing" (swindling) during the last two years of his life
(1591-92). Also of interest is Thomas Harman's Caveat
for Commen Carsetors (1566) which provided a warning,
along with an outline of various deceits, for the vagabond.
The popularity of the works of Greene and Harman

prompted others to take up this style, and it became increasingly fictionalized, eventually reaching pure fiction in Fielding's Jonathan Wild. Aydelotte includes a discussion of legislation against vagabonds and a study of the origins of vagrancy, which he relates to the change from medieval feudal systems to the modern system of land tenure.

Bartlett, Willard William. The Man by the Side of the Road. Westerville, Ohio: Albert, 1938. Pp. 62.
Individuals encountered by the author as he travelled through the United States and around the world are depicted. The central figures of the portraits usually are marginal in some way. Most are spiritually or mentally broken and isolated.

Beck, Frank O. Hobohemia. Rindge, N.H.: Richard R. Smith, 1956. Pp. 95.
A minister to "low road" society recounts experiences and observations of personalities encountered early in the 20th century. He includes character pieces of hobo types (a "mission stiff," a skidder, a "richman, poorman, beggarman, thief,") and some famous persons (Jane Addams, Emma Goldman).

Benson, Ben (Hobo). Hoboes of America: Sensational Life Story and Epic of Life on the Road. New York: Hobo News, 1942. Pp. 96.
Ben Benson, writing after his re-election as King of the Hobos in August, 1941, discusses the history of the Hobo conventions (first held in Britt, Iowa, in 1900). The text is a series of articles on hobo life, including discussions of methods of travel, various hobo age groups, personal feelings and perceptions, female hoboes, and the community spirit of hoboes. Illustrations and cartoons are included.

Brissenden, Paul F. The I. W. W.: A Study of American Syndicalism. New York: Russell & Russell, 1919. Pp. 438.
This detailed history of the I. W. W. contains an account of its attempts to organize the homeless man.

Brown, Edwin A. "Broke": The Man Without the Dime. Boston: Four Seas, 1920. Pp. 370.
Beginning with some experience among homeless men in Denver, the author visited about 30 cities, often staying in uptown hotels but spending his days in informal questioning among the homeless. He pleads for the construction of a municipal emergency house in every city.

Brown, John. I Was a Tramp. London: Selwyn & Blount, 1934. Pp. 280.
Born in the north of England in 1907, Brown left school at 16 and went to sea. Later he was an unemployed tramp, occasionally working as an itinerant laborer in England, living in workinghouses and casual wards. Having developed an interest in socialism, he subsequently began work as a political organizer in England. Finally he entered Durham University and then Oxford, where he took a degree in Economics and Political Science.

Carew, Bampfylde-Moore. An Apology for the Life of Bampfylde-Moore Carew, Commonly Known Throughout the West of England by the Title of "King of the Beggars" and "Dog Merchant-General." London: Goadby, 1750. Pp. 151.
A shorter version of the following work.

Carew, Bampfylde-Moore. The Life and Adventures of Mr. Bampfylde-Moore Carew, Commonly Called "The King of the Beggars." London: Printed for A. Millar, E. Dilly, J. Hodges, and J. and R. Tonson, 1782. Pp. 246.
The author left school and joined the gypsies at age 15. Numerous European and American experiences as well as his motives and feelings are recorded in this autobiographical account (written in the third person). Gypsy life is described in considerable detail. This work served as a model for much of the later autobiographical writing on mendicancy.

Chaplin, Ralph. Wobbly: The Rough-and Tumble Story of an American Radical. Chicago: University of Chicago Press, 1948. Pp. 433.

Written by one who "helped to lay the foundations for radicalism" in the labor movement, this account includes some references to work among the homeless men.

Chesterton, Mrs. Cecil. In Darkest London. London: Stanley Paul, 1926. Pp. 255.
The author learned about homelessness by becoming a homeless woman for a time. The book describes her search for each night's lodging, the various facilities for homeless women, and the types who frequent them. She vividly describes nights in shelters for women, lodging houses, Salvation Army houses, and the life on the street. Unable to get work, she sells matches, begs, and spends nights wandering the streets. She maintains that homeless men receive better treatment than homeless women.

Clapp, Charles, Jr. Drinking's Not the Problem. New York: Thomas Y. Crowell, 1949. Pp. 179.
By use of his own story, informal case histories of friends, and personal research the author hopes to aid the potential alcoholic. Essential to his argument is the idea that alcoholism is symptomatic of a greater, underlying problem. Given individual will and commitment, and with the aid of the numerous available church, medical, and social service groups, the alcoholic can find direction in life.

Clouston, Harry. The Happy Hobo. London: Stanley Paul, 1937. Pp. 288.
On a bet with friends, this New Zealander started out from a local hotel (with neither money nor clothes) to bum his way around the world. This work is a series of anecdotes about the first five years of his adventures, which are varied and vividly described. The motivations and perceptions of this world traveler are perhaps different from the average hobo, but his experiences and feeling of wanderlust are similar to those expressed in other works in this field. He supported himself by working at various odd jobs, including seaman and pavement artist. In the United States he "rode the rails." He spent time on London's skid row, and comments: "Once

a man sinks below a certain level of decency, not only does he find it hard to retrieve his position, but he also loses the desire to lift himself out of the morass."

Couch, W. T. (ed.) These Are Our Lives: As Told by the People and Written by Members of the Federal Writers' Project of the Works Progress Administration in North Carolina, Tennessee, and Georgia. Chapel Hill: University of North Carolina Press, 1939. Pp. 421. Life histories of common people were gathered by the Federal Writers' Project. Writers conducted informal interviews with their subjects and stories are told in the subject's words. Among the life histories are "Didn't Keep a Penny," the story of a Negro who had worked at various odd jobs and was reduced to down-and-out circumstances through marriage and subsequent divorce. In "I Can Read and I Can Write," the protagonist encounters union difficulties because of his race and loses his job on the railroad even though he had over 30 years' experience.

Cowdrey, Robert H. A Tramp in Society. Chicago: Francis J. Schulte, 1891. Pp. 288.
A novel about a tramp who finds a patron and eventually proves he can make it in upper class society.

Crawford, James Hunter. The Autobiography of a Tramp. London: Longmans, Green, 1900. Pp. 328.
The narrator, of gypsy parentage, relates the story of his life and illustrates the difficulties and simple pleasures of transiency. The account is a series of anecdotes about growing up and living as a rural 19th century vagabond.

Davies, William Henry. The Adventures of Johnny Walker, Tramp. London: Jonathon Cape, 1926. Pp. 256. This account of the travels of the author through the United States and England begins at the Chicago World's Fair. After a brief period as a cowboy in the West, Davies decided to give up work and live as a beggar, considering it a noble life. Differences between begging in the United States and England are noted, and the British situation preferred. Methods of begging and obtaining lodging are described. Davies points out how the Salvation Army, missions, and workhouses have had an ill effect on the begging profession.

Day, Beth. No Hiding Place. New York: Henry Holt, 1957. Pp. 273.
Vincent Tracy's alcoholic descent leads from a secure and well-to-do childhood, a place in cafe society, and a promising Fifth Avenue job to poorer hotel rooms, the Bowery, the streets, sanatoria, public hospitals, and jails. Both the descent and the hard trip back are traced in this biography. Believing that alcoholism is not a disease, but rather a problem of will, he "dried out" and proceeded to help other alcoholics, first informally and finally at the Tracy Farms, which he established in upstate New York.

Devere, William. Tramp Poems of the West. Tacoma, Washington: Cromwell, 1891. Pp. 102.
The generally humorous narrative poems in this anthology are based on the author's experience in a mining camp. Main themes are gambling, drinking, and un—forgettable characters. The dialect seems authentic, but the verse is uneven.

Digit (pseud.) The Confessions of a Twentieth Century Hobo. London: J. Jenkins, 1924. Pp. 192.
The experiences of an Englishman traveling and working at odd jobs in the United States in the early 1920's are recounted in this autobiography. Except for a cursory description of a one-night stay in Bryant Park (New York), most of the author's attention is devoted to the verbatim recall of conversations with various people encountered in his travels. He maintains that human nature is "pure gold" and that Americans are not nearly as bad as most Englishmen suspect.

Dow, Father John (pseud.) Sobriety and Beyond. Indianapolis: S. M. T. Guild, 1958. Pp. 387.
An Alcoholics Anonymous member attempts to outline all the steps necessary for control over drinking, stressing attitude and prayer as the most significant points in the growth of the sober soul. A number of examples illus-

trating this outline are drawn from the author's experience, and there are many interesting anecdotes.

Douglas, Robin. Sixteen to Twenty-One. London: A. M. Philpot, 1925. Pp. 283.
This book contains a young man's recollections of London low-life. Douglas, falsely punished for theft at cadet school and refused a commission into the navy, begins his tramping at 16 and supports himself by entertaining with his banjo-mandolin in taverns and on the streets. He has some contact with the Salvation Army. Douglas takes the advice of a man on the street who tells him to look for "religion, ambition, and love." As the memoir ends, he has found love.

Edge, William. The Main Stem. New York: Vanguard Press, 1927. Pp. 212.
The author spent about a year on the road as a young man, and here describes his experiences as a casual laborer. Of particular interest is his interaction with an intelligent and articulate tramp. Edge's perspective reflects middle-class values, yet he is sympathetic and understanding of the tramp's predicament.

Floyd, Andress. My Monks of Vagabondia. Union, New Jersey: Self Master Press, 1913. Pp. 146.
A collection of stories from the files of Self Master Magazine illustrates life at the Self Master Colony. Chapters are introduced by relevant quotations ("When a boy goes to prison, a citizen dies."--Jacob Riis), and consider particular facets of vagabond life. The author wants to educate the public to the difficulties and potentials of the vagabonds, and the humor and tragedy of their lives. He maintains that, given understanding, most vagabonds can be helped to live more fruitful and decent lives.

Foster, William Z. Pages From a Worker's Life. New York: International Publishers, 1939. Pp. 314.
This work is described as a sequel to From Bryan to Stalin, a history of left-wing trade unionism in the United States. Foster recalls the 26 years (1891-1917) in which he rambled around the United States as a casual laborer. There is a chapter on hoboes. The conclusion is a plea

for the more general recognition of 1) the unrewarded toils of the masses and 2) the great success of socialism in the U.S.S.R.

Fox, Richard Michael. Drifting Men. London: Hogarth, 1930. Pp. 150.
Some previously published pieces are reprinted in this personal account of London vagabonds, English prison life, and European travels. Included are discussions of vagabonds' attitudes, literary interests, and poems and songs.

Free, James Lamb. Just One More: Concerning the Problem Drinker. New York: Coward-McCann, 1955. Pp. 211.
Written by a former alcoholic, this book is directed to problem drinkers and their families. Jellinek's list of phases and symptoms of alcoholism and Seliger's list of questions, "Are you an Alcoholic?" are included for self-diagnostic purposes. Classifications of types of drinkers and treatments are presented, and various forms of therapy are considered. The adjuvant roles of the physician, the clergyman, Alcoholics Anonymous, and other organizations are noted, and there are lists of committees and outpatient clinics of the National Committee on Alcohol.

Friedman, I. K. The Autobiography of a Beggar. Boston: Small, Maynard, 1903. Pp. 350.
This fictionalized autobiography and a collection of anecdotes about the Beggars' Club is an attempt to portray the "flavor" of begging as a way of life.

Fuller, Arthur F. An Odd Soldiery. Fort Worth: Solar Musical & Literary Bureau, 1910. Pp. 151.
A man plagued by bad health makes a plea for understanding. Beginning his career as a musician--choirmaster, organist, and composer--he was forced to abandon his lifework because of heart and nervous conditions. This book is an account of his life as a wandering peddler.

Fuller, Ronald. The Beggars' Brotherhood. London: George Allen & Unwin, 1936. Pp. 253.
Tramps and beggars in sixteenth - century Britain are described. Readers are warned that time and distance often romanticize beggar life and that high-waymen, beggars, and cheats were bestial creatures, "living in circumstances of appalling squalor." Yet the author himself does not avoid a certain romanticizing of tramp life as he records tramp folklore, poetry, and songs.

Gape, W. A. Half a Million Tramps. London: George Routledge & Sons, 1936. Pp. 352.
Gape ran away from home in 1914 after being punished by his father. This account describes the following 22 years in which he tramped through England, Canada, the United States and South America. His attempts to intro-duce mystery and surprise into the narrative are suc-cessful and entertaining. In a concluding statement he criticizes the inadequacies of private charities and con-cludes that public funds and public awareness of the tramp problem are the only avenues by which both the tramp and society can be helped.

Gardner, John E. Spin the Bottle: The Autobiography of an Alcoholic. London: F. Muller, 1964. Pp. 238.
The autobiography of the alcoholic son of a clergyman attributes alcoholism to an insecurity born of a bleak childhood milieu. Significant incidents on the road to al-coholism are recounted, all of which involve evaluation and reaction to the values and opinions of his family and friends. Gardner's description of the cause of the disease includes his life in the army and as a priest, alcoholic breakdown, and rehabilitation.

Gibbs, Archie. U-Boat Prisoner: The Life Story of a Texas Sailor. Boston: Houghton Mifflin, 1943. Pp. 208.
The hard life of a World War II hero is chronicled in this autobiography edited by Eugene Leuchtman. When Gibbs was a child, his mother was committed to a mental insti-tution and his father abandoned the family, leaving him to the care of a reform school. On the road at age 16,

he made his way hopping freights, panhandling, and doing migratory work in the South and West. Later he joined the merchant marine, but his employment remained sporadic and he spent many nights in flophouses. During the war he was prisoner on a U-boat for four days, changing his image from vagrant to hero.

Gleason, William F. The Liquid Cross of Skid Row. Milwaukee: Bruce, 1966. Pp. 256.
This portrayal of six days in the life of a priest who works with alcoholics on Chicago's skid row and of a man he is trying to help includes realistic descriptions of skid row and its men. The life histories of several alcoholics are related, and the institutions of skid row (Alcoholics Anonymous meetings, bottle gangs, jackrollers, panhandling, the revolving door, sickness and death) are seen in action.

Goldthorpe, Harry. Room at the Bottom. Bradford, England: Sunbeam Press, 1960. Pp. 48.
Depression and post-Depression experiences of the author in a career of rejection and rallying against authority are described. Much of the book reviews his experience as secretary of an Unemployed Association which rebelled and demonstrated against the poverty of the unemployed. Dealings with the Salvation Army, employment as car auctioneer, and travel to Africa also are related. The manifest purpose of the book is the demonstration that there is no room at the top. Hopefully, when men recognize this they will be prompted to greater cooperation.

Gray, Frank. The Tramp: His Meaning and Being. London: J. M. Dent & Sons, 1931. Pp. 268.
As a tramp in England the author spent most of his time on the road between workhouses and "casual wards" in rural areas, but also lived on skid row in London. An evaluation of the history of vagrancy and vagrancy legislation in England in terms of the author's personal experience concludes that a national effort is needed to coordinate and expand the care and rehabilitation of tramps currently undertaken at local levels. Interesting photographs of tramps are included.

Hapgood, Hutchins. Types from City Streets. New York:
Funk & Wagnalls, 1910. Pp. 379.
Part one of this account of the "low life" of New York
City is a description of Bowery men, thieves, and bo-
hemians. Part two, while still descriptive, attempts to
generalize about the life styles and perspectives of the
lower class. Hapgood contends that low-life characters
have an "instinctive dignity" which makes them "aristo-
crats."

Harris, Sara. Skid Row, U. S. A. New York: Doubleday, 1956. Pp. 285.
In the forward by John Murtagh, Chief Magistrate of the
City of New York, this is called a work that "offers us
an opportunity to understand these people, to understand
how they became what they are, and to determine how we
might make it otherwise." In separate chapters for each
respondent, the author tells the personal stories of a
group of skid-row denizens, and sketches the many and
complicated aspects of skid-row life.

Heath, Sidney. Pilgrim Life in the Middle Ages. London: T. Fisher Unwin, 1911. Pp. 352.
The author aims "to serve and entertain the general
reader who is interested in the religious pilgrimages of
older days," and portions of the work are directly relevant to the study of homelessness, e. g., "Hermits,
Anchorets, and Recluses" and "Pilgrim Inns." Pilgrim
shrines, pilgrim itineraries, and the religious context
are treated at length.

Higgs, Mary. My Brother the Tramp. London: Student
Christian Movement, 1914. Pp. 82.
The inadequacy and severity of legislation on vagrancy
is documented. The public interest and Christian charity would both be served by better regulated and more realistic treatment of tramps. Rehabilitation oriented to
improving the physical health and mental outlook of the
tramp would result in the eventual elimination of vagrancy.

Higgs, Mary. Down and Out: Studies in the Problem of Vagrancy. London: Student Christian Movement, 1924. Pp. 110.
In this revised edition of My Brother the Tramp, the author continues her appeal for Christian treatment of tramps and vagrants. This work is an overview, supported by anecdotes and references by an author who has immersed herself in the problems of vagrancy. The book is not a systematic study, but rather an intelligent and purposeful description.

Higgs, Mary. Glimpses into the Abyss. London: P. S. Kind & Son, 1906. Pp. 331.
English shelters, workhouses and cheap lodging facilities for derelict women are evaluated. The author and a companion undertook several "tramping" tours and their experiences are recounted in detail. The conditions of filthiness and discomfort allowed by superintendents of workhouses and shelters led her to conclude that such shelters should be maintained by the police. The establishment throughout England of regular facilities would improve the physical and the moral condition of vagrant women.

Holbrook, Stewart H. The Story of American Railroads. New York: Crown, 1947. Pp. 468.
Chapter 34 of this history of the railroads traces the rise of "Riders of the Rods and the Blinds" after the Civil War. Men who traveled illegally on railroads risked many dangers and cost the railroads a good deal. There are a number of interesting anecdotes.

Horsley, Terence. The Odyssey of an Out-of-Work. London: John Lane, 1931. Pp. 272.
After serving in World War I, Horsley was unable to find work in his chosen occupation of electrician, and took to the road in search of employment. Descriptions of lodging houses, Salvation Army posts, missions and jails are vivid and detailed. Included are accounts of meetings with prostitutes, thieves, and professional tramps. He is sympathetic to those who turn to drink

because of the strain of unemployment. While writing this book (age 35) he was still hoping to find a job.

Hotten, John C. (trans.) The Book of Vagabonds and Beggars: With a Vocabulary of Their Language (Liber Vagatorum), ed. by Martin Luther in 1528. London: John Camden Hotten, 1860. Pp. 64.
In addition to a classification of beggars and advice about how to treat each type, this work includes Martin Luther's original preface and 16 pages of vagabond vocabulary. Hotten's preface traces the history of the book.

Hough, Henry Beetle. An Alcoholic to His Sons. New York: Simon & Schuster, 1954. Pp. 245.
Although writing about an anonymous alcoholic subject, the author's goal is not a life story but rather a description of patterns of alcoholism, danger signs, public attitudes, and the attractive aspects of alcohol preceding addiction. Remembrances of pre-1914 U.S.A. and attitudes toward alcohol at that time are followed by discussions of college life, social drinking, marriage and 25 years of problems with alcoholism. Eventual hospitalization and involvement with Alcoholics Anonymous lead to a cure. The final note is a condemnation of the traditional legal and judicial approach to alcoholism and praise for the ideals, ideas, and methods of Alcoholics Anonymous.

Hueffer, Oliver. A Vagabond in New York. New York: John Lane, 1913. Pp. 229.
This autobiographical discussion of non-skid-row homelessness by one of the "literary vagabonds" recounts the adventures of a British vagrant in New York.

Jackson, Holbrook. All Manner of Folk. London: Grant Richards, 1912. Pp. 206.
There is a brief chapter romanticizing the vagabond. All men have something of the vagabond in them. They are drawn to the rakish figures of history and literature as well as to contemporary tramps who have answered the call of the open road, abandoning all care and participating in the full current of life.

Jackson, Jason. Overland Slim the Maverick. New York: Greenwich Book Publishers, 1957. Pp. 99.
A hobo's experiences are traced from placement in an orphanage through many years of travel on the road (including terms in a reformatory and a prison) to his eventual marriage and settling down as a small business man. He outlines his life as "the seven ages of the eventful life of a genuine American": orphanage, school for the blind, reform school, hobo, penitentiary, professional beggar and business man. During his traveling he spent time on the Bowery.

Jennings, Frank L. Tramping with Tramps. London: Hutchinson, 1932. Pp. 288.
After a several-week tramping excursion that included about 400 miles of walking, a London minister attempted to present a complete picture of tramp life. The result is typical of many similar works, although the religious-moral perspective reflects the author's vocation. Jennings, known as "The Tramp Parson," also wrote In London's Shadows, a description of similar excursions in several city slums.

Jusserand, Jean Adrien Antoine Jules. English Wayfaring Life in the Middle Ages. 4th ed. London: Ernest Benn, 1950. Pp. 315.
The environmental context is established in a discourse on roads and bridges in the fourteenth century, and of ordinary travellers, inns and alehouses, and roadside hermits. Following an evaluation of the security of the roads (there was little safety against either robbers or the sheriff's officers) the wayfarers are discussed at length. Considered separately are lay wayfarers (herbalists, charlatans, minstrels, jugglers, tumblers, messengers, itinerant merchants and peddlers, outlaws, wandering workmen, and peasants out of bond) and religious wayfarers (wandering preachers and friars, pardoners, and pilgrims). This classic historical work has been published in several editions since it first appeared (in French) in 1884.

Keeler, Ralph. Vagabond Adventures. Boston: James R. Osgood, 1872. Pp. 274.
Highly anecdotal and often discontinuous in its narrative and basic outline, this work describes the author's tramps about the United States and Europe. Although sometimes verbose and rather pretentious in philosophizing, Keeler presents an interesting picture of vagabond life after the Civil War.

Keen, Maurice Hugh. Outlaws of Medieval Legend. London: Routledge & Kegan Paul, 1961. Pp. 235.
This work is a scholarly, literary treatment of romances and ballads as sources of outlaw stories. In the conclusion outlaws are glorified as representing a violent effort to put down tyranny and injustice. The forest as a refuge, tales of Robin Hood, and other less well-known legends are considered.

Kemp, Harry. The Cry of Youth. New York: Kennerly, 1914. Pp. 140.
Some poems on poverty and vagabondage are included in this collection. Sample titles are: "The Boxcar," "A Tramp's Confession," and "In a Chop-Suey Joint."

Kemp, Harry. Tramping on Life: An Autobiographical Narrative. Garden City: Garden City Publishing, 1922. Pp. 438.
The wanderings and early loves of a literary tramp are described. His experiences include travel by freight car, arrests for vagrancy, common labor, travel as a seaman to the countries of the Pacific, college in Kansas, and publication of his first book.

Kennedy, Bart. A Tramp's Philosophy. London: John Long, 1908. Pp. 317.
The author of several other works on tramps and tramping here turns to more diverse aspects of life, including art, millionaires, women's suffrage, friends, sailors, and "doing nothing." Each chapter is an essay; all are tied together by the author's witty prose, frequent skepticism, and considerable insight. In this work, a tramp's view of the world is rational and entertaining.

Kerouac, Jack. On the Road. New York: New American Library, 1957. Pp. 254.
This novel of the modern tramp is of the same mold as Jack London's The Road. Driven by wanderlust and romantic thirst for experience, the tramp is now a hitchhiker instead of a train-jumper and uses marijuana instead of whiskey. Kerouac depicts the asocial existence of the tramp and the flexibility of his life.

Kromer, Tom. Waiting for Nothing. New York: Alfred A. Knopf, 1935. Pp. 187.
This first-person account is an excellent description of the thoughts, attitudes and problems of a skid-row man. There is no discussion of causes or background; the story begins and ends with the narrator homeless and unrehabilitated.

Larson, Melvin G. Skid Row Stopgap: The Memphis Story. Wheaton, Illinois: Van Kampen Press, 1950. Pp. 112.
The Memphis Union Mission, founded in 1945 under the leadership of Jimmy Stroud, became a center for both homeless men needing shelter and Memphis Youth for Christ. This book describes the first four years of the mission (which bases much of its work on an evangelical and fundamentalist Christianity) and conveys the "spirit" of Memphis as perceived by the author.

Lee, Edward. Prison, Camp and Pulpit. Oswego, New York: R. J. Oliphant, 1889. Pp. 288.
The life story of a runaway boy, soldier, criminal, and finally revivalist preacher and mission worker is the basis for a moralistic volume written in the hope that many will profit from the story and avoid the ways of evil and intemperance. The author worked among Bowery men in 1887-1888.

Light, Lou. The Modern Hobo: Ocean to Ocean. Santa Ana: Warden, 1913. Pp. 79.
One of the most egotistical of the hobo autobiographies, this work includes photographs of the author atop a passenger train leaving New York, being saved from falling off a freight in motion, etc. Drawing on his experiences

while hoboing from New York to San Francisco, Light contends that the main causes of vagrancy are economic, particularly the activities of trusts and permissive immigration laws.

Lindsay, Nicholas Vachel. A Handy Guide for Beggars. New York: Macmillan, 1916. Pp. 205.
Lindsay describes his adventures as a penniless wanderer among the people of southern and eastern United States.

Livingston, Leon R. (A-No. 1). The Curse of Tramp Life. Cambridge Springs, Pennsylvania: The A-No. 1 Publishing Company, 1912. Pp. 133.
Livingston warns of the dangers and hardships of tramping, particularly tramping on the railroad. The style is characteristically anecdotal, and is complemented by illustrations. At the beginning there is the story of a boy running away from home; the conclusion finds the author visiting the parents of this boy and learning of his death.

Livingston, Leon R. (A-No. 1). From Coast to Coast with Jack London. Erie, Pennsylvania: The A-No. 1 Publishing Company, 1917. Pp. 130.
In these anecdotes and descriptions of an adventure with Jack London, Livingston's style is unchanging. He continues to avoid "the least mention of anything that would be unfit reading for ladies or children." Numerous illustrations and the author's moralizing are scattered throughout.

Livingston, Leon R. (A-No. 1). Life and Adventures of A-No. 1, America's Most Celebrated Tramp. Cambridge Springs, Pennsylvania: A-No. 1 Publishing Company, 1910. Pp. 137.
Livingston left home at age 11 and travelled by boat and rail in the western hemisphere, working at odd jobs, stealing, and begging. His personal experience as well as his dealings with other tramps lead him to attribute the tramp problem to two main factors: wanderlust and the corrupting influence on youth of urban skid rows.

Livingston, Leon R. (A-No. 1). Mother Delcassee of the Hoboes and other Stories. Erie, Pennsylvania: The A-No. 1 Publishing Company, 1918. Pp. 136.
The central figure of this story--a Mrs. Delcasse of New Orleans--provided a lodging house for hoboes, many of whom wintered in New Orleans. In addition to tramp tales, the book contains a list of 47 types of tramps, e. g., moochers, sticks, stew bums, gay cats, and yeggs. In this ninth of his series, the author is typically concerned with moral ramifications of the tramping wanderlust.

Livingston, Leon R. (A-No. 1). The Snare of the Road. Erie, Pennsylvania: The A-No. 1 Publishing Company, 1916. Pp. 134.
The seventh of the author's works on tramp life, this volume focuses on the problem of youth being "snared" into vagrant life by the romantic tales of railroad hoboes. The story is based on the attempts of one neighborhood to protect its youth.

London, Jack. The People of the Abyss. New York: Macmillan, 1903. Pp. 317.
Life among London's lower classes, including skid-row men, is reported by one who lived among them in 1902 and 1903. The text is illustrated with very good photographs. London suggests that extreme variations in the distribution of wealth impugn the value which Western man has egotistically ascribed to "civilization."

London, Jack. The Road. New York: Macmillan, 1907. Pp. 224.
The life of a tramp depends on his ability to "hold down a freight," i. e., to hitch a ride on a train, and London explains all the subtleties of this and other tramp techniques. Also necessary to the professional tramp is the ability to suspend one's humane or social feelings and honor the "law," whether it be the law of a prison workyard, a gypsy camp, or a train yard gang. The tramp exists outside society and its standards but his longevity depends on knowledge of these standards and manipulation of them to satisfy his own ends.

Love, Edmund G. Subways Are for Sleeping. New York: Harcourt-Brace, 1956. Pp. 186.
Homeless persons the author has known in New York City are described. This is one of the few recent books directing attention to homeless persons who do not live on skid row.

McCarthy, Peter H. Twenty-two Years on Whiskey Row. Joliet, Illinois: 602 Collins Street, 1931. Pp. 48.
A reformed alcoholic describes his conversion and organization of a mission in a skid-row section of Joliet, Illinois. A few brief case histories illustrate the efficacy of religion in alcoholic rehabilitation.

Meriwether, Lee. The Tramp at Home. New York: Harper, 1889. Pp. 296.
A description of the working conditions and life styles of lower-class people in many parts of the country is based on the author's experience as a special agent for the United States Bureau of Labor. He spent one night on the Bowery. It is suggested that the worker's plight may be greatly improved through tariff reduction and a graduated land tax.

Milburn, George. The Hobo's Hornbook: A Repertory for a Gutter Hongleur. New York: Ives Washburn, 1930. Pp. 295.
This anthology of the literature of hobodom was compiled by the author as he traveled as a hobo in the United States. A distinction is made between hoboes and tramps: hoboes are seen as a special class of migrant laborer. A general introduction and comments on the selections demonstrate the basis in social experience of specific examples of hobo stories, songs, and poetry.

Miller, Harry. Footloose Fiddler. New York: McGraw-Hill, 1945. Pp. 326.
In this novel a young fiddler goes south with a sideshow act, west with gamblers, to Mexico with an opera company, and home again to Ohio.

Milligan, James. I Didn't Stay Honest. London: Sampson Low, Marston, 1936. Pp. 244.

The autobiography of an alcoholic adventurer describes his experience tramping in the midwestern United States. Some of the adventures recounted are bizarre and implausible.

Moore, Bob. Don't Call Me a Crook: My True Autobiography. London: Hurst, Blackett, 1935. Pp. 304. An English ship's engineer in and out of ports from Hoboken to Yokohama manages to get involved with alcohol, opium or smuggling at every turn. His inability to keep a wife, a shore job or to stay sober or out of trouble with the police does not stop him from picking up another bottle and boarding another ship.

Morgan, Murray. Skid Road: An Informal Portrait of Seattle. New York: Viking Press, 1951. Pp. 282. Acknowledging that formal histories of Seattle already exist, the author states that "this is the story of the others, of some who tried and failed and of some who achieved success without becoming respectable, of the life that centered on the mills and on the wharves." This is a journalistic, anecdotal history of Seattle, and the bulk of the narrative is not concerned with skid road.

Mullin, Glen H. Adventures of a Scholar Tramp. New York: Century, 1925. Pp. 312. A young college graduate who lived on the road in the early 1920's describes the character development and experiences of certain fellow tramps.

Neville, Hippo. Sneak Thief on the Road. London: Jonathan Cape, 1935. Pp. 349. A youthful Englishman travels hobo-style around England in order to purge a feeling of alienation. During the course of his travels, he begs, steals, and associates with many tramps and itinerants whose casual conversations are recorded in this work.

Norman, Frank. Stand on Me; a True Story of Soho. London: Secker & Warburg, 1959. Pp. 207. This book is the colorless story of a hippie down and out in the Soho district of London. The bulk of the story is devoted to an autobiographical narrative of his experiences with drugs and "birds," i.e., women. There is extensive use of cockney slang terms making the book somewhat difficult for the American reader.

O'Connor, Philip. Britain in the Sixties: Vagrancy. Baltimore: Penguin Books, 1963. Pp. 186.
O'Connor sees the problem to be not vagrancy but the poverty of the Establishment and the society in which the modern vagrant finds himself. The vagrant is merely trying to follow the Christian way, as did St. Francis or Christ himself, but modern society is too materialistic, judging a man by what he possesses rather than what he is. The vagrant who owns nothing attains a purity of self which cannot be reached by the man bound to possessions and to the ideology constructed to protect them. The vagrant has failed in modern society because that society is inconsistent and pathologically materialistic, and traits that made vagrants "failures" might make them successes in a future, idealistic, saner society. O'Connor discusses the philosophy of vagrancy, his own experiences on the road, and vagrants he has known.

O'Connor, Philip. The Lower View. London: Faber & Faber, 1960. Pp. 220.
This memoir tracing the life of a writer from isolation to social integration includes discussions of the same path with other writers (Stephen Spender, Francis Cornford) and personal insights into English society of the '40's. O'Connor's peculiar definition of the "lower view" tends toward an all-embracing and manipulative conception of society. He points out that this is not an affirmation of what he considers to be an ill-established social norm, but it is rather a compromise of isolationism with a concern for the improvement of society.

O'Connor, Philip. Memoirs of a Public Baby. London: Faber & Faber, 1958. Pp. 232.
The setting of O'Connor's autobiography is England between the 1920's and 1945. Preoccupied with his own depression and "a distaste for all that was deemed normal," O'Connor discusses the character traits that made him a social isolate: a cowardice manifested in individuality, and an inability to compete. Particularly revealing is his attitude of disgust toward publishers who ac-

cepted his automatic and unfinished poems; his delight in success was always soured by the thought that he had cheated to achieve the success.

Orwell, George. Down and Out in Paris and London. New York: Harper, 1933. Pp. 292.
This excellent account of the life styles, attitudes, and emotions of vagrants and slum dwellers in Paris and London includes a depiction of life in a London skid-row lodging house.

Petty, John. Five Fags a Day: The Last Year of a Scrap-Picker. London: Secker & Warburg, 1956. Pp. 233.
Petty relates his experiences as a down-and-outer in England during the 1930's. His characteristic mental attitude is one of hoping for the best but expecting to be disappointed. His loves, hates, anguishes, and continual oppression are portrayed convincingly.

Pfau, Ralph (with Al Hirshberg). Prodigal Shepherd, Philadelphia: Lippincott, 1958. Pp. 250.
Father Pfau is a priest who overcame his own alcoholism while a member of Alcoholics Anonymous and afterward assisted others to use A.A. The book illuminates the origins, methods, and clientele of A.A. Pfau knew Doherty Sherrin, its founder.

Phelan, James Leo. Jail Journey. London: Secker & Warburg, 1940. Pp. 384.
This account of life in an English jail during the 1930's was intended by its author to be a modern version of John Mitchell's Jail Journal. The underworld of prison life is described.

Phelan, James Leo. The Name's Phelan. London: Sidgwick & Jackson, 1948. Pp. 298.
This portion of Phelan's autobiography recounts his childhood and early adulthood, which occurred against a background of domestic strife and the Irish Civil War. The author's vagrancy is not explained by him in terms of his life history; instead he asserts that he is a tramp by instinct. The narrative, which ends with Phelan in

jail under a life sentence for murder, suffers from a lack of continuity and deals only obliquely with homelessness and the road.

Phelan, James Leo. Tramping the Toby. London: Burke, 1955. Pp. 244.
These impressionistic reminiscenses are based on a few months on the road in rural England. Tramps and their life styles are described.

Phelan, James Leo. Turf-Fire Tales. London: William Heinemann, 1947. Pp. 203.
Impressions of lower-class life in Dublin and the surrounding countryside are summarized in human-interest tales, some of which concern tramps, street urchins, and gypsies.

Phelan, James Leo. We Follow the Roads. London: Phoenix House, 1949. Pp. 220.
The author's theories of the road, based on his own personal experiences, are put forward, and the life-style and personality of the tramp are extolled. The book's main contention is that the tramp is not simply an unemployed social parasite upon whom work must be forced but rather a person who regards the complex life of the towns as a mistake. It is asserted that the instinct to tramp is inborn ("a man is a tramp before his mother is born") but that "civilization" may extinguish this instinct. There are numerous character sketches of tramps known by the author and vignettes of life on the road.

Pinkerton, Allan. Strikers, Communists, Tramps and Detectives. New York: Carleton, 1878. Pp. 412.
The massive unrest of labor in 1877 is seen as a consequence of "outside agitation" of the Communist Internationale operating through labor unions. A cursory description of tramps and their patterns of life helps to establish them as one of the classes most involved in the strikes. The author sees tramps as unwitting accessories to communist subversion.

Rickett, Arthur. The Vagabond in Literature. London: J. M. Dent, 1906. Pp. 206.

Several writers in whom the wandering spirit ("opposed to the routine and conventions of ordinary life") was dominant are discussed in this work. Subjects include Hazlitt, DeQuincey, Stevenson, and Whitman. The emphasis is on the authors' personal lives rather than their literary contributions.

Rosenfield, Joe, Jr. The Happiest Man in the World. Garden City: Doubleday, 1955. Pp. 292.
This book is the autobiography of a reformed alcoholic who began drinking heavily before age 15. Except for six months spent on a skid row in New Orleans he maintained strong family ties throughout life. His heavy drinking led to deterioration of his social relationships and irresponsibility, but he was rehabilitated through Alcoholics Anonymous. Descriptions of A.A. meetings and the writer's post-rehabilitation efforts as an A.A. official are emotional and vivid. Later he participated in a charity radio show, the "Happiness Exchange," and has since worked in charitable organizations to help alcoholics and drug addicts in New York.

Sanborn, Alvan Francis. Moody's Lodging House and Other Tenement Sketches. Boston: Copeland & Day, 1895. Pp. 175.
Descriptions of homeless men in Boston lodging houses are based on the author's experience as a participant-observer. Conversations are recounted, and there are several brief character sketches. The author is sympathetic, seeing the homeless man as an honest "noble savage" who need not conform to hypocritical or superfluous social conventions.

Seabrook, William Buehler. No Hiding Place. New York: Lippincott, 1942. Pp. 405.
In this autobiography of a writer, adventurer, and tramp the problems of reality perception and alcoholism are placed in the context of childhood experiences, family situations, sexual fantasies, and the difficulties of becoming a writer. Suffering rom acute alcoholism the author was voluntarily committed to an asylum. The psychological and physical suffering leading to rehabilitation are described.

Sinclair, Andrew.   The Halleluja Bum.   London: Faber
& Faber, 1963. Pp. 207.
An Englishman, suffering from "claustrophobia inside
a moat," tramps through the United States and reports
the adventures of a truly modern "beat" bum.

Smyth, Joseph H.   To Nowhere and Return. New York:
Carrick & Evans, 1940. Pp. 311.
The autobiography of a New England writer includes
childhood, travels as a writer, marriage and its collapse,
excessive drinking, destitution on the Bowery, and eventual rehabilitation. The story is made more meaningful
by the author's public stature (editor of several widely
known periodicals).

Stoneham, C. T.   From Hobo to Hunter.   London: John
Long, 1956. Pp. 222.
The career of this British wanderer includes "life of an
underdog" as a Canadian vagrant, hunting, and exploring.
He describes his experiences as farm worker, waiter,
cook, carpenter, traveling salesman, soldier in World
War I, pioneer and big game hunter in Africa, and final-
ly, as a writer.

Stuart, Frank S.   Vagabond.   London: Stanley Paul,
1937. Pp. 281.
At age 16 the author was dismissed from school after
his father was executed for gun-running. Since that time
he has wandered through Germany, France, and England.
This account dramatically relates his dealings with prostitutes, criminals, and other vagabonds. Stuart searched
for identity, seeking facts about his family. He relates
stories of the various jobs he held, particularly peddling,
and gives advice on fire-making, food gathering, and other
vagabond concerns.

Tully, Jim.   Beggars of Life.   Garden City: Garden
City Publishing, 1924. Pp. 336.
An orphan tires of working for slave wages and takes
to the road. He supports himself by begging, stealing,
selling his vote to a ward heeler, and various other
sporadic menial and spot jobs. The book stresses the

harsh realities of tramp life. The author rationalizes his years on the road as the gratification of a wanderlust.

Tully, Jim. Shadows of Men. New York: Doubleday, Doran, 1930. Pp. 330.
This author alternately lived on and off the road all his life, producing many novels, short stories, articles and documentaries about his experiences. Although he seems to have been more hobo than writer, all his works are well-written and lively. Six books preceded this one. Many of its episodes concern the discomforts of life in jail and the types of men encountered there.

Whitney, Elizabeth D. The Lonely Sickness. Boston: Beacon Press, 1965. Pp. 178.
Mrs. Whitney, the director and founder of the Boston Committee for Education on Alcoholism, relates the histories of several alcoholics who attempted rehabilitation with her help. Alcoholism is a disease that springs from deeper personality problems, and it requires both medical and psychiatric treatment. Regular counseling and participation in Alcoholics Anonymous are helpful. There is an appendix of questions and answers about alcoholism.

Willard, Josiah Flynt. The Little Brother: A Story of Tramp Life. New York: Century, 1902. Pp. 254.
This quasi-tragic novel deals indirectly with the adventures of a runaway boy while on the road. "The little brother" is thought to be the ward of his older sister, the schoolteacher, but when he dies in a hobo camp following a train accident, it is revealed that he was her illegitimate son. She swoons; the boy's father realizes his thoughtlessness and carries her away into the sunset.

Willard, Josiah Flynt. My Life. New York: Outing, 1908. Pp. 365.
Flynt's main interest is the other side of the hill (referred to as Die Ferne in this memoir). He serves as a fireman aboard an Atlantic freighter, studies geography and vagrancy in Germany, and tramps about Russia, enjoying his travels and making political comments.

Willard, Josiah Flynt. Tramping with Tramps: Studies and Sketches of Vagabond Life. New York: Century, 1899. Pp. 398.
Having tramped in the United States, Germany and Russia, the author reports about tramp life. The work is divided into four parts: 1) "studies" of the tramp way of life (e. g. , boy tramps, criminals, city tramps), 2) accounts of trips to far-away places, 3) character sketches, and 4) a discussion of the tramp language.

Willard, Josiah Flynt. The World of Graft. New York: McClure, Phillips, 1901. Pp. 221.
Exiles from organized crime give their opinions about the efficacy and ethics of municipal police forces in Chicago, New York, and Boston. Most informants were relatively well-to-do ex-thieves or police department bureacrats. There are systematic recommendations for reform and an amusing glossary of thief vocabulary.

Worby, John. The Other Half. New York: Lee Furman, 1937. Pp. 307.
This autobiography of a tramp who rode the rails in the United States and England dwells on the author's sex life and the sexual practices and perversions common among hobos and in skid-row subculture. The clear intent is to be racy and shocking; the book accomplishes neither and in the process sacrifices much credibility.

Wyckoff, Walter. A Day with a Tramp and Other Days. New York: Charles Scribner's Sons, 1901. Pp. 191.
Fresh from college in 1891, Wyckoff spent 18 months on the road as a casual laborer, traveling from Connecticut to California. He makes no pretense of being a scientific observer, but his recollections, perceptions and insights provide an interesting and sympathetic account of the life of the wanderer.

ARTICLES

Anderson, Paul Ernest. "Tramping with Yeggs," Atlantic Monthly, 136 (December, 1925), pp. 747-755.
Experience as a pseudo-tramp in northern Oklahoma and southern Kansas is the basis for this description of tramp life. Tramp life is seen as a type of fraternal existence complete with initiation rites and codes of ethics.

Benton, James. "Rest for Weary Willie: Life in a Federal Transient Camp," Saturday Evening Post, 209 (September, 1936), pp. 14-15, 87-90.
The funeral of a hobo in a federal transient camp is described. In an attempt to portray the meaning of being a transient, the personal life, feelings, and social circles of the hobo are portrayed. Details of the funeral service are noted, e. g., the difficulty of planning a service that would be meaningful to the circumstances of hobo life, the characteristics of transients who attended the service.

Blau, Raphel David. "Magnificent Hobo," Holiday, 18 (December, 1955), pp. 178-185.
A brief history of "General" Daniel Pratt's life and experiences as a wandering hobo centers upon one of his visits to Dartmouth College and the welcome he received from the students. Various examples of Pratt's lecturing style and his poetry give this article much color. It is noted that of all the persons listed in Dictionary of American Biography, Pratt is the only one whose occupation is recorded as "vagrant."

Carter, Barbara. "The Jalopy Nomads," The Reporter, 30 (May 7, 1964), pp. 31-33.
Little is known about those who wander from place to place by car. The problem is illustrated by selected cases, e. g., families who have been traveling for months in search of opportunities, but have found only hardship. The National Travelers Aid Association is cited for its increasing attention to poverty on the highways. Strict residency requirements for welfare and other assistance

indicate a general failure to recognize the plight of the jalopy nomads.

Cooke, John, "Vagrants, Beggars and Tramps, "Quarterly Review, 209 (October, 1908), pp. 388-408.
The history of vagrancy in Europe from Saxon times to the present is artfully summarized and spiced with numerous literary references (e. g., Erasmus, Scott, Hugo, Cervantes, Jonson, and Shakespeare). Centuries of legislation and official concern have not erased the problem; a 1905 census of vagrants in England and Wales counted over 60, 000. Laws against vagrancy have failed, but putting vagrants to work has not been properly attempted. It is recommended that Britain establish labor colonies patterned after such institutions in Belgium, Holland, and Germany. But vagrancy is best checked during childhood, and a useful first step would be the compulsory education in industrial schools of the estimated 30, 000 abandoned children in England.

Davies, William H. · "Beggars' Review, " Living Age, 263 (December, 1909), pp. 630-632.
Davies discusses the point of view of a beggar without spiralling into philosophy. Varieties of beggars are mentioned (e. g., "cattle stiff, " "mission") and the methods of each are outlined.

Dunn, Martha Baker, "Philosophy and Tramps, "Atlantic Monthly, 97 (June, 1906), pp. 776-783.
An erudite tramp introduced Montaigne's writing to the author; the consequences for the author's personal philosophy about individualism and tramps are considered. The spirit of errancy constitutes, in itself, a sort of individualism.

Edwards, Albert. "The Beggars of Mogador, " The Outlook, 101 (August, 1912), pp. 929-936.
Types of beggars found in Mogador (Morocco) include nomads from the South, ordinary beggars, various orders of begging friars, orphans, various types of entertainers, and divinity students. A brief treatment of the Moslem ethic of mendicancy is included.

Ellison, Jerome. "The Shame of Skid Row," Saturday
Evening Post, 225 (December, 1952), pp. 13-15, 48-51.
Using Detroit for specific illustrations of the dimensions
of homelessness, the author comments on the number of
skid-row men in the United States and their cost to tax-
payers (approximately $40, 000, 000 annually). Various
characteristics of skid-row life are described. A brief
outline of the rehabilitation of a homeless man illustrates
the means available if the government, private agencies,
and the general public would make active and concerted
efforts to meet the problems dramatized by skid row.

Franck, Harry A. "Three Hoboes in India," Century
Magazine, 79 (March, 1910), pp. 774-781.
The author tries to capture the flavor and local color of
Indian culture. There is a brief description of that as-
pect of the colonial administration which deals with the
vagrant.

Hoffer, Eric. "The Role of the Undesirables," Harper's
Magazine, 205 (December, 1952), pp. 79-84.
The author spent several weeks in a federal transient
camp in California in 1934. This experience is described,
primarily in terms of the characteristics of the approximately 200 men in the camp. It is noted that many of the
pioneers who settled America and Australia were failures, fugitives, and felons much like the men in the
transient camp. Those on the lower side of society must
be remembered, for they are an essential and sometimes
dynamic portion of the society.

Jacobs, Paul, "The Forgotten People," The Reporter,
20 (January, 1959), pp. 12-20.
Migrant workers are unprotected by federal welfare laws,
unions, or minimum-wage laws, and laws explicitly designed for their protection are ignored by the farmer
employers. One of the major problems is that child
labor must be used, illegally, to supplement the family
income. Also, there is no care available for children
too young to work. Recently, private organizations such
as the Catholic Council for the Spanish Speaking and the
American Friends Service Committee have attempted

to help the migrants. Some states are appointing invest-
tigating committees, and it is hoped that the needs of the
"forgotten people" will soon be more widely recognized
and met.

Keatley, Vivien B., "America's Displaced Persons,"
American Mercury, 63 (October, 1946), pp. 405-411.
The conditions of migrant workers and other farm laborers are described. Farm owners and government agencies have been indifferent to their plight. The problem
derives from the rapid industrialization of agriculture
and from the indifference of the American people to long-
term social inequalities.

Kemp, Harry. "Lure of the Tramp," The Independent,
70 (June, 1911), pp. 1270-1271.
This article contains an account of the irresponsible and
asocial condition of the hobo, description of a hobo
camp, and a presentation of a less common derelict
type, the "gay cat," who works occasionally for drink
money.

Kent, Mariner J. "The Making of a Tramp," The Independent, 55 (March, 1903), pp. 667-670.
After a business failure, the author spent several months
on skid row before obtaining steady employment once
more. He reproves those who scorn the unfortunate
homeless men and emphasizes the difficulties of the
homeless life.

Kerouac, Jack. "The Vanishing American Hobo," Holiday, 27 (March, 1960), pp. 60-61, 112-113.
This essay elegizes the past as a more pleasant time for
hoboes. Increased police surveillance and harrassment
of hoboes indicate a general public attitude of increased
disdain for them. Some of the old customs of hoboes are
noted. Famous men, (Franklin, Einstein, Buddha, and
Jesus) are cited as examples of the great spirit of freedom of the hobo. Informal conversations of Bowery men
illustrate the present state of the skid-row bum; he en-
joys few of the pleasures of his predecessors.

Levine, Faye. "India's Holy Men," Atlantic Monthly,
220 (October, 1967), pp. 18-28.

An American journalist's report of the Hindu "festival of Aquarius" includes comments on American hippies, poets, and wanderers who come to India and behave like Indian holy men. The author comments on the place of disaffiliation in Indian life: "Orthodox Hindus place a high value on detachment from family, job, and possessions, and consider the solitary, intinerant life a noble one. 'Dropping out, ' whether from school or adult responsibility, is not only universally approved, but actually prescribed (to all good Hindus) by ancient scripture." Examples of Indian and American "dropouts" are given.

Love, Edmund G., "Subways are for Sleeping, " Harper's Magazine, 212 (March, 1956), pp. 54-60.
Henry Shelby, one of the thousands of homeless vagrants in New York City, is a graduate of the University of Michigan with a master's degree in economics. He roams the streets of New York, picking up odd jobs and managing his money carefully. He sleeps in the subway or in the park, being careful not to become too familiar to the police, and spends his days going to art galleries and museums, riding the ferry, or looking at microfilm in the N.Y. Public Library. He is content, waiting and living, to see where his life will take him.

McGhee, Peter S. "Bowery Bums' Rush, " The Nation, 198 (May 11, 1964), pp. 483-485.
Written for the layman, this article concerns itself mainly with the "cleaning up" of the Bowery for the World's Fair. It includes a brief description of the physical aspects of the Bowery and follows the Bowery resident through a normal day's routine. McGhee describes the "revolving door" of arrest, trial and conviction, sentence to the workhouse, and return to the Bowery. At the time of this writing Bowery men were being arrested almost wholesale, and comparatively severe sentences were given to keep them off the streets.

McNaspy, C.J. "Escape from Skid Row, " America, 104 (February, 1961), pp. 700-703.
In its 26-year history the New York City Department of Welfare's camp for homeless men, Camp LaGuardia,

has served more than 100,000 men. The facilities and services are briefly explained. The author regrets only that the Camp LaGuardia is principally supportive rather than rehabilitative. Also included is an anonymous autobiographical sketch of a lawyer becoming a skid-row man and eventually regaining self-control through his friends, his church, and Alcoholics Anonymous.

Meynell, Alice. "The Last Outrage," The Catholic World, 167 (April, 1948), pp. 76-77.
The typical treatment of beggars in England is deplored. The main point is that to communicate with beggars on the streets is more human than simply to ignore them. Passing beggars without even an acknowledgement of their presence is "the last outrage."

Mitchell, Joseph. "Joe Gould's Secret," New Yorker, 40 (September 19 and September 26, 1964), pp. 61-125, 53-159.
This is a history of Joe Gould, archetypal skidder and a friend of poets (e.e. cummings, Ezra Pound) and the author of a mammoth dream--"An Oral History of Our Time." Gould's preoccupation with the common man carried him to Greenwich Village to document the "low life." The low life absorbed him, but Gould retained his individuality and maintained existence by means of his intellect, his loquaciousness, and his tendency toward exhibitionism. The "oral history" was an underground legend in his time, but save for an occasional section appearing in little magazines it was never published, and apparently did not exist. Gould died in 1957.

Murtagh, John M. "The Derelicts of Skid Row," Atlantic Monthly, 209 (March, 1962), pp. 77-81.
The chief justice of the Court of Special Sessions in New York City describes his experiences presiding at night court, the "dismal dumping ground for the also-rans of society." An example of the stereotypical "once promising" assistant district attorney who "hit the skids" and became a Bowery derelict is recounted. The history of

the Bowery is traced briefly, and the changes in the City's official approach to skid-row derelicts are noted. New York City's approach to the problem is described as more humane than most; the public intoxication statute is not used; instead arrests of derelicts are said to be limited to instances in which the drunk is disorderly or dangerous. It is asserted that the usual "revolving door" treatment of chronic inebriates is archaic, inhumane, and farcical.

Numelin, R. "Les tramps," Les Annales Politiques et Litteraires, 113 (February, 1939), pp. 161-163.
This brief essay on the American hobo emphasizes the romantic elements such as comaraderie and the freedom of the road. Josiah Flynt and Nels Anderson are cited as authorities. Rootlessness and habit are said to be the main reasons for the existence of tramps.

Sarcey, Y. "Mendigots et pauvres," Les Annales Politiques et Litteraires, 110 (October, 1937), pp. 183-184.
In an editorial also entitled "Grains de Bon Sens," the writer distinguished between professional panhandlers and poor unfortunates, disparaging the former and sympathizing with the latter.

Van Swol, Erwin. "The Hoboes' Secret Code," Coronet, 48 (August, 1960), pp. 35-38.
Hoboes, tramps and bums are characterized, respectively, as ambulatory workers, dreamers, and drinkers. The origins of homeless wandering are seasonal work, low mentality, physical handicaps, drug or alcoholic addictions, racial discrimination, and wanderlust. Twenty-one examples of signs which hoboes use to communicate with subsequent hoboes are given. This unspoken language, scribbled wherever convenient, is said to be well known throughout the United States and in several other countries.

Velie, Lester. "The Americans Nobody Wants," Colliers, 125 (April 1 and April 8, 1950), pp. 13-15, 48-50 and 26-27, 54-57.
Although more than half of the seasonal farm laborers of California's San Joaquin Valley have settled down into

shantytowns and run-down shacks, they are not recognized as residents and don't receive the benefits of federal minimum-wage laws, Social Security, or union protection. Attempts to correct these inequities are frustrated by those who don't recognize the residency of the workers. Investigations of their conditions, begun in 1950 by state committees and farm organizations, led to demands for the rights of farm workers to bargain, to get federal benefits, and to form a union. New industries in the area may provide jobs for the overflowing labor pool, and eventually it is possible that the seasonal farm laborer, along with other displaced persons, can achieve the standard of living other Americans enjoy.

Vorse, Mary Heaton. "America's Submerged Class: the Migrants," Harper's Magazine, 206 (February, 1953), pp. 86-93.
Although few states have made any efforts to deal with the problems of migrant workers (among those that have are New Jersey, New York, California and Wisconsin), interest in migrant problems is growing, as evidenced by an increasing amount of research about their conditions. However, only a beginning has been made. The President's Commission on Migratory Labor proposed a plan which was blocked in the legislature; the American people must realize the extent of the migrant workers' misery and press for reform. Moreover, not only do migrant workers entering illegally from Mexico constitute a social problem in their squalid and powerless condition, but the ease of their crossing constitutes a breach in national security.

Waters, Theodore   "Six Weeks in Beggardom," Everybody's Magazine, 12 (January, 1905), pp. 69-78.
A mission worker disguises himself as a beggar and spends six weeks among New York's skid-row society. Waters advocates a central control center to which all beggars might be referred and where they would receive lodging, food, advice, and possibly work.

OTHER WORKS

Willard, Eugene B. "The Bowery--The World's Premier Port of Homeless, Unemployed and Unemployable Men." New York: New York Public Library (privately bound), 1937. Pp. 54.
The following titles are included in this series of magazine articles and unpublished manuscripts: "Abnormal Personality Traits," "Sex Life of Homeless Men," "Bowery Men and Their Fetishes," "Queer Types of the Bowery," "Rendezvous of Humanity's Dregs," "Gravitating to the Bowery, " "The Varying Shores of the Bowery, "and "Broken Dreams, Broken Hearts, and Broken Lives," These literary and anecdotal pieces convey Willard's impressions of the Bowery and the sad condition of its inhabitants.

EMPLOYMENT AND UNEMPLOYMENT

BOOKS

Alden, Percey, and Hayward, Edward E. The Unemployable and Unemployed. London: Headley Brothers, 1908. Pp. 155.
A chapter on the historical background of unemployment in Britain is followed by consideration of three types: the unemployable (including vagrants and the physically or mentally disabled), the under-employed, and the unemployed. Various policy measures are discussed, including labor colonies and public or private work projects. An explicit assumption is that the industrial system must be regulated and modified to prevent the human suffering that has accompanied industrialization.

Bakke, E. Wight. The Unemployed Worker. New Haven: Yale University Press, 1940. Pp. 465.
The findings reported in this book derive from an eight-year program of research on the unemployed worker and his family conducted by the Institute of Human Relations. The central problem concerned adjustments, perspectives, and behavior patterns of workers and their families when the breadwinner is unemployed. Investigation took place in New Haven, Connecticut and included: 1) participant observation, 2) case studies and budget investigations of 25 families, 3) interviews with 200 families, 4) a survey of patterns of unemployment compensation, 5) interviews with social workers, ministers, public officials, and employers, and 6) examination of various reports and other documents. The report describes the life style of the unemployed worker. Research findings and suggestions for social policy are mentioned throughout but both are more adequately and systematically formulated in a companion volume, Citizens Without Work.

Bakke, E. Wight. Citizens Without Work. New Haven: Yale University Press, 1940. Pp. 306.

This continuation of The Unemployed Worker emphasizes
adjustments made by unemployed workers and their families in relation to their neighborhood, friends, religious
organizations, and political life. The first section of
the book concerns the unemployed worker and his place
in his community, the second concerns family adjustments and stability, and the third is a summary of findings drawn from both volumes. The summary is directed to two areas, 1) unemployment and self reliance, and
2) social service policy implications. The author focuses
on the worker's need for social respect, economic
security and a sense of control over his affairs. Regarding social service policies, it is maintained that middle-
class assumptions and values are often different in degree, if not also in kind, from those of the working class,
and that these differences must be perceived and taken
into account in the formulation of social welfare policies
and practices.

Calkins, Clinch. Some Folks Won't Work. New York:
Harcourt, Brace, 1930. Pp. 202.
The author attempts to refute the popular notion expressed in the title by examining the circumstances of
persons unemployed during the winter of 1929-30. The
focus is on people who have become the victims of seasonal unemployment, or who have lost their jobs because
of industrial dislocations. The case histories are truly
heart-rending. Calkins concludes that industry and
initiative do not invariably find their markets, that the
problem of unemployment must be faced, and that the
right to work should be recognized.

Dague, R. A. An Act to Give Employment to the Unemployed. Chicago: Charles H. Kerr, 1899. Pp. 20.
A bill introduced in the California legislature is reprinted in this work. Its content provides for the release of
state funds to create jobs on public works projects for
the unemployed. The legislative history of the bill is
briefly delineated. Selected comments of the press and
political and religious leaders are quoted and there is an
analysis of the economic forces that have made the bill
necessary and of the economic and social consequences

if it is not passed. The discussion establishes a quasi-Marxian dichotomy between the honorable laborer and the greedy capitalist. The comments have a strong populist flavor.

Friedmann, Eugene A., and Havighurst, Robert J. The Meaning of Retirement. Chicago: University of Chicago Press, 1954. Pp. 197.
The perceived significance of work and attitudes of workers toward retirement are considered in this collection of studies. The authors see in modern life an inexorable trend toward more leisure time both during working life and after retirement, and suggest that Americans must learn to apply the principle of "equivalence of work and play" if they are to adjust. Two pieces particularly relevant to problems of social isolation are "The Older Worker and the Meaning of Work" and "A Comparison of the Meanings of Work and Retirement Among Different Occupational Groups."

Hathway, Marion. The Migratory Worker and Family Life. Chicago: University of Chicago Press, 1934. Pp. 240.
A random sample of 100 Washington State migratory families were studied during the years 1929-1931. Data were obtained from family interviews, employers' interviews, and questionnaires given to various community groups and state agencies concerned with migratory families. The families' work and travel histories, family relations, school attendence, and contacts with social agencies are described. The findings support an argument for public and governmental adjustments to ameliorate strains upon family life created by migration. For example, it is suggested that school terms be adjusted to crop care and harvest patterns.

Higgs, Mary. How to Deal with the Unemployed. London: S.C. Brown, 1904. Pp. 196.
Problems of unemployment in England are treated. The social process leading to unemployment is a degenerative process, and the unemployed are a cancerous growth in the body social. Historical attempts to resolve the

problem, particularly the workhouse system, are seen as ineffectual. There are three types of unemployed persons--confirmed loafers, "incapables," and the inefficient. It is dangerous to allow any of these to reproduce and hence swell the ranks of social misfits. Possible solutions to the problem are the organization of labor markets, penal treatment of loafers, promotion of education, and restriction on the "breeding of ineffectives."

Klein, Philip. The Burden of Unemployment. New York: Russell Sage Foundation, 1923. Pp. 260.
This study of the administration of unemployment relief in 15 U.S. cities, 1921-22, discusses types of unemployment, under-utilization of job skills, criteria for relief, and the complex social-political-bureaucratic milieu in which unemployment relief is administered. There is a 20-page section on homelessness and transiency, as well as useful chapters on "The Use of Employment Statistics" and "Statistical Indices Available in a Community."

Parker, Carleton H. The Casual Laborer, and Other Essays. New York: Harcourt, Brace & Howe, 1920. Pp. 199.
Four papers on migrant labor and labor unrest by a professor of economics are contained in this volume. The theoretical base of the work is an instinctual theory of economic behavior, ostensibly derived from Freud and Darwin. Labor unrest is a consequence of "mal-adjustment between a fixed human nature and a carelessly ordered world." A 1913 strike by migrant laborers in the California hop-fields is analyzed in terms of the author's thesis. A general conclusion inferred from attitudes and behavior of strikers is that the strike was an instinctual reaction of the mob to a "suppression of normal instincts and traditions" rather than a response to infiltration and organization by subversives.

Purcell, Theodore V. Blue Collar Man. Cambridge: Harvard University Press, 1960. Pp. 300.
Purcell develops a theme introduced in an earlier book, The Worker Speaks His Mind: the worker tends to de-

velop an allegiance to both his company and his union. The present book is based on 800 interviews with workers, union leaders and company administrators in three meat-packing plants in the Midwest. Purcell did the interviewing himself. Sections of the book of particular interest for the study of disaffiliation include a chapter on workers' aspirations for their children and an entire section on workers' attitudes and behavior with regard to unions. Also directly relevant is a chapter on patterns of rank-and-file union participation. Purcell rates each worker on his degree of union participation according to eight criteria. He reports that the nature of worker involvement within unions varies but in general the amount of participation does not. In all three unions the rank-and-file workers were largely inactive.

Rogers, Thomas Wesley. The Occupational Experience of One-Hundred Unemployed Persons in Bloomington, Indiana. Bloomington: Indiana University, 1931. Pp. 61.
Extensive employment histories were obtained from 100 persons who were given work through the Citizens Committee on Unemployment Relief. Each history is presented separately, along with brief descriptive comments. There are several summary tables. None of the histories represents stereotypical homelessness.

Shotwell, Louisa R. The Harvesters. New York: Doubleday, 1961. Pp. 242.
This work grew out of a pamphlet for the National Migrant Committee of the National Council of Churches. Journalistic accounts are presented of several migrant families from different ethnic backgrounds. The migrants' points of view are considered, as are the problems they present for communities, the national economy, farm managers, and schools. Legislatures, unions, and communities must demonstrate greater concern for migrants and their problems. There is an excellent bibliography.

U.S. Department of Labor. Farm Labor Fact Book. Washington, D.C.: U.S. Government Printing Office, 1959. Pp. 240.

This report describes agricultural workers and the man-power problems of farm labor. Case studies depict hardship, but there are no recommendations beyond the usual generalizations. There is a survey of recent leg-islation dealing with the substandard conditions described. Appendices include useful statistical summaries (em-ployment statistics, type of workers, income) and maps illustrating patterns of migration.

Webb, John N., and Brown, Malcolm. Migrant Families. Washington, D. C.: U.S. Government Printing Office, 1938. Pp. 192.
Migrant families that received aid from the Transient Program of the Federal Emergency Relief Administration are described on the basis of 5,489 migrant families' records held by the FERA. The authors note two serious methodological shortcomings: unattached individuals are not represented, and urban dwellers are over-represent-ed. Characteristics such as sex, family size and dura-tion and length of transiency are presented. There are numerous tables and descriptions of subgroups of the transiency streams. The main policy conclusion is that residence requirements for relief should be eliminated.

ARTICLES

Clark, Robert E. "The Relationship of Alcoholic Psy-choses Commitment Rates to Occupational Income and Occupational Prestige," American Sociological Review, 14 (August, 1949), pp. 539-543.
The hypothesis that "alcoholic psychoses commitment rates are inversely related to the amount of income and prestige associated with various occupational groups" is supported. The sample consists of the white males age 20-69 studied by Faris and Dunham (Mental Disor-ders in Urban Areas). The paper concludes that ex-cessive drinking is more frequent among lower prestige groups who have little reputation to lose than among high status groups (teachers, lawyers, clergymen, etc.) where individuals must maintain their dignity.

Curtis, Richard F. "Income and Occupational Mobility," American Sociological Review, 25 (October, 1960), pp. 727-730.
Curtis considers the general hypothesis that "occupationally mobile persons differ from non-mobile persons in the same occupational stratum in terms of other rank systems." Using data from six annual sample surveys from the Detroit Area Study, he finds an inverse relation between mobility and income of family heads. The relation strengthens with age, and is most striking in the lowest and highest occupational strata.

Curtis, Richard F. "Occupational Mobility and Membership in Formal Voluntary Associations: A Note on Research," American Sociological Review, 24 (December, 1959), pp. 846-848.
In a secondary analysis of sample surveys in the Detroit area, Curtis finds that intergenerational occupational mobility has no significant effect on rates of membership in a number of types of formal associations (women's clubs, charitable and welfare organizations, youth-serving, fraternal, sport team or hobby club, and neighborhood improvement associations). The class differences are in the traditional direction, with white collar membership rating higher than blue collar in every case but one: sports teams or hobby clubs. In this instance, "stable" blue collar families are as likely to belong as are "stable" white collar families.

Dollard, John. "Some Casual Data on Drinking Habits Among Two Strata of Civilian War Workers," Quarterly Journal of Studies on Alcohol, 3 (September, 1942), pp. 326-345.
This study of drinking habits of migrant workers compares 225 clerical workers with 300 war plant workers. Social and occupational differences of the two samples are briefly ennumerated. Heavy drinking is more attributable to transiency than to type of occupation. Heavy drinkers tend to be unhappy or unsuccessful, mostly because of recent migration as a result of the war.

Draper, Jean E., Strother, George B., and Garrett, Doris E. "The Effect of Training and Previous Experience on the Re-employment of Military Retirees," Journal of Gerontology, 18 (January, 1963), pp. 71-79. Personal characteristics, attitudes, and employment status of retired U.S. Air Force enlisted personnel are evaluated in an analysis of questionnaires received from 943 persons retired at least two years (333 were disability retirees). Findings show a significant relationship between level of civilian employment and the transfer of military skills.

Dubin, Robert. "Industrial Workers' Worlds: A Study of the 'Central Life Interests' of Industrial Workers," Social Problems, 3 (January, 1956), pp. 131-142. A 1952-53 study of approximately 1,200 employees in three midwestern industrial plants provides support for the propositions that 1) persons will perform adequately in areas of social experience where performance is mandatory but not valued, i.e., they will do their work but will not necessarily like it; 2) individuals may become attached to nonvalued social experiences, particularly in terms of obvious features of the situation, i.e., although workers do not consider their work as a central life interest, they recognize their job as a focal point for their experience with technology and formal organization; and 3) primary social relationships develop only in situations where social experience per se is valued by the individual, i.e., the human relations school of industrial management notwithstanding, workers do not view their workplace as providing opportunities for their preferred associations. Dubin suggests that the aspects of workplace thought to be disturbing and alienative may in fact be the features that make the nature of technological interdependence obvious to workers. Most workers do not consider their work a central life interest--only 24 percent of all the workers could be classed as "job-oriented."

F., I. J. "Alcoholism: An Occupational Disease of Seamen, Approaches to a Solution of the Problem in the Port of New York," Quarterly Journal of Studies on Alcohol, 8 (December, 1947), pp. 498-505.

The high incidence of alcoholism among seamen is attributed to lack of outlet for release of tension while at sea and the relative absence of family and other social connections. Group processes aboard ship which have tended to institutionalize the drinking ethic and enforced isolation are discussed. A catalog of facilities in the Port of New York for the care of alcoholic seamen is included as well as specific recommendations for expansion of these facilities. The author is Executive Secretary of the New York City Alcoholics Anonymous Seamen's Club.

Gilbert, Jeanne G. and Healey, James C. "The Economic and Social Background of the Unlicensed Personnel of the American Merchant Marine," Social Forces, 21 (October, 1942), pp. 40-43.
Data for this study of the personal backgrounds and characteristics of seamen are from a survey of 326 residents and visitors to Seamen's House YMCA in New York City. The findings reflect the lack of domestic ties among these seamen: only one-ninth are married and only one-fourth have any residence which might be termed a home. U.S. Maritime Service statistics are cited for comparison; these show that 82 percent of those enrolled in maritime service are single; about 13 percent are married; and 5 percent are divorced or widowed. Since the "basic sentiment" of a home is "mutual dependence," statistics on dependence meaningfully reflect the solitariness of seamen: over 75 percent have no dependents, and 16 percent have only one dependent. "The seaman without dependents is the seaman without attachments to a therapeutic responsibility. Dependents may be something of a burden, but they bring to the seaman a saving sense of responsibility."

Goodchilds, Jacqueline and Smith, Ewart E. "The Effects of Unemployment as Mediated by Social Status" Sociometry, 26 (September, 1963), pp. 287-293.
Experimental studies of two groups of unemployed men (180 subjects in all) reveal that subjects of high occupational status "not only did not become debilitated under unemployment stress, but actually showed increases in a number of positive self-perceptions and behav-

iors. The longer the period of unemployment, the   more defensive and self-critical the higher social status subjects became.

Hartle, Douglas C. "The Characteristics of the Unemployed: Some Implications of the James Report to the Senate Committee on Manpower and Employment," Canadian Journal of Economics and Political Science, 28 (May, 1962), pp. 254-262.
The James Report is a summary of characteristics of the unemployed based on 17,000 questionnaires completed by registrants at the National Employment Service of Canada. Each local office selected a random sample from its files on a particular day in 1960. The report indicated that many of the registrants were "marginal members of the labour force," i.e., they either did not want full-time permanent work, or it was not necessary for them to work. The press treated the report as an expose of fraudulent claims for unemployment insurance. Hartle questions the value of the unemployment insurance law itself. Moreover, since increased training and education lead to a greater output for the same wages, the use of more training and education as a solution to unemployment is questionable.

Hartle, Douglas. "Seasonal Unemployment in Canada, 1951-7," Canadian Journal of Economics and Political Science, 24 (February, 1958), pp. 93-98.
Winter unemployment in Canada seems to be increasing despite several programs designed to reduce it. Possible explanations for the increase are 1) the seasonal sub-industries of the main industries are expanding relatively more rapidly than other less seasonal industries, 2) the seasonal pattern of demand is shifting, 3) changes in industrial cost structure make winter work less desirable, and 4) with increasing unemployment insurance, workers are less anxious for winter work. The first two of these can be investigated with existing data, and it is suggested that the government consider collecting data relevant to 3) and 4).

Hayner, Norman S. "Taming the Lumberjack," American Sociological Review, 10 (April, 1945), pp. 217-225.
This article discusses the "increasing domestication" of the lumberjack. Anecdotes and previous research on lumberjacking are cited and contrasted with conditions in 1945. Loggers and their families were interviewed informally. In the past most loggers were single and transient, but the "new" loggers are usually married and live in a "company town." The logger of 1945 was found to be a good family man, the undisputed head of the household. Conservation and changes in logging methods are briefly discussed. Technological changes increasing the accessibility of logging camps have prompted the shift from transient to regular labor in the logging industry.

Heath, Robert G. "Group Psychotherapy of Alcohol Addiction," Quarterly Journal of Studies on Alcohol, 5 (March, 1945), pp. 555-562.
Twenty percent of the admissions to the Merchant Marine Rest Center are alcoholics. Certain personality traits of alcoholics are postulated and a program of group therapy which attempts to redirect these traits is delineated. Seamen are considered a special group whose occupation fulfills much the same purpose as alcohol (e.g., escape) while also acting to reinforce personality traits associated with alcoholism.

Hoyt, Elizabeth E. "Voluntary Unemployment and Unemployability in Jamaica with Special Reference to the Standard of Living," British Journal of Sociology, 11 (June, 1960), pp. 129-136.
Jamaica has a high rate of unemployment and at the same time a shortage of labor. In exploring the reasons for this paradox the author discusses the possible incentives to become employed as they relate to the standard of living. The topics include family system, markets, and social welfare agencies. She concludes that more study is needed on the inter-relationship of parts of the standard of living to other parts and to the whole economy, especially for underdeveloped countries.

Johnson, Leroy and Strother, George B. "Job Expectations and Retirement Planning, " Journal of Gerontology, 17 (October, 1962), pp. 418-423.
The basic hypothesis is that the attitude with which the individual approaches retirement must be viewed in the light of job attitudes and experiences. A large food-processing plant (3, 300 employees) was the research site. Structured interviews with a sample of employees were supplemented by attitude check lists. The general conclusion is that those for whom work has the most positive values will also be most successful in finding positive values in retirement.

Leavy, Stanley A. and Freedman, Lawrence Zelic. "Psychopathology and Occupation, Part One, Economic Insecurity, "Occupational Psychology, 35 (January, 1961), pp. 23-35.
This study considers the relationship of economic conditions and personality traits. Clinical material consisted of 500 case records of psychoneurotic patients, mostly from New Haven, Conn., who had been treated between 1946 and 1951, a period of high employment and relative prosperity. Approximately one-half of these patients were hospitalized for some period of time; the other half were seen as outpatients. Findings indicate a positive relationship between unemployment, unsteady economic conditions, and neurosis.

Maxwell, Milton A. and Observer. "A Study in Absenteeism, Accidents, and Sickness Payments in Problem Drinkers in One Industry, " Quarterly Journal of Studies on Alcohol, 20 (June, 1959), pp. 302-312.
Medical files of a United States company with over 10, 000 employees are the basic data for this study. Forty-eight problem drinkers are contrasted with two matched control groups. The problem drinkers are shown to be more accident-prone, more often absent, and to receive substantially larger sickness payments.

Meltzer, H. "Age Differences in Happiness and Life Adjustments of Workers, " Journal of Gerontology, 18 (January, 1963), pp. 66-70.

Interviews with 257 employees in an industrial setting
are analyzed in a study of the relation between aging and
life satisfaction. Findings indicate that feelings that one
has his share of happiness increase with age, as do the
significance of work and interest in steady work. Significance of leisure activities and hope for advancement decrease with age. Feelings that one has received his
share of recognition show little variation with age.

Page, Robert C., Thorpe, John J., and Caldwell, D. W.
"The Problem Drinker in Industry," Quarterly Journal
of Studies on Alcohol, 13 (September, 1952), pp. 370-396.
This study of workers whose drinking interferes with
their efficient job performance is based on a review of
the literature, consultation with professionals dealing
with the problem, case studies of industrial problem
drinkers, and company records. There are 36 case
histories (1 female); most of the workers were over 40.
It is concluded that estimates of the extent of problem
drinking based on company medical records are usually
underestimates, and that more preventative measures
should be taken.

Paster, Samuel. "Alcoholism--an Emergent Problem
Among Veterans," Mental Hygiene, 32 (January, 1948),
pp. 58-71.
Many alcoholics are neurotics whose drinking is rooted
in early, turbulent parent-child relationships. They
are distinguished from nonalcoholic neurotics in that
they are unable to evoke the common neurotic defenses
to allay anxiety and diminish internal conflicts. Three
detailed case histories show the impact of various forces
on veterans who began their drinking after returning
from the army. One of these, a comparatively well-
integrated man who had experienced good family relationships, recovered quickly. The recovery of others was
hindered because of unfortunate parent-child relationships.

Pearson, Margaret. "The Transition from Work to
Retirement," Occupational Psychology, 31 (April and
July, 1957), pp. 80-88 and 139-149.

Employment histories of 220 aging (between 60 and 65) employees of a Liverpool manufacturing firm were analyzed. The men also were sent a questionnaire about their attitudes toward retirement. Findings reveal that with age the men tended toward easier jobs and day work rather than varying shifts. Most respondents favored a fixed retirement age, and 41 percent favored that age at 65 or earlier. Two years after these studies 74 of the respondents who had retired were re-interviewed. Fifteen men had found some employment, 34 wanted employment. Reasons given were need of money, boredom, and loneliness. The passive acceptance of their new way of life was one of their most noticeable characteristics. The author cites similar findings in other studies, laments the "functionless interregnum" between retirement and death, and asks what can be done with those years.

Rapoport, Robert, and Rapoport, Rhona. "Work and Family in Contemporary Society," American Sociological Review, 30 (June, 1965), pp. 381-394.
A consideration of theoretical orientations to the relation between work and family centers about the following points: family and work have become increasingly differentiated, they vary in relative salience, work and family modes of interaction tend to be isomorphic, and relations between them vary depending on the stage of the life cycle. "Salience" refers to the "potency" of work in the individual's life-space. This variable might be very useful in the study of social isolates. Relative salience is seen as probably the most important factor determining the patterns that are developed to integrate work and family. The authors concentrate on critical points of major role transition, hypothesizing that new patterns of interrelationship between work and family are "crystallized" within a brief period, perhaps a few weeks, after the initial critical period of intensive involvements in new situations. Their generalizations are based on exploratory interviews with a dozen couples undergoing both marriage and graduation. Although stresses are multiplied when transitions in two spheres occur simultaneously, beneficial consequences may result.

Robinson, H. A. and Finesinger, Jacob E. "The Significance of Work Inhibition for Rehabilitation," Social Work, 2 (October, 1957), pp. 22-31.
Work inhibition is a situation in which the individual is physically able to work but psychologically disabled. Factors relevant to vocational rehabilitation are discussed, including motivation for job placement, the meaning of work for the individual, and the dynamic social setting of the work situation.

Smith, J. M. "Age and Re-employment: A Regional Study of External Mobility," Occupational Psychology, 41 (October, 1967), pp. 239-244.
Analysis of unemployment records of workers in Liverpool reveals that in comparison with young workers (aged 20-25), older workers (aged 40-45) tend to be unemployed longer between jobs, are less likely to be hired for a different kind of work than their previous employment, and manifest more diversity in socioeconomic status among themselves. There was no apparent tendency for older workers who did change the nature of their employment to drift into jobs with either lighter or heavier physical requirements.

R. L. Smyth, "Male Unemployment Problems in Large Ports and Urban Areas, With Special Reference to Kingston-upon-Hull," Yorkshire Bulletin of Economic and Social Research, 5 (August, 1953), pp. 155-178.
Unemployment in the Port of Hull is analyzed using a random sample of 500 employment record cards from the Hull Employment Exchange Register in 1952. Two percent of the sample were itinerants, and 15 percent were "long-term unemployed." The main unemployment problem in Hull is shown to be the lack of jobs for a surplus unskilled labor force. In Hull, as elsewhere in Britain, there is a "hard core of unemployment," and the main burden of unemployment is borne by comparatively few workers. Although length of unemployment increases with age, age per se does not seem a major factor. Only one-eighth of the men had indicated they were willing to leave Hull to seek work. The long-term

unemployment problem in Hull has persisted due to factors such as 1) decline in basic industries that employ
manual labor, 2) failure of the non-basic industries to expand,3) Hull's inability to attract new industry.   Possible
remedial action is recommended. Apparently this is the
first analysis of a local unemployment register. The
author notes the advantages of the study of such small
units in revealing facts about unemployment which are
overlooked in the more common "aggregative approach."

Speck, Peter. "The Psychology of Floating Workers, "
Annals of the American Academy of Political and Social
Science, 69 (January, 1917), pp. 72-78.
Three kinds of laborers are distinguished, 1) steady
workers, 2) floating workers, and 3) unemployables or
down-and-outs. Speck suggests that there exists a psychological condition that corresponds to each of these
types. The process by which individuals sink from steady
worker to down-and-out is characterized in terms of a
continuing reinforcement of hopelessness and despair.
Legislation to alter working conditions is the least costly
means to reduce the number of casualties of this process.

Straus, Robert, and Bacon, Selden D. "Alcoholism and
Social Stability: A Study of Occupational Integration in
2, 023 Male Clinic Patients, "Quarterly Journal of Studies
on Alcohol, 12 (June, 1951), pp. 231-260.
Male alcoholics being served by nine public outpatient
clinics in the United States are described. The theoretical premise is that social integration or degree of socialization is the most important factor in determining
recovery from alcoholism. Data are presented on the alcoholic's marital status, type of residence, age, and occupational status. The role of the outpatient clinic is described; most alcoholics live within "normal" society
and hence an outpatient clinic makes a positive contri-
bution.

Strayer, Robert. "A Study of the Employment Adjustment of 80 Male Alcoholics, "Quarterly Journal of Studies
on Alcohol, 18 (June, 1957), pp. 278-287.
In this study occupational adjustment--measured in terms

of job satisfaction, goal achievement, reaction to supervision, relations with fellow employees and number of job changes--is examined in relation to excessive alcohol use. Data are from 80 case histories of the Bridgeport Clinic of the Connecticut Commission on Alcoholism, and were selected on the basis of the completeness of their social history files. While employment was usually maintained as drinking became more severe, the subjects experienced periods of loss of time from work, drinking on the job, and increased hostility to supervisory personnel. Most of these subjects came to the clinic before their problems became overwhelming.

Street, David, and Leggett, John C. "Economic Deprivation and Extremism: A Study of Unemployed Negroes," American Journal of Sociology, 67 (July, 1961), pp. 53-57.
Ninety-two Negro heads of households in two Detroit residential areas were interviewed in 1958 with respect to their attitudes about the concomitants of economic depression. Additional data from a sample of 375 male manual workers interviewed in 1960 are added for comparative purposes. The hypothesis that widespread unemployment in a community leads to extreme political views among those most affected by the unemployment is supported.

Trice, Harrison M. "The Job Behavior of Problem Drinkers," pp. 493-510 in Pittman, David J. and Snyder, Charles R. (eds.), Society, Culture and Drinking Patterns. New York: John Wiley and Sons, 1962.
Work histories of two samples of employed alcoholics (N's of 286 and 635) were analyzed in an attempt to determine effects of alcoholism on job behavior. Subjects were male members of Alcoholics Anonymous. The effects of drinking on work efficiency, absenteeism, cover-up, turnover, and work accidents vary with the type of job. Hence research must also take into account how specific work situations influence the etiology and expression of alcoholism.

Wilensky, Harold L. "Orderly Careers and Social Participation: The Impact of Work History on Social Integration in the Middle Mass," American Sociological Review, 26 (August, 1961), pp. 521-539.
Based on interviews with 678 males of the "middle mass," this paper explores the relation between "orderliness" in occupational history and social participation. Two other major dimensions of the job history, direction and amount of movement, are considered. These dimensions are components of the concept "career." Analysis of respondents' career patterns reveals that traditional indicators of social class no longer discriminate among styles of leisure and degrees of social integration for the "middle mass," and "chaotic experience in the economic order fosters a retreat from both work and the larger communal life."

Wilensky, Harold L. "Work, Careers, and Social Integration," International Social Science Journal, 12 (No. 4, 1960), pp. 543-560.
Some of the most fascinating clues to the shape of modern society can be found in the labor-leisure problem. Wilensky here makes explicit the theoretical foundation upon which his study of labor and leisure in Detroit is based. Although much social behavior varies by class, for a growing middle class traditional indices of status (present income and occupation) no longer distinguish styles of life and social integration. Other attributes of social structure that predict behavior in the middle class must be discovered. The two most common patterns of "underdog" response are "individuation" (apathetic retreat or explosive "compensation") and family-home localism. Implications for the urban-industrial future include an organization of work in which a small group of expert professionals work hard to control the masses, who in turn "take it easy" in jobs having short hours and requiring little brawn and shrewdness but emphasizing reliability and trained intelligence.

Wilensky, Harold L., and Edwards, Hugh. "The Skidder: Ideological Adjustments of Downward Mobile Workers," American Sociological Review, 24 (April, 1959), pp. 215-231.
In a secondary analysis of 495 questionnaires from non-supervisory employees of two factories, the authors test several hypotheses relating political conservatism to downward mobility. They categorize the main explanations for conservatism of the downwardly mobile into 1) resistance to failure in a society which emphasizes success values, and 2) early, retrospective, anticipatory or later socialization. Findings indicate that early or retrospective socialization leading to denial of failure is a possible orientation, but do not support the later socialization and anticipatory socialization hypotheses. Skidding is shown to have a conservative impact on values and beliefs about stratification.

Youmans, E. Grant. "Objective and Subjective Economic Disengagement Among Older Rural and Urban Men," Journal of Gerontology, 21 (July, 1966), pp. 439-441. The "disengagement theory" suggests that withdrawal from social ties is an inevitable concomitant of aging. In an assessment of "adaptive" reactions to economic disengagement and of the influence of the rural-urban factor on adaptive reactions, data were obtained by interview from rural Kentuckians (72 men aged 60-64 and 102 men 75 or over) and from an urban sample (49 men aged 60-64 and 57 over 75). Employment and income were used as objective indicators of economic disengagement. Subjective information was obtained by asking questions regarding the respondents' feelings about their condition. It was found that although the older men had less income and were less involved in work roles, they felt less economic deprivation; apparently they had adjusted to their status. With one exception, there were no differences between rural and urban men: the older rural men expressed less dissatisfaction about opportunities to work for pay.

Young, Pauline V. "The Human Cost of Unemployment,"
Sociology and Social Research, 17 (March-April, 1933),
pp. 361-364.
Attention is directed to the "new class of poor and dependents, " laborers who formerly were steadily employ -
ed but who lost their jobs as a result of the Depression.
Neither former employers nor an overburdened welfare-
charity system have met their needs. The author pleads
that the plight of these unemployed persons be taken
seriously, and that creative thought, better organization,
and more funds be devoted to their problems.

Zawadzki, Bohan, and Lazarsfeld, Paul. "The Psychological Consequences of Unemployment, " The Journal
of Social Psychology, 6 (May, 1935), pp. 224-251.
The Institute for Social Economy in Warsaw, Poland,
conducted a contest in which prizes were given for the
best autobiographies of unemployed persons. Fifty-seven
of these autobiographies (chosen from 774), published
in 1933 under the title Memoirs of the Unemployed, are
the basic source of data for this paper. The authors discuss psychological states, home situations, changes in
perceptions and experiences of hardship associated with
unemployment. Homelessness is seen as one of many
consequences of unemployment. The treatment is primarily descriptive, and the authors acknowledge the
difficulties and possible inaccuracies implicit in the
use of the autobiographical data.

OTHER WORKS

Barnett, Gordon James. "A Study of Satisfied and Dis-
satisfied Chronically Unemployed Men, " unpublished
doctoral dissertation, Columbia University, 1950.
Barnett administered a battery of tests to 174 chronically
unemployed persons who applied for food and/or lodging
at the Salvation Army Men's Social Service Center in
New York City between July 1948 and February 1949.
He found that two factors differentiated between chronic
and nonchronic unemployment. These were father's
occupation and the "LO" score, a measure sometimes

interpreted as an indicator of an individual's degree of aspiration. The study is a useful source for information on the social characteristics of homeless men.

Bradwin, Edmund W. "The Bunkhouse Man," unpublished doctoral dissertation, Columbia University, 1928. Pp. 308.
The conditions in Canada's casual labor camps are described by one who worked in them, first as a laborer and later as a teacher. The main emphasis is on the need for reform in the laws governing work relations in the labor camp. There is a general treatment of life in the camps and of the characteristics of workers who live there.

Davis, Robert. Some Men of the Merchant Marine, unpublished master's thesis, Columbia University, 1907. Pp. 46.
An essay on the characteristics and activities of merchant seamen is based on the author's voyage on a steamship from New York to Galveston and back. He worked in the steward's department of the ship, and most of his observations refer to the stewards, cooks, mess-men, porters, and pantrymen. Among the topics discussed are recreation on shipboard and ashore, seamen's missions and why they are not more successful, the attraction of the sea, women and home in the lives of seamen, and religious, moral, and political views of seamen. There are no statistical data.

Leiserson, William Morris. "Unemployment in the State of New York," unpublished doctoral dissertation, Columbia University, 1911. Pp. 199.
Widespread unemployment and coexistent labor shortages are examined in terms of supply-and-demand economics. It is skilled labor that is in short supply, but most of the unemployed workers are unskilled. Occupational training schools and centralization of statewide employment offices are suggested as remedies. Vagrants, tramps, and skidders are mentioned only as consequences of economic depression.

Oregon Bureau of Labor. . . . And Migrant Problems
Demand Attention, Salem: Oregon Bureau of Labor,
1959. Pp. 218.
Interviews were conducted with 1, 603 migrant workers ,
representing 6 percent of the state's migrant workers.
General questions were asked with a view toward identifying the characteristics of the typical migrant worker.
The social and economic position of the migrants vis a
vis the community and state is examined and recommendations are made for the improvement of their position.

Pollitt, Daniel H. The Migrant Farm Worker in America. A report prepared for the Subcommittee on Migrant Labor, Washington, D. C.: U. S. Government
Printing Office, 1960. Pp. 79.
The tone of this report sometimes verges on that of
campaign oratory (a frequent source is the congression-
al record), but for the most part it is a systematic and
well-documented account of the plight of the migrant
worker. His life style is described and compared with
that of the industrial laborer. There are several case
studies. The dynamics of the agricultural system which
the migrant serves are examined, the extent of the use
of migrant labor in the United States is presented in
terms of locale and crops, and the general conclusion
is that the migrant is a victim of blatant exploitation.
His situation might be ameliorated either through unionization or legislation. Previous legislation which af-
fects the migrant is outlined.

VOLUNTARY ASSOCIATIONS

BOOKS

Hausknecht, Murray. The Joiners. New York: Bedminster Press, 1962. Pp. 141.
A description of the voluntary association membership of Americans is derived from a secondary analysis of two national surveys. Until this study there were no reliable data on the extent of membership in voluntary associations for the nation's population as a whole. One sample was a 1954 American Institute of Public Opinion sample and the other a 1955 NORC survey. Sample sizes, respectively, were 2,000 and 2,379. Of most interest to the study of social isolation are chapters on membership and stratification and on membership and integration. Hausknecht suggests that low rates of affiliation in voluntary associations indicate a relative lack of integration among the young and the old. The working class stands to benefit most from membership in voluntary associations, yet has an extremely low rate of such memberships . This low level of affiliation is a greater restriction for the lower-class person than it would be to the middle-class individual. "The worker remains the underdog in our society partly because the conditions of his existence create a pattern of life making it difficult to see his opportunities or even to comprehend them."

Kornhauser, William. The Politics of Mass Society. Glencoe: Free Press, 1959. Pp. 256.
The central argument of this work is that the mass society is vulnerable to political movements which endanger democratic institutions while the pluralist society provides a context in which these institutions are strong. Kornhauser uses data from many nations in elaborating this theme. After discussing the theory of mass society he describes the social sources of mass movements and analyzes their social composition. Chapters on unattached intellectuals, marginal middle classes, and iso-

lated workers are relevant to the study of disaffiliation.

Langner, Thomas S. and Michael, Stanley T. Life
Stress and Mental Health. New York: Free Press of
Glencoe, 1963.
This sequel to Srole's Mental Health in the Metropolis
reports the relation of mental health to certain "stress
factors," mainly childhood symptoms, pathology of the
family of orientation, "adult factors" (including worries,
health, and social affiliation), and social mobility. Mental health is closely associated with present socio-economic status, but not to parental status when present
status is held constant. Fairly extensive data on social
affiliation are presented.

Nisbet, Robert A. The Quest for Community. New
York: Oxford University Press, 1963. Pp. 303.
Organizations are important integrative mechanisms
for society. Nisbet deals with "the political causes of
the manifold alienations that lie behind the contemporary
quest for community." Modern Western man is seen as
frustrated, anxious, and isolated precisely because the
state has, as it were, replaced the functions of many of
the organizations which previously served to integrate
individuals. In order for constitutional guarantees to
be meaningful, there must be integrated and powerful
small areas of society (organizations of the middle-
range). Political enslavement depends upon the detachment of men from the authorities and memberships which
insulate them from external political power. The total
state is monolithic; the only protection against it is
autonomous organizations on lower levels. Hence, to-
talitarian governments try to re-make all organizations
as agencies of the state. Social groups thrive only when
they have significant functions and authorities in the
lives of their members, and under true totalitarianism
the role of the autonomous social group is destroyed.
Liberal democracy can thrive only if autonomous formal groups prosper. The apathy of the isolated individual under totalitarianism resembles the apathy of
the homeless man.

Queen, Stuart A. and Gruener, Jennette R. Social Pathology: Obstacles to Social Participation. New York:
Thomas Y. Crowell, 1940. Pp. 662.
This is a textbook on social pathology. Part I deals with
the nature of social problems considered pathological
and outlines the authors' methods. Part II offers an
encyclopedia of "obstacles to social participation,"
such as senescence, feeble-mindedness, and unemployment; about 30 pages of explanation and description are
accorded to each of 20 "obstacles." A chapter on transience presents limited data on transience in the United
States and illustrates possible causes and ramifications
of transience in three case histories. The presentation
is objective, well-ordered, and relatively thorough.

Rose, Arnold M. Theory and Method in the Social Sciences. Minneapolis: University of Minnesota Press,
1954. Pp. 351.
Rose traces the rise of modern "mass society" and reactions to it, outlining the widespread occurrence and
isolative effects of the unstable "audience" and the
importance of the "public" in integrating persons in modern social life. He hypothesizes that voluntary associations support political democracy by distributing power
among a large proportion of the population, that they
help ordinary citizens see democratic processes in
action, and that they provide a social mechanism for
continually instituting social change. Changes accompanying and following the Industrial Revolution led to a
decline in the influence of the community, church, and
extended family. Reaction to this decline varied; in
many Western countries, including the United States, a
dominant reaction was the forming of voluntary associations. Associations are seen as vital substitutes for
the weakened extended family, church, and community
ties. Relevant chapters include: "The Problem of a
Mass Society," "A Theory of the Function of Voluntary
Associations in Contemporary Social Structure" and
"Voluntary Associations in France."

ARTICLES

Babchuk, Nicholas and Thompson, Ralph V. "The Voluntary Associations of Negroes, " American Sociological Review, 27 (August, 1962), pp. 647-655.
The extent of Negro participation in voluntary associations and the situational and personal determinants of that participation are investigated in a survey of 120 adult Negroes in Lincoln, Nebraska. Negroes belong to more voluntary associations than whites, especially at the lower-class levels. The high level of participation in voluntary associations is viewed as a pathological condition reflecting exclusion from the organized life of white Americans. The Negro association provides an opportunity for self expression and status recognition, and may provide a functional equivalent of the strong kinship ties among lower-class whites.

Beiser, Morton. "Poverty, Social Disintegration and Personality, " Journal of Social Issues, 21 (January, 1965), pp. 56-78.
This psychologically-oriented discussion of the relation between social disintegration (lack of social ties) and poverty emphasizes individual rather than social causes and effects. General traits, skills, and psychological well-being of the disintegrated poor are considered. Results of the Stirling County mental health survey of a disintegrated community and the programs for community development that followed are discussed. A successful program for community development requires a knowledge of the attitudes, lack of skills, and psychopathology of the disintegrated poor.

Brager, George. "Organizing the Unaffiliated in a Low-Income Area, " Social Work, 8 (April, 1963), pp. 34-40.
Delinquency rates have been shown to be low in well-integrated, community-oriented neighborhoods. But in lower-income areas adults are unlikely to become involved in community affairs. Mobilization for Youth, an

experimental action-research project on Manhattan's Lower East Side, tried to increase the organization of the unaffiliated, keeping in mind the distinctive characteristics of the area. The already-present informal groups were encouraged to work together to plan cultural or social programs. Group leaders were sought out and given special training in the hope that the presence of indigenous organizers rather than outside help would make it easier for lower-income persons to identify with the leaders and cooperate in the program. Although the project met with mixed success, it remains an exemplary effort to overcome common obstacles by taking into account the peculiar life style and prevalent attitudes in a target area.

Breton, Raymond and Pinard, Maurice. "Group Formation Among Immigrants: Criteria and Processes," Canadian Journal of Economics and Political Science, 26 (August, 1960), pp. 465-477.
This paper is an examination of those aspects of a person's interpersonal network that lead to the establishment of personal ties. The authors are concerned with the bases of the interpersonal attraction that leads to the formation of groups. Interviews were conducted with 230 immigrants in Montreal. Merton's idea of "status homophily" (the tendency for people to choose friends or join groups having members like themselves) is supported. Occupational homophily was found except where occupation did not correspond to education. A high degree of ethnic homophily was related to language or educational deficiencies which limited respondents' ability to communicate with persons outside their group.

Cohen, Albert K. and Hodges, Harold M., Jr. "Characteristics of the Lower-Blue-Collar-Class," Social Problems, 10 (Spring, 1963), pp. 303-334.
Cohen and Hodges describe aspects of the lower-lower-class (LL) person's life-situation. Their generalizations are based on approximately 100 LL's, part of a larger sample of 2,600 male heads of families in San Francisco, San Mateo, and Santa Clara counties in California. The

LL's life-situation is viewed as characterized by 1) sim-
plification of the experienced world, 2) powerlessness,
3) deprivation, and 4) insecurity. The LL adaptation to
the situation is to establish a series of "helping" solidary
relationships, particularly with kin. The LL differs
from other classes in its more nearly exclusive dependence on such relationships, and in the units involved--
individuals may act not on their own behalf but as representatives of collectivities. Relatives and friends are
more likely to press claims for help after marriage, and
more effort is devoted by each spouse to maintaining the
wide structure of such relationships that existed before
marriage than is the case with other classes. The LL
spends little time in "purely social" activities, and the
socializing he does is mainly with relatives and neighbors. The LL is unlikely to belong to voluntary associations, or if he does belong, is unlikely to attend meetings.
One of the striking features of the study is the preference
for the familiar among the LL--they value and seek out,
more than any other class, "the routine, the familiar,
the predictable." The LL is characterized by anti-in-
tellectuality, authoritarianism, and pessimism.

Duines, Russell R. "The Consequences of Sectarianism
for Social Participation," Social Forces, 35 (May, 1957),
pp. 331-334.
Mailed questionnaires returned by 360 Protestants in the
Columbus, Ohio metropolitan area included a 24-item
church-sect attitude scale. For the sectarian, the religious group was found to be a meaningful association
and source of friendship.

Dyckman, John W. "Some Conditions of Civic Order in
an Urbanized World," Daedalus, 95 (Summer, 1966),
pp. 797-811.
Forms of contemporary urban growth capable of upsetting
the established social and political order and likely to
impede orderly social change are examined. Topics
considered include runaway urbanization, scale and
density of metropolitan areas, urban costs and economic
development, urban institutions under pressure, expecta-

tions of the new urbanites, segregation and conflict, the casualties of efficiency, control by communication, and the urban outsiders. The city is seen as a "powerful integrating device for a society undergoing rapid social and economic change, " but modern urban society has not communicated adequately with several nonintegrated or alienated groups, who form "explosive residues of discontent . . . everywhere in the world urban order. "

Erbe, William. "Social Involvement and Political Activity: A Replication and Elaboration, " American Sociological Review, 29 (April, 1964), pp. 198-215.
Data from a survey of three small midwestern towns indicate that socioeconomic status, organizational involvement and alienation all are associated with political activity. There is an excellent review of studies of social involvement and political activity; usually the two are directly related.

Greer, Scott and Orleans, Peter. "The Mass Society and the Parapolitical Structure, " American Sociological Review, 27 (August, 1962), pp. 634-646.
The relation between urbanism and the mass society is examined with reference to the parapolitical structure (ostensibly nonpolitical organizations that could represent the political interest of their members if necessary). Respondents are residents of the St. Louis metropolitan area; 1, 285 suburbanites and 515 city-dwellers were interviewed in 1957. Four types of social participators are distinguished (isolates, neighbors, community actors, and deviants). Relations between sub-area population type and the parapolitical structure, between parapolitical structure and political process, and between sub-area population type and political process are explored through tests of 13 specific hypotheses. The strength of the parapolitical structure varies widely within the metropolis. Political involvement in the central city may be mediated through the local parapolitical structure, through a larger-scale parapolitical structure, or chiefly through the mass media. The majority of the

citizens are involved through the first two of these. In the suburbs, political involvement through the local parapolitical structure is the predominant form.

Keedy, T. C., Jr. "Anomie and Religious Orthodoxy," Sociology and Social Research, 43 (September, 1958), pp. 34-37.
Previous studies have shown a correlation between religious orthodoxy and ethnocentrism and between ethnocentrism and anomie. This study tested the relation between anomie (measured by the Srole scale) and orthodoxy (measured both by attitudes and church attendance) among a sample of 108 middle-class Protestant undergraduates at a small liberal arts college in the "Bible-Belt." Religious orthodoxy was found to be correlated with ethnocentrism, but anomie was not.

Knupfer, Genevieve. "Portrait of the Underdog," Public Opinion Quarterly, 11 (Spring, 1947), pp. 104-114.
Drawing on findings from 30 studies completed between 1927 and 1944, the author attempts to show that economic and educational deficiencies prompt lower-class people to withdraw from participation in certain important areas of American social and cultural life. Topics discussed include organizational participation, informal social activities, participation in the "thought life" of the community, access to information on public affairs, interest in public affairs, voting behavior, and aspirations.

Levens, Helene. "Organizational Affiliation and Powerlessness: A Case Study of the Welfare Poor," Social Problems, 16 (Summer, 1968), pp. 18-32.
In 1966 many Welfare Recipients Leagues were formed by people on welfare. This study of one of the League chapters worked from the hypothesis that members of the League would have fewer feelings of powerlessness (as manifested by a fatalistic outlook on life, feelings of incapability of controlling problems, and lack of participation in activities designed to alter their circumstances) than would non-members. The sample consisted of 131 Negro and Puerto Rican mothers living in the same neighborhood and receiving welfare. Interviewers were three

Negro women of the same neighborhood who were also
on welfare. Members of the League did not differ from
non-members in age, education, number of children, or
number of organizational affiliations. However, they
manifested significantly less powerlessness. League
members were more likely to have active work histories
and had not been on welfare as long as non-members.

Lundberg, George A. and Lawsing, Margaret. "The
Sociography of Some Community Relations," American
Sociological Review, 3 (June, 1937), pp. 318-335.
Moreno's sociometric techniques are applied in an analysis of friendship relations in a small community. Information about friends, visiting, social correspondence,
and other community contacts were gathered in a house
to house canvass of a small Vermont town. Only three
of the 256 persons interviewed appeared to be "completely
isolated," and these were all older people without relatives.

Maccoby, Herbert. "The Differential Political Activity
of Participants in a Voluntary Association," American
Sociological Review, 23 (October, 1958), pp. 524-532.
Voting statistics of Warren County, Virginia are analyzed
with special reference to membership in a recreational
association. The voting statistics are examined at two
points in time, making possible inferences about the role
of the association in influencing persons who join it to be
more active in politics. This study is distinctive because it relies on official records of formal association
activity rather than self-reporting. It is concluded that
in comparison with non-participants, participants are
more likely to vote, to remain voters, and to become
voters if they previously have been nonvoters.

Rose, Arnold M. "Attitudinal Correlates of Social Participation," Social Forces, 37 (March, 1959), pp. 202-
206.
An analysis of 110 questionnaires mailed by persons migrating to Minneapolis in the spring of 1955 reveals that
respondents who report many friends and some organizational affiliations are more optimistic, satisfied, and

confident than persons having few friends or affiliations. The hypothesis that non-participants are anomic is supported.

Smith, David Horton. "The Importance of Formal Voluntary Organizations for Society," Sociology and Social Research, 50 (July, 1966), pp. 483-494.
The effects and implications of formal voluntary organizations in industrial society are explored in this theoretical essay organized around Talcott Parsons' system problems. In addition to providing facilities for communicating ideas and values and for mobilizing human and societal resources, voluntary organizations are responsible for much goal attainment, integration, and pattern maintenance.

Spinrad, William. "Correlates of Trade Union Participation: A Summary of the Literature," American Sociological Review, 25 (April, 1960), pp. 237-244.
A summary of 35 published reports of trade union participation concludes that participation in unions is enhanced by factors that increase identification with occupational situation and occupational community and diminished by influences that foster contrary orientations. "Ultimately, union activity is a result of the acceptance of work, work place, work mates, and working class as somehow constituting a very meaningful part of the union member's life--not merely as instrumental features which are useful for the achievement of gratifications elsewhere."

Stark, Rodney. "Class, Radicalism, and Religious Involvement in Great Britain," American Sociological Review, 29 (October, 1964), pp. 698-706.
A secondary analysis of a 1957 survey of British adults (N = 1, 669) supports the hypothesis that the lower classes find radical politics a better outlet than organized religion for their status dissatisfactions. Consequently the lower-class religious apathy in Britain may be partly accounted for by the strength of lower-class radicalism.

Teele, James E. "Measures of Social Participation, " Social Problems, 10 (Summer, 1962), pp. 31-39.
Studies of social participation often assume that some of the variables (different types of participation) lie along a single dimension, but this assumption is almost never tested by studying the intercorrelations between various components of social participation. Teele examines the inter-relationship among several social participation variables using data from a 1959 survey of 649 relatives of ex-mental patients. He concludes that prior researchers have combined social participation variables which appear to be unrelated. A scale of "voluntary social isolation" is suggested, based on three variables (attendance at club meetings, visits with friends, and participation in social hobbies) which are moderately correlated.

Walters, O.S. "The Religious Background of Fifty Alcoholics, " Quarterly Journal of Studies on Alcoholism, 18 (September, 1957), pp. 405-416.
A group of problem drinkers was compared to a control group to determine if there were differentials in early religious training. Subjects were male patients at the Topeka Veterans Administration Hospital. Fifty patients admitted for treatment of alcoholism and 50 men chosen from other wards of the hospital were interviewed. Religious activity appeared slightly more prominent in the backgrounds of the problem drinkers; it is suggested that somehow religion may have contributed to the development of alcoholism. The author states that among the alcoholics the persistence of childhood religious faith into adult life was striking; 44 of the 50 men reported that their religious beliefs either had not changed or had become stronger.

Wilensky, Harold L. "Life Cycle, Work Situation, and Participation in Formal Associations, " pp. 213-242 in Kleemeier, Robert W. (ed.) Aging and Leisure. New York: Oxford University Press, 1961.
Wilensky assumes that participation in secondary organizations is the basis of integration into community and society, while primary group participation is the basis

of personal adjustment. He summarizes the literature
on participation by age, giving supporting evidence for
the generalization that number of memberships is lowest for people under 30, rises until age 44, and then de-
clines gradually, with the rate of decline increasing after
age 60. Such generalizations are hypothetical, however,
in view of the difficulties which beset attempts to relate
participation and age. He discusses four of these difficulties: lack of relevant controls, the probable over-
estimation of participation in cross-sectional surveys
because of an undersampling of social isolates, the lack
of information about quality of social participation, and
the fact that there is an "ebb and flow" of participation.
His attempts at explaining variations in number and
strength of secondary ties revolve around 1) shifts in
social structure (the decline of the extended family system with its functions being absorbed by secondary organizations), 2) interlocking cycles of work, family,
consumption, and participation, and 3) career-connected
patterns of participation for mobile men and mass apathy and family localism among nonmobile men. Some
attention is given to the functions of secondary attachments in the lives of older people. There is an excellent bibliography.

Wright, Charles R. and Hyman, Herbert H. "Voluntary
Association Memberships of American Adults: Evidence
from National Sample Surveys," American Sociological
Review, 23 (June, 1958), pp. 284-294.
In a secondary analysis of two nationwide surveys conducted by the National Opinion Research Center (1953
and 1955) the authors test hypotheses concerning the
membership of Americans in voluntary associations.
Membership in churches is not counted as voluntary
association membership. Union membership is also
excluded from most of the tables, although some figures
on it are given in the text. Among the major findings:
voluntary association membership is not characteristic
of the majority of Americans; few Americans belong to
two or more voluntary associations; and membership
varies directly with socioeconomic status, urbanization

of residential area, voting, support for charities, interest in public affairs, and family status. Membership does not seem to be related to situational factors such as length of residence in the community, commuting time to work, and length of residence at the same address.

Zborowski, Mark. "Aging and Recreation, " Journal of Gerontology, 17 (July, 1962), pp. 302-309.
Changes in recreational activity accompanying aging are examined in a questionnaire study of 204 members of the Age Center of New England. Subjects were asked to list their recreational activities at age 40 and at the time of the survey (median age of respondent was 69). Although the findings indicate decreasing recreational activity, there was no evidence of increased solitary activity or social isolation with age. Major decreases occurred in activities associated with physical exertion and in activities shared with family members. In general, aged subjects tended to retain the patterns of recreation established in earlier adulthood. It is concluded that aging itself has little influence on recreational patterns and preferences. The findings support the activity theory of aging and do not support disengagement theory.

Zborowski, Mark and Eyde, Lorraine E. "Aging and Social Participation, " Journal of Gerontology, 17 (October, 1962), pp. 424-430.
Current and retrospective data gathered by interview are used in a test of the hypothesis that the social relationships of a sample of 204 aged members of the Age Center of New England had not changed markedly between subjects' age 45 and the time of the study. Changes in social participation of males and females are discussed separately. Respondents indicated a strong reluctance to reduce their social interaction and were fairly successful in maintaining participation at past levels, although subjects from lower economic strata showed a greater decrease in social participation than did more well-to-do respondents. Contact with friends declined somewhat in frequency, but there was

no decline in number of friends. The results give no
evidence of a relationship between aging and voluntary
withdrawal from social participation. The decreased
participation that occurred in certain types of participation is not attributable to aging alone but rather to an
"interdependent constellation of age, sex, socio-economic, and occupation variables."

Zetner, Henry. "Primary Group Affiliation and Institutional Group Morale," Sociology and Social Research,
40 (September-October, 1955), pp. 31-34.
The aim of the study was to determine if Shils' finding
that primary group affiliation is a determinant of institutional group morale in the military also applies to an
educational institution. A sample of 92 native-born,
white, male freshmen at Stanford University in 1951-52
was divided into two equal groups according to whether
the student was one of many from his high school at
Stanford or was its only representative on campus. It
was hypothesized that students with more extensive informal group affiliation and those whose affiliation was
of longer duration would have higher morale than their
counterparts with fewer or more brief affiliations. Extent of affiliation had only limited effect on morale.

OTHER WORKS

Vinter, Robert Dewhirst. "Social Goals and Social Participation Among Urban Lower-Class White Males,"
unpublished doctoral dissertation, Columbia University, 1957. Pp. 211.
On the basis of 50 interviews with lower-class fathers
in Springfield, Massachusetts during 1953-54, Vinter
proposes that there is a relation between deterioration
of primary group relations, anomie, and low levels of
organizational participation. Persons who lack positive
involvement with primary groups also are found to lack
extensive secondary affiliation. A good review of the
literature relating to organizational participation of the
lower class is included. The author develops an index
of participation based on Chapin's social participation

scale, and reports an inverse relation between anomie and all forms of social participation. Kinship association is most typical of persons who lack the goals of monetary success; however, the presence or absence of locally available kin is related to aspiration level. A norm of organizational participation is reported: although the respondents belong to few organizations, they are apologetic about it and indicate that they should be more affiliated.

AGING AND DISAFFILIATION

BOOKS

Bott, Elizabeth. Family and Social Network: Roles, Norms, and External Relationships in Ordinary Urban Families. London: Tavistock, 1957. Pp. 252.
Intensive interviews were conducted with members of 20 "ordinary" London families of varying economic status. Families were contacted through schools, and child welfare clinics, or were recommended to the researchers by friends or ministers. The author empha - sizes that the study is exploratory and generalizations apply only to its "sample." Essentially the book is a comparative analysis of 20 families; its description of factors affecting social networks, conjugal roles and social networks, and relationships with kin is relevant to the study of social isolation and integration.

Drake, Joseph T. The Aged in American Society. New York: Ronald Press, 1958. Pp. 431
Among the topics discussed in this text for College courses in gerontology and geriatrics are the sociocultural environment in which America's aged persons live, the possibilities for continuing employment of older workers, sources of income for older persons, and current efforts to make old age more meaningful. A major goal of the author is to bring understanding of "the older person as a physical, psychological, and social entity rather than a social statistic." Relevant to the study of social isolation is a discussion of the personal adjustment of aged persons. It is concluded that the aged cannot unequivocally be considered a social minority, but they possess many of the character - istics of racial and ethnic minorities.

Kleemeier, Robert W. (ed.) Aging and Leisure. New York: Oxford University Press, 1961. Pp. 447.

Articles related to the topic "the use of time and the
meaning of activity in the later years of life" are included in this collection. Selections are grouped into three general areas: 1) how older people use their
leisure time, 2) the significance of their use of leisure, and 3) problems of conceptualization in the study
of leisure. Sections especially relevant to the study of
social isolation are Margaret Gordon's "Work and Patterns of Retirement," Thompson and Streib's "Meaningful Activity in a Family Context," Harold Wilensky's
"Life Cycle, Work Situation and Participation in Formal
Association," and Max Kaplan's "Toward a Theory of
Leisure for Social Gerontology."

Kutner, Bernard, Fanshel, David, Togo, Alice M. and
Langner, Thomas S. Five Hundred Over Sixty. New
York: Russell Sage Foundation, 1956. Pp. 345.
This book reports the results of a survey of 500 elderly people from the community of Kips Bay, York-
ville, New York. It attempts to trace the impact
of urban social forces upon older persons from various
backgrounds and circumstances. Case histories illustrate adjustment to changes in family status and employment which accompany aging. Variables such as sex
differences, socioeconomic position, health and marriage are related to morale. In general, married persons with high socioeconomic position and good health
score highest on the measures of adjustment. A
negative evaluation of retirement is associated with
feelings of deprivation, social isolation, and poor health.
Of all the factors involved in adjustment to retirement,
the feeling of being useful and wanted seems most important. There is discussion of the relationship between morale and self-concepts, and on activity and
isolation as aspects of the aging process. Also considered are attitudes toward and use of community health
resources and the implications of the findings for planning future facilities.

Lowenthal, Marjorie Fiske, Berkman, Paul L., et al.
Aging and Mental Disorder in San Francisco. San Francisco: Jossey-Bass, 1967. Pp. 341.

A "hospital sample" of 534 patients aged 60 or over admitted in 1959 to psychiatric screening wards of San Francisco General Hospital is compared to a 600-case sample of similarly aged uninstitutionalized residents of San Francisco interviewed in 1960. Follow-up interviews were obtained in 1961 and 1962, permitting longitudinal as well as cross-sectional analysis. The volume emphasizes "detection and correlates of mental illness among the community-resident aged, and the circumstances under which they are maintained or survive in the community." The discussion of the influence of "deprivational factors" and the "social visibility hypothesis" are particularly relevant to the study of homelessness. Some skid-row men were included in the sample. Methodologically this is a very useful work, containing detailed descriptions of psychiatric disability rating methods and various indexes and scales.

Rosow, Irving. Social Integration of the Aged. New York: Free Press, 1967. Pp. 354.
Interviews were conducted with a purposive sample of 1,200 elderly persons in the Cleveland metropolitan area. The general problem was an investigation of the friendship and informal associational patterns of the aged with reference to their residential concentration. Findings confirm the hypotheses that the number of friends varies with the proportion of aged neighbors,and that the friends of elderly persons tend to be drawn from among neighbors. On the basis of amount of contact with friends and desire for friends respondents are classified as "cosmopolitan," "phlegmatic," "isolated, " "sociable," and "insatiable." Also considered are the reference groups of the aged. Results highlight the sharp age-grading that isolates the aged in America . There is an excellent bibliography of almost 300 items.

Townsend, Peter. The Last Refuge--a Survey of Resi - dential Institutions and Homes for the Aged in England and Wales. London: Routledge & Kegan Paul, 1962. Pp. 552.
This survey of the residential institutions and homes for the aged in England and Wales is concerned with

old-age residential accommodation as provided under the
(British) National Assistance Act of 1948. Designed to
complement a previous work by the author (The Family
Life of Old People), the present work is an attempt to
establish some guidelines and obtain basic information
about old persons living with their families as compared
to those living in institutions. The non-institutional
sample consists mainly of working-class residents of
Bethnal Green in East London. In addition, forty public assistance insitutions were visited. Interviews,
questionnaires, and observations are the main source
of data. Results point to the need for more equitable
treatment of old persons in pensionable status. There
are many detailed case histories and an extensive bib -
liography.

Young, Michael and Willmott, Peter. Family and Kinship in East London. London: Routledge & Kegan Paul,
1957. Pp. 232.
A study of kinship among families in a predominately
lower-class London borough is based on interviews with
933 persons in the borough (Bethnal Green), including
interviews in depth with 45 couples having young children. Also studied were 47 couples (41 of them were interviewed two years after the initial interviews, thus
providing longitudinal information) who moved from
Bethnal Green to the public housing at nearby Greeleigh.
The observed kinship network, much wider than anticipated, is explained in terms of respondents' previous
family patterns in London. Relevant to the study of the
study of social isolation are analyses of contacts of
men and women with their siblings and other relatives,
of the links of the kinship systems with the larger community, and of the relation between social mobility and
contact with kin.

ARTICLES

Albrecht, Ruth. "The Parental Responsibilities of Grandparents," Marriage and Family Living, 16 (August ,
1954), pp. 201-204.

The responsibilities assumed by grandparents for their descendants beyond the second generation are analyzed via interviews with a representative sample of the aged population (65 and over) in a midwestern community. The most common relationship is active social participation by visits, but it does not involve responsibility in either direction. Almost two-thirds of the grandparents make such visits. Letters are the only means of communication between generations for 10 percent of the grandparents and almost half of the great-grandparents. Privileges and responsibilities of grandparents vary by region and urban situation.

Albrecht, Ruth. "Relationships of Older People with Their Own Parents," Marriage and Family Living, 15 (November, 1953), pp. 296-298.
Findings about intergenerational attitudes and responsibilities are based on focused interviews with a sample of 100 persons over 65 years of age in a midwestern town. Other members of the subjects' families also were interviewed. Subjects reported that the care of their aged parents was their responsibility only when the parents were in the U.S.: 11 percent had such responsibility, which usually fell to single or widowed women rather than married women or men. Negative attitudes towards aged parents were largely based on feelings of being rejected during adolescence, memories of being forced to work too hard, or shame because of parents' occupation or socially unacceptable behavior.

Anderson, Barbara Gallatin. "Stress and Psychopathology Among Aged Americans: An Inquiry into the Perception of Stress," Southwestern Journal of Anthropology, 20 (Summer, 1964), pp. 190-217.
Patterns in stress perception are analyzed using data from interviews with 127 aged persons one year after their admittance to a hospital psychiatric ward in San Francisco in 1959. Interviews focused on the place of the stressful situation in the life history and on the respondent's reaction to it. Certain kinds of stress were associated with particular times of life, and the response

to the stress was related to whether the subject had a psychogenic or an organic disorder. In comparison with other phases of life middle-age was perceived as relatively stress free.

Anderson, Nancy N. "Effects of Institutionalization on Self-Esteem" Journal of Gerontology, 22 (July, 1967) , pp. 313-317.
Institutionalization may increase or decrease self-esteem, depending on its effect upon social interaction. In order to correct for the association between low self-esteem and choosing to live in an institution, residents of an institution were compared to those on a waiting list for admission to the institution. The research site was a church-related home for the aged with 127 "boarding house care" and 33 "nursing care" residents. Most respondents were married females. Questionnaires were completed by 56 of 151 applicants and 101 of the residents. Findings indicate that the amount and quality of interaction is more closely related to self-esteem than to institutionalization, but institutionalization provides opportunities for interaction.

Bell, Tony, "The Relationship Between Social Involvement and Feeling Old Among Residents in Homes for the Aged, " Journal of Gerontology, 22 (January, 1967), pp. 17-22.
Fifty-five single elderly people residing in three California institutions were interviewed in an examination of the relationship between social involvement and feeling old. Roles considered were organization member , shopper, friend, acquaintance, neighbor, and relative. Types and frequency of interaction and perceptions of being old were recorded. Feeling old is associated with low total social involvement. It may be that as interaction with family and close friends decreases, positive reinforcements are decreased, and feeling old is a consequence of the decline in positive reinforcement.

Berardo, Felix M. "Widowhood Status in the United States: Perspective on a Neglected Aspect of the Family Life-Cycle, " The Family Coordinator, 17 (July, 1968), pp. 191-203.

Despite its emergence as a major phenomenon of American Society, widowhood has received little attention
from social scientists. A socio-demographic profile
of the American widow reveals that widowhood is largely a problem for the aged woman, that her economic
status is insecure, and she faces higher risks of mor-
taility, mental illness, and suicide than her married
counterparts. Extensive, systematic research is needed to discover the factors associated with successful
adaptation to widowhood.

Botwinick, Jack. "Cautiousness in Advanced Age, "
Journal of Gerontology, 21 (July, 1966), pp. 347-343.
Cautiousness was investigated in relation to age, sex,
and education in the context of 24 "life situations" divided into sets of 12. One set was designed to reflect the problems of later life and the other set
concerned problems more typical of younger adults.
There were two alternatives for each situation, one rewarding but risky, the other less rewarding but safer.
Among 47 respondents aged 67-86 and 111 aged 18 -
35, the older subjects were more conservative and
cautious, shying away from risky actions regardless
of likelihood of success. Each group tended to be more
cautious with the problem concerning their own age group.
Neither sex nor education seemed related to cautiousness.

Brown, Robert Guy. "Family Structure and Social Iso -
lation of Older Persons, " Journal of Gerontology, 15
(April, 1960), pp. 170-174.
This paper records a study of the physical and social
isolation of older persons from their children, and of
the loneliness resulting from this isolation. The sam -
ple consisted of 260 persons aged 60 and over. The
hypothesis that feelings of neglect in older people result from isolation due to children's geographic mobil -
ity or changed family structure was supported only in
the upper-status segment of the sample. Although physically separated, elderly persons and their children
may maintain close ties. In fact, many older persons
do not follow the stereotypical pattern of physical and
social isolation.

Clark, Margaret. "The Anthropology of Aging, A New Area for Studies of Culture and Personality," The Gerontologist, 7 (March, 1967), pp. 55-64.
Previous anthropological studies on aging and on popular attitudes toward aging are reviewed. Data from interviews conducted in 1963-64 with 80 aged residents of San Francisco (40 "normals" and 40 respondents institutionalized for psychiatric care) are analyzed, with particular emphasis on respondents' self-esteem. It is concluded that successful adaptation to aging must include modification of the basic orientations (achievement, aggressiveness, acquisition, individualism) characteristic of American life. If they are to avoid conflict, people must learn the "proper" manner of growing old.

Davis, Robert William. "The Relationship of Social Preferability to Self-Concept in an Aged Population," Journal of Gerontology, 17 (October, 1962), pp. 431-436.
An examination of the relationship between self-concept and social functioning among 33 aged institutionalized subjects reveals that elderly persons preferred by their peers have more positive self-concepts than the non-preferred.

Dean, Lois R. "Aging and the Decline of Affect," Journal of Gerontology, 17 (October, 1962), pp. 440-446 .
This report is concerned with the four affective states of anger, irritation, boredom, and loneliness. The author attempts to determine if either the methods of self-definition of the incidence of these four states changes with increasing age. The data are drawn from the Kansas City Study of Adult Life, a six-year investigation of socio-psychological factors accompanying the transfer from middle to old age. A panel of 200 men and women aged 50-95 was interviewed at regular intervals. Findings support the hypothesis that "active" emotional states--such as anger and irritation--decrease with age. Contrary to the initial expectation, boredom seems to be an active affect, and loneliness seems to increase with age, although self-definitions of being lonely change with age.

Dean, Lois R. "Aging and the Decline of Instrumental-
ity, " Journal of Gerontology, 15 (October, 1960), pp. 403-
407.
Data from the Kansas City Study of Adult Life are analyzed in the context of disengagement theory,   which
postulates an inverse relation between age and the number of obligatory personal interactions. Also discussed
is the application of the instrumental-expressive dichotomy to the   personality system, giving   it   meaning
analogous to Parson's description of its place in social
systems. The data support disengagement theory.

Desroches, Harry F. and Kaiman, Bernard D. "Stability of Activity Participation in an Aged Population, "
Journal of Gerontology, 19 (January, 1964), pp. 211-214 .
In Experiment 1, 99 domiciliary residents were questioned about the frequency of participation in various
activities. Four years later 33 of these men were still
living in the domiciliary; 18 were interviewed again,
using the same instrument. In Experiment 2, the activity questionnaire was administered to 26 of 52 domiciliary transfers shortly after transfer between institutions
and again five months later. These data support   two
inferences: 1) activity participation does not change as
a function of time,   and 2) a change in institutional
environments produces   only minimal decrements   in
activity participation.

Emerson, A. R. "The First Year of Retirement," Occupational Psychology, 33 (October, 1959), pp. 197-208 .
As part of a study of the effects of retirement, 124 men
were interviewed a week prior to their 65th birthday ,
six months later, and again a year later.   Physical
health, mental health, activities and social contacts, and
general attitudes were measured.   The   investigation
was intended as a re-evaluation of the "retirement impact" hypothesis (retirement leads to ill-health or death).
Conclusions are: 1) the first year of retirement has no
apparent effects on physical or mental health; 2) atti -
tudinal changes take place which indicate that some ten -
sion is experienced; 3) passive, rather than active ,

adjustments are made in activities; and 4) patterns of social contact are modified. The authors conclude that the detrimental effects of retirement may be overrated .

Farber, Arthur. "Noninstitutional Services for the Aged," Social Work, 3 (October, 1958), pp. 58-63. The need for non-institutional services for the aged has arisen because of the high cost of hospital care and over-crowding in homes for the aged. Many communities have the components for a good system of over-all community planning and cooperation, but have not put them together effectively. Examples of professional and non-professional programs by public, private, and commercial agencies include a homemaker service for those who find housekeeping too much of a burden, counseling services, and a foster home program for elderly persons. New programs take time to be accepted and become well established, and during that time the needs of the aged become more pressing.

Filer, Richard N. and O'Connell, Desmond D. "Motivation of Aging Persons," Journal of Gerontology, 19 (January, 1964), pp. 15-22. The sample of 102 aging disabled male veterans in a domiciliary community was divided into two groups. Both groups were faced with definite expectancies but only one group was provided with incentives for performance. The performance of the motivated group was superior. Some of the deterioration of behavior observed in aging, institutionalized persons seems to be fostered by the institutional climate and is not merely the result of aging. Such persons may be working far below capacity; functional levels rise when they are exposed to greater incentives and opportunity.

Friedman, Alfred S. and Granick, Samuel. "A Note on Anger and Aggression in Old Age," Journal of Gerontology, 18 (July, 1963), pp. 283-285. The question "Is it ever right to be angry?" was asked of a socially heterogeneous sample of 140 respondents . The sample was divided into two groups by age. The "young" group responded affirmatively with significantly

higher frequency than the "old" group.   This finding,
along with the results of a self-description derived from
the Clyde Wood Test, supports the hypothesis that "the
aged tend to regard anger as undesirable but yet perceive themselves as free to show such feelings."

Friedman, Edward P.   "Spatial Proximity and Social
Interaction in a Home for the Aged," Journal of Gerontology, 21 (October, 1966), pp. 566-577.
The sample consisted of 58 elderly Episcopal women
living in a home for the aged in an eastern city.   Spatial
proximity is shown to be a significant factor in friendship choices; it is more significant when reciprocity is
part of the relationship.   Even when subjects had lived
at the home for an extended period spatial proximity re -
mained a significant factor in friendship.

Gordon,   Margaret S.   "Changing Patterns of Retirement," Journal of Gerontology, 15 (July, 1960), pp. 300-
304.
A somewhat impressionistic picture of various patterns
of retirement includes identification of four common
patterns and discussion of the function of retirement
pensions within each pattern.   The issue of compulsory
versus voluntary retirement is also considered.

Hyman, Dorothy K. and Jeffers, Frances C.   "A Study
of the Relative Influence of Race and Socio-Economic
Status Upon the Activities of a Southern Aged Popula -
tion, "   Journal of Gerontology,   19 (January, 1964),
pp. 225-229.
Analysis of the activities and attitudes of a biracial
older population (260 volunteers over 60 years of age)
in a southern community indicates that differences in
activity patterns are socio-economic rather than racial,
but differences in attitude are associated with both socio-
economic and racial factors, especially religion   and
economic security.

Kerckhoff, Alan C.   "Husband-Wife Expectations and
Reactions to Retirement," Journal of Gerontology,   19
(July, 1964), pp. 510-516.

The sample consisted of 90 white married couples in which the man was within five years of retirement and 108 couples in which the man already had retired. Both groups of husbands were more pleased about retirement than were their wives. Men retired for less than five years showed the greatest satisfaction. When the couples were grouped according to the occupation (or pre-retirement occupation) of the husband, upper-level (professional and managerial) couples did not welcome retirement, but their experiences were comparatively favorable and their reactions to retirement generally were rather positive. Middle-level (white collar and skilled) couples welcomed retirement and seemed to have relatively positive experiences, but they did not respond as favorably as upper-level couples.

King, Charles E. and Howell, William H. "Role Characteristics of Flexible and Inflexible Retired Persons," Sociology and Social Research, 49 (January, 1965), pp. 153-165.
"Role biographies" obtained by interview from 128 retired persons were evaluated for evidence of role flexibility. Roles judged to have significant influence on retirement include the school role, occupational role, community role from age 15 to 25, marital role, spousal role, organizational participation role, organizational performance role, change in interpersonal association role, and loss of spousal role. The basic finding is that people who have been "flexible" throughout their lives adjust to retirement more readily than the "inflexible." Organizational participation and proficiency are associated with flexibility.

Knupfer, Genevieve, Clark, Walter and Room, Robin. "The Mental Health of the Unmarried," American Journal of Psychiatry, 122 (February, 1966), pp. 831-851. A random sample of 1,268 residents of San Francisco interviewed in 1962 as part of a longitudinal study of drinking practices were reinterviewed in 1965 (N=785). Information obtained from mailed questionnaires was combined with interview data. Symptoms of maladjustment are analyzed by sex and marital status. Single men are shown to be more isolated and antisocial than either single women or married men. There is evidence that the never-married men were psychologically impaired to begin with (they are likely to have experienced greater stress in childhood than did men who married) and that a vicious circle of "reactive factors" tend to make the unmarried male antisocial.

Lipman, Aaron and Marden, Philip W. "Preparation for Death in Old Age, " Journal of Gerontology, 21 (July, 1966), pp. 426-431.
Open-ended questions dealing with preparation for incapacity and death were included in a questionnaire administered to 119 residents of Public Housing Projects in Miami. All respondents lived alone. Most had made some provision for death. The only significant background factors distinguishing those who had made some preparation from those who had not were source of income, race, and education. The educated, the whites, and those with incomes independent of welfare were most likely to have made provisions for death .

Lowenthal, Marjorie Fiske. "Antecedents of Isolation and Mental Illness in Old Age, " Archives of General Psychiatry, 12 (March, 1965), pp. 245-254.
It is hypothesized that social isolation is an intervening variable between certain personality and social factors and mental illness in old age. Analysis of life history data from 534 respondents hospitalized in psychiatric observation wards in San Francisco General Hospital (including material from multiple interviews and diagnoses with these respondents over a three-year period) indicates that anticipated antecedents of isolation (e. g., physical illness, never having married, sporadic employment) are predisposing factors for mental disorder but not for social isolation. It is concluded that psychogenic disorders in old age derive from various psychological, social, and genetic antecedents and that social isolation among the aged tends to be a consequence rather than a cause of the mental illness.

Lowenthal, Marjorie Fiske. "Perspectives for Leisure and Retirement," pp. 118-126, in Brockbank, Reed and Westby-Gibson, Dorothy (eds.), Mental Health in a Changing Community. New York: Grune & Stratton, 1966.
An increasing number of aged people are "at leisure" with the problem of finding something to occupy their time. Five studies based on comparative analyses of 534 psychiatrically hospitalized elderly persons and 600 persons living in the community (San Francisco) provide information on factors relevant to aging and isolation. Sample findings; lifelong isolates tend to be drawn from the lowest socioeconomic class; isolation does not derive from maladjustment in old age; morale and social isolation are inversely related, although many isolates do not have low morale; potentially isolating circumstances have greater effect on mental health than upon extent of isolation. It is concluded that older people need norms for growing old, just at they needed norms for growing up. A possible solution is the establishment of educational institutions run by and for older people.

Lynn, Richard. "Personality Changes with Aging," Behaviour Research and Therapy, 1 (March, 1964), pp. 343-350.
An attempt is made to integrate Eysenck's theory of personality and the research on aging by taking the view that aging involves shifts in four independent areas of personality: neuroticism, introversion - extraversion, psychoticism, and general intelligence. Laboratory experiments indicate a tendency in older persons towards introversion and enhanced inhibitory, rather than excitatory, potentials. The author's thesis is that the advantages of aging lie in the former characteristic, and the disadvantages in the latter.

Maddox, George L. "Activity and Morale: A Longitudinal Study of Selected Elderly Subjects," Social Forces, 42 (December, 1963), pp. 195-204.
Longitudinal data on aging, attitudes, and activity were obtained from 182 non-institutionalized volunteer subjects 60 years of age and over, with a second survey

three years after the initial interviewing. Analysis of the interview data supplemented by medical, psychiatric, and psychological evaluations reveals a positive relationship between changes in activity and changes in morale. However, interpretation of this finding is complicated by certain intervening or contextual test factors, such as physical and psychological health, social structural characteristics (e. g., marital status), and type of activity. The apparent influence of these test factors underlies the importance of specifying the exact conditions under which there is a positive relationship between activity and morale.

Maddox, George L. "Some Correlates of Differences in Self-Assessment of Health Status Among the Elderly," Journal of Gerontology, 17 (January, 1962), pp. 180-185.
An investigation of correlates of differences in self-assessment of health among 251 non-institutionalized elderly subjects reveals that the most important determinant of an elderly person's conception of his health status is his objective state of health. General anxiety about health and poor adjustment to the environment are associated with pessimism about one's health status. Optimism about health varies directly with social status.

Maddox, George L. and Eisdorfer, Carl. "Some Correlates of Activity and Morale Among the Elderly," Social Forces, 40 (March, 1962), pp. 254-260.
An investigation of the relationship between age and activity and between activity and morale among 250 non-institutionalized respondents 60 years of age and over supports the view that activity decreases with age and that morale and activity are positively associated. However, some of the respondents are "disengaged persons" who maintain morale in the absence of activity.

Pollack, M., Karp, E., Kahn, R. L. and Goldfarb, A. I. "Perception of Self in Institutionalized Aged Subjects: I. Response to Patterns of Mirror Reflection," Journal of Gerontology, 17 (October, 1962), pp. 405-408.

Responses to self-mirror reflection were studied among a random sample of 568 subjects in residential institutions for the aged and 128 non- institutionalized respondents in New York City. All respondents were at least 65 years of age. Self-derogatory responses were about twice as frequent among the institutionalized as the non-institutionalized respondents (19.5 percent versus 8.6 percent). Self-derogation was not significantly related to age or mental status, although some state hospital patients did not recognize their own images. Women were significantly more self-derogatory than men. The authors conclude that a mirror reflection test is an efficient index of self-depreciation and suggest that it be included as part of the mental examination of aged persons.

Rose, Arnold M. "Aging and Social Integration Among the Lower Classes of Rome, " Journal of Gerontology, 20 (April, 1965), pp. 250-253.
Interviews were conducted with 142 women and 109 men in lower-income communities in Rome. Findings are that the aged are less socially integrated than younger persons. However, some forms of integration are directly associated with age; church attendance and acquaintance with local storekeepers and peddlers are examples.

Rose, Arnold M. "Class Differences Among the Elder -ly: A Research Report, " Sociology and Social Research, 50 (April, 1966), pp. 356-360.
A survey of 210 elderly residents of Minneapolis and St. Paul indicates that middle-class respondents have better health (self-defined), have fewer disrupted in -terpersonal relationships, have fewer personal prob -lems, participate more in voluntary associations, vote more frequently, and manifest greater interest in increased religious and family life than do lower - class respondents.

Rosow, Irving and Breslau, Naomi. "A Guttman Health Scale for the Aged, " Journal of Gerontology, 21 (October, 1966), pp. 556-559.

A six-item Guttman scale for determining the health status of the aged in survey research is described. The scale is based on respondents' judgements but derives from objective referrents of activity and functional capacity. The scale is validated on a sample of 1, 200 aged residents of Cleveland. There is a reasonably high correlation between patients' subjective and physicians' objective health assessment, but even without this association subjective perceptions of health are valid sociological concepts.

Schwartz, Arthur N. and Kleemeier, Robert W. "The Effects of Illness and Age upon Some Aspects of Personality, " Journal of Gerontology, 20 (January, 1965), pp. 85-91.
The hypothesis was that the psychological effects of illness and aging tend to be similar and in the same direction. One hundred males were divided into four groups of equal size on the basis of health and age. Criterion measures were the twenty statements problem, the semantic differential, and the Picture-Frustration test. The attitude of the old and ill toward the self was more negative than that of the young and well, but illness rather than age seemed the main factor contributing to negative self-perceptions.

Shanas, Ethel. "Family Responsibility and the Health of Older People, " Journal of Gerontology, 15 (October, 1960), pp. 408-411.
The author studied a national sample of 1, 734 older people (aged 65 and over) and a sample of 2, 507 adults (21 and over). This paper considers only those aged people with at least one child. Information on two topics was obtained: 1) the physical proximity of the subject to his children and the relation of health to such proximity; and 2) attitudes toward suitable living arrangements for older persons. Despite the high geographic mobility in American society most aged parents have children living nearby and one-third of them share the same household with one of their children. The more unhealthy an aged parent, the more likely he is to live close to his children. The questions

on attitudes revealed that most people feel that aged parents, especially if ill, are the responsibility of the children, and that sometimes a joint household is necessary.

Stone, Jane Livermore and Norris, Arthur H. "Activities and Attitudes of Participants in the Baltimore Longitudinal Study, " Journal of Gerontology, 21 (October, 1966), pp. 575-580.
Activity and attitude inventories were administered to 463 participants in the Baltimore Longitudinal Study. Findings reveal no significant relation between attitude or activity and chronological age.

Streib, Gordon F. "Participants and Drop-outs in a Longitudinal Study, " Journal of Gerontology, 21 (April, 1966), pp. 200-209.
Analysis of characteristics of participants and dropouts in the Cornell longitudinal study of retirement (N=3, 793) shows that native-borns, females, and persons of higher social status and good health are most likely to continue participation. With respect to adjustment and life satisfaction there are no substantial differences between participants and drop - outs, and inclusion of all the drop-outs would not have affected the final results of the study.

Thompson, Wayne E., Streib, Gordon F. and Kosa, John. "Effect of Retirement on Personal Adjustment: A Panel Analysis," Journal of Gerontology, 15 (April, 1960), pp. 165-169.
This paper challenges the view that maladjustment among retired persons is due to the lack of clearcut social roles and loss of status associated with retirement. The sample was 1, 559 males born between 1887 and 1889. The respondents were contacted several times, both before and after retirement. Maladjustment in retirement is related to pre-retirement attitude, the effect of retirement on economic well-being, and the use of free time. Extreme personal maladjustment among the aged cannot be attributed to retirement.

Tobin, Sheldon S. and Neugarten, Bernice L.   "Life
Satisfaction and Social Interaction in the Aging, " Journal of Gerontology, 16 (October, 1961), pp. 344-346.
A survey of 187 persons aged 50 and over (including 79
aged 70 or more) provides evidence that refutes the disengagement theory of aging.   Social   interaction and
life satisfaction are positively related, and the strength
of the relationship increases with age.

Youmans, E. Grant.   "Family Disengagement Among
Older Urban and Rural Women, " Journal of Gerontology,
22 (April, 1967), pp. 209-211.
Women's family visiting and helping relationships were
examined in a test of the disengagement theory of aging.
Data were obtained from an urban Kentucky sample of
103 women aged 60-64 and 112 women 75 or over.   A
comparable rural sample included 94 women aged 60-64
and 76 women in the older category.   Only the rural
sample manifested family disengagement.   There was
little difference in extent of disengagement between the
older and younger subsamples.

Young, Michael and Geertz, Hildred. "Old Age in London and San Francisco: Some Families Compared, "
British Journal of Sociology, 12 (June, 1961), pp. 124-141 .
This is a report of a preliminary study to determine the
extent to which older people become isolated from their
families, and which family ties remain strongest.   Two
communities were chosen: Woodford in London and
Menlo Park in San Francisco: sample sizes were 98
and 210, respectively.   Names were drawn from the
lists of local doctors.   All female respondents were
over age 60, and male respondents were over 65. In -
terviews included many open-ended questions. The two
groups were found to be similar in that parents in their
old age maintain close ties with their adult children and
daughters consistently are more important than sons in
maintaining family ties.   A major intersample differ -
ence was that the respondents in the United States were
more aware of their ancestry; this finding was   borne
out by an additional study of 3, 964 people in the United
States and 900 in Britain. Possible explanations   are
offered for the differentials in concern   with ancestry.

OTHER WORKS

Berardo, Felix M. Social Adaptation to Widowhood Among a Rural-Urban Aged Population. Pullman: Washington Agricultural Experiment Station Bulletin 689, 1967. Pp. 31
A random sample of residents of   Thurston   County, Washington were interviewed in 1956. Of the 549 persons in the original sample, 225 were widowed. A secondary   analysis of these   interviews   reveals that the aged married persons are better off than the widowed. The report   includes   information on health, economic circumstances,   living   circumstances,   use of time, social isolation, friendship relations, and formal social participation. Although   the aged   widow   suffers   the greatest economic deprivation,   the widower   is most isolated and is worse off than the widow in almost every other respect.

ANOMIE, ISOLATION, AND MARGINALITY

BOOKS

Becker, Howard S. Outsiders. New York: Free Press of Glencoe, 1963. Pp. 179.
Becker begins this approach to the understanding of deviant subcultures and subgroups with the premise that laws and rules define certain acts as deviant and consequently certain classes of people as deviants or "outsiders." To understand deviance, therefore, one must understand the process by which new rules are created and the motivation of the "moral entrepreneurs." As an example, the history of the legislation outlawing marijuana is described. Some of the processes by which an individual accepts or rejects membership in a deviant group are analyzed with reference to dance band musicians.

Blauner, Robert. Alienation and Freedom. Chicago: University of Chicago Press, 1964. Pp. 222.
Blauner begins with Marx's theory of alienation and applies it to modern industry. Drawing heavily on Seeman's dimensions of alienation, he analyzes alienation among four types of industrial workers--printers, textile workers, auto workers and chemical operators. Most of the data are from a 1947 job attitude survey by Elmo Roper, supplemented by other case studies of industrial plants. Blauner reports a consistent pattern in the relation between alienation and freedom in the modern industrial factory. Craft industries are characterized by low alienation. Alienation is highest among assembly line industries, and decreases as industry becomes automated and the worker's control over work process results in a more cohesive, integrated industrial climate. The "alienation curve" in any particular industry is likely to decline as employees under automation gain "new dignity from responsibility and a sense of individual function."

Clinard, Marshall B. (ed.) Anomie and Deviant Behavior: A Discussion and Critique. New York: The Free Press of Glencoe, 1964. Pp. 324.
Papers in this collection originally were presented at a 1962 conference on social deviation, sponsored by the American Sociological Association. A comprehensive inventory of empirical and theoretical studies of anomie (prepared by Stephen Cole and Harriet Zuckerman) has been added. The utility of anomie theory in the study of several forms of deviant behavior (gang delinquency, mental illness, drug addiction, alcoholism) is evaluated. Edwin M. Lemert criticizes the structural view of deviation upon which the original statements of anomie were based, noting that it "rests upon reified ideas of culture and social control" and proposing an alternative "risk-taking" view. Robert K. Merton comments on previous criticisms and suggests additional research. An overview, extending from Durkheim's work to the papers contained in this book, is presented by the editor.

DeGrazia, Sebastian. The Political Community: A Study of Anomie. Chicago: University of Chicago Press, 1948. Pp. 258.
As described by Durkheim, anomie includes uneasiness or anxiety, a feeling of isolation from group standards, and feelings of pointlessness. Two types of anomie are distinguished: simple anomie (the psychological result of conflict between systems of belief) and acute anomie (the result of the deterioration of belief systems). The prevalence of simple and acute anomie in modern democracies is discussed. Mass unemployment is seen as indicating acute anomie. Adaptations to acute anomie include mental illness and suicide and affiliations with mass movements which seek to substitute a new moral order for the present one. DeGrazia concludes that anomie is unrelated to any particular system of belief. It occurs only when there is no clear, consistent belief system. The political community is essential; without the cooperative help of the community, the individual perishes.

Fromm, Erich. Escape From Freedom. New York:
Holt, Rinehart & Winston, 1941. Pp. 305.
Fromm's thesis is that the industrial revolution and the
Reformation freed Western man from the traditional
bonds of medieval society without substituting other integrative bonds, and as a result left him feeling isolated
and powerless, a ready prey to mass movements such
as Nazism which give him feelings of belonging and power. Although "negative freedom" makes the individual
isolated and alone, free individuals can be integrated
through "spontaneous activity," including "work" and
"love" for one's fellows. Fromm concludes that the
isolation and alienation that accompany freedom weak-
en and frighten man, and make him ready to submit to
new kinds of bondage. "Positive freedom, on the other
hand, is identical with the full realization of the individual's potentialities, together with his ability to live
actively and spontaneously."

Hoskisson, J. B. Loneliness: An Explanation, A Cure.
New York: Citadel Press, 1965. Pp. 128.
Loneliness is the experience of being cut off. Types of
loneliness are described (general loneliness, interest
loneliness, nostalgic loneliness, faithless loneliness,
specific loneliness, incompletion loneliness, and loneliness for God). Avoidance of loneliness requires the
willingness and ability to communicate with others.
Solutions to loneliness are occupation, preoccupation,
and self-realization. Hoskisson favors the latter. Practical steps for banishment of loneliness are given, including details for special exercises and a system of
self-induced deep relaxation.

Josephson, Eric and Josephson, Mary (eds.) Man
Alone: Alienation in Modern Society. New York: Dell,
1962. Pp. 592.
The editors state that their purpose in this collection of
articles is to describe particular conditions in modern
industrial society that have led to man's estrangement
and to show some of the ways in which men and women
have responded to that estrangement. In the introduction the concept of alienation is defined and its intellect-

ual history traced; it is distinguished from anomie and social isolation. The sections of the book on "social isolation, " "work and leisure, " and "rebels, deviants, and retreatists" are most relevant to the study of disa-filiation. There is a 74-item list of suggested readings.

Mizruchi, Ephraim Harold. Success and Opportunity: A Study of Anomie. New York: Free Press of Glencoe, 1964. Pp. 204.
An extended theoretical discussion--with numerous quotations--is combined with a report of a 1958 survey of 223 housewives in Cortland, New York. Findings include the statement that "among the active participants in formally organized voluntary associations, those from the lower classes tend to more anomie than those from the middle classes." Table IX might be re-percentaged on the other axis to give social participation by anomie scores, rather than vice versa.

Moustakas, Clark E. Loneliness. New York: Prentice-Hall, 1961. Pp. 107.
Isolation and loneliness are not results of modern industrial society but rather are inevitable parts of life. Much of modern "alienation" is "loneliness anxiety, " a fear of being alone and an implicit rejection of the "central and inevitable fact of human existence: loneliness." Although "loneliness is almost always regarded as destructive and the common social urge is to rescue the lonely one, " the author feels that man can only come to grips with reality by recognizing the positive value of isolation and loneliness. "The 'never be lonely' theme is a reflection of man's estrangement from himself in the world today." Many examples and personal, as well as historical, experiences are included which demonstrate the value of loneliness. Of particular interest are chapters on "concepts of loneliness, " "the isolated man, " and "the loneliness of public life."

Tunstall, Jeremy. Old and Alone. London: Routledge & Kegan Paul, 1966. Pp. 344.
This book reports the third of a series of studies of old age. The previous studies were of old people living in

private households in Britain, the U.S. and Denmark, and of old people living in residential institutions in Britain. The present study was of the "alone minority." A sample of 195 aged persons manifesting aloneness and isolation was obtained by a "screening interview" administered to 538 old people chosen at random from physicians' lists in four contrasting areas, Harrow, Northampton, Oldham and South Norfolk (over 99 percent of old people in Britain are registered with physicians). Follow-up interviews were conducted with the "alone." Forms of being alone include living alone, social isolation, loneliness, and anomie. Groups having high probabilities of aloneness (the single, the recently widowed, and the housebound) are discussed in separate chapters. The "private pursuits and public provision" of the alone are considered, as are implications of the findings for social theory and social policy. There are many direct quotations and illustrative case histories. Appendices describe research methods in detail and the questionnaires are reproduced. There is also an excellent selected bibliography (90 items).

Weil, Simone. The Need for Roots. New York: G. P. Putnam's Sons, 1952. Pp. 256.
Perhaps the most important and least recognized human need is to be rooted. Roots are achieved via participation in community life. Uprootedness accompanies military conquest, but may also develop within a country, from factors such as 1) desire for gain becoming the most important social motive, or 2) specialized, technical education which does not bring one in contact with the real world, nor satisfy one's spiritual needs. Uprootedness is extremely dangerous because it is self-propagating. It fosters two kinds of behavior, spiritual lethargy resembling death, and frantic activity designed to uproot, often violently, those not yet uprooted, or only partly so. A discussion of uprootedness in urban areas, towns, and in nations is followed by reflections on "The Growing of Roots."

Wilson, Colin. The Outsider. Boston: Houghton Mifflin, 1956. Pp. 288.
The outsider is not a social problem, but rather the
one man able to see. He maintains a higher purpose and
awareness of life; it is the rest of mankind who drift aim-
lessly. Because he is different from other men, the outsider suffers a problem of identity: he seeks to know himself and his potentialities. Nevertheless, he also seeks
balance, escape from triviality, vividness of sense perception, and sometimes escape from being an outsider.
The resolution of his difficulties may lie in the way of the
visionary. These ideas are illustrated in a careful syn-
thesis of the writings of literary and philosophical outsiders, including Tolstoy, Camus, T. E. Lawrance, Van
Gogh, Hemingway, Dostoevsky, Fox, Hesse, Buddha,
Nietzsche, and Blake.

Wood, Margaret Mary. Paths of Loneliness. New York:
Columbia University Press, 1953. Pp. 237.
Societal forces which tend to isolate individuals and
personal adaptations to these "isolating precesses" are
described. The emphasis is on intra-group rather than
inter-group isolation. Isolation is related to sex and
family life, aging, unemployment, heavy responsibility
("men in great places"), deviant behavior, and stigma-
tizing diseases (leprosy, syphilis, and mental illness).
"Adaptations" include "the far-wanderer," "the lonely
egotist," and the "authoritarian escapist." There is a
good bibliography (250 items), largely items published
before 1940.

Wood, Margaret Mary. The Stranger. New York: Columbia University Press, 1934. Pp. 198.
The author attempts to explain behavior toward strangers
in terms of pre-existing relationships in society. After
an outline of social relationships as units of social structure and a discussion of the concepts "stranger" and
"group," she analyzes the relationship between the stranger and the social order ("the obligations of kinship,"
"the principle of authority," "the principle of mutual

obligations"). A section on the stranger and the community pattern considers alien communities (immigrants and foreign colonies), isolated communities (frontier settlements), country communities, and the city. There are also observations on "the stranger and the specific situation."

ARTICLES

Angell, Robert C. "Preferences for Moral Norms in Three Problem Areas," American Journal of Sociology, 67 (May, 1962), pp. 650-660.
Eight hundred respondents in a Detroit Area Study sample were asked to select among several standards of conduct in hypothetical situations involving religion and civil liberties, family privacy, and race relations. Seven causal factors are evaluated (ethnicity, age, schooling, occupation, income, anomie, and religiosity). Race and schooling are the most powerful factors determining intersample differences in preferences for moral norms. Of special interest to students of homelessness is the finding that schooling, occupation, and income are inversely correlated with anomie.

Antonovsky, Aaron. "Toward a Refinement of the 'Marginal Man' Concept," Social Forces, 35 (October, 1956), pp. 57-62.
Marginality (a condition wherein one has ties to two partially incompatible societies and does not wholly belong to either) is distinguished from alienation and anomie, terms referring to a feeling that one does not belong anywhere. Responses to marginality among 58 Jewish males in New Haven are analyzed. The author concludes that marginality is an important source of problems in the pluralistic environment but notes an absence of traditional concomitants of marginality such as instability, perpetual conflict and uncertainty.

Berreman, J. V. "The Escape Motive in Alcoholic Addiction," Research Studies of the State College of Washington, 18 (March, 1950), pp. 139-143.
The escape motive hypothesis of alcohol addiction is

over-used and over-simplified. Sixty case histories from the records of the Oregon Liquor Control Commission Clinic, supplemented by interview data, reveal varying motives for compulsive drinking. As drinking becomes heavier, motives tend to be individual rather than social, but in all cases many years of drinking preceded the establishment of a compulsive pattern. A crisis preceded the onset of the compulsive pattern for about two-thirds of the sample, while the remaining third noted no such crisis or shock. It is concluded that alcohol addiction is a complex form of behavior and cannot be explained by a simple theory of escape motivation.

Bordua, David J. "Juvenile Delinquency and 'Anomie': An Attempt at Replication," Social Problems, 6 (Winter, 1958-59), pp. 230-238.
In a replication and critique of Lander's study of anomie in Baltimore, Bordua uses Lander's methods but adds the Srole anomie scale and a measure of social isolation based on the frequency of involvement in voluntary social relationships (including neighbors, co-workers, and organizations). Education is found to be the variable most closely related to isolation. Independent of income, education predicts anomie and other variables related to social instability, and it is a better predictor of these variables than is income. The anomie concept used by Lander is really misnamed, and the components of the anomie factor are in no way causes of delinquency. The anomie concept in this case obscures rather than clarifies the analysis; delinquency does not flow from anomie but rather is a form of it.

Cohen, Albert K. "The Sociology of the Deviant Act: Anomie Theory and Beyond," American Sociological Review, 30 (February, 1965), pp. 5-14.
Merton's anomie theory of deviant behavior is seen as an important step toward a general theory of deviance, but it has several "imperfections and gaps." Cohen stresses the deviant act as the result of a long interaction process rather than an abrupt "leap from a state of strain . . . to a state of deviance." The interaction

between deviance and milieu needs further exploration. A typology of responses of the opportunity structure to ego's deviance is presented. Investigation of the inter-penetration of two major sources of deviance (anomie, and role validation through exhibition of behavior cul-turally expected of the given role) is necessary before they can be fused in a single theory.

Cohen, Lillian. "Los Angeles Rooming-House Kaleido-scope," American Sociological Review, 16 (June, 1961), pp. 316-326.
Responses to a survey of 600 rooming house inhabitants in three areas of Los Angeles highlight the anonymity of urban life; most of the residents we re unmarried and socially disaffiliated. The entire sample was divided in-to Hollywood and Downtown sections; the Hollywood dwellers largely aspired to fame or professional stand-ing while Downtown aspirations were for higher wages, better housing, or a more satisfying sex life. The room-ing house inhabitants, especially the poorer Downtown sample, embody the conflicts characteristic of modern urban society.

Cressey, Donald R. and Krassowski, Witold. "Inmate Organization and Anomie in American Prisons and So-viet Labor Camps," Social Problems, 5 (Winter, 1957-58), pp. 217-230.
Relationships among inmates and between inmates and officials in Soviet and American prisons are compared. Soviet camps differ principally in their need for inmate labor and their view of political prisoners as a class to be exploited. Anomie is defined as individualism and as under-organization or pluralistic ignorance. Conditions of anomie include psychological and social isolation.

Dubin, Robert. "Deviant Behavior and Social Structure: Continuities in Social Theory," American Sociological Review, 24 (April, 1959), pp. 147-164.
In Social Theory and Social Structure, Merton proposed four types of deviant adaptation to anomie. Dubin's theoretical analysis yields a total of 14 deviant adapta-tions, all of which exist in real life. The author illus-trates each of the types derived from his analysis.

Dubin's typology is not designed for prediction, but sets the boundaries of outcomes. He makes two major additions to Merton's typology: he adds group to the category of actors, and he emphasizes the effect of multiple cultural goals.

Faris, Robert. "Cultural Isolation and the Schizophrenic Personality," American Journal of Sociology, 40 (September, 1934), pp. 155-164.
Data from hospital records, accounts of prisoners in solitary confinement, and descriptions of spatially isolated peoples indicate that extended periods of isolation ("separation from intimate and sympathetic social contacts") produce a "seclusive" personality that is prone to schizophrenia. Schizophrenics are over-represented in areas of marked social disorganization and limited social life. Treatment of schizophrenia by re-establishing social contacts appears promising.

Feuer, Lewis. "What is Alienation? The Career of a Concept," pp. 127-147 in Stein, Maurice and Vidich, Arthur (eds.), Sociology on Trial. Englewood Cliffs, New Jersey: Prentice-Hall, 1963.
Feuer traces the history of the concept of alienation from Calvin, who saw man estranged from God because of original sin, through Marx and Engels, who used the concept extensively in their early writings but later rejected it and stressed instead economic conflict. The concept and use of alienation has returned to sociological analysis, particularly through the neo-revisionist Marxism. Various sociological usages of the term alienation are outlined: alienation of class society, of competitive society, of industrial society, of mass society, of race and of the generations. Feuer gives examples of each of these and outlines some of the scales that have been used to measure alienation. He concludes that the concept of alienation still has overtones of political theology and that in sociological and political analysis it often confuses rather than clarifies.

Freyhan, F. A. "Emotional Vacuum and Alcoholism," Deleware State Medical Journal, 18 (May, 1946), pp. 122-125.

Alcoholism is associated with certain socio-pathological factors, the most important of these being an "emotional vacuum;" many people drink to break the monotony of their lives. Alcoholics are not primarily escapists but rather persons who lack focus or orientation toward society. Re-education and re-orientation are the processes of therapy, with emotional maturity, self-discipline, and personal and social responsibility the chief goals of rehabilitation.

Kerckhoff, Alan C. "Anomie and Achievement Motivation: A Study of Personality Development Within Cultural Disorganization, " Social Forces, 37 (March, 1959), pp. 196-202.
Variations on the Thematic Apperception Test were given to Indian and white students in grades 5-8 in five Wisconsin schools. Strong achievement motivation was associated with maturity, majority group status and strong identification with the majority group by members of the minority. The Chippewa Indians are seen as an anomic group with little social participation in white society, no voluntary organizations or clearly defined social groups of their own, and limited social control. Anomie among the Chippewa is a result of deculturation or cultural disintegration. Disorganization, anomie, and demoralization are used synonymously.

Killian, Lewis M. and Grigg, Charles M. "Urbanism, Race and Anomie, " American Journal of Sociology, 67 (May, 1962), pp. 661-665.
The effects of race, class, and urban residence on anomie (measured by Srole's scale) are investigated in a study of two southeastern United States communities, a city and a rural county seat. The authors report that the findings "cast further doubt upon the validity of the traditional assumptions concerning the relationship between urbanism and anomia. " Level of education, rather than urban residence, seems to account for the urban-rural differences in anomia scores. In small towns, being a Negro is directly related to anomia; in cities, low occupational status of Negroes is associated with high anomia, but for whites low education and low self-

placement rather than low occupational status seem most associated with anomia. The white collar Negro in the city is less anomic than his counterpart in the small town.

Levinson, Perry. "Chronic Dependency: A Conceptual Analysis, " Social Service Review, 38 (December, 1964), pp. 371-381.
Applying Etzioni's theory of social control to social work, this paper suggests a typology of chronic dependency whereby clients are classified as "moral, " "calculative" and "alienative. " The central point is that chronic dependency and long-term assistance are not synonymous, and that conceptual as well as therapeutic confusion results when the terms are used interchangeably. Adequate identification of the types of chronically dependent clients requires specification of the proportionate distribution of each type and of the social characteristics associated with it.

Lowenthal, Marjorie Fiske. "Social Isolation and Mental Illness in Old Age, " American Sociological Review, 29 (February, 1964), pp. 54-70.
The relation between isolation and mental disorders in old age is analyzed in an assessment of the prevalent assumption that age-linked isolation is an important correlate (if not cause) of mental illness in old age and in an attempt to extend understanding of social isolation in general. The sample consists of four subgroups drawn from the 1, 200 institutionalized and non-institutionalized elderly subjects of a series of studies in geriatric mental illness. Social, physical, and psychological characteristics of the four groups are analyzed; illustrative case materials show the development of isolation and its relation to subjective and objective indicators of maladjustment.

Lowenthal, Marjorie Fiske and Boker, Deetje. "Voluntary vs. Involuntary Social Withdrawal, " Journal of Gerontology, 20 (July, 1965), pp. 363-371.
A sample of 269 survivors from a parent sample of 600 community-resident aged people are classified by extent and nature of social interaction and compared on selected

demographic, psychological, and social variables including morale and attitudes. Results lend support to
the disengagement theory of aging. Certain deprivations
among the aged may obliterate the relationship between
social interaction and morale.

McClosky, Herbert and Schaar, John H. "Psychological
Dimensions of Anomy," American Sociological Review,
30 (February, 1965), pp. 14-40.
Anomy is conceived as moral-psychological state pro-
ceeding from impeded socialization and learning which
may occur when 1) congitive capacity is impaired, 2)
persons have overly anxious, hostile, or uncertain personalities, or 3) extreme or deviant views are held.
Social impediments to socialization and learning do exist,
but they have been given undue weight. Self-administered
questionnaires containing scales of agree-disagree items
were given to cross sections of the Minnesota (1955; N=
1, 082) and national (1958; N =1, 484) populations. High
correlations in the directions expected were found between responses to anomy items and those on cognitive
functioning, psychological inflexibility, anxiety, ego
strength aggression, extreme beliefs, and misanthropy.
The principal sources of anomy may reside in social
settings, individual personalities, or a combination of
setting and personality. Anomy appears to be symptomatic of a despairing outlook toward oneself and one's
community.

Miller, Curtis R. and Butler, Edgar W. "Anomie and
Eunomia: A Methodological Evaluation of Srole's Anomia
Scale," American Sociological Review, 31 (June, 1966),
pp. 400-406.
Tests of unidimensionality and scalability of a set of
items are described and applied to responses to Srole
scale items. The authors recommend that a scale first
be factor analyzed for dimensionality, then tested for
scalability and typological construction by means of
Guttman scaling and latent class analysis. The Srole
scale was found to be unidimensional, but does not scale
in the Guttman sense. Latent class analysis of the Srole
scale revealed only two classes, indicating that the
scale should not be used as a continuum.

Mizruchi, Ephraim Harold. "Social Structure and Anomia in a Small City, " American Sociological Review, 25 (October, 1960), pp. 645-654.
An investigation of anomia (measured by the Srole scale) in a small city in New York is based on 618 completed interviews. Anomia is found to be universally associated with social class, income (but when education is held constant, the relationship disappears), class identification, and social participation in both formal and informal groups, but it is not associated with sex or urbanism.

Pieris, Ralph. "Bilingualism and Cultural Marginality, " British Journal of Sociology, 2 (December 1951), pp. 328-339.
British attempts to acculturate Sinhalese-speaking Ceylonese by teaching them English resulted in a cultural marginality resulting from bilingualism. Problems of this kind can be eliminated by the establishment of a world language; such a step would also eliminate the association between language and culture, so that adoption of one culture by members of another would not be hindered by old associations and problems of communication.

Powell, Elwin H. "The Evolution of the American City and the Emergence of Anomie: A Culture Case Study of Buffalo, New York: 1810-1910. British Journal of Sociology, 13 (June, 1962), pp. 156-168.
This paper is an attempt to delineate some of the historical and institutional sources of the anomie of urban life. Buffalo, New York from 1810 to 1910 is described as the typical American city. Two tables covering population, property, crime and unemployment for males over ten years of age are included with the description of Buffalo as a community and a class society. Powell considers anomie the product of capitalism. In the evolution of Buffalo from a cohesive community to an atomized society the decisive factor in producing anomie seems to be the process of urbanization rather than the development of the economic institutions.

Rose, Arnold M. "Living Arrangements of Unattached
Persons," American Sociological Review, 12 (August,
1947), pp. 429-435.
Housing for the unattached is presently inadequate.
Part of the problem is due to a cultural lag; unattached
persons are still considered unusual or temporary
cases. Three groups of the unattached are distinguished: immigrants, indigent native migrants, and
self-supporting native migrants. The housing problems
of each group are discussed. The solution to the problem consists in obtaining government or private capital
to finance large housing projects for the unattached.

Rose, Gordon, "Anomie and Deviation-A Conceptual
Framework for Empirical Studies," British Journal of
Sociology, 17 (March, 1966), pp. 29-45.
After a review of the uses of the concept, Rose defines
anomie as a loss of norm legitimacy sufficient to cause
avoidance behavior. The concept may be theoretically
distinguished on individual and social levels. Considering both levels, legitimacy loss is due to 1) lack of
knowledge about norms 2) weakness of norms or 3) norm
conflict which results in apprehension about the norm's
validity. The cultural structural approach to anomie has
been difficult to operationalize, partly because vague
terms such as "success" and "middle class status" are
crucial to the theory. A more complex theory of deviation is necessary; relative deprivation must be taken
into account. Research on deviation and anomie must
consider 1) the indicators and processes involved in the
norms of working class culture and their relation to frustration 2) relative deprivation itself 3) goal internalization 4) the relationship of goals to the specific society
in terms of equilibrium between norms and conventional
goals. Suggestions for future research include ten test-
able hypotheses.

Tec, Nechama and Granick, Ruth. "Social Isolation and
Difficulties in Social Interaction of Residents of a
Home for Aged," Social Problems, 7 (Winter, 1959-60),
pp. 226-232.
This study explores the relation between social isolation

of aged persons before they enter a home for the aged and subsequent difficulties they experience in social interaction. A measure of social isolation based on contact with relatives, presence of children, length of unemployment, and whether or not a person lives alone is proposed. The effects of previous isolation on subsequent adjustment in the home for the aged are analyzed, using data from records of all residents of the home who were transferred to mental institutions between 1943 and 1954 (N = 50) and a control group of 50 individuals who were not transferred. The hypothesis that there is a relation between social isolation and subsequent adjustment in the home is supported. Social skills can survive in old age if social isolation does not occur simultaneously with biological aging.

Wittermans, Tamme, and Kraus, Irving. "Structural Marginality and Social Worth," Sociology and Social Research, 48 (April, 1964), pp. 348-360.
Structural marginality is a condition of non-availability of meaningful institutionalized roles, and it operates to depress social participation. Implicit in role assignment is social worth, i.e., a recognition of competence, rights, and status. Structural marginality connotes low worth. The structural marginality of youth is related to changes in the bases of the division of labor.

Yinger, J. Milton. "On Anomie," Journal for the Scientific Study of Religion, 3 (April, 1964), pp. 158-173.
This theoretical piece emphasizes the relationship between anomie and socio-cultural structures. A typology of social situations ranging from cultural unity to full anomie is offered, based on the degree, disruptiveness, and cumulative effect of value disagreements in the society. Race relations are classified according to a hypothetical development in America to illustrate the scheme. Several interpretaions of anomie are discussed. Yinger inquires into minimum cultural unity necessary in a heterogeneous society, suggesting the role that religion may play in the "cooling out" functions. Due to an increase in functional interdependency among societal elements anomie may not be as pervasive as

some writers have suggested. However, social chaos and individual alienation are "universal facts of our time" and anomie has increased with modernity. The question of anomie involves a general inquiry into the nature of the moving equilibrium in modern society that permits change, pluralism, and individuality while avoiding personal demoralization and also providing a core of shared values without coercion and totalitarianism.

Zorbaugh, Harvey W. "The Dweller in Furnished Rooms: An Urban Type, " American Journal of Sociology, 32 (July, 1926), pp. 83-89.
The rooming house is a social situation which produces from the raw material of unmarried young workers and students a distinct social type. The mobility and anonymity of rooming house dwellers tends to attenuate stable social situations and to obstruct fulfillment of individual wishes. Possible alternatives for the urbanite are the fabrication of a dream world, the substitution of a pet, suicide, or, most frequently, individualized and impulsive behavior. This article is an earlier and simplified version of the chapter "The World of Furnished Rooms" in the authors's The Gold Coast and the Slum.

OTHER WORKS

Advisory Subcommittee of the West Side In-Building Committee. The World of 207. New York: Housing and Redevelopment Board. Pp. 47.
The West Side In-Building Committee in New York City selected an SRO (single room occupancy building) to be observed. A 91-unit, six-story building was chosen and 31 residents were interviewed. Goals of the committee were to understand the needs of the tenants, to discover what specific service might be rendered, and to learn if tenants would respond and use preferred services. An in-building program providing regular counseling services and opportunities for tenants to meet in structured activities is discussed. Appendices include case histories.

Granick, Ruth. "Social Isolation Experienced Prior to Entry as a Factor in the Adjustment of Residents of a Home for Aged," unpublished doctoral dissertation, Columbia University, 1962. Pp. 223.
It was predicted that social isolation prior to admittance to a home for the aged would hinder social adjustment in the home; that the longer the isolation had existed, the more difficult adjustment would be; that socialization into a home is an intervening process between prior isolation and social adjustment; and that the components of social adjustment (integration, evaluation, and conformity) are functionally interrelated. One hundred consecutive new admissions to a home for the aged were interviewed upon admission and again one or two months later. The first interview focused on personal history and background factors, the second was concerned with socialization into the home. Social work records were also used as a source of data about adjustment in the home. Prior isolation was found to hinder adjustment in the home, but length of prior isolation was not important. The components of adjustment were more closely related to each other than to isolation, and the extent of their intercorrelation increases over time. Socialization serves as an intervening variable between isolation and both integration and evaluation, but not conformity; deviant behavior in the home takes time to develop; initially most persons conform.

Hurewitz, Paul, "The Neutral Isolate: Some Personality, Behavioral, and Role Perception Dynamics of Pre-Adolescent Sociometric Isolates Compared With a Group of Sociometric Leaders," unpublished doctoral dissertation, New York University, 1961. Pp. 306.
Using sociometric instruments 19 isolates were chosen from 1,167 elementary school students in Brooklyn, New York. These isolates were contrasted with a matched group of sociometric leaders from the same population with reference to personality and role-perception variables. The two groups were clearly distinguishable on various personality measures. Compared to the leaders the isolates were more emotionally

unstable, tended to overestimate their social relations with others, were more apt to manifest perceptions which reflected wish-fulfillment, were less accurate in predicting their role status, had poorer school adjustment and achievement, and were less accurate in predicting the status roles of classmates.

Nahemow, Lucille Davis. "Persuasibility, Social Isolation and Conformity Among Residents of a Home for Aged," unpublished doctoral dissertation, Columbia University, 1963. Pp. 279.
Ninety-six admissions to a home for aged were interviewed after one to three years residence to test the hypotheses that 1) persuasibility is related to social isolation, and 2) persuasibility is not related to conformity to social norms. In the main the hypotheses were confirmed, although the support for the first varied with the measure of persuasibility used. Most residents of the home were highly persuasible; the isolates tended to be more persuasible than the others. Anomia seemed to be more important than social isolation in determining persuasibility. Persuasibility and conformity are independent behaviors, hence social conformity does not presuppose the loss of independence of thought.

Teele, James Edward. "Correlates of Social Isolation," unpublished doctoral dissertation, New York University, 1961. Pp. 235.
Two-hour interviews were conducted with 649 adult relatives in the households of formerly hospitalized patients. All respondents resided in or near Boston. Six measures of social participation were correlated with various background, personality, and belief items. Voluntary participation, visiting relatives, and church attendance each manifest distinctive background and attitudinal correlates. Personality as well as socio-cultural factors are related to the various dimensions of social participation.

Sisenwein, Robert Julian. "Loneliness and the Individual as Viewed by Himself and Others," unpublished doctoral dissertation, Columbia University, 1964. Pp. 83.

The hypothesis that feelings of loneliness derive from the discrepancy between one's self-perception and others' perceptions of him is tested in a study of the freshman cadets (N = 255) at the U.S. Merchant Marine Academy. The questionnaire included self-ratings and measures of loneliness. Ratings of subjects by their roommates and other peers were also obtained. The hypothesized relationship did not appear. In explaining the negative findings, the author suggests that in assessing peers' perceptions he may have been looking at the wrong variable. It may be the disparity between one's self image and his own perceptions of how others view him that is the important factor in producing loneliness.

INDEXES

NAME INDEX

Abeles , H. , 192
Adams, F. D. , 175
Adler, L. M. , 69
Advisory Social Service
  Committee of the Munic-
  ipal Lodging House, 126
Aikenhead, R. S. , 226
Al-Issa, I. , 201
Albrecht, R. , 358–359
Alden, P. , 318
Alfor, J. A. , 190
Alkie, 281
Alksne, H. , 249
Allen, E. B. , 246
Allen, W. H. , 105
Allport, G. , `80, 85
Allsop, K. , 281
Anant, S. S. , 187
Anderson, B. G. , 359
Anderson, D. , 282
Anderson, H. E. , 163–164
Anderson, N. N. , 360
Anderson, N. , 3, 20, 26–27
  29, 30– 31, 40, 94,106,127,
  136, 163, 282, 315
Anderson, P. E. , 309
Angell, R. C. , 381
Antonovsky, A. , 381
Apple, D. , 184
Armstrong, C. P. , 276
Armstrong, J. D. , 188, 195,
  246
Armstrong, R. G. , 271
Asbury, H. , 14–15, 20
Asher, R. W. , 188

Augustin, J. , 282
Aydelotte, F. , 282

Babbie, E. R. , 80
Babchuk, N. , 343
Bacon, S. D. , 150,188, 247–
  248, 333
Bahr, H. M. , 3, 26, 39, 41,
  106 - 109, 128
Bailey, M. B. , 219, 248–
  249, 271
Bain, H. G. , 128
Baker, M. A. , 129
Bakke, E. W. , 318
Bales, R. F. , 184
Barbour, L. L. , 164
Barnett, G. J. , 337
Baron, S. , 116
Bartholomew, A. A. , 250
Bartlett, W. W. , 283
Bassett, L. A. , 129
Bateman, N. I. , 219
Bauer, C. , 175
Beasley, R. W. , 176
Beck, F. O. , 283
Beck, S. M. , 150
Becker, H. S. , 375
Beiser, M. , 343
Belcher, J. C. , 69
Bell, R. G. , 189
Bell, T. , 360
Bellin, S. S. , 69–70
Bendiner, E. , 94
Benjamin, B. , 65, 67
Benson, B. H. , 283

SUBJECT INDEX

Abstinence, from alcohol, 5, 205, 214, 252, 269; see also Drinking

Achievement, 385

Adaptation, 6, 9, 44, 51-54, 57, 63-64, 380, 385

Addicts, 105, 212, 316

Adolescents, 212, 276-281, 297

Adjustment, 53, 56, 65, 72, 203, 248, 272, 318-319, 334

Affiliation, 4, 5, 7, 41-45, 48, 81, 128, 340-341, 376; see also Disaffiliation, Voluntary associations

Africa, 291

Age Center of New England, 352

Aged persons, 24-26, 51-52, 55, 58, 60, 62, 69-72, 103, 116, 133-134, 139-140, 164-165, 172, 175, 283, 320, 324, 332, 355-374, 378, 390; activity and morale, 368-369, 371; anger and aggression, 364; cautiousness of, 361; community planning for, 364; Cornell study, 372; courtship opportunities, 72; family structure among, 361, 371, 373; homes for, 357,365, 390; institutionalized, 360, 365; kinship ties,51,71, 355-356, 358; health of, 69, 356, 370-371; motivation of, 364; noninstitutional services for, 364; role characteristics, 366; self-concepts, 60-61, 362, 365, 369-371; social integration of, 357, 360, 370, 373-374; see also Aging, Retirement

Aggression, 261, 387; see also Antisocial behavior

Aging, 56, 69, 74, 128, 330, 336, 352-353, 355-359, 361-363, 365-373, 386-387, 389-390, 392-393; activity theory, 352, 368-369, 371; anthropology of, 362;and disaffiliation, 128, 355-374; disengagement theory, 56, 336, 352, 363, 373, 387; leisure, 355, 368; church attendance, 370; and marriage, 365; mental disorder, 356-357, 366-367, 386; personality changes, 368, 371; preparation for death, 69, 74, 367, 372; and race, 365-366; and religion, 365; stress of, 359, 366, 369; see also Aged persons